Born and brought up in Irela
England. After taking a degree
a pilot in RAF Coastal Comma
leader. After working on the *Ir*
University where he lectured in
in 1954.

He has written two books on the history of psychical research, *Natural and Supernatural* and *Science and Parascience*. Since his editorship of the *Spectator* in 1959–62, he has worked in television as writer/presenter for *What the Papers Say* and *All Our Yesterdays*, and written a number of books, including *The Forbidden Game: A Social History of Drugs*, *Roger Casement*, *Natural Medicine* and *The Disease of Civilization* (which is also published by Paladin Books). He was elected a Fellow of the Royal Society of Literature in 1974.

BRIAN INGLIS

The Paranormal

An Encyclopedia of Psychic Phenomena

PALADIN
GRAFTON BOOKS
A Division of the Collins Publishing Group

LONDON GLASGOW
TORONTO SYDNEY AUCKLAND

Paladin
Grafton Books
A Division of the Collins Publishing Group
8 Grafton Street, London W1X 3LA

Published by Grafton Books 1986

First published in Great Britain by
Granada Publishing 1985

Copyright © Brian Inglis 1985

ISBN 0-586-08463-0

Printed and bound in Great Britain by
Collins, Glasgow

Set in Bembo

CONTENTS

ACKNOWLEDGEMENTS

My thanks to Renée Haynes for her comments and suggestions about the original typescript – very helpful they were! – and to Bernard Levin, Andrew MacKenzie and Margaret Van Hattem, who joined me in reading the proofs. My thanks, too, to Eleanor O'Keeffe and Nick Clark-Lowes at the Society for Psychical Research. But I also owe a debt of gratitude to people who helped me in the early stages of my research into the paranormal, by pointing me in profitable directions and warning me about blind alleys: in particular Rosalind Heywood, who was always a fund of useful and entertaining information, and Arthur Koestler, with whom I had many a spirited argument over what should legitimately be classified as paranormal, and what ought to be discarded as – in his view – parapornography.

NOTE ON ILLUSTRATIONS

Illustrations for any book about the paranormal raise intractable problems. Photographs of ectoplasmic materializations, for example, inevitably look bogus; and there is no way of proving that the phenomena were genuine, except to take the word of witnesses. Those I have used were accompanied in the books where they originally appeared by the descriptions of reliable witnesses; what looks static in the photographs, they agreed, developed and then faded away before their eyes.

INTRODUCTION

Anybody who attempts to describe paranormal phenomena is immediately confronted with a problem. For an influential minority of people, they do not exist. To relate accounts of them is consequently to court derision.

Nevertheless I have presented the evidence as if the events described actually happened. It would be easy, but tiresome, to hedge: with qualifications such as 'alleged' where, say, witnesses claim to have seen a person, or an object, floating in the air in defiance of gravity. I have preferred to work on the principle (which most historians accept) that if a phenomenon is reported sufficiently often by people of standing, its existence can be assumed, even if individual reports may be untrustworthy. Readers can make up their own minds, from the evidence, which reports can be trusted, and which should be rejected.

Sceptics claim that with the paranormal, this criterion should not apply, because people of the highest intelligence and integrity have held beliefs which have subsequently been shown to be fallacious. This is true: we now know that the sun does not go round the earth. But that was an interpretation, not a fact. The fact was, and is, from our viewpoint, that the sun rises, and sets. That interpretations and beliefs can be mistaken is all too obvious; but this does not apply in the case of events.

Of course people can be fooled by tricks or delusions; but these cannot account for the great mass of reports of paranormal events by eye-witnesses. Some I have included are admittedly less to be relied upon than others – those in the Old Testament, for example, or accounts of miracles performed by saints. Yet even these often have details which lend them a measure of credibility; and they show that the same types of phenomena were being reported in all ages as are still being reported today.

A second problem has been to decide what to exclude. Just as the cartographers of old used to let their maps peter out at the edges, with 'Here be Savages' and pictures of mythical beasts, so on the fringes of the paranormal there are vampires and were-wolves, Yetis and lake monsters, flying saucers and hobgoblins. I have included a wider range than most parapsychologists would accept; but my main concern has been with the phenomena which parapsychology has been concentrating upon: extra-sensory perception, psychokinesis, ghosts and divination – concentrating for the most part on the actual evidence, rather than speculative interpretations. This has meant, for example, that I do not deal, except in passing, with movements and cults such as the Cabala, the Rosicrucians, or the Hermetic Order of the Golden Dawn – they can be found in *The Encyclopedia of the Unexplained*, edited by Richard Cavendish (London, 1974) – or with Spiritualism except in the years when it was intermeshed with psychical research, up to the 1920s. It needs to be said, though, that evidence of many of the forms of paranormal phenomena, often well-attested, continues to pour out in Spiritualist journals the world over. *A Popular Dictionary of Spiritualism*, a small-scale encyclopedia, was published in London in 1961.

This brings up a further problem: presentation. Entries in encyclopedias are usually presented in alphabetical order. But this was not always so; and although I began the compilation with the now standard procedure in mind, I soon had to abandon it, for a variety of reasons. The term 'paranormal' is a relative newcomer: indeed it is only within the past ten years or so that it has come to be used colloquially. 'Psychokinesis', for the action of mind on matter, is still groping its way into common usage. And there are many terms which parapsychologists have introduced which have yet to establish themselves. It would be foolish, I thought, to present the information under technical headings which to most readers would be unfamiliar.

Another consideration was that terms which *are* familiar are often misleading: 'ghosts', for example – as I show in the section on the subject. But the main reason for splitting the work up into sections, under the main headings, is that it puts the phenomena in their context, showing how they interlock and inter-react.

Yet another problem has been to strike a balance between the historical evidence, on the one hand, and the experimental evidence, on the other. During the past century the emphasis has been on research projects designed to prove to scientists that the paranormal is a reality; particularly over the past fifty years, very little attention has been paid to the experiences of ordinary men and women. This, I am sure, has been a mistake; and I have tried to restore what some psychologists contemptuously dismiss as 'anecdotal' evidence to its rightful place.

This does not mean that the experimental evidence lacks credibility; but much of it is of a technical kind which cannot easily be summarized. It is surveyed in the massive *Handbook of Parapsychology*, compiled by Benjamin B. Wolman in 1977; and in *Psychical Research* (1982), edited by Ivor Grattan-Guinness. And Michael A. Thalbourne has provided a useful *Glossary of Terms Used In Parapsychology* (1983).

1 THE PARANORMAL

A Historical Survey

Attitudes to those phenomena which are now regarded as paranormal, and beliefs about their origins, have altered many times in the course of history; but the accounts of the phenomena themselves have remained strikingly consistent, as far back as the records go – and further back, if we accept the evidence from tribal communities.

Tribal shamans were ordinarily marked out for the post in youth, or even in childhood, by the fact that they displayed indications that they were capable of divination – through extrasensory powers; and, better still, if they could work magic – through psychokinetic powers. Ghosts and apparitions, too, were very much a part of the life of a tribe; as were witches and sorcerers, who were assumed to have the powers of a shaman, but to be using them for their own, sometimes malign, ends, rather than for the tribe's benefit.

These powers were thought to reside in those individuals who had access to the spirit world. Inevitably this prompted the view among missionaries, who for centuries were the chief source of information about tribal beliefs, that the power which was being exploited by shamans, spirits and sorcerers alike was diabolic – even when it was being used for the tribe's benefit; the devil could well be aiding shamans, the better to keep his hold on them and their tribes. But a few of the shrewder observers eventually began to realize that some tribes, at least, had more sophisticated ideas about the source of the energy which was being tapped. It could be put to a variety of uses, but it was assumed to be neutral – in the sense that gravity is neutral. It was 'a kind of material fluid devoid of personal intelligence but capable of receiving, incorporating and reflecting the impression of ideas and spirits', as the French investigator, Pierre Saintyves, put it in *La Force Magique* (1914); 'a kind of impersonal spirit without ideas proper to it, in which the intentions of men and of spirits can be incorporated so that they can fulfil their aims'.

The 'fluid' went by many different names, but the one which came into most common use to describe it in English was *mana*, the term used for it by the islanders of the South Pacific.

A similar belief, uncovered by members of the East India Company who took the trouble to investigate Hindu lore, was in 'prana' – a subtle form of energy believed to permeate the universe, but manifesting itself through human beings, some of whom could exploit it.

A distinction gradually arose between occult phenomena, for which there was no identifiable reason, their cause being hidden; and magical phenomena, obtained by shamans or sorcerers exploiting the energy flow, through clairvoyance or through mind-over-matter displays, both of which were a commonplace in tribal communities.

But the concept of *mana* was eroded by two processes: the emergence of states, with ruling castes who were not prepared to allow their subjects to submit to the dictation of tribal shamans; and the development of hierarchical notions about the spirit world, leading to a belief in gods as its rulers – and eventually, as portrayed in the Old Testament, to a belief in a single, all-powerful God.

The Israelite community was still recognizably shamanist. But because the shamans' successors, the prophets, were in communication with a single master, the Lord, the powers that he gave them – whether extra-sensory, as in the many accounts of precognitive dreams, or magical, as when Elijah called down fire from heaven – were taken to be divine; even when the Lord leased them to the devil, to allow him to tempt Job from his faith. The *mana* concept faded. The energy must, it was assumed, all come from the Lord, whether it was used by his spirits (angels) or by his prophets; whether exploited by the devil and *his* spirits (demons), or by witches in the devil's clutch. And this was a view which Christianity took over. Fortified by the accounts of the miracles of Jesus and his disciples, and by St Paul's faith in the power of the Holy Spirit (a spirit emanation, direct from God), the early Christians believed that any of the faithful could work miracles – magic – too. The essence of the early Christian faith was, in effect, 'we can all be shamans, now' – if the powers are used for God.

The Supernatural

The energy supplied by the Holy Spirit might be taken to be divine, but it was still assumed to be natural. What else could it be, if it were God's handiwork? After the Renaissance, however, scientists began to find that certain familiar forces operated through fixed – and it came to believed, immutable – laws, which they described as natural; the term 'supernatural' coming into use to describe those phenomena which appear to defy the laws of nature.

For a time this implied no disrespect to God. He had laid down the laws, after all, merely reserving for himself (and certain leaseholders, such as the devil) the right to break them. When they were reportedly broken, the manifestations were regarded either as miraculous, as in accounts of holy men and women levitating, or as diabolic, as in the spells cast by witches. Natural and supernatural enjoyed a brief period of co-existence, with phenomena which were not clearly enough defined being left in the occult category as, simply, unexplained.

In the 18th century, however, scepticism began to emerge about the existence of miracles, the case against them being forcefully put by the Scots philosopher, David Hume; and by the mid-19th century disbelief in them had advanced to the point where the historian William Hartpole Lecky could observe that 'nearly all educated men receive an account of a miracle taking place in their own day with an absolute and even derisive incredulity, which dispenses with all examination of the evidence'. The supernatural, in other words, was being discounted, even by Christians, as a workaday force. Catholics still allowed for occasional miracles, including remarkable cures at Lourdes; but the Vatican subjected the evidence to such stringent investigation that official sanction was rarely forthcoming. Protestants still prayed for the sick (and occasionally even for rain, during a protracted drought), but few retained any firm belief in God's willingness to intervene to break nature's laws on earth, even if they took for granted that he could, if he wanted to.

This still largely holds, today. In his *Miracles* (1947), C. S. Lewis set out the Christian viewpoint succinctly. To him, the Supernatural (he gave it a capital S) implied the existence of something 'not beyond this nature, but beyond any and every nature'; a distinction which he clarified by citing angels (it made

15

no difference, he insisted, whether the reader believed in angels or not). 'All angels, both the "good" ones and the bad or "fallen" ones which we call devils,' he claimed, 'are equally "Supernatural" in relation to *this* spatio-temporal Natural: they are outside it and have powers and a mode of existence which it could not provide.' To a Christian, in other words, the supernatural is on a different plane of existence.

For Catholic theologians, however, Lewis's distinction was a little inadequate, in view of the widespread belief, among the faithful, in miraculous intervention. They were also faced with the difficulty that some 'miracles' were beginning to look a little shop-worn; it was becoming more difficult to cite clairvoyant powers or levitations as evidence of holiness, in putting the claims for a beatification, when the same effects were being reported by the hundred from seances; and to describe those effects as diabolic – though they were, and sometimes still are, so described – was to credit the devil with more influence than was comfortable.

As a compromise, 'preternatural' was brought in to perform the required service. In *On Time* (1983), Michael Shallis credits a Dominican friar, whom he does not identify, as giving an example of the distinction:

It was said that when St Dominic celebrated mass, as he raised the host, the communion bread, he levitated off the ground. The transformation of the bread into the body of Christ, the monk said, was a truly supernatural event; the levitation of St Dominic was, however, simply preternatural. All preternatural phenomena, he said, were purely illustrative of the supernatural, and not supernatural as such.

Animal Magnetism

Towards the end of the 18th century, a new theory was put forward by Franz Mesmer to account for some of the phenomena which Hume and his followers dismissed as contrary to the laws of nature. Essentially it was an up-dated version of *mana*, attributing the unexplained energy flow to a form of magnetism reaching the earth from the stars. Like magnetism, it could be made to enter into inanimate objects, such as iron bars or bowls of water; but it could also be tapped by certain individuals, and transmitted through them (or through objects they had magnetized) to others, chiefly for the purpose of curing illness.

Mesmer himself adopted a technique very similar to one in common use by shamans; he would direct the magnetic 'fluid' at patients; they would go into trance states, often into convulsions, followed by comas; and when they recovered, they would usually feel much the better for the treatment. An investigation by eminent doctors and scientists, set up by Louis XVI of France at the behest of Marie Antoinette, confirmed in 1784 that patients did actually appear to benefit; but the reason, the report claimed, was that the mesmeric technique worked on the patients' imaginations. No evidence had been found of any magnetic force.

The implication was that mesmerism, in so far as it worked therapeutically, worked within the laws of nature. One member of the committee, however, demurred: the respected scientist Laurent de Jussieu. He had observed the way in which patients who were facing in other directions nevertheless reacted to a stick or a finger, pointed at them by the 'magnetizer', behind them, several feet away. Although Jussieu was not prepared to commit himself to acceptance of the 'animal magnetism' hypothesis, he felt compelled to admit at least the possibility 'of the existence of a fluid, or force, which is exercised by man on man, and which sometimes produces a perceptible effect'.

Jussieu's observations were soon to be confirmed by Mesmer's disciples, in different parts of Europe; notably Count Chastenet de Puységur, a former President of the Medical Society of Lyon, who found that he could induce a trance state in some patients which would not develop into convulsions and coma, and which sometimes led to patients becoming clairvoyant, describing pictures they could not see, or picking up what was in the Count's mind by thought-transference. One patient could be stopped in full flow of talk simply by the Count mentally telling him to stop.

The French Revolution and the Napoleonic wars ended such research, or drove it underground; but after 1815 it emerged again, particularly in France, and although animal magnetism (as its exponents still believed it must be) continued to be used chiefly in the treatment of patients, the 'higher phenomena', as they came to be known – clairvoyance, thought-transference, and occasionally magical effects – were continually reported, and were vouched for by some of the most eminent scientists of the era, in different countries. And when another commission of inquiry was appointed by the French Academy of the Sciences, its report in

1831 confirmed that some of the 'higher phenomena' had been witnessed, and confirmed by tests, clairvoyance among them.

This was too much for the great majority of members of the Academy. By this time belief in the existence of immutable laws of nature had become a faith; the ability to 'see' an object which was hidden, or an event taking place at a distance, was held to break them. A fresh commission, hastily appointed, repudiated the 'verdict of its predecessor; and to be on the safe side the members of the Academy agreed to investigate animal magnetism no further – not even its therapeutic potential. The trance state which the magnetizers induced, the assumption remained, must itself be spurious. Patients must simply be pretending to be entranced.

Hardly had animal magnetism been thus unceremoniously ditched, however, when the 'higher phenomena' resurfaced in a new guise, even more threatening to scientists' peace of mind because not merely were they magical, in that inanimate matter appeared to be moving around without the application of sufficient physical force – or, sometimes, without any physical force at all – but also because the movements could be, and were, brought about, witnessed and reported by hundreds of men and women of unblemished reputations, in the United States, in Britain and all over Europe.

'I have no doubt that there are *thousands* of tables turning every night in London,' the popular author Sir David Brewster wrote in the spring of 1853, 'so general is the excitement.' The contagion spread even to the royal residence at Osborne, where Queen Victoria and her consort Prince Albert were amazed by the table's antics. Reports appeared by the score of tables not merely turning, moving and tilting, but occasionally actually floating. Careful experiments conducted in Switzerland by the French statesman and scientist, Count Agenor de Gasparin, and a Professor of Physics, Marc Thury, revealed that there were indeed forces, apparently emanating from individuals or groups, capable of making tables and other objects act as if they were being manipulated by an invisible and powerful being.

Spiritualism

When a table appeared to take on a life and personality of its own in this way, some of those who witnessed its antics felt that supernatural forces must be at work. A controversy arose among Protestant clergy whether or not the forces involved were diabolic; and the pastime was condemned as such by the Catholic Church. But another interpretation was that the motions must be the work of spirits – not necessarily of evil spirits, but spirits of the dead.

Belief in the existence of a spirit world inhabited by the spirits of the dead, and by non-human or quasi-human 'elementals' (as for convenience they can be described, though the term has sometimes been used in different senses), had survived – just – under Christianity, and occasionally individuals claimed that they could, and did, enjoy communication with spirits; one of the most celebrated being Friederica Hauffe, 'the Seeress of Prevorst', treated as a patient and carefully investigated in the 1820s by Justinus Kerner of Weinsberg in Germany, who was compelled to accept that, whether or not, as she believed, spirits were responsible, she certainly had striking clairvoyant and magical powers. By the 1840s belief in spirit communication had become sufficiently common to be known as 'spiritism' on the Continent, and 'spiritualism' in Britain; but it was the table-turning craze which finally established it – initially chiefly as a pastime, then as a cult, and eventually as a religion, but also, in all these stages, as a means to produce, and to investigate, the 'higher phenomena', much the same as those of mesmerism, but with a greater emphasis on magical manifestations.

The effective re-birth of spiritualism is usually formally dated from 1848, when two of the daughters of the Fox family, living in Hydesville, New York, challenged a presence which was haunting their home with noises to reply to their 'raps', which it did. The sisters, Margaret and Kate, then began to demonstrate that they had psychic powers, not just to produce what sounded like raps, at a distance, but also to make tables and other objects move, or tilt, and answer questions by the raps, or the tilts – the method usually employed being to run down the alphabet until a rap, or a tilt, indicated the appropriate letter. Whole sentences could be spelled out in this way, sometimes providing information of a kind that the group round it could not have provided, and intimating that it came from a spirit source; either from a spirit 'control' who directed the proceedings, or from 'communicators' – the spirits of people who had died and were anxious to reassure their loved ones that all was well with them.

It had soon been found not to be necessary to have either of the Fox sisters as the 'medium' between the spirits and sitters; found, indeed, that it was not essential to have *anybody* with known psychic powers in the company, if the table was to perform – which was one of the reasons why table-turning so rapidly became a craze. For many groups, it was enough to get the table to give whatever display it chose, for their night's entertainment. But others became intrigued by the information that its raps, or tilts, could provide; particularly when they indicated that the 'communicator' was a dead friend or relation. Sceptics claimed that gullibility on the part of sitters was responsible for their acceptance of the raps and tilts, and even those who could not dispute the evidence of their own eyes and ears were often reluctant to concede that spirits had a role in producing it. Nevertheless there were occasions when the messages spelled out appeared to have come from somebody deceased; as they did in the case of the celebrated mathematician Augustus de Morgan, who in 1853 received information through a medium, which, he felt, could only have been known to himself and his dead father. Attempts to attribute the information to other sources, he observed, were insufficient: the spirit hypothesis was sufficient, 'but ponderously difficult'.

From the 1850s to the 1870s, the dominant figure in spiritualist (as it came to be known) mediumship was Daniel Dunglas Home, who in drawing-rooms or dining-rooms around Britain and Europe produced not merely raps and tilts of tables, but disembodied hands, and music from instruments placed at a distance from him, as well as occasionally himself levitating. He performed in society, for kings and queens, professional men, scientists and *savants*; the seances were conducted in light sufficient for all to see that he could not be physically responsible for what was happening; and he was never detected in any attempt at trickery. Largely because of his influence, from this time mediumship took two courses: displays of the physical phenomena – movements of objects, materializations, and so on; and seances to obtain messages, usually communications from what seemed to be spirits. Home had never taken payment for his seances; but soon there were scores of professional mediums, a few of whom were reported as producing even more spectacular manifestations, such as 'full-form materializations', to all appearances human.

Paradoxically, then, although the great majority of educated men and women would in all likelihood have agreed with Lecky's assertion in his *History of Rationalism*, when it was published in 1865, that they would dismiss accounts of miracles 'with absolute and even derisive incredulity', a socially influential minority had witnessed and accepted as genuine manifestations which were embarrassingly like those which in the past had been regarded and revered as miracles, and were still so regarded in predominantly Catholic countries. Few of those who had attended Home's seances, however, were Catholics; and if they were, were rarely of the type who readily accepted miracles in the traditional sense. Many of those he had convinced, too, remained unconvinced by the spiritualist hypothesis. The assumption that such effects must be regarded as miraculous no longer sufficed. Another category was required; and in 1866, the French astronomer, Camille Flammarion, suggested in *Des Forces Naturelles Inconnues* that they should be given house-room until ways were found to incorporate them into nature's laws, or until those laws were revised.

For this there was a precedent. In the 18th century astronomers had rejected meteorites on the grounds that they were a superstition dating from classical times, when they had been believed to be Jove's thunderbolts. What was rejected as supernatural or miraculous, Flammarion argued, might also be the product of natural but as yet unexplained forces. And as 'occult' had by then become too entangled with the supernatural in the minds of his fellow-scientists for rehabilitation, Flammarion suggested 'psychic' as a new label for them.

The term caught on. When, in 1882, the first organization dedicated to research in the field was founded in London, it called itself the Society for Psychical Research ('psychical' to avoid the confusion which would otherwise have arisen from 'a psychic researcher'). 'Psychical', Edmund Gurney – Hon. Secretary, with Frederic Myers, of the SPR – claimed, did not involve any hypothesis about the nature of the forces; it was simply a convenient term 'under which to embrace a group of subjects that lie on, or outside, the boundaries of recognized science, while seeming to present certain points of connection among themselves'.

The territory which the psychical researchers planned to explore and map was laid down in the aims of the committees set up by the Society; and they show that it was much the same as the territory today regarded as 'paranormal'. But they are also revealing of the kind of problems with which parapsychologists have been confronted: as, for example, in the case of the committee set up to investigate 'the forms of the so-called mesmeric trance state', one form of which was contesting for recognition by medical scientists in a new guise, 'hypnosis'.

For a century – apart from the brief period in the early 1830s when the second of the investigations by the French Academy of the Sciences had reported favourably, and before its report was overturned by the third – orthodox medical science had held that there was no such thing as the mesmeric trance state, or animal magnetism. The introduction by the Scots doctor James Braid in the 1840s of a different theory to account for the trances – that they were induced by a process which was part physiological, part psychological, rather than psychic – had helped gradually to convince scientists that the trance state was a reality; and just about the time that members of the SPR were embarking on their investigations, hypnosis was being accorded grudging recognition. This did not banish the psychic element: in the wave of reports from doctors and psychologists who experimented with hypnosis during the 1880s, several were of the 'higher phenomena', in particular 'community of sensation', or 'exteriorization of sensibility' – the capacity of some hypnotized subjects to 'see' objects behind their backs, or to 'taste' what the experimenter was tasting. But hypnosis itself was taken out of the occult category – though it never quite lived down its occult associations.

The other SPR committees were set up to investigate the influence which a mind could exert on another, other than through the recognized modes of perception – telepathy, as Myers called it; 'sensitives', as people with psychic capabilities were sometimes called; apparitions and hauntings; and 'the various physical phenomena called Spiritualistic'. From the start, there was a divergence between those researchers who accepted that the phenomena, whether physical or mental, *were* Spiritualistic (or, as the Continental researchers still preferred, spiritist) and those who believed, or hoped, that the forces could all be, and in due course would all be, accounted for naturally, for example by telekinesis, as the Russian investigator Alexandre Aksakov called the action of mind on matter.

There was fairly general agreement on the need for psychical research to rid itself of the traditional concept of the supernatural: the assumption that the forces involved broke the laws of nature. To call a *fact* supernatural, Alfred Russel Wallace insisted, was a contradiction in terms; his implication being that the psychic phenomena he had himself observed were facts, and as they did not accord with the established scientific canons, then the scientific canons must be revised – just as the established view of the Creation had had to be revised following his and Darwin's presentation of their theory of evolution.

In France, however, the physiologist Charles Richet took a rather different line. He, too, insisted that the phenomena must be accepted as facts. But they did not, he believed, contradict any accepted scientific truths: 'they are new; they are unusual; they are difficult to classify; but they do not demolish anything of what has been so laboriously built up in our classic edifice'. People who denied their existence on *a priori*, 'against the laws of nature', grounds were simply unable to distinguish between the unusual and the contradictory.

The two attitudes foreshadowed the divergent courses which leading psychical researchers have since taken. Wallace, Crookes, Lodge and others came to accept spiritualism: science, they believed, would have to accept the reality of spirit forces and the process of incorporating them into the framework would require more than minor adjustments. Richet, Baron Schrenck-Notzing and those who shared their standpoint continued to argue that there was nothing wrong with orthodox materialist doctrine; it was simply being too narrowly and arbitrarily defined by scientists who continued to reject the evidence for what Richet called the 'unrecognised latent powers in the human organism'.

A new term was needed for the new science which would accommodate both viewpoints. 'Psychic', admittedly, was useful, and had established itself. But in certain respects it was unsatisfactory, as it was also used by psychologists concerned simply to distinguish psychological from physical reactions. Myers proposed 'supernormal'. To describe something as 'abnormal', he pointed out, meant that it was unusual and perhaps inexplicable, but did not carry the implication that it was contrary to the laws of nature:

a 'supernormal' phenomenon would simply be 'one which exhibits the action of laws higher, in a physical aspect, than are discerned in action in everyday life' – 'higher' implying a more advanced stage of evolution.

Charles Richet, however, preferred 'metapsychic', the counterpart of metaphysics, which Aristotle had adopted to describe those laws which transcend those of simple physics; and at an International Congress in 1923 it was decided to accept Richet's term. Not for the last time, however, the formal decision proved abortive. Emile Boirac had earlier suggested that the study of psychic phenomena should be called parapsychology, 'alongside psychology'; but Richet had objected, saying that it carried the connotation of 'erroneous psychology', a verdict which the congress accepted. In Germany, however, Max Dessoir had begun to describe the research as parapsychology; and it was this term – ironically, in that Dessoir was sceptical – which caught on, as Richet reluctantly had to concede.

Two of the lines of research which the SPR committees had embarked on produced striking results. A surprisingly large number of people provided accounts of apparitions, and other psychic phenomena; and the quality, as well as the quantity, of the evidence, carefully checked by Gurney, disposed of the then prevailing idea that hallucinations (of sounds and feelings, as well as visions) were experienced only by the feeble-minded or the mentally deranged. And protracted tests of the Boston medium Leonora Piper by, among others, William James established beyond reasonable doubt that she was picking up information by extra-sensory means – though whether it came from the spirit world, or from some telepathic ability of a kind never before disclosed under test conditions, remained in dispute.

Investigations of mediums who produced physical phenomena also gave remarkable results – ironically, all too remarkable for the comfort of some of the leading psychical researchers. In particular the President of the SPR, Henry Sidgwick, and his wife Eleanor could not bring themselves to believe that spirits, assuming that they existed, would present themselves in such uncouth and vulgar forms (one of the most commonly encountered of the spirit 'controls', John King, claimed to have been a pirate in his life on earth); and they suspected that the evidence for telekinesis had been based on deception of the kind which the Italian medium,

Eusapia Palladino, had been known to practise whenever she could, 'levitating' tables with her feet.

Eusapia made no attempt to deny that she cheated. In her trance state, she pointed out, she was not aware of what she was doing; it was up to her investigators to control her movements. And in one respect, her record was far more impressive even than Home's: for twenty years she was subjected to tests in rigorously controlled laboratory conditions by dozens of the most eminent scientists in Europe. In light good enough for them to watch what she was doing, the great majority of her investigators reported that they had witnessed movements of objects at a distance from her, and levitations of tables, as well as feeling themselves tapped, nudged, even kissed, as if by an invisible being with a childish sense of humour, who would untie their shoelaces or play with their spectacles.

The Sidgwicks, however, took the results of a test at Cambridge in 1895, at which she was allowed to cheat, as evidence that she was fraudulent; a let-out repeated by sceptics in the United States fifteen years later, to discredit her. Similar tactics were used to damn another physical medium, 'Eva C', Marthe Béraud; and a mass of well-attested evidence of her powers, backed by photographs, was brushed aside not merely by sceptics, but by members of the SPR who felt that the phenomena were repellent (as indeed they often were) and had best be set aside.

Although the British medium Mrs Osborne Leonard was providing evidence of mental mediumship even more impressive than Mrs Piper's, by the 1930s it was evident that the hopes of the founders of the SPR were not being fulfilled. The academic world was even more hostile to psychical research than it had been fifty years earlier; the public, more apathetic. It was only with the publication in Boston of J. B. Rhine's monograph *Extra-Sensory Perception* in 1934, describing research at Duke University undertaken not with mediums but with students, most of whom had not been aware of possessing psychic powers, that parapsychology – as Rhine chose to describe psychical research done along his lines – caught the attention of the public, and compelled academics to take notice.

Psi

'Parapsychology' and 'psychical research' have since been running largely in tandem, the emphasis being on laboratory-type trials with large numbers of participants to find whether there are statistical indications of 'psi' – a term which, though it has yet to acquire colloquial status, is increasingly being used as an umbrella to cover the force, or forces, involved. It was introduced by Dr R. H. Thouless, of the Department of Education at Cambridge University, who wanted a neutral term that would nevertheless indicate the subject, and he thought that the letter of the Greek alphabet would serve as shorthand for the whole psychic range – as it still can; but it is most commonly employed as descriptive of psychic forces, as in 'psi–mediated' which expresses the difference between, say, a message conveyed by thought-transference picked up through sensory clues, and a telepathic communication.

The implication of 'psi', then, and of 'paranormal' is that forces exist – or perhaps a single force, taking different forms – which will eventually be 'naturalized', though this will almost certainly require a fundamental change in scientific thinking to accommodate them, because there is an element in them which distinguishes them from the forces which are accepted as natural. If all forms of life were to be wiped from the face of the earth in some holocaust, gravity would still influence the tides, and electricity would continue to be generated in thunderstorms; but there is nothing to suggest that psi would manifest itself. In one respect it resembles magnetism, which is ordinarily noticed only when arrangements are made to enable it to be, as with compass needles. But psi seems to need living beings (not necessarily human beings) to work through. The most plausible explanation is that the energy is there, permeating space, awaiting its Newton to bring it within science's grasp; but for the present we can observe it only through its effects on and through the living.

Or on, and through, the dead? There is a great deal of evidence pointing to survival of human life, in some discarnate form, after death; and also for the ability of the spirits (or 'discarnate entities', as some purists prefer to describe them) to exert an influence not only on the minds of the living but, in poltergeist-type effects, on matter. Strenuous efforts have been made, however, to account for these phenomena by postulating an extension of the paranormal powers and faculties of the living; and the issue is still in dispute. Either way, in any case, the assumption is that psi needs animate beings or entities to display itself.

The significance of this element in psi has too often been missed by scientists when they call for demonstrations of the force at work, and expect them to be of the kind that can be given with magnetism. For research purposes it is safest to regard psi as the equivalent of the force which prompts people to fall in love: that is, something which happens to and through people, but cannot be laid on in the way that a piece of steel can be magnetized. Some people are more susceptible than others, and become the channel for psi; a few – mediums, or psychics – can sometimes switch on the current, as it were, at will. But nobody has ever been able to switch it on, and keep it on, sufficiently consistently to convert sceptics.

Over the past half-century, the status of the paranormal in the public mind has been rising, though erratically. After the initial impact of Rhine's *Extra-Sensory Perception* in the mid-1930s a reaction set in in academic circles, and the war and its aftermath tended to drive the subject out of serious consideration. In 1949, however, Alister Hardy, Professor of Zoology at Oxford, avowed his belief in telepathy and its importance at the annual meeting of the British Association for the Advancement of Science; the following year the Royal Institution, whose members had been notoriously unsympathetic, opened its doors to a debate on the subject; and in 1955 the independent scientific foundation CIBA held an international symposium on ESP in London. In the United States, recovery after the war took longer, but parapsychology was gradually accepted as a subject for courses at universities; and in 1969 the American Association for the Advancement of Science allowed the Parapsychological Association, an international body, to become an affiliate.

So far as the general public was concerned, however, what brought the paranormal into the household were Uri Geller's television performances in the early 1970s, in which he succeeded in bending metal objects and starting up clocks and watches which had long ceased to work not only in the studio but, as hundreds of viewers wrote in to testify, in homes all over the country. And although subsequently many of those who had been convinced by what they had witnessed changed their minds, coming to believe that Geller must have been a very accomplished conjuror, reports of 'mini-Gellers', not only in Britain but from many other parts of the world, and of laboratory trials conducted with them, kept interest, particularly in psychokinesis, alive. In the United States

Geller's public performances, though the results were less spectacular than in England, sufficed to disturb sceptics, and in 1975 a group of them came together to found the Committee for the Scientific Investigation of Claims for the Paranormal (CSICOP); but it was not long before members who had joined it in good faith began to resign when they realized that some of its leading lights appeared to be interested only in demolishing those claims, and were using distinctly unscientific methods in the process.

Until the 1970s, 'the paranormal' had remained, for most people, little more than an up-market synonym for 'the supernatural'; but by the 1980s it was establishing itself in its own right, as articles in the popular papers and television programmes began to show. When readers of the London *Times* were asked in a 1981 questionnaire about their beliefs, over 80 per cent said that they accepted ESP and telepathy; and although this was a self-selected sample, in that it was of readers who took the trouble to fill in the questionnaire and post it off, in a poll taken nationally that year the proportion of believers was almost as high. This represented a marked increase over the proportion in a national poll taken fifteen years earlier, when over half the sample had replied that they did *not* believe in telepathy.

On another level, too, interest in psychical research has clearly grown since the war, though it is shrouded in official secrecy. The International Astronautics Federation Conference in Paris in 1963 was told by an official of the American National Aeronautics and Space Administration that experiments were being carried out in the United States in 'energy transfer phenomena', a field of research, he admitted, which had been largely ignored by Western scientists; with specific investigation of the relationship between 'the physical fields of particles and the non-demonstrable "personal" psi-plasma field' – in other words, psychokinesis. The results of such research, positive or negative, have not been released; but both the Americans and the Russians have been exploring the possibility of using ESP or PK for military purposes, as Ronald M. McRae has shown in his *Mind Wars* (1984).

Yet it remains difficult to establish that the paranormal deserves serious academic study. Partly this is due to the reluctance of people who have had psychic experiences to admit to them – sometimes from uncertainty whether they really were psychic, when the possibility remains that coincidence, say, is responsible;

sometimes from a reluctance to be regarded as a 'kook'. Kipling, for example, had many experiences of the type which could be regarded as paranormal, but he was careful to insist in his autobiography 'I am in no way psychic', explaining that he had 'seen too much evil and sorrow and wreck of good minds on the road to En-Dor to take one step along that perilous track'. He never grasped that one of the primary aims of psychical researchers was to purge the paranormal of the sinister type of occultism he had in mind, and had warned against in his verse.

> And nothing has changed of the sorrow in store
> For such as go down on the road to En-dor.

2 EXTRA-SENSORY PERCEPTION

GENERAL ESP

We ordinarily acquire information through the five senses of hearing, sight, smell, taste and touch. Its acquisition through other – paranormal – channels was given the German equivalent of 'extra-sensory' by a German psychical researcher, Rudolf Tischner, in the early 1920s, embracing telepathy – perception of thoughts and feelings; clairvoyance – perception of objects, or events; precognition – glimpses of the future; and retrocognition – glimpses of the past. J. B. Rhine adopted *Extra-Sensory Perception* as the title of his 1934 monograph on the research at Duke University: the term caught on, and has been in use ever since, though commonly abbreviated to ESP.

It has had critics. In his *Treatise on Parapsychology* (1960) René Sudre pointed out that information acquired paranormally does not necessarily have the characteristics of a perception; 'it emerges like a memory from the subconscious mind'. It is extrasensory, too, only in the sense that it does not use the five senses as a channel of *entry* for the information. The information, however, reaches consciousness from the subconscious (or, as Frederic Myers preferred it, the subliminal mind, which lies below consciousness's threshold) *through* the senses; so that people may 'see' apparitions or 'hear' voices which appear to them to be real.

The origins of ESP remain obscure. 'We do not even know whether, in evolutionary terms, psi is an emergent faculty – somehow related to man's spirituality – which gradually unfolds, like sentience and consciousness, with each upward step on the evolutionary ladder,' Arthur Koestler observed; 'or whether on the contrary extra-sensory perception is an archaic and primitive form of communication which has been superseded by more efficient forms of sensory perception.' The two possibilities are not mutually exclusive: the ability to exploit ESP may have been latent, and revived by man's spirituality. But whatever the answer,

Koestler emphasized that the question is of fundamental importance; and 'this alone would make the pursuit of parapsychology an immensely worthwhile undertaking'.

What can hardly be disputed is that the most primitive forms of life must have survived and evolved with the assistance of a kind of ESP, as they lacked the five senses – except (and this only to a limited extent) touch. Nevertheless they were capable of exploiting their resources in ways which make the term 'primitive' inappropriate, as Sir Alister Hardy, Professor of Zoology at Oxford University, showed in *The Living Stream* (1965). Single-celled amoebas are commonly referred to as the simplest form of life; yet their near relatives, the *Foraminifera*, 'secrete calcareous shells of many chambers which, in different species, take on almost every imaginable arrangement', and 'build houses which are little short of marvels of engineering and constructional skill'.

There are other examples, notably the case of sponges. The cells which go to form a sponge also have different roles, as described by Lyall Watson in *Supernature* (1973) – the first attempt to provide a synthesis of the qualities of miscellaneous information collected by biologists, naturalists and zoologists, of the kind which orthodoxy cannot satisfactorily explain. Some bring in the sponges' food and digest it; some are sex cells; some are 'cells that build supporting skeletons of such superb geodetic construction that they serve as inspiration for aircraft designers'. Yet if a sponge is cut and macerated, to separate the individual cells which compose it, 'the gruel gets together and organizes itself – and the complete sponge reappears like a phoenix to go back into business again'.

That animals in a more advanced stage of evolution enjoy extrasensory powers has been well-documented. Natural explanations for some still mysterious faculties, such as homing, have been advanced: birds, for example, appear to be able to navigate with reference to the sun, and to the stars, and also to have a built-in bio-magnetic component. But these, though they may help to explain the flight path, do not account for the flight *plan*. Pheromones, too – free-floating scent molecules – have been presented as the explanation for some types of otherwise inexplicable forms of communication, such as those which bring the males of a species to a female on heat; but they hardly account for some of the exploits of, say, lost or stolen pets in finding their owners, many miles away.

Stories abound of pets which have inadvertently or deliberately been left far from their homes, yet have managed to find their way back. Rarer, but well-documented, are cases where the owner has left his old home, and the pet has found him in his new one. The most remarkable achievement so far recorded was by the dog, Tony, who managed to track his owners, the Doolens, from Aurora, forty miles west of Chicago, to Lansing, 170 miles to the north-east of Chicago, the other side of Lake Michigan, in six weeks. And Tony had not gone by water; on his collar there was a tag indicating that he had been in temporary adoption on his way round the lake. In his *Parapsychology* (1964), Gaither Pratt, who had a keen interest in animal ESP, cited other examples, including an account of a dog which once, and only once, started a continuous whining and barking, refusing to come out from under a New Jersey house; later, it was found that the elder son of the family had just been killed in an automobile accident on his way home from college. A homing pigeon, too, which a boy had adopted, managed to find him after he had been taken to a hospital seventy miles away.

Pratt hoped to do some experiments designed to test further the possibility of homing to the owner, as distinct from homing to the pigeon loft; but this proved technically too difficult. There have, however, been some carefully conducted trials with animals, the best known being those carried out in 1912, and demonstrated to scientists by Karl Krall of Munich, who had trained horses to tap out replies to questions with their hooves, spelling names, or solving mathematical problems. One of them, Muhamed, could give the square root of numbers in a few seconds. Sceptics assumed that Krall had found ways to transmit the answers to the horses by signals, so that all their training had consisted of was learning to tap to his nods; and even when he showed that he did not have to be present, the suspicion remained that he might be feeding them the information by sound. But Maeterlinck, when he visited the 'Elberfeld horses' as they came to be known, thought up a way in which even this possibility could be eliminated. In Krall's absence, he shuffled a pack of cards which had numerals on them and placed three face downwards in front of Muhamed:

there was therefore, at that moment, not a human soul on earth who knew the figures spread at the feet of my companion, this creature so full

33

of mystery that already I no longer dare to call him an animal. Without hesitation and unasked, he rapped out correctly the number formed by the cards.

The experiment succeeded as often as Maeterlinck tried it, as it also did with two of the other Krall horses. After his initial amazement, Maeterlinck decided that it was not so surprising, after all, 'that these subliminal faculties not only exist but are perhaps keener and more active than in us, since our conscious and abnormally individualized life atrophies them'.

But why, if the faculty developed early in evolutionary development, has it not matured more satisfactorily for the benefit of mankind? Accounts of what appears to be ESP are quite common; but its actual occurrence, for many of us, is rare. The most plausible explanation is Bergson's: that the human brain is primarily a filter, to process information and sensations coming into the mind, so that they can be dealt with expeditiously on a system of priorities. ESP can only get through when the mind is off-guard, as in dreams and trances; or through certain individuals, such as mediums, in whom the faculty has not been repressed; or perhaps when a signal is particularly urgent, as in 'sixth sense' premonitions.

ESP can be broken down into its different categories, as some examples which follow later will show. But it has to be borne in mind that the distinction is often arbitrary. In *The Invisible Picture* (1981) Louisa Rhine provided an interesting example: the story of a man who, as he was double-parked, was nervously waiting for his wife to come out of a drugstore. By the time she appeared he was so irritated that when she said, 'Guess what I bought!' he replied, sarcastically, 'three dozen wooden clothes pins' – which was precisely what she *had* bought. Assuming that this was ESP, rather than simple coincidence, it could be attributed either to his 'seeing' the pins being bought – clairvoyance; or to reading his wife's mind when she asked him the question – telepathy; or to realizing what was going to happen before the purchase was made – precognition; or to recalling what had happened at the time the purchase was made – retrocognition.

Where it is difficult or impossible to decide which type of ESP is involved, parapsychologists have begun to prefer the classification GESP – general extra-sensory perception – and the results of many trials are best interpreted as indicating GESP rather than, say, telepathy or clairvoyance.

Experimental GESP

Early in the 17th century Sir Francis Bacon proposed ways in which 'binding of thought' might be tested. Among other methods, he suggested trials with cards, which would show whether people reputed to have second sight could demonstrate their faculties. He added that investigators should note 'whether it hit for the most part, though not always', which is precisely what modern investigators have realized they must do, in order to check whether the 'hits' – the correct guesses – exceed the proportion, in any 'run' of guesses, which chance expectation would predict.

If a coin is flipped a hundred times, it will come down 'heads' approximately fifty times, and 'tails' fifty times. It occasions no surprise if there are small deviations either way; but if, in a series of runs of a hundred flips, 'heads' comes uppermost *consistently* more often than 'tails', the suspicion will arise that some factor other than chance must be at work. In the 1880s Charles Richet invoked this principle, testing subjects for their ability to 'thought-read' with the help of a pack of playing cards. He would turn up a card and ask what suit it was; spades, hearts, diamonds or clubs. His reasoning was that if they consistently made more than one correct guess in four, telepathy could be responsible.

The possibility of clairvoyance – the subject 'seeing' the card itself – was not taken seriously. In fact when the psychologist J. E. Coover began testing students at Stanford University, shortly before the first world war, he thought the simplest way to control the experiments was for the transmitting 'agent' to look at half the cards he turned up; his student 'percipients' would then try to guess the cards, and if they succeeded at a rate significantly higher than chance expectation with those cards which the agent looked at, by comparison with those the agent did *not* look at, this would constitute evidence for telepathy. As he expected (he was a sceptic), there was no difference in the rate of correct guesses, whether the agent saw the cards or not.

When J. B. Rhine began conduction tests at Duke University in the early 1930s, using packs of 'Zener cards' with their five different symbols, he took the possibility of clairvoyance into consideration, and found evidence that a few subjects could produce scores consistently higher than chance even when the agent did *not* look at the cards. Re-examination of Coover's figures, too, disclosed that most of his percipients who had scored significantly above chance had scored above chance both with the cards the agent saw and those which he did not see, suggesting that they might have been demonstrating clairvoyance.

Perhaps, Rhine speculated, there is no such thing as telepathy. Perhaps clairvoyance could explain the high scoring when the cards were looked at, as well as when they were not? But at this stage, a joker appeared in the pack. Suppose – it could be surmised – that another component of ESP might be involved – precognition? If so, high scoring in trials might be attributable to the ability of subjects to guess (the term 'guess' also attracted criticism, as it implied a conscious process dissimilar from the one which psychics employ; but like ESP, it has stuck) what card was *next* in the pack? And trials have subsequently shown that some subjects do indeed guess 'precognitively'.

From the point of view of establishing the existence of the paranormal, however, the decision whether telepathy or clairvoyance is responsible for the results is of less importance than the demonstrations which the results gave of GESP, not just at Duke but in trials in other universities.

Perhaps the most spectacular scoring was recorded in 1937 by Bernard Riess of the Psychology Department at Hunter College, New York. Riess found a subject willing to work with him in trials in which he turned up the Zener cards in his study – usually two 'runs' of 25 cards each evening – while she made a note of her 'calls' at home. Out of 1,850 guesses, she made 1,349 'hits' – an average of around eighteen in each run through the Zener pack. But then illness intervened, and in the next series her scores were at chance level.

Although card (and picture) guessing have remained the standard method of testing for ESP, some ingenious variations have been tried, such as the experiment set up in the 1960s by Douglas Dean, of the Newark College of Engineering, exploiting the functioning of the autonomic nervous system – on much the same principle as lie-detector tests. The subject to be tested was given a list of names of people calculated to arouse some emotional impact on him; these were put on cards and shuffled in with names drawn at random from a telephone directory. The blood flow in the index finger of the subject, measured by a plethysmograph, was then monitored – while the names were being called by the agent from a distance. Fluctuations in the flow, it was found, occurred significantly more often when the 'impact' names were called.

In the early 1970s experiments of a different kind were undertaken by two physicists at the Stanford Research Institute, Hal Puthoff and Russell Targ, to test for 'remote viewing' as they chose to call it: 'the ability of certain individuals to gain access to and describe, by means of mental processes, information sources blocked from ordinary perception, and generally accepted as secure against such access'. Subjects in a laboratory were asked to describe, and draw, their impression of target sites at varying distances from the SRI, elaborate precautions being taken to ensure that the 'target demarcation team', which travelled by automobile to the target sites, would not know until they opened their fresh, randomized instructions, where they were going. In addition the comparison of the pictures with the photographs taken at the sites was conducted independently both of investigators and subjects (one of whom, Pat Price, was a former California police commissioner who had found he had psychic abilities).

Three principal findings emerged. It was possible to obtain significant amounts of accurate information about remote locations; distance from the lab. base was not a factor; and it made no difference when the subjects were shielded in a Faraday cage against possible electro-magnetic impulses. The drawings, when approximating to the target photographs, also suggested that the subjects were picking up shape, and sometimes colour, rather than function or name.

Puthoff and Targ's description of their trials was published in the *Journal of the Institute of Electrical and Electronic Engineers* in 1976. In a letter published in *Nature* (17 August 1978) the psychologists David Marks and Richard Kamman of the University of Otago, New Zealand, claimed that the comparison of the target photographs and the percipients' drawings had not been conducted fully 'blind' as the judges had been given some verbal clues; they added that their own experiments to replicate the results had failed. Replying in *Nature* with Puthoff and Targ (13 March 1980) Charles Tart, Professor of Psychology at the University of California, who had not been involved in the original trials, described how he had sent the photographs and drawings to a different judge, randomizing them in ways suggested by Marks and Kamman for future trials; and her assessment had revealed similarly significantly positive correlations to those of the earlier judges. (Trials in some other laboratories using the Marks/ Kamman protocol have since achieved significantly positive replication). The data, Tart concluded, 'continue to confirm the original conclusion that remote viewing is a viable human perceptual capability'.

Ordinarily the weight of experimental evidence for ESP would long since have sufficed to convince doubters. By the early 1950s, unless there were 'a gigantic conspiracy involving some thirty University departments all over the world, and several hundred highly respected scientists', Professor Hans Eysenck of London University commented (and as a Behaviourist psychologist, his scrutiny of the evidence had been critical), 'the only conclusion the unbiased observer can come to must be that there does exist a small number of people who obtain knowledge existing either in people's minds or in the outer world, by means as yet unknown to science'.

Sir George Thomson, physicist and Nobel Prize winner, had taken the same view. The reality of ESP, he claimed in 1952, would certainly have been accepted had it not involved 'such a fundamental upsetting of systems of thought'. Orthodox scientists, however, did not and still do not like to have their systems of thought upset; and although questionnaires have revealed a willingness among a majority of people with academic posts to accept the possibility of ESP, the proportion who are prepared to accept it as proven has remained small. And as it happens, the resistance has been made easier by the inability of parapsychologists to satisfy the criteria which orthodox science lays down, before it can accept research findings; in particular, that they must be repeatable. Experience has shown that there are far too many, and complex, 'variables' for repeatability to be attained.

Psi: the Variables

The most obvious variable is that some people are more psychic than others; and parapsychologists have been unable to decide whether this is primarily the consequence of nature or nurture.

The old assumption was that a few individuals were psychic from birth, but that most people were not; if they had a psychic experience it was the result of some atavistic hiccup. Rhine held this view initially; but gradually, as a result of his experiments, he moved away from it 'completely to the other extreme', as he admitted in 1955: 'subjects are *made*, not *born*' and 'exceptional performance represents a combination of circumstances within and around the subject'.

This would help to account for the many cases on record where subjects have appeared to be exceptionally gifted with psi, and then totally lost it; but it hardly fits with the number of mediums who have retained it all their lives. The most widely accepted proposition today is that some are born with psychic faculties and display them from childhood; others are born with them, but they remain latent until something triggers them into action; and most people either have only limited ESP capabilities, or have too powerful a 'censor' in the brain to display them, though they may break through sporadically – most people have occasional psychic experiences, such as 'dreaming the future'.

A considerable amount of research has been carried out with the aim of discovering whether there are any personality characteristics which individuals who display psychic abilities have in common. Much of the exploration has been with the help of personality inventories of the kind pioneered by Eysenck, differentiating between extraversion and neuroticism. But – as so often, exploring psi territory – initially promising leads have often turned out to end in blind alleys; and surveying the evidence in 1977 John Palmer, Associate Professor of Psychology at the University of California, expressed the view that the only reasonably clear findings to emerge are that people who are successful in laboratory-type ESP tests tend to be (a) 'relatively well-adjusted' and (b) to 'believe in ESP' – particularly when (a) and (b) interact.

As people who do well in laboratory-type tests are not necessarily the most psychic of individuals in everyday life, as many of the celebrated psychics in history have been far from well-adjusted, and as belief in ESP may be not so much a personality characteristic as a product of conditioning or experience, the discovery of these two personality characteristics has been of little value in identifying individuals who would be most likely to provide evidence for psi. Nevertheless, as Palmer points out, 'if theoretical principles uncovered through personality-ESP research can provide insights for those working with other approaches, this research will have been well worth the effort'.

As in many types of psychological test, the possibility that variations of mood may influence results has to be considered – as G. N. M. Tyrrell realized in the 1930s. When R. H. Thouless, reviewing Rhine's *Extra-Sensory Perception* for the *SPR Journal*, urged caution until the Duke experiments had been repeated in Britain, he was taken to task by Tyrrell, whose experience conducting trials himself had made him aware of the problems. 'Dr Thouless seems to regard it as an easy matter for anyone to repeat Dr Rhine's experiments; but what I wish to stress is that anyone who "repeats" them without reproducing the psychological atmosphere has not really repeated them at all.' Tyrrell warned, 'The psychological atmosphere is elusive, but it is clearly of the greatest importance: and if the investigator disregards it, nature will not.'

This comment provoked the derision of Dr E. J. Dingwall, a former Research Officer to the Society, who pointed out that to accept such a variable might entail having to take into account how a subject reacted to what he had had for breakfast. But the evidence for the significance of mood (in the broadest sense) as a variable has continued to grow.

The mere knowledge that they are being tested can affect subjects. As Tyrrell, again, pointed out, expecting a subject who had demonstrated psychic prowess spontaneously to demonstrate it to order in trials was like asking somebody who had said witty things at dinner one night, making the company laugh, to repeat them 'cold' next day.

Attitudes to psi may influence the results of tests. In the 1950s Gertrude Schmeidler, Professor of Psychology at the City University, New York, asked some colleagues and students if they would like to be subjects in an ESP trial. Most expressed mild interest, but two were deeply hostile: a colleague told her that even if ESP were true, he would not believe it; and a secretary expressed the view that such research was not respectable. When the trial was held, Schmeidler found that the mildly interested subjects on balance scored slightly better than chance expectation; the two who were hostile (they had co-operated only because they hoped that she would realize that she was wasting her time, and perhaps jeopardizing her academic prospects) scored well *below* chance.

This gave Schmeidler an idea; and over the next ten years she conducted a number of series of trials to find whether, separating the goats from the sheep by ascertaining which of the participants rejected ESP and which accepted it, at least as a possibility, would make a difference to the results. It did. In every series the sheep, taken as a flock, averaged slightly above chance: the goats, about the same amount below. And since then, most of the trials conducted by other researchers on similar lines have confirmed these findings.

Scoring consistently lower than chance expectation, therefore, so far from providing sceptics with additional evidence against ESP, can actually be held to suggest that ESP is being employed to demonstrate the subject's distaste. But the sheep/goat effect, revealing though it has been to parapsychologists, has done little to convince sceptics, partly because the distinction between the two is subjective, but also because they do not care for the idea that their subconscious may be collaborating with the enemy. And there is the further problem that 'psi-missing' is not just a matter of belief. It can be related to mood – as Rhine found in the course of trials with one of his best subjects, A. J. Linzmayer. Linzmayer had been scoring an average of nearly ten hits in each run of 25 Zener cards – five more than chance; but on one occasion, when he wanted to stop but was persuaded by Rhine to continue, his 'hits' fell to 3.5 in each run.

If this had been an isolated case, it could have been attributed to chance; but there have been many reports of the effects of boredom on subjects undergoing trials. In one of the earliest (and most successful) investigations ever conducted on behalf of the SPR, by Malcolm Guthrie, a Liverpool businessman, and the young Oliver Lodge, newly-appointed Professor of Physics at Liverpool University, two girls who worked in one of Guthrie's shops showed a remarkable talent for card-guessing, and for drawing pictures which matched closely those which their investigator had drawn, in conditions which were as fraud-proof as Lodge could make them, and which no critic has subsequently been able to fault. But the results were not consistent. 'When the children were in good humour, and excited by the wonderful nature of their successful guessing, they very seldom made a mistake,' Lodge reported.

Once, one of them had had 17 successive 'hits'. But periodically they needed the stimulus of some new 'game'. At one point when their powers appeared to have waned they were revived by a switch from guessing pictures to guessing tastes.

Another of the earliest discoveries made by psychical researchers using laboratory-type guessing procedures was that those subjects who began to score above chance expectation rarely kept it up for long. Gradually, in the course of a series of runs, their scores would fall to chance level.

'Decline effect' was observed and recorded by Charles Richet. In the course of his experiments with a hypnotized subject in the 1880s he found she could guess playing cards at a higher rate than chance expectation even when she was not under hypnosis, though her results were less impressive; but he also found that her scoring rate tailed off during sessions, leading him to advocate brief 'runs' in trials. The powers of the young Creery sisters, whose ability to guess cards correctly led to their being used in the earliest formal tests the SPR laid on after its foundation, also showed a deterioration – because, Myers surmised, 'the experiments had become of weighty importance to us, and of somewhat prolonged strain and tediousness to them.' (Eventually the sisters were reduced to cheating with the help of a code, to continue to impress visitors – though as William Barrett pointed out, when he had been testing them earlier they could not have cheated, as his precautions had been more stringent.)

Sometimes what is not so much decline effect as débâcle has been reported. The most successful of the clairvoyants at Duke was Hubert Pearce; but one day he came into the laboratory to tell Gaither Pratt he had had some very worrying news from his home, and from that point on his ability to score above chance left him, never to return. (Nearly thirty years later Pratt went to visit Pearce, by that time a Methodist minister in Arkansas; 'the visit served to renew our friendship', Pratt reported, 'but it did not, alas, revive our professional partnership'.)

Inevitably, sceptics have attributed decline effect to the fact that successful subjects have come under suspicion, or at least aroused more attention, when getting good results, and have consequently been unable to continue to cheat. But in hundreds of trials a few individuals have scored consistently *slightly* higher than chance; getting, say, six or seven, rather than five, 'hits' in runs of

Zener cards. If they were cheats, would they all have contented themselves with cheating at that feeble level? In such trials, too, neither the initial scoring above chance nor the decline effect is registered until after the trial has ended; the individuals concerned would not have been under special observation any more towards the end than at the start.

That performance should be influenced by mood is not in itself surprising; the ability to display ESP may have some affinity with other performances where mood has, or can have, a decisive role – as it can for an actor. The analogy has in fact proved close in a number of respects; particularly in the response of subjects to observers. 'Our worst experiments before strangers have invariably been when the company was dull and undemonstrative,' Lodge noted in his report of the Guthrie experiments, adding that in his opinion, 'the fault rests, for the most part, with the thinkers rather than the thought-readers' – a view most actors, confronted by a torpid or restless audience, would echo.

If the attitude or reactions of witnesses can have an effect on psi scores, so also, it can reasonably be surmised, can the personality of the investigator. The discovery that some investigators appear to be 'psi-inhibitors' was made in the early days of psychical research, because the first President of the SPR, Henry Sidgwick, was one ('the liberal heart which he possessed', William James was to recall, 'had to work with an intellect which acted destructively on almost every particular object of belief that was offered to its acceptance'). Since then, there has rarely been a period when psychical research has lacked psi-inhibitors. They need not consciously be sceptical, any more than Sidgwick was; the mechanism by which they block ESP may have nothing to do with their opinions about psi, or about the performer. The blockage is in the subconscious; or, perhaps, in the lack of psychic rapport with the others involved in a trial.

Yet another complication has been found, making even more difficult the task of judging whether the guesses which percipients make in trials for ESP should be regarded as 'hits'. Where the choice is simple, as in 'heads' or 'tails', the guess must be either right or wrong; but even with playing cards, there are snags. People tend to guess certain cards, such as the Ace of Spades, much more often than others; should the Ace of Spades happen to be among the target cards there will be a higher proportion of 'hits' – but not from ESP.

With drawings, the problem is even greater. Not merely are some objects more likely to be guessed than others, but the possibility has to be allowed for that the percipient will 'see' the object correctly, but interpret it incorrectly; describing an orange, say, as 'a ball', or as 'the sun', or simply as 'a circle' – which, reduced to two dimensions in the drawing, it has become. Displacements of this kind occurred in the tests Upton Sinclair did with his wife; the pictures she 'saw' and drew for him were often strikingly similar to those which he had drawn, but she had put her own interpretation on them.

The problems posed by displacement were to be encountered later in the 1930s by Whately Carington, a psychical researcher who had given up a successful career in the civil service to concentrate on investigating ESP. Dissatisfied with the standard card tests, he evolved a different method, inviting about 250 people to join him in an experiment in which at a specified time each evening, he hung up a drawing, chosen by opening a dictionary at random and finding a drawable object on the page. When the percipients' drawings came in, they were examined to see which of them matched the target drawing; but quite often displacement made judgment difficult, as Rosalind Heywood was to recall in *The Sixth Sense* (1959). She was helping Carington by doing the target drawings, one of which was a peach, which she drew on a twig, with two leaves. A percipient living twenty miles away drew an almost identical picture, but she labelled it 'orange' because, she explained, 'I know it is not an apple as the skin is rough.' The meticulous Carington would not allow this as a 'hit'.

The displacements, he found, could also be in time. Matching the percipients' drawings with the targets, whether done by Carington himself or by an independent assessor, revealed that the number of 'hits' was significantly higher than chance; but it also showed that if the target were, say, an arrow, a slightly higher proportion of drawings of arrows would be sent in both on the day before it was the target and on the day after.

Recognizable displacements of these kinds could be spotted and allowed for; but others could easily be missed, as Gardner Murphy found when he was carrying out trans-Atlantic trials with René Warcollier in France. On one occasion when an agent tried to transmit the idea of prayer by putting himself in the position of somebody praying, the percipient described a curtain, which would have been registered as a 'miss' had not somebody realized that it was in fact an accurate description of the curtain which hung behind the agent, while he was 'at prayer'.

That displacements of these kinds should occur is not surprising, in view of the fact that the transmission of information by ESP is not from conscious mind to conscious mind. An agent's subconscious may be otherwise engaged; a percipient's subconscious may be 'scanning' on its own. But the existence of displacement effect has continued to make life difficult for those parapsychologists who long for precise, easily quantifiable results.

Yet another problem has been posed by experimenter-effect. That investigators may unconsciously influence the results of their experiments in a great variety of ways has long been recognized by psychologists (though often brushed under the carpet as an unwelcome intruder). The fact that some investigators get better results with subjects in ESP tests than others consequently excites no surprise; not, that is, among psychologists prepared to accept the existence of ESP. But what has disconcerted psychical researchers has been the consistency with which some investigators, not themselves sceptics, appear to put a blight on a normally effective subject so that, even when they do not meet, tests give negative results. Can it be that experimenter-effect may work not just at the psychological, but also at the parapsychological level, so that individuals who are psi-inhibitors may be exercising their inhibitory influence on subjects through ESP?

That 'psi experimenter-effect' needs to be taken into consideration in trials was demonstrated in a simple but ingenious experiment carried out by G. W. Fisk, a member of the Council of the SPR, in the 1950s. He had had encouraging results with the aid of a variant on card (or picture) guessing: he sent out cards with clock faces on them, in sealed opaque envelopes, inviting percipients to guess the time on each card. Without informing the percipients, Fisk had half of the clock-face times set by Dr D. J. West, another council member who had tended to be a psi-inhibitor in experiments. Although there was no way in which the percipients could have known whether the time was set by Fisk or by West, when the cards were returned it was found that the correct guesses for Fisk's cards were significantly above chance, while those for

West's were, with one exception, at the chance level. A follow-up test, with a single percipient, produced the same result.

Surveying the accumulating evidence for psi experimenter-effect in Wolman's *Handbook of Parapsychology* (1977), Rhea White has contended that 'it is probably one of the most important variables of all'. If some investigators cannot get results, while others can with the same subject, the investigator cannot be regarded as outside the experiment: 'if psi is a reality, it would be impossible to rule out the experimenter in the results of any investigations'.

One other possible variable on the parapsychological plane has to be taken into account: the existence of discarnate intelligences, of the kind that are assumed to be spirits, intervening in trials. Intervention of this kind has commonly been reported in investigations of poltergeists, and occasionally in connection with ESP tests – for example, through unaccountable disruption of recording equipment at critical junctures. It is now more commonly attributed to 'exteriorization' – psychic energy emanating from a living person, or persons.

With all these complications to face, it is hardly surprising that some investigators have felt, as Dr (now Professor) Donald West has put it, that ESP phenomena appear to retreat before investigators 'like a will o' the wisp' – or, in Koestler's version, like the ink-fish, which baffles predators by enveloping itself at the last moment in an inky cloud, enabling it to escape. And although the proliferation of variables does not destroy the credibility of the phenomena, their presence has effectively spoiled chances of convincing orthodox scientists of the reality of the paranormal by depriving them of repeatable experiments which they can do in their own laboratories with their own subjects, and get the same results.

CLAIRVOYANCE

As defined by Michael Thalbourne in his *Glossary of Terms used in Parapsychology* (1983), clairvoyance is 'the paranormal acquisition of information concerning an object or contemporary physical event'; and he adds the warning that it should not be confused 'with the vulgar interpretation of "clairvoyance" meaning "knowledge of the future"'. Attempts have been made by psychical researchers to remove the confusion by introducing a new term, but without success: whereas Myers's 'telepathy' soon caught on, his 'telesthesia' did not. We are stuck with clairvoyance, and the confusion.

There is a further complication. Clairvoyance, strictly speaking, should be used only when the information is paranormally conveyed by 'seeing' – as in the case of visible apparitions. Information conveyed by 'hearing voices' has a term of its own, clairaudience, which is beginning to acquire colloquial status; so also (though more slowly) is clairsentience, for paranormally transmitted physical effects. Such terms have yet to establish themselves for the paranormal acquisition of information through smell, or of taste; 'olfactory psi' and 'gustatory psi', which have been suggested, have to serve as stopgaps. For convenience these are commonly grouped under clairvoyance, though they may be telepathic, precognitive and retrocognitive. Premonitions of the kind traditionally attributed to the 'sixth sense' may also be included.

Second Sight

Clairvoyance in the narrower sense of 'seeing' paranormally used to be called second sight; and for clarification, the expression might well be revived.

In tribal communities, explorers and missionaries often found, second sight was so commonly experienced that it was taken for granted, the only difference from the other senses being that it was ordinarily used only when required for some particular

47

purpose. Among the Zulus, a century ago, anybody who had mislaid something tried to go into a state of abstraction until the vision of its whereabouts came to him: 'the sight is so clear that it is as though it were not an inner sight', Bishop Callaway, a shrewd and careful observer of Zulu ways, recorded; 'but as if he saw the very thing itself and the place where it is'.

Tribal shamans were expected to be clairvoyant, as were the Old Testament's prophets and the 'seers' of classical times. The Old Testament is packed with examples. Jesus frequently displayed second sight, according to the gospels; so did his contemporary, the Greek traveller and philosopher, Apollonius of Tyana. While in Ephesus he suddenly began to describe an attack on the cruel emperor, Domitian, in Rome, urging on the assassins with growing fervour, to the astonishment of the bystanders; they were subsequently still more startled to find that Domitian had in fact been assassinated at the time.

In the 15th century Joan of Arc's second sight helped to make her a legend in her own lifetime; but perhaps the most celebrated demonstration of 'seeing' what was happening at a distance was provided three centuries later by Emanuel Swedenborg while he was at a reception at Gothenburg, attended by several local notables, some of whom were to testify to the accuracy of the story. Suddenly going into a trance, Swedenborg 'saw' and described the disastrous fire which was sweeping Stockholm 300 miles away, relating the course which it was taking in vivid detail. When, later, a courier arrived from Stockholm it was found that the course which the fire had taken exactly matched Swedenborg's running commentary. In modern times the most celebrated clair-voyant has been the Dutchman, Gerard Croiset, who worked closely with one of Europe's leading parapsychologists, Professor Willem Tenhaeff of the University of Utrecht, and also with the Dutch police, helping to solve many mysteries. Croiset was particularly in demand in cases where people had disappeared without trace; depressingly often he had to tell anxious relatives that the missing person was dead, because he had 'seen' the corpse, and could direct the police to where it lay.

Croiset refused payment for his services, feeling that he had received a divine gift which, if he tried to exploit it for gain, might be lost to him. His readiness to be tested made it possible to monitor many of his cases; and analysis revealed that he obtained his information through visual images which presented themselves as if in clips of film, showing him what was happening or had happened, at a distance – or what was going to happen.

Because he was frequently involved in cases which made headlines, Croiset aroused some suspicion among psychical researchers, who feared he was a publicity-seeker; and sceptics found little difficulty in picking holes in some of his cases, particularly those which had received over-enthusiastic newspaper coverage. Sometimes, too, he had to admit failure. More often he provided leads, but not the full story. A typical example was in connection with the case of the kidnapped wife of a London newspaper executive. Croiset, consulted, correctly said that she was no longer alive, and that two coloured men who were in an old farm dwelling were involved in the crime; and he gave the route that the kidnappers had taken. It petered out before it led the detectives in the case to the farm, leaving them unimpressed. Members of the victim's family, however, pointed out how accurate his account had been; in particular, his claim that at one point on the route there was an aeroplane which he described as 'pre-war' or 'not of this decade'. No such aircraft was found, which helped to cast doubt on his story; only subsequently was it realized that a cinema at the time had been showing the film *Battle of Britain*, and for promotional purposes a full-size mock-up of a Spitfire was exhibited on the roof.

Among recent stories of second sight coming to people who did not look upon themselves as clairvoyant, one of the most remarkable was recounted by Beverley Nichols in *Powers That Be* (1966). Asked by the Canadian Broadcasting Company to do a broadcast from London on British royalty, he decided he would like to end it with a word picture of the Queen driving down the Mall in her golden coach, flanked by the Horse Guards. He was doing so when

without any warning, I had a sharp feeling of discomfort, almost of nausea, accompanied by an acute headache. The picture of the Queen and her cavalcade vanished as swiftly as if it had been blacked out in a theatrical performance, to be replaced by an equally vivid picture of President Kennedy driving in an open car, flanked by his escort of motor-bicyclists with their snarling exhausts. And, as though it were being dictated to me, I began to describe the scene.

The Kennedy scene happened to fit the producer's theme, as Nichols could contrast the elaborate security precautions surrounding the President with the relatively insignificant ones thought necessary then for the Queen. The broadcast over, they were leaving complacently for a drink, when

> . . . a little man with a white face turned the corner. He came to a halt in front of us. He stared at us, not quite seeing us.
> 'President Kennedy,' he blurted out, 'has been assassinated. Six minutes ago.'

In this vision, Nichols had 'seen' the President not in Dallas, but in New York, as if from the window of the apartment from which he had actually seen Kennedy drive by the previous winter. Yet because of the nature of his feelings when he was in the studio, he could not accept the stock 'coincidence' interpretation; they had actually been reflected, he had noticed, on the tape when it was being played back to him – his voice's tempo had changed, while he was describing the Presidential cavalcade, returning to normal when he resumed his description of the scene in the Mall. Cases of spontaneous clairvoyance of this kind, where there is objective supporting evidence, as Nichols realized, are unusual. His was different: he had the tape to lend confirmation.

Ordinarily, second sight shows events, or places; but one other type has quite often been reported in which the clairvoyants are presented with knowledge about somebody they have only just met, as if providing them at a stroke with the kind of background information which they would ordinarily have only about someone whom they knew well.

The renowned German-Swiss administrator, author and playwright, Johann Zschokke, had many experiences of this kind in the early 19th century. A little diffident, he was to recall in his autobiography that occasionally, while he was in company with strangers, their lives would suddenly be revealed to him; and he would find when he questioned them that the portraits, presented ready-made as if he had known them all their lives, were correct.

On one occasion when this happened, the man whose life-history he had obtained in this way began to jeer at the Swiss people; whereupon Zschokke, having first politely asked his permission, proceeded to tell him about his schooling, his youth, and a fault committed in connection with a black money-box belonging to his employer, along with precise details of the room where the box had stood, on a table to the right of the door. 'The startled young man confirmed every particular' – even the money-box episode.

Jung was to relate similar experiences in his *Memories, Dreams, Reflections* (1963), including one in which, to illustrate a contention about the psychology of a criminal made by one of the company he happened to be sitting with at a wedding, he made up a story, complete with details; only to find to his horror that, as some of the other guests knew, he had 'told the story of the man opposite to me, exactly and in all its details'.

That neither Zschokke nor Jung regarded their faculty as an asset (it had never been the slightest service, Zschokke lamented, as it manifested itself independently of his will, often in connection with people 'he cared little to look through') was not unusual. In Britain, people of the old Celtic stock were popularly supposed to enjoy second sight; the fact that they did *not* enjoy it, and wished they did not have it, impressed Samuel Johnson on his tour of the Hebrides, where it was endemic. He had been sceptical, but he found that 'those who profess to feel it do not boast of it as a privilege, nor are considered by others as advantageously distinguished'; consequently 'they have no temptation to feign; and their hearers have no motive to encourage imposture'.

Later, as the conviction grew among scientists and the public that second sight was contrary to the laws of nature, clairvoyants came to be regarded as charlatans, which was one of the reasons why the early psychical researchers often shied away from investigating them. But from time to time individuals emerged who were not professional clairvoyants, whose reputations were such that they could not easily be dismissed as publicity seekers and who were willing to allow their abilities to be tested.

Twice – in 1923, and again in 1933 – members of the Society for Psychical Research tested the Polish psychic, Stefan Ossowiecki, with drawings enclosed in sealed opaque envelopes. In both cases he was able not merely to provide his own drawing of the object, but to make it closely resemble the one which was used in the test. Yet clairvoyance remained a sideline to him, a genial hobby – until the German invasion. Then, he began to use it seriously to warn friends and acquaintances when they were in danger until, in the Warsaw uprising, he met the death he had predicted for himself from a German execution squad.

Although clairvoyants such as Ossowiecki provided impressive evidence, the attitude of British psychical researchers still tended to be that of Frank Podmore – the Society's chief *rapporteur* and historian, but a man with a deeply sceptical outlook, accepting telepathy, precognition and, reluctantly, a few mediums, but little else: clairvoyance *might* occur, but not often enough to bother about. This assumption was only overturned when Rhine began to investigate ESP at Duke in the early 1930s, asking Gaither Pratt to try to find subjects who would do well in tests for 'pure' clairvoyance. Pratt went ahead, sceptically, and for a time obtained only negative results; but when Hubert Pearce, whose mother had displayed psychic powers, volunteered to be tested with the Zener cards, he began to score at an average of about ten on each run – five more than chance expectation.

For eighteen months, Pratt and Rhine tested Pearce under a variety of conditions, making them gradually more stringent: using new packs; putting screens between him and the cards; sitting him at a distance from where Pratt was turning over the cards, sometimes in another building. Yet the high scoring level was maintained. Once, Pearce actually went through the entire pack without a 'miss': 25 'hits' out of the 25. When the series was complete, and the odds against chance being responsible for Pearce's 'hits' were worked out, they were 1 in 10,000,000,000, 000,000,000,000.

Pearce's career as a psychic was relatively brief; not so that of the Czech, Pavel Stepanek, a protégé of the biochemist Dr Milan Ryzl of Prague, who in the 1950s evolved a way of releasing ESP potential in subjects with the help of hypnosis. Curiosity brought Stepanek to his laboratory in 1961; and following the preliminary training through hypnosis, he found that he could enter into an altered state of consciousness without its help, and in that state, score far above chance in trials with cards. The system was simpler than the one used at Duke: all he had to guess was whether the cards, which were kept out of his sight, had a white or a black side uppermost. In the first formal trial he made 2,000 guesses, 1,114 of which were right: a score for which the odds are heavily against chance being responsible.

Unusually, Stepanek's clairvoyance appeared to be largely

immune to decline effect. Investigators came to test him from all over the world; however rigorous their controls, very rarely did he fail to satisfy them that he must have a degree of second sight (appropriately, one of those rare occasions was when he was tested by Dr John Beloff, who had gained the reputation of being a psi-inhibitor; Stepanek provided what could be regarded as confirmation by scoring *below* chance). When he went to the United States for tests there with Gaither Pratt, his prowess showed no sign of falling away in trials of various kinds. They were also to reveal a curious feature of this guessing: it was more likely to be correct on certain cards than on others, as if his psychic self had favourites – 'focusing effect', as Pratt described it.

Year after year, Stepanek submitted to many different trials. 'He's managed to keep on clairvoyantly identifying cards longer than anyone in history,' Sheila Ostrander and Lynn Schroeder commented in their *Psi: Psychic Discoveries behind the Iron Curtain* following their tour of the Soviet Union and its satellites in the late 1960s; as a result, more than anybody else he helped to open the gates of the scientific establishment to psi and 'for that alone he deserves a niche in the history of psychic research'. Echoing an opinion expressed by many of his investigators, astonished at the good-humoured patience with which he underwent tests, Ostrander and Schroeder added that 'it couldn't happen to a nicer person'.

Although many other people have demonstrated the ability to score significantly above chance in clairvoyance tests (at least until decline effect sets in), only a few have displayed abilities comparable to Stepanek's: notably Ingo Swann.

A New York artist, Swann relished off-beat types of test, and one of his specialities was 'seeing' and describing as it were from above, looking down – what the terrain looks like at any point of the world's surface. In 1973 a sceptical colleague of the physicists Hal Puthoff and Russell Targ of the Stanford Research Institute, knowing of their interest in psychical research, challenged them and Swann to do a test, but under more stringent controls than those to which he had been accustomed. Seated in an SRI laboratory, he was asked to describe what he would 'see' at a certain place; the only information which he (and his SRI investigators) were given was the precise latitude and longitude; and to ensure that he had not performed the barely credible feat of knowing what maps would reveal to anybody who had taken the trouble to learn all the co-ordinates, the world over, off by heart, he was asked to give details which maps would *not* show, of a place 3,000 miles away. He did: at the same time drawing a rough sketch indicating where there were buildings, a road, a fence and trees. 'Not only was Swann's description correct in every detail,' the challenger had to concede, 'but even the relative distances on his map were to scale.' To perform such a feat once would alone have strained the 'coincidence' explanation beyond credibility; but Swann was able to pass such tests time and again.

Travelling Clairvoyance

The mesmerists of the first half of the 19th century were continually reporting cases of 'travelling' clairvoyance among the 'higher phenomena', but in a loose sense. They would tell a mesmerized subject to visit another room in the same building, or a room in another town – and describe it, along with an account of anything that was happening in it at the time; the details could be checked later.

Of all the 'travelling clairvoyants' the best known was Alexis Didier, who gained an international reputation in the 1840s for his ability to tell strangers, often curious and sceptical foreigners, what he could 'see' when he 'travelled' to any place which they cared to nominate; an ability vouched for after tests even by the leading conjuror of the time, Robert-Houdin. Once M. Séguier, the President of the French Law Courts, thought he had caught Alexis out in error when, describing on request the contents of his study, Alexis included a bell, sitting on his desk. Séguier knew it had not been on his desk that morning; but when he returned home, he found his wife had put it there. Alexis's manager and mesmerist, J. B. Marcillet, amassed a quantity of such accounts, attested by well-known public figures – Victor Hugo among them. The only explanation which his detractors could think up was that Marcillet must have planted agents all over Europe, to find out in advance who were going to test Alexis, and provide him with the required information about them; a hypothesis so farfetched that it constituted an unintentional testimonial to Alexis's powers.

But did Alexis actually 'travel' – did he have a psychic component which actually visited the places he described? One of the beliefs associated with shamanism was that the shaman's spirit could, if he wished, leave his body while he was in his trance and visit places ten or a hundred miles away to collect information. The French missionary Father H. Trilles described in his *Fleurs Noires et Ames Blanches* (1914) how on one occasion, when a Yakibou witch doctor said he was going to forgather with others, in the spirit, at a place four days' march away, Trilles decided to test him by asking him to call on one of Trilles' converts, who had some cartridges he needed, and tell him to bring them. Trilles was careful to keep an eye on the witch doctor for the day-long duration of his trance. Three days later, the convert appeared with his cartridges; he had heard the witch doctor, he explained, calling to him from outside his hut, to tell him to bring them to Trilles at once.

With the setting-up of the Society for Psychical Research in the 1880s, and the collection by Gurney and others of all the reliable anecdotal evidence they could lay their hands on for psychic phenomena of any kind, a few cases with an element of actual 'travel' were submitted and investigated. The Rev. P.H. Newman described how when he was still sceptical in such matters, he dreamed he had seen the woman who was to become his wife going up a flight of stairs, and had put his arm around her waist; he had noted the time, ten o'clock; and when he awoke next morning, had written to her describing the dream. His letter crossed one from her saying that, as she was going to bed, at ten o'clock, she had distinctly heard his footsteps on the stairs and felt his arm around her waist.

Some experiments followed in which amateur psychical researchers tried to 'travel' to visit loved ones or fellow-researchers, and in a few cases the visited person reported some vision or 'voice' to confirm that the 'traveller' had indeed manifested himself. But interest in this type of investigation faded, and when experiences of travelling clairvoyance began again to be reported, the emphasis had switched to a rather different type of phenomenon: reports from individuals who while asleep, or dozing, or unconscious, felt that they had left their bodies and floated up towards the ceiling, thence to watch, and sometimes listen to, what was going on below.

Out-of-the-Body Experiences

An out-of-the-body experience has been succinctly defined by

Susan J. Blackmore in her book on the subject as one 'in which a person seems to perceive the world from a location outside his physical body'. She stresses that it refers to an *experience*, 'not to any objective fact of separation'; in other words it may be hallucinatory. When the term first came into use the stage had been set for it by Sylvan Muldoon and Hereward Carrington's *The Projection of the Astral Body* (1929), whose title indicated the assumption that there is actual separation in such cases; a belief derived from the teachings of the Theosophists, who held that there is an 'astral body' which can leave the physical body and travel. To psychical researchers, this was taking too much for granted; so the term 'Out-of-the-Body Experiences', initially abbreviated to OOBEs but recently more commonly to OBEs, has been adopted as a less loaded alternative.

In a survey in 1954 of what he called 'ESP projection' Hornell Hart, Professor of Sociology at Duke, made the distinction between simple experiences of being out of the body and those cases which provided evidence that the individuals concerned had actually 'travelled' because they had 'seen' something which was actually happening at the time – as about one in three had, in his sample. Since then other surveys derived from the answers to questionnaires in the US and in Britain have shown that OBEs are surprisingly common (though few people have more than one), and are most frequently encountered when unconscious – as after an accident, or while under an anaesthetic. Easily the commonest varieties consist simply of the experience of floating in the same room, near the ceiling, seeing the unconscious body on the bed below, which does not in itself constitute evidence either for ESP or for 'travel'; and most of the accounts of 'travelling', though often they confirm that what was 'seen' was subsequently found to be veridical, contain indications that what was seen did not exactly match up with what was happening, which favours clair-voyance or chance rather than 'travel'.

The first detailed account of the use of self-induced OBEs with a view to exploring the possibilities of 'travelling' appeared in 1971: *Journeys Out of the Body*, by Robert Monroe, an American businessman. Monroe was initially alarmed by the experience, but came to enjoy it, and to use it to make 'visits'. On one occasion, for example, he thought he would find how a friend who had been ill was faring, and was surprised to 'see' him up and about –

as inquiry afterwards revealed that he was; dressed, too, in the same clothes as Monroe had 'seen' him in. Monroe's most spectacular achievement was to 'visit' a friend on holiday, at a distance in a country cottage. Unable to attract her attention, when he found her talking to a friend, he decided – though out of his body and invisible – to try to give her a playful pinch. She duly started, as if sl.: had felt something. When she returned, he asked her if she recalled feeling anything; she replied by showing him a small bruise where the pinch had been made.

Although Monroe and others were able to provide a great deal of evidence of 'travel' it was too anecdotal to satisfy those parapsychologists who, though prepared to accept out-of-the-body experiences *as* experiences, doubted whether there is any paranormal component – and still more, that any 'extrasomatic' power is involved, enabling the 'OBE-er' to exercise any physical influence at a distance from his physical body. Karlis Osis of the American SPR worked out a way for a psychic, Keith Harary, to demonstrate that something actually travelled, by having Harary in one room, periodically inducing trances and, while in them, 'visiting' another room to see if he could make his presence there felt by human detectors. They were not told when to expect his OBE activity; their function was simply to report anything unusual in the way of their own feelings or sensory images. At the end of the first session it was possible to ascertain whether the detectors' responses were significantly more frequent during Harary's OBE periods; they were. Even more remarkably, he influenced a kitten; it stopped meowing when, while out of the body, he stroked it. And although tests with instruments proved in general negative, on one occasion a magnetometer behaved eccentrically.

The psychiatrist Jan Ehrenwald has distinguished between three interpretations of the condition in which 'the experiencer's body turns into a depersonalized soulless object', watched by the observing self 'hovering above or localized far away from his physical habitat'. It can be regarded either as a psychiatric syndrome, charged with colourful detail from folklore or the subject's imagination; or as a condition which, though derived from an altered state of consciousness, does, or can have an ESP component; or as actually involving the separation of a disembodied entity from the body, facilitating 'travel' on a psychic plane. The evidence for the second of these interpretations is strong; for the third – the extrasomatic hypothesis – though still inadequate to satisfy those who demand rigorous scientific proof, it is at least sufficient to lend some confirmation to the historical evidence which the early SPR experimenters provided.

'Finger-tip Vision'

One other form of clairvoyance has often been reported, called by a variety of names, of which 'finger-tip' is perhaps the most familiar. In so far as this implies that only finger tips have some mysterious quality that can occasionally enable them to stand in for eyes, it is misleading; in many of the accounts, psychics have used other parts of their anatomies. In his psychiatric practice in the late 19th century, the Italian criminologist, Cesare Lombroso, had to treat a girl for hysteria who, he found, 'saw with her ears'; she could read lines of print if they were held to the side of her head. When in the 1920s the curiosity of the French writer, Jules Romains, was roused by accounts of the way in which sleep-walkers have performed a variety of intricate actions while their eyes appear to be tightly closed, it prompted him to ask himself whether there might not be some other organ in the body which, in certain circumstances, could stand in for normal vision; and he found that some of the subjects tested displayed what he described as 'para-optic' ability, which enabled them to detect colours and read sentences. Some used their fingers, others used different organs in order to 'see'.

The most celebrated displayer of para-optic vision in recent times has been Rosa Kuleshova, a nearly blind girl from the Urals, who found in the early 1960s that she could 'see' with her fingers. Understandably sceptical, her doctor tested her and was surprised to find that she could. Subsequently Rosa was to give successful demonstrations for the members of the Soviet Academy of Science, and to undergo numerous tests designed to discover whether one of the other five senses might be responsible – for example, to find if finger tips were unusually sensitive to texture (enabling her to read ordinary print as she read braille) or to dyes (enabling her to 'feel' colours). No explanation of this kind could be found; and eventually her investigators settled for acceptance of a new faculty, 'bio-introscopy'.

Investigating the 'higher phenomena' the mesmerists had often encountered what they called autoscopy: the ability of certain subjects in trances to 'see' into their own bodies, or the bodies of other people. One of them had greatly impressed the members of a committee of the French Academy of the Sciences by pronouncing a diagnosis on a sick woman which contradicted the one made by her doctors: when she died, shortly afterwards, the autoscopic diagnosis was found to be correct.

The most plausible explanation for para-optic, bio-introscopic or autoscopic vision is that it is basically clairvoyant, the fingers or other organs being no more than a pointer, concentrating the faculty. Recent reports from China of the discovery of children who can 'see' with various portions of their anatomies, even their backsides, tends to confirm this hypothesis. Soviet investigators, desperately anxious as they have been to avoid committing themselves to anything which can be derided as paranormal, have emphasized that Rosa was not psychic in other respects; but she was in fact subject to fits – traditionally linked in shamanism with psychic capabilities (fits were one of the indicators in tribal communities of a potential shaman). Mentally unstable though Rosa also was, making it easier for a sceptic to dismiss the claims made for her, reports on her abilities make up an impressive dossier; in any case, as so often has happened, the publicity attaching to her led to the discovery of many other people with similar powers.

Clairaudience

The term clairaudience came into use among mesmerists and spiritualists in the middle of the 19th century to describe sounds, or voices, heard in the inner ear as if they were real; and it has come to be regarded as one of the forms of clairvoyance, in the loose sense of that term. It can, however, be telepathic, or precognitive; or it may take the form of an apparitional experience.

Shamans often believed that the information reaching them from spirits was spoken out loud. So did the prophets in the Old Testament. The chronicler of the first book of Samuel recalled that clairaudient communication 'was precious in those days; there was no open vision' – no visual clairvoyance; so when old Eli found that the child Samuel could hear the Lord's commands, he knew that Israel had another prophet in the making, 'and all Israel, from Dan even to Beer-sheba, knew that Samuel was established to be a prophet of the Lord'.

Socrates heard his daemon's instructions clairaudiently. 'The divine faculty of which my voice is the source has constantly been in the habit of opposing me even about trifles, if I were going to make some slip or error in any matter,' he told the judges who had condemned him to death; but the voice had not prompted him on this occasion. 'What do I take to be the explanation of this silence? I will tell you. It is the intimation that what has happened to me is a good, and that those of us who think that death is an evil are in error.'

As Myers noted, Joan of Arc's voices are particularly well documented, because she was condemned mainly on the strength of them; her words at her trial resemble those of Socrates, in their 'resolute insistence on the truth of the very phenomena which were being used to destroy her'. She began to hear the voices in childhood, attributing them to angels; they usually came while she was awake; and what they told her was usually correct – as when they said that a sword would be found behind the altar of the Church of St Catherine of Fierbois, and warned her she was about to be wounded in battle. 'Her answers are clear and self-consistent, and seem to have been little, if at all, distorted by the recorder,' Myers observed. 'Few pieces of history so remote as this can be so accurately known.'

People who heard voices were usually careful not to disclose the fact, in view of the risk of condemnation to the same fate as Joan. But a clairaudient experience was reported of Calvin, who had no reason to fear the stake. According to Theodore Beza, who was to succeed him as leader of his party, on the night of 19 December 1562 Calvin heard 'a very loud sound of drums used in war', and although it was stormy at the time, he could not shake off the feeling that they were real. 'I entreat you to pray,' he told his friends the following day, 'for some event of very great moment is undoubtedly taking place.' It was: the Huguenots were suffering a catastrophic defeat at the battle of Dreux.

Although the threat of execution as a witch faded in the 18th century, it was replaced for clairaudients by the threat of incarceration in a lunatic asylum; 'hearing voices' came to be regarded as an indication of incipient insanity. It was only with the publication of the range of psychic experiences collected by

Gurney and Myers in Britain and by Flammarion in France that, as with apparitions, it came to be recognized as something which anybody might experience – though recognition was slow to spread to the public.

Sometimes the messages heard represented telepathic communications. Flammarion cited the case of Count Gonemys, a doctor in the Greek army, who was approaching the destination to which he had been posted when he heard an inner voice telling him 'Go and see Volterra'. Gonemys did not know Volterra; he remembered having once seen him, ten years before, but he had not been thinking of him. Hardly had he reached his hotel when Volterra arrived, begging Gonemys to treat his son, who for five years had been crazy, continually in paroxysms 'accompanied by whistlings, howlings, bayings and other animal cries'. Hypnotized, the son calmed down, and recovered his sanity – as Volterra was to testify.

Precognitive clairaudience has often been reported. Two of the cases are unusual, in that both were linked to broadcasts. In *The Invisible Picture* Louisa Rhine records the case of a man who was dozing in a chair on 7 December 1941 when he woke up suddenly to express his shock at President Roosevelt's radio announcement of the Japanese attack on Pearl Harbor. His wife, who had been listening to the radio, told him he must have been dreaming; there had been no such announcement. While they were still talking about it, an announcer broke into the programme: 'Flash! The President has announced that the Japanese are bombing Pearl Harbor.'

At 8.30 on the morning of 3 June 1964 Lady Rhys Williams, a former governor of the BBC, told her daughters she had heard on the radio that Goldwater had defeated Rockefeller in the California primary. So he had; and some other details she had mentioned were correct. But the first announcement of Goldwater's victory was not made until seven hours after she had 'heard' the broadcast.

Sometimes clairaudience has provided a useful warning. One such case, reported in the Boston *Transcript* in 1894, was checked later by Richard Hodgson on behalf of the Society for Psychical Research. A Boston dentist was at his work-bench, using a copper vessel to make the substance then employed to set false teeth, when he heard a voice telling him 'Run to the window, quick!' Without thinking, he ran to the window to look out; and as he reached it, the copper vessel exploded with such force that it broke the work-bench, and left bits of copper embedded in the ceiling. The report in the *Transcript* came from a patient who arrived for treatment. The dentist had been alone at the time, he admitted to Hodgson, so he could not verify the story; but the appearance of the dentist's workshop had substantiated it.

In his autobiography Tito Gobbi recalled how on an occasion when he was driving up a mountain road with a precipice alongside, he suddenly heard the voice of his brother, Bruno, saying 'Stop at once.' He stopped: moments later an articulated lorry whose brakes had failed careered down the road towards him; if he had not stopped, he believed, he 'would have been swept away to my death at the corner'. His brother had died not long before, killed in an air crash; Tito Gobbi was certain that it was his voice he had heard: 'I know it to this day.'

Out of nearly two hundred cases of clairaudience collected by Louisa Rhine, only one gave a warning of this kind – she noted in some surprise – by somebody living. A trucker who had fallen asleep at the wheel described how he was woken, just in time to swerve his truck away from a wall, by hearing his mother calling him, just as she had done when he was a child. His mother, Louisa Rhine found, had not been aware of feeling any alarm about him at the time.

One other type of clairaudience has quite often been reported by musicians: they have 'heard' compositions, as if an orchestra were playing them in advance. Saint-Saëns told Flammarion that on the last day of the Franco-German war, he and his fellow soldiers at the front had been able to dine unexpectedly well ('upon an excellent horse') and were feeling well-satisfied with themselves when 'suddenly I heard, running through my head, an unusual dirge of melancholy chords'; a profound sadness overcame him, with the certainty of some misfortune. Later, he heard that his close friend Henri Regnault had been killed at that very moment: 'I experienced, therefore, the reality of telepathy before the word was invented.' The dirge which he heard was to become the opening of his Requiem.

Clairsentience

The term clairsentience, used to describe the transmission of psychic information through direct physical impulses, has yet to establish itself among parapsychologists: it does not feature in Thalbourne's *Glossary*. It presents problems, too, of definition, usually being hard to distinguish from the process by which the body responds to stimuli without the intervention of the conscious mind. A telepathic clairvoyant or precognitive 'flash' may alert the body to take the appropriate action in such a manner that, to the individual concerned, it will appear that his body has been moved by an invisible agency.

This was G. N. M. Tyrrell's explanation of a case he had come across. In *The Personality of Man* (1946) he recalled an occasion described by a woman he knew who had lost a ruby out of a ring while doing some washing, and who had assumed it must have gone down the drain. The next morning, in the same room, she seemed to hear someone say 'What about the ruby?' and, forgetting she was alone, she replied 'Oh, that's gone for good.' At that moment 'I seemed to be grasped by the shoulders and twisted round, and the first thing my eyes rested upon was the ruby on the floor, shining in a shaft of sunlight.' She was careful to explain that she did not actually feel her shoulders grasped, any more than she had heard a particular person's voice. It was unlikely, Tyrrell thought, that she had been acted upon by any force from outside; 'she merely *felt* as if she were being moved.' The signals sent by the subliminal self, in other words, 'may take the form of inner feelings or impulsions.'

Such inner feelings have been fairly frequently reported, particularly if the individual who has been impelled feels that they have taken him out of danger. In 1844 N. P. Tallmadge, Governor of Wisconsin, was invited to join the Presidential party on a trip down the Potomac in the warship *Princeton*; one of the events being the firing of a cannon, so powerful that it had been facetiously named 'The Peacemaker'. Standing beside the breech, he witnessed three discharges without a qualm; but just before the fourth, and last, was due, he was suddenly seized with such dread that he found himself irresistibly impelled to go down to the cabin to join the ladies of the party. 'The Peacemaker' thereupon exploded, killing five of the group standing round it, including two cabinet ministers. 'I rushed on deck,' Tallmadge recalled, describing the occasion, 'saw the mangled and lifeless bodies, and found that the gun had burst at the very spot where I had stood at the three former fires, and where – if I had remained at the fourth – I should have been perfectly demolished.'

Winston Churchill was moved by such impulsions on a number of occasions; as when, escaping from his Boer captors, he felt he was 'guided' to the only house in a settlement whose owner would not immediately have handed him over to the authorities. And in her autobiography, Lady Churchill recalled another example, from her own experience.

At the end of a tour of inspection he made during the Blitz, Churchill refused to go back to Downing Street in the armoured car in which he had been travelling, complaining that it was too uncomfortable. Instead he commandeered a staff car. He was about to get in on the nearside, as he always did, when 'for no apparent reason he stopped, turned, opened the door on the other side of the car himself, got in, and sat there instead' – something Lady Churchill had never known him do before. While he was being driven back a bomb fell near the car, the blast lifting it on to its two nearside wheels. Had he been sitting on the nearside, the car would have turned over: 'Only Winston's extra weight had prevented disaster'. When she heard what had happened, his wife asked Churchill why he had changed his mind, getting into the car. Something had made him stop, he said, in a way that told him he was meant to sit on the other side. 'I sometimes have a feeling – in fact I have had it very strongly – a feeling of interference,' he told a miners' gathering later in the war. 'I want to stress it. I have a feeling sometimes that some guiding hand has interfered.'

Intervention by what seems to be a guiding hand is not the only form clairsentience can take. 'Touch', in this context, is not a clearly defined sense; it embraces perception of changes of temperature, for example, and also the effect of radiations. It is possible, and indeed likely, that the body has psi-receivers, capable of picking up psychic emanations or transmissions; Dr H. G. Heine has argued that the vehicle of the sixth sense is the reticulo-endothelial system, its cells providing a chemical communications network. Clairsentience, through some such process, may eventually be found to account for perception of changes of temperature in seances or hauntings when no actual change of temperature has occurred; perhaps also for the perception psychics report of the presence of 'ley lines', or of underground streams.

Psychic Odours and Tastes

If psychic communications sometimes have to try to force their way into our awareness through one or other of the five senses, it need come as no surprise that there is an extensive literature about psychic smells. In hagiography, the 'odour of sanctity' was commonly reported as pervading the atmosphere around holy men and women, or even around their corpses; people in haunted houses have often encountered odours of a very different kind – usually of corruption or putrefaction; and sitters at spiritualist seances have also occasionally reported a specific smell associated with a spirit, or 'control'.

Taste – in any case largely dependent upon the sense of smell for recognition – has rarely been reported in a psychic context. But both 'olfactory' and 'gustatory' (as the Swiss psychologist Theodore Flournoy labelled them) psychic experiences have been elicited by experiments.

Playing his 'telepathy game' with his family and friends, Gilbert Murray, Regius Professor of Greek at Oxford University, occasionally picked up part of the information through smell. When he caught the odour of burning oil or paint, which linked up with his impression that the scene was Italy, it led him to the correct guess that the target subject was Savonarola's Florence, with the people burning their possessions. On another occasion he got 'a sort of smell of wild animals – carnivorous animals'; the target was a lion in the zoo trying to trap meat outside its cage. And when the target was an opium den off Piccadilly Circus, he smelled 'some incensy stuff – I should think it was opium or hashish'.

In *The Confessions of an Octogenarian* (1942) L. P. Jacks, editor of the *Hibbert Journal* and Professor of Philosophy at Oxford for over forty years, observed that he had never seen a ghost, 'but I think I can claim to have smelt one' – not the ghost of a human being, but of a cigar. His father-in-law, Stopford Brooke, had been in the habit of smoking a dozen or more strong Manila cigars a day. Writing Brooke's biography, Jacks finished a chapter one night at one A.M. and was about to put out the lights and go to bed when quite suddenly the room filled, almost overpoweringly, with the unmistakable odour of Manila cigars, which 'lasted for some minutes before going as suddenly as it came'. A sceptical friend suggested that Jacks might have picked up the smell of the cigar of a policeman on the beat under the open window; but the window was shut and the house a lonely one, on no beat.

Although it is little known, the experimental evidence for psychic smell and taste is strong, largely because of a discovery in the 1780s by one of the disciples of Mesmer, Dr J. H. Petetin, a past President of the Lyon Medical Society. Testing one of the patients to find what she could 'see' when she was in a mesmeric trance, Petetin found that the patient could also 'taste' food simply by touching it. And from that time on, one of the ways in which the mesmerists sought unsuccessfully to convince conventional scientists of the reality of the 'higher phenomena' released in a few subjects in their trances was to show that the subjects could identify objects by taste or smell which they could not taste or smell in the ordinary way: 'community of sensation'.

In his *Letters on Animal Magnetism* (1851), William Gregory, Professor of Chemistry at Glasgow University, described tests which had been made of this form of psychic communication. In one of them a servant girl working for the Rev. Andrew Gilmour of Greenock (clergymen were more willing to do this kind of research than scientists, and servant girls were their most readily available subjects) could, when mesmerized, tell him correctly what he was tasting. William Scoresby too – Fellow of the Royal Society, and credited in the *Dictionary of National Biography* with having laid 'the foundation stone of Arctic Science' – conducted similar tests, finding one subject who could tell him not merely that what he was tasting was a biscuit, but also what kind of biscuit it was. And Wallace, before he made his name as a naturalist, having heard about community of sensation, did tests with boys at the school where he taught, and found one who could 'taste' whatever Wallace put into his own mouth, and 'smell' whatever Wallace was smelling.

When, in the 1880s, the Liverpool businessman Malcolm Guthrie was testing two clairvoyant show-room assistants, and found that, after initial success, the girls appeared to lose their faculty, he was embarrassed, as he had been so impressed by them that he had invited Myers and Gurney of the newly-formed SPR to test them. Could the girls perhaps regain the faculty, if the guessing was switched to test for community of sensation? The idea proved fruitful. One of the girls, Myers and Gurney found, could indeed come close to 'tasting' what they were tasting.

Substance	Guess
Carbonate of Soda	Nothing 'tasted'
Cloves	Cloves
Citric acid	Salt
Acid jujube	'Pear drops'
Candied ginger	'Something sweet and hot'
Home-made noyau	Salt
Bitter aloes	'Bitter'

Although the girl had scored only one direct 'hit' the overall score was clearly far higher than chance expectation; particularly as one of the substances, noyau (a liqueur), would have been unfamiliar, and others, though familiar as ingredients, are rarely tasted on their own.

Such tests have sometimes been performed since, ordinarily with hypnotized patients, with positive results. But largely owing to a lingering disinclination to the use of hypnosis in experiments, felt even by parapsychologists, trials of community of sensation have not established themselves as a standard experimental procedure.

TELEPATHY

Historically, the idea of communication between mind and mind, as distinct from second sight or clairvoyance in general, is a relative newcomer. Even its immediate predecessor 'thought-reading', by which the distinction was first conveyed, only entered the language around the middle of the 19th century. As a result, though there is evidence from all eras and all parts of the world of belief in such communication, it is rarely possible to make a clear-cut distinction between it and other types of extra-sensory perception. When, for example, the King of Syria complained that there must be a spy in his camp and a servant told him that the 'spy' was the prophet Elisha, in Israel, who was telling his king 'the words thou speakest in thy bedchamber', the implication was that Elisha must be picking up the information by ESP; but whether by telepathy or clairaudience was not indicated.

During the earlier part of the 19th century, the notion began to emerge that thoughts and feelings could be transmitted, person to person, at a distance: a different, and a higher, more personal form of communication than clairvoyance, which was acquiring its gypsy-fortune-teller, fairground image. Stories began to circulate of well-known men and women who had suddenly found themselves, for no obvious reason, cast into deep gloom, only to hear by the next mail that some close relation or friend had died. Working on some compositions in 1833, Schumann was haunted for four days by a certain passage, which filled his mind with pictures of coffins and despairing faces; and when he came to cast around for a title, *Leichenphantasie* (Funereal Fantasy) came to mind. Only when a letter from his sister-in-law arrived telling him of the death of his brother did Schumann feel that 'everything was explained'; and the composition was renamed a Nocturne.

The first formal presentation of thought-reading in its own right was in a paper by William Barrett, Professor of Physics at the Royal College of Science in Dublin. Barrett had been observing a friend's experiments with mesmerism; and one of the village children who was being tested, Barrett had noticed, could 'feel' and 'taste' what the mesmerist was feeling or tasting in ways which Carpenter's theory of hyperacuity of the senses could not account for. There must be some as yet undiscovered channel of communication, he told the British Association for the Advancement of Science at its annual meeting in 1876, to account for this 'community of sensation' – and not only of sensation: 'ideas or emotions occurring in the operator appear to be reproduced in the subject without the intervention of any sign, or visible or audible communication'.

Some members of the British Association were disgusted that such a subject should have been aired. E. Ray Lankester, who had emerged as the scourge of the mediums, wrote to *The Times* to complain that its discussions had been 'degraded' by the introduction of spiritualism. But the paper gave encouragement to those who, like Myers and Gurney, had become convinced that there must be some channel of communication other than those provided by the five senses; and one of the first objectives of the Society for Psychical Research when it was formed six years later was to examine 'the extent of any influence which may be exerted by one mind upon another, apart from any generally recognized mode of perception'.

Myers realized, however, that a new term was needed, as 'thought-reading' had come to be used to describe an act popular with audiences in music halls, in which performers would pretend to be able to read minds while in fact employing some deception. He proposed 'telepathy', defining it as 'the communication of impressions of any kind from one mind to another independently of the recognized channels of the senses'; and unlike so many attempts to graft on refinements of terminology, this term 'took', not only with psychical researchers but with the public.

Most of the accounts of ostensibly telepathic communication collected in the early years of the SPR should in retrospect be put in the broader ESP category, as a clairvoyant element cannot be excluded; but in some, telepathy is indicated, as in the description by Canon Warburton of an occasion when he had come up to London from Oxford to stay a night or two with his brother, who, he found, had left a note saying he had gone to a dance and would be back at one. Dozing in a chair, Warburton 'saw' his brother leaving the ballroom, catching his foot on the top stair and falling headlong, saving himself with his hands and elbows. Half an hour later his brother arrived and told him how narrow an escape he had just had: 'coming out of the ballroom, I caught my foot, and tumbled full length down the stairs'.

There are so many accounts of what appear to have been telepathic dreams that it is a relief, ploughing through them, to come across one with an unusual twist, told by Ann Bridge in *Moments of Knowing* (1970). Archdeacon Bevan had been a close friend of a former headmaster of Charterhouse, Dr Haig-Brown; and when Haig-Brown died, his wife asked Bevan if he would read the lesson at the funeral service. The night before, he had a disturbingly vivid dream that when he had reached the lectern, there was no Bible, and the chaplain told him he was expected to know the lesson by heart. Unnerved, the archdeacon decided to take a small prayer book with him; and although when the time came there was a Bible on the lectern, he read from his familiar book. Afterwards, Mrs Haig-Brown told him how thankful she had been that he had read from the Authorized Version, as her husband always had – rather than the Revised Version, which the chaplain preferred. She had lain awake, she told Bevan, much of the night, wishing she had the courage to ask the chaplain whether, on this occasion, he would mind if the Authorized Version were used.

There have also been many accounts of 'shared' dreams, in which two people find they have had the same or a startlingly similar dream on the same night. Andrew Lang heard about, and took the trouble to verify, a remarkable example. A Miss Ogilvie told her brother, the Laird of Drumquaigh, that she had had an odd dream in which the household poodle, Fanti, had gone mad. 'That *is* odd,' the Laird replied. 'So did I!' They agreed not to tell their mother, for fear it would make her nervous. Their mother, however, reported when they saw her that she had dreamed that Fanti had gone mad, and bit. Later in the day when her two other daughters, who had been away for the night, arrived home, they said they had slept badly. 'I was dreaming that Fanti went mad,' one of them explained, 'when Mary wakened me and said she had dreamed Fanti went mad and turned into a cat, and we threw him into the fire.' Lang, intrigued, sought and obtained confirmation of the tale from the Laird – and also heard that the poodle had lived out its life-span 'sane and harmless'.

One of the most striking accounts of a telepathic-type dream was published in *The Times* of 21 July 1904 in a letter written by Rider Haggard. A couple of weeks before he had experienced two nightmares, leading to his wife waking him up to ask why he was making such weird noises. One had simply conveyed to him a sense of terrified oppression and struggling, such as drowning would involve: the other, that his daughter's black retriever, Bob, was lying on its side amongst brushwood, beside water, and apparently trying to communicate to Rider Haggard that it was dying. At first he assumed that these were simply disagreeable dreams; but when he was told the dog was missing, he organized a search and found the body of the dog floating against a local weir. Subsequently two platelayers on the local railway told him that they had discovered the dog's collar beside the line, the morning after Rider Haggard had his nightmares. They had found it on a bridge over the river; and they had formed the view that the last train the night before had struck the dog, hurling it into the reeds beside the river's edge.

Both in his judicial and in his personal capacity, Rider Haggard's letter concluded, he had been accustomed all his life to the investigation of evidence; and reviewing the episode, 'if we may put aside our familiar friend "the long arm of coincidence", which in this case would surely be strained to dislocation', he was forced to accept that the mutual attachment which had existed between him and the dog had enabled it to call his attention to what had happened through 'whatever portion of my being is capable of receiving such impulses when enchained by sleep'.

Although many people have experienced what they take to be quite frequent telepathic communication with a friend or a relative, the occasions when it occurs cannot as a rule be regulated. There is one instance, however, of a man who throughout his life was able to induce in himself a condition in which he could pick up information almost at will: Gilbert Murray, one of the most highly regarded academic figures of his time, who had discovered that he had the faculty, and had developed it in the course of the 'guessing game' he played with his family. It was derived and adapted from the 'willing' game, a popular late-Victorian pastime in which somebody who had been sent out of the drawing-room returned to try to find an object selected by the remainder of the guests, who would 'will' him or her to the target. Murray found that he could pick up more ambitious targets: quotations; scenes from books; family episodes. After a while, the targets and his responses were written down, and the complete records were eventually published by the SPR. Over a period of about half a century, in the course of making hundreds of guesses, the outcome was almost startlingly consistent; around a third of his guesses were correct, a third part-correct and a third either wrong or not attempted.

Murray would go out of the room while members of his family and guests decided on a subject; it would be written down; and he would be called back and asked to guess it. Typical examples were:

Subject: Sinking of the *Lusitania*.

Murray: I've got this violently. I've got an awful impression of naval disaster. I should think it was the torpedoing of the *Lusitania*.

Subject: The scene in *Marie Claire*, where she finds the nun, Soeur Marie Aimée, crying.

Murray: This is a book – it's not English, not Russian – it's rather a – I think there are nuns in it – there are a lot of people – either a school or a laundry – and one of the nuns is weeping – I think it's French. Oh, it's a scene in *Marie Claire*, near the beginning – I can't remember it, but something like that – it's in the place where she goes – one of the nuns crying – a double name – no I can't get the – Marie Thérèse –

In his Presidential address to the SPR in 1915 Murray made an attempt to explain how, in examples like this, the information reached him. Initially it was not through any one of the senses, he had found; it came through 'a sort of indeterminate sense of quality, or atmosphere'. Often he would get a feeling about the country in which the scene, or incident, had taken place; and also a sense of whether it was a scene or incident from life, or out of a book. Sometimes he would then 'see' the target in his mind's eye, or 'hear' it, or pick up a revealing smell.

For a while, Murray believed that his faculty was not telepathic, but the product of hyperesthesia: in his case, unconscious hyper-acuity of hearing. He did not, as a rule, get the answers right if the target words were written down, but not spoken; and sometimes his near-misses appeared to be through mis-hearing, as when he got 'Masefield' in his reply when the word in the target sentence was 'Mansfield' or when he seemed to 'hear' correctly but got the wrong person – Doughty the travel writer when the target was Doughty the Elizabethan sailor.

There were some occasions, however, when he picked up targets which had been written down, and had not been spoken; and others when he picked up not merely the target episode but something which had been in the mind of the setter (who might be a member of the family but was often a visitor). For example, on one occasion the subject was a scene in a book by Alexandre Aksakov about children being taken by their parents to see their grandparents; Murray, who had not read the book, said it was a scene in which children were travelling with their parents – he thought, across the Volga – to see their grandmother. The Volga had not been referred to in the setting of the target; but it featured in family crossings in the book, and had been in Murray's daughter's mind when the subject was set. And eventually, in the course of his SPR Presidential Address during his second term of office in 1953, Murray said that he had settled for telepathy as the most plausible explanation of his faculty.

Nevertheless from time to time attempts have been made to explain away Murray's faculty as hyperacuity of hearing: or even simply as conscious hearing. The notion that the high-principled Murray should have continued throughout his life to pretend to his family that he was out of earshot, when in fact he had his ear to the key-hole, hardly merits rebuttal; it is the kind of trick a man might play once or twice to fool his children, but it is inconceivable that he would have gone on playing it, at the risk of being humiliatingly caught, when they were grown up. As for unconscious hyperacuity, its existence, as Lord Rayleigh pointed out in his Presidential Address to the SPR in 1942, had never been demonstrated; he thought it a myth. Admittedly there have been a number of examples of individuals picking up information at distances too great for ordinary hearing-power; but these raise the possibility of clairaudience as the explanation.

With the advent of controlled trials on the Rhine model, it became rarer for anecdotal evidence for telepathy to appear in print; but in *The Living Stream* (1965) Sir Alister Hardy described a couple of experiences he had had as a young officer during the first world war, with a woman who, though not a professional, had occasional psychic visions. On one occasion when he was having tea with her she told him she had just 'seen' his brother, who at the time was in a German prison camp, 'painting what seems to be squares and oblongs of red and blue' on a large sheet of white paper. This was precisely what Hardy himself had been doing earlier that afternoon, preparing maps for a lecture on military history. There was no way, Hardy knew, she could have known what he had been doing, either then or on a second occasion, a year later, when she asked him what he had been doing, as she 'saw' a 'large pink square' on a table in front of him. There had been such a square, that afternoon, in the course of some experiments he was conducting into camouflage effects.

These instances, Hardy admitted, were of no scientific value; but for him, they had been just as real as any of the observations he had made in Natural History. And if telepathy existed, it must be of importance for biologists: 'this faculty whereby one individual influences another by means other than through the ordinary senses is surely one of the most revolutionary discoveries'.

Because the possibility of clairvoyance was hardly taken into account in the early years of psychical research, positive results of trials in that period can rarely be attributed to 'pure' telepathy; but one series of experiments pointed strongly to mind influencing mind. When in the 1880s the brothers Pierre and Jules Janet went with Julian Ochorowicz to Le Havre to test 'Mme B', to investigate the 'higher phenomena' which she displayed while under hypnosis, they wanted to make sure that she was not picking up their suggestions by hyperacuity of hearing; so they began to increase the distance between her and the hypnotist. Eventually tests were conducted with the two of them half a mile apart; in one house the hypnotist endeavoured to put 'Mme B' into a trance, and later to wake her out of it, noting the time as he did so, while in another house one of the other investigators would be with her, watching her and noting the times at which she entered and came out of a trance state. In the course of 25 such tests, the times corresponded on 18 occasions, and on another four they were close. 'Mme B', too, reacted while in her trance to suggestions put to her by the hypnotist.

This was not what the Janets had expected, let alone wanted to find. As for Ochorowicz, he had embarked on research hoping to discredit the 'higher phenomena', which he had regarded as a barrier to the acceptance of Braid's interpretation of hypnosis as a physiologically-induced condition. He left Le Havre, he was to admit, deeply emotionally disturbed, because he could no longer reject the 'extraordinary phenomenon of action at a distance, which upsets all currently received opinions'.

It was not until fifty years later, however, that confirmation was obtained of the existence of thought transmission through extra-sensory perception. When Rhine and his assistants at Duke realized that what had been taken to be evidence for telepathy could just as well have been evidence for clairvoyance, because the subject might in fact have been 'seeing' the cards, they began a fresh series of tests in which the agent simply *thought* of the target – say, one of the Zener card symbols. Only after the subjects had signalled that they had made their guesses did the agent write down, or draw, the target that he had chosen. As with the clairvoyance tests, the distances between agent and subjects were varied to see if that made any difference. It did not. 'There were several pure telepathy experiments conducted at Duke with significant results,' Rhine reported in *The Reach of the Mind* (1947). 'There was less evidence for telepathy than there was for clairvoyance, but it was similar in kind in so many respects that the two types of research to some extent reinforced each other.'

In 1962 there was further confirmation for the reality of telepathy from an unexpected source: Soviet Russia. In the early years of communist rule, scientists had enjoyed a fair measure of freedom; and one of them, L. L. Vasiliev, managed to conduct a series of experiments into paranormal phenomena by claiming that he was anxious to find whether electro-magnetism could account for them. One of his experiments resembled those which the Janet brothers had undertaken with 'Mme B' in the 1880s. The aim was to find whether a susceptible subject could react to hypnosis at distances ranging from a few yards to a thousand miles; and it was discovered that he could be put into a trance, or brought out of it, within six minutes, the distance making no appreciable difference.

As no link could be found with electro-magnetism, the results were unlikely to find favour with the increasingly conservative science establishment in Russia; and they remained unpublished until, following the death of Stalin and the rise of Khrushchev, scientists again enjoyed a more relaxed atmosphere. Vasiliev's *Experiments in Distant Influence* was published in Russia in 1962, and the following year in an English translation by C. C. L. Gregory and his wife Anita, the research protocol meeting with the guarded approval of Professor Eysenck, who thought the experiments had been conducted under properly controlled conditions and that the statistical evaluation of the results had been sound.

Orthodox scientists still have not accepted telepathy; but the public has been becoming increasingly willing to recognize its existence. A poll conducted in Britain by the Opinion Research Centre in 1968 revealed that only 45 per cent of the population was prepared to believe that messages or ideas could be transmitted telepathically, as against 52 per cent who thought they could not. But the proportion of believers was very much higher – 65 per cent – in the age group 21–4; and a further poll carried out in 1980 by the Independent Audience Selection organization has shown that the trend has been towards belief at all ages: 73 per cent of adults in the sample said they were believers, including two out of three of the over-65s.

PRECOGNITION

During the 17th century the terms 'prevision' and 'precognition' came into use to describe examples of second sight in which the vision appeared to relate to some future event. Prevision came then to be the stock term; but parapsychologists now prefer precognition, as the psychic perceptions are not necessarily 'seen'.

In all parts of the world, and in all eras, it has been assumed that certain individuals can look into the future. Discovery of what the future would hold was one of the main functions of tribal diviners – shamans, witch doctors or medicine men. Unluckily few of the earlier explorers took the opportunity to test the precognitive abilities of the diviners they encountered; and missionaries, though often prepared to accept psychic abilities as genuine, tended to attribute them to the devil, and were not inclined to investigate for fear of falling under diabolic influences themselves.

One of the few who published the results of an investigation of the psychic powers of African witch–doctors was the French missionary, Fr P. Boilat. In his *Esquisses Senegalaises* (1853) he described how, hoping to prove to himself that a witch doctor's powers were not genuine, he put an unspoken question. The witch doctor told him that the documents he was awaiting would be arriving in fifteen days' time; thereby not merely correctly guessing the question, but also providing what turned out to be the correct answer.

Some shamans divined the future spontaneously, as if they had had a flash of insight into what was going to happen. Others went into a trance and either consulted the spirits or were 'possessed' by a spirit who would talk to the tribe through them. Shamans also often used their dreams, or dreams reported by members of the tribe, as indications of events to come; interpreting them if the material in the dreams was symbolic.

The extent to which information through these channels was relied upon comes out very clearly in the Old Testament, where 'prophets' are held in awe. In its original sense, prophecy did not mean predicting the future: merely that the words, whether reported by the prophet or spoken through him while he was possessed, were taken to be divinely inspired. But as the messages were so often about what would happen if the word of the Lord were not heeded, prophecy tended to become equated with divination of the future. The seers and soothsayers of classical times made their reputation chiefly by the accuracy with which they foretold coming events – all the more so when, as in Cassandra's case, or 'Beware the Ides of March', they were ignored, with fatal consequences.

The first well-documented and attested case history of an individual with the precognitive faculty is in the records of the interrogation of Joan of Arc. In addition to her 'voices', she periodically had spontaneous visions of the 'flash' type in which she saw, or sensed, what was going to happen to people, as when she warned a colleague that he would die 'without losing blood' in three days – during the attack on Tournelles, he fell into the Loire and was drowned – or when she told the Dauphin that she herself would be wounded by an arrow or a bolt in the siege of Orleans, a prophecy that was actually recorded by a Flemish diplomat, who happened to be present, a fortnight before the event.

Reports of spontaneous precognition of this kind often suggest that it is akin to hallucination: the psychic suddenly 'sees' not the person she is looking at, but a scene in which that person will later feature – as in a story Samuel Pepys related that originated with the Earl of Clarendon. A Scot who had come to dine with the Earl's father in 1662 was observed to be looking with great intensity at another of the guests, Lady Cornbury; and when asked why, he replied, 'I see her in blood.' Her husband thought no more about it, as she was in excellent health. But the following month she caught the smallpox; on the ninth day of the illness, her nose bled for a short time; and that afternoon 'the blood burst out again with great violence at her nose and mouth, and about eleven of the clock that night she died, almost weltering in her blood'.

Shortly before the outbreak of the French Revolution, a dinner was held in Paris attended by members of the aristocracy who were numbered among the reformers. According to the account of Jean François La Harpe, most of the guests were enthusiastic about the prospects. The Marquis Cazotte, however, who had a reputation for second sight, described bluntly what the fate of each person present would be: Condorcet would take poison, to avoid execution; Bailly, Malesherbes, the Duchess of Gramont and Cazotte himself (as well as 'the highest in the land') would perish on the scaffold. As for the freethinker, La Harpe, something 'at least as wonderful' would happen to him; surviving the Revolution he would die a Christian (he did).

So strikingly accurate were the predictions that in spite of the insistence of Mme de Genlis, who claimed she had often heard La Harpe tell the story before the Revolution broke out, there was a tendency to dismiss them; but eventually the discovery of the memoirs of the Baroness d'Oberkirch revealed that she had heard about Cazotte's 'dreadful omens' from La Harpe in 1789, before the Revolution had begun to devour its children.

Dramatic accounts of precognition inevitably tend to be remembered, where others, which are chiefly of curiosity value, are forgotten. But Goethe was to recall that when he had to leave his Frederika in Sesenheim in 1771, he had a vision of himself going back there; it struck him as odd, in that he had on a grey coat of a kind he had never worn, fringed with lace, but it gave him hope that he would be able to return. He did, eight years later, wearing, 'although it was not my will which had made me assume the costume', the identical coat.

A glimpse of a more immediate future published in *Annales des Sciences Psychiques* in 1916 is unusual in that although it referred back to an episode over twenty years earlier, it had the backing of attestation by three friends of the doctor who had had the precognitive 'flash', as he had told them about it before the publication of the news to which it referred. He had been at his studies when suddenly 'an unexpected phrase was imposed upon his mind with such force that he could not help writing it down':

M. Casimir-Perier is elected President of the Republic by 451 votes

His fellow-students were derisory; but later in the day, four of them went to a café to await the result of the election. When the papers arrived, they revealed that out of 845 votes, Casimir-Perier had received 451.

A number of the precognitive experiences which Flammarion included in his collections were of this 'flash' type. When an artist friend was showing Saint-Saëns a picture which he was submitting for the annual Exposition at the Palais de l'Industrie, Saint-Saëns saw 'it hanging in a particular place at the top of the stairs'; the picture was accepted, and it was hung precisely where he had foreseen. And when his application to enter the Académie des Beaux-Arts was turned down, Saint-Saëns told himself, looking in irritation at the Egyptian lions that adorn, 'in such bizarre fashion', the façade of the Institute, 'I shall present myself again *when the lions turn round.*' Some time afterwards, 'the lions were turned!' – though not, Flammarion wrote back to him to insist, psychokinetically: 'Your mind saw an aspect of the future, without suspecting it.'

A remarkable instance of a 'flash' precognitive experience has been related by Air Marshal Sir Victor Goddard in his *Flight Towards Reality* (1975). Flying south from Scotland in 1935 he ran into bad weather, became disorientated and, after going into a tail-spin which nearly resulted in a crash, decided to re-orientate himself by flying over a disused first world war airfield, Drem. He had just paid a visit to it by road, in order to find whether it was still available for landings; but he had found that it had been converted into farm land, the near-derelict hangars being used as barns. Flying over it, however, he saw to his astonishment that the hangars appeared to have been refurbished, and on the new tarmac were four aircraft, one of them a monoplane of a type unknown to him. They were coloured yellow; and the mechanics who were working on them were in blue dungarees.

In 1935 there were no monoplanes in RAF service; no aircraft coloured yellow; and airmen wore brown dungarees. Baffled, Goddard told his Wing Commander, who advised him to 'lay off the Scotch'; and when he wrote to tell his hostess in Scotland, she was also incredulous. Four years later, after the outbreak of war, Drem reopened as a flying training school, with monoplanes of the kind Goddard had seen, coloured yellow to distinguish them from operational aircraft; and airmen's dungarees were by this time blue.

There are a few cases in which 'flash' precognition appears to have acted through the subconscious mind to provide protection from some danger by clairsentience. In his *Foreknowledge* (1938) H. F. Saltmarsh cited the experience of Lady Craik, who had been just about to cross a street in front of a stationary bus 'when she felt a strong hand on her shoulder which pulled her back sharply', just in time to save her from being run down by a speeding motor-cyclist. 'She turned to thank whoever had saved her, but, to her surprise, there was no one within reach.' The subliminal mind of Lady Craik had become aware of the danger, Saltmarsh thought, 'and conveyed the warning to the normal consciousness by means of a tactile hallucination'.

In this case the 'tactile hallucination' acted as a restraint: in another, a hallucination may have prompted a positive course of action which saved a life, though the reason for the sequence of events will never now be known.

The story was related by Arthur Koestler in *The Challenge of Chance* (1973) as one of the case histories sent in to him when he appealed for accounts of striking coincidences. A young man suffering from a nervous breakdown had thrown himself in front of a tube train which had stopped just in time, injuring him severely but not fatally. The driver of the train, however, had not been responsible for putting on the brakes in time: 'quite independently,' Koestler's informant told him, 'some passenger on the train had pulled down the emergency handle.' The passenger had even been interviewed, later, in case there were grounds for prosecuting him for pulling it without reasonable cause.

'Anybody familiar with the London Underground system,' Koestler commented, 'can confirm that it is quite impossible for a passenger to see what is happening in front of the engine.' Even had it been possible, he could not have pulled the handle in time. A journalist friend of Koestler's checked the story, and found it was correct. Maddeningly, though, it proved impossible to persuade the authorities to disclose the identity of the passenger, to find what had prompted his action. 'If we assume that the unknown passenger acted on a telepathic impulse,' Koestler commented, 'we must also assume that it was a precognitive impulse, anticipating the event by a couple of seconds to stop the train in time.'

Another tale in Koestler's collection was of an experience related to him in a letter from Sir Alec Guinness. When Sir Alec was in a London play, he was in the habit of going to an early mass on Sunday morning before catching the 9.50 train to his home in the country. Ordinarily he was an early riser, both by instinct and habit; to be on the safe side he set *two* alarm clocks, but he usually awoke before they rang. On one occasion, however, he managed to sleep through both; he misread the time when he woke up, and it was not until he found he was at the nine o'clock mass that he realized he would miss his usual train. When he arrived to catch the next one, he was told there would be a delay; the train he would have travelled on, had he not slept through the alarms, had been derailed. His habit had been to sit at the front of the front coach; it projected out from under the roof of Waterloo station, giving more light for reading, and it was usually less crowded. He found later that it had been the front coach which had toppled on its side; and although there had been no fatalities, some of the occupants, badly knocked about, had had to be taken to hospital. Had precognition preventing him from being woken that morning saved him from injury or worse?

It is not always possible to be sure of the state of mind in which predictions of the future have been made; but in Nostradamus's case, he appears to have put himself into a state of trance in order to compose the quatrains which were published in his *Centuries* in 1555. Three examples cited by James Laver in his biography of Nostradamus seem respectively to have been four years, a century, and two-and-a-half centuries, ahead of his time.

One quatrain described how an older man would be overcome by a younger one in single combat: 'in a cage of gold, his eyes will be pierced, two wounds in one, then die of a cruel death'. Jousting in 1559 with the young captain of his Scots guard, King Henri II of France was struck by a lance which penetrated his gilt visor, wounding him in the eye and throat; he died a few days later.

The second quatrain spoke of 'the Sicilian Nizaram' attaining high honours 'when Innocent shall hold the place of Peter'; but he would then be plagued by civil war. Mazarin (anagrams were common in the quatrains), who was a Sicilian, ruled France during the Papacy of Innocent X. He was apparently firmly in control until the Fronde rebellion drove him out, for a time, in the early 1650s.

The third quatrain was the most remarkable of all.

> By night will come through the forest of Reines
> Two married people by a circuitous route –
> Herne, the white stone,
> The monk in grey – into Varennes,
> Elected Cap; result, tempest, fire, blood, slice.

In 1792 Louis Capet (Louis XVI), the first king of France to be confirmed on the throne by the vote of an Assembly, left Paris with Marie Antoinette to try to escape from France by a circuitous route; they were stopped at Varennes, and sent back to Paris – both, a few months later, to be guillotined. Many of Nostradamus's other quatrains can be interpreted as applying to future e··nts, but none so clearly as these; and they represent what is perhaps the most disturbing long-term evidence for some form of predestination.

In recent times the most startling case of precognition emerging in a book has been the plot of a work of fiction, *Futility,* published in 1898. It told the story of a new monster liner, the largest ever built, designed to be unsinkable and consequently carrying only the regulation minimum of lifeboats. The assumption was that the bulkheads separating her 19 watertight compartments would close automatically on any impact: even if at full speed she ran into an iceberg, 'at the most, three compartments would be flooded'. But destiny was not to be thwarted; on her Atlantic crossing the liner struck an iceberg and sank with heavy loss of life.

The story bore an astonishingly close resemblance to what was actually to happen, fourteen years later, when the *Titanic,* with similar specifications and limitations, struck an iceberg and sank with heavy loss of life on its maiden voyage; but what made the resemblance even more uncanny was the name which the American author of *Futility,* Morgan Robertson, had given his fictional liner: the *Titan.*

Some of the *Titanic*'s features might have been predicted by a Jules Verne or an H. G. Wells; but there is nothing to show that Robertson had the necessary inside knowledge. In any case, he did not claim to write from inside knowledge, but as a medium. 'He implicitly believed,' a friend of his wrote, 'that some discarnate soul, some spirit entity with literary ability, denied physical expression, had commandeered his body and brain for the purpose of giving to the world the literary gems which made him famous.' Another friend, describing how Robertson would relax in a comatose condition waiting for the stories to pour into his mind and 'marshal themselves into a coherent narrative', recalled that the discarnate writer would suddenly cease to provide the material, from time to time, leaving Robertson with no alternative but to take up some other employment, as he knew he could not himself write the stories by which he had made his reputation, and earned his living.

Of countless other reports of trance mediums telling customers about future events, one of the more impressive came from Sir Oliver Lodge. The medium had described a house where Lodge would eventually live, giving details of a number of its features, including a door of a kind ordinarily seen in churches. Seven years later Lodge went to live in a house whose existence he had not previously known about; it turned out to be as the medium had described it, including the church door. But there was a twist to the tale. Lodge was subsequently informed that the door had been added, 'independently and so to speak accidentally' by the previous owner. It had not been there at the time when the medium had described it to Lodge.

Easily the most commonly reported examples of precognition are dreams in which something is seen or experienced which later *is* seen or experienced. Professor Ian Stevenson has estimated that at least five thousand reasonably well-attested cases have been published in the English language alone; and in the collection Louisa Rhine made at Duke, of three thousand reports of psychic experiences, of which a third were precognitive, three out of four of those were in dreams.

Admittedly there is often a problem in distinguishing precognition in dreams from other forms of ESP, as Dame Edith Lyttelton noted in her survey of the subject in 1937. She cited as an example the experience of Miss H. N. Mudie, one of the joint principals of New Brighton High School, who dreamed she had been told of a murder in a hotel beside the school, her informant insisting that the murderer had slept in the school. Three weeks later, a maid at the hotel was shot by her lover, who then shot himself. As Miss Mudie herself observed, there was the possibility that the murderer had found shelter in the school grounds. 'Did my subconscious mind contact the mind of the culprit,' she asked, 'when he was planning to kill the girl?' In that case telepathy, rather than precognition, would be indicated.

Either way, the communication would have been extra-sensory; and sceptics prefer to take the line that chance coincidence is sufficient as an explanation, because with so many millions of dreams each night, there are bound to be frequent similarities between the dreams and subsequent events – particularly in the case of those dreams which are most dramatic: every time a plane crashes, a few people will surely have dreamed the night before of an airline crash. So attempts have been made to lay down guidelines as to what may, and what should not, be admitted as *prima facie* evidence of dream precognition.

In 1965 G. W. Lambert, for many years a member of the Council of the SPR, put forward the criteria necessary, he believed, for a decision to be reached as to whether a precognitive element may be present in a dream.

1 The dream should be reported to a credible witness before the event.

2 The time interval between the dream and the event should be short.

3 The event should be unexpected at the time of the dream.

4 The description should be of an event destined literally, and not just symbolically, to happen.

5 The details of dream and event should tally.

These criteria can help to sieve out unsatisfactory cases; but with two reservations. It is not always possible to report dreams to a credible witness, because frequently the dream is only remembered when, or just before, it is 'broken' by the event it has foreshadowed; in such cases we have to rely on the credibility of the dreamer. And although a long time interval between the dream and the event may in some cases make chance coincidence more likely – to meet somebody we have not seen or heard of for years the morning after we have dreamed of meeting him is obviously more impressive than a meeting months later – in other cases, the greater the time span the more remarkable the predictive element becomes – as when, for example, a particular day, months ahead, is named for a particular event of a kind which could not be predicted by ordinary means.

The possibility of chance coincidence being responsible for 'seeing' the future in a dream has incidentally had one curious advantage. It has enabled sceptics to accept the evidence without feeling the need to cast doubt on the veracity of the dreamer. Thus in *The Philosophy of Sleep* (1830) Robert McNish recalled a dream he had had that a near relation, who lived a hundred miles away and had been in perfect health, had died; he awoke 'in a state of inconceivable terror', and for the next three days remained in 'a state of the most unpleasant suspense', feeling a presentiment that 'something dreadful had happened or would happen'. It had: a letter arrived telling him that his relative had died of a stroke the morning after McNish's dream. Because McNish regarded belief in the capacity of the human mind to see into the future as a superstition and philosophically untenable, he felt compelled to as·ert that his dream about his relation's death had been coincidental, and his presentiment no more than a childish weakness. Yet anybody who accepts the possibility of precognition need not accept McNish's interpretation.

Inevitably the most celebrated dreams which have accurately predicted some forthcoming event have been about disasters: often about assassinations. In May 1812 John Williams, the well-to-do manager of a number of tin mines in Cornwall, dreamed he was in the lobby of the House of Commons, where he witnessed the assassination of Spencer Perceval, the Prime Minister. He related his dream to his wife and fell asleep again, only to have the same dream; and when it was repeated a third time, he was so agitated that he contemplated going to London to warn Perceval – a course from which his friends dissuaded him. Perceval was assassinated in the lobby of the House of Commons a week later.

To dream of such an event, it might be argued, is not unusual. What made it unusual – apart from the fact that Williams had the same disturbing dream three times – was that when he next visited London he happened to see a portrayal of the assassination in a print shop; 'the colours of the dresses, the buttons of the assassin's coat, the white waistcoat of Mr Perceval, the spot of blood upon it, the countenances and attitudes of the parties present were exactly what I had dreamed'. This account, admittedly, was written twenty years later, but he had told members of his family and friends encountered at the time; the 1832 version, he explained, was necessary to correct some of the inaccurate versions which were circulating, including one in *The Times*.

In 1865 Abraham Lincoln told his wife and his friend, Ward H. Lamon, of a dream he had had of sounds of mourning in the White House. Anxious to discover the cause, he went from room to room until, in the East Room, 'there was a sickening surprise. Before me was a catafalque on which rested a corpse wrapped in funeral vestments. Around it were stationed soldiers who were acting as guards, and there was a throng of people, some gazing mournfully upon the corpse.' As the face of the corpse was covered, Lincoln asked who it was. The President, he was told, had been killed by an assassin. Lincoln slept no more that night, and the dream continued to haunt him. A week later, he was assassinated at the Ford Theatre.

Presidents, it can be argued, must always fear assassination and this fear might have congealed into the dream coincidentally; but some of the dreams recorded by famous men are hard to fit into the coincidence category.

While staying at his sister's house, Mark Twain dreamed that he saw his brother Henry's corpse lying on a burial cask in a sitting-room, with a bouquet of white flowers, in the centre of which was a single red flower, on his breast. So shaken was he by the dream that he actually got up and dressed, intending to pay his respects to his loved dead brother, before he realized thankfully that it had been a dream. But then came the news of an explosion in the boiler room of the steamboat Henry worked in near Memphis; Henry was one of the many who had been killed. When Mark Twain arrived in Memphis he 'saw his brother lying exactly as he had seen him in his dream, lacking only the bouquet of white flowers with its crimson centre – a detail made complete while he stood there, for at that moment an elderly lady came in with a large white bouquet, and in the centre of it was a single red rose'.

Dreams of more trivial events may provide just as impressive, or even more impressive, evidence for precognition; but they are naturally less likely to be published and remembered unless they happen to somebody famous who relates them in his memoirs, or to his biographer. In 1863 Dickens dreamed that while at his office he saw a lady in a red shawl with her back to him, whom he thought he knew; but when she turned round, he realized that he had not met her before, and she introduced herself as 'Miss Napier'. Dressing the next morning, he thought how preposterous such dreams were: 'Why,' he asked himself, 'Miss Napier?' He had never heard of anybody of that name. That evening, while he was reading, some visitors arrived, along with 'the lady in the red shawl, whom they presented as "Miss Napier"'! According to his biographer, John Forster, Dickens insisted that 'these were all the circumstances, exactly told'.

Precognitive dreams feature extensively in the evidence collected in the early years of the SPR; and some were agreeably light-hearted. Mrs Atlay, wife of the Bishop of Hereford, described how she had dreamed that, going into the dining-room after reading morning prayers in the hall of the episcopal palace, she had found an enormous pig standing between the dining table and the sideboard. Before reading prayers she told the children and their governess of the dream; after prayers, she opened the dining-room door and there was the pig, which had just escaped from its sty.

Flammarion, too, gave several examples of precognitive dreams; some of them macabre, as in the case related by the scientist, Baron Lazare Hellenbach. He had an appointment with M. Hauer, of the Vienna Geological Institute; and the night before, he dreamed that he saw a man 'pale and trembling, supported by the arms, by two men'. On arrival at the Institute in the morning, he found the door of the laboratory locked; and looking through a window he saw a scene exactly as it had been in his dream, the two men 'supporting Hauer, who had just poisoned himself with cyanide'.

In times of impending catastrophe, such as the weeks before the outbreak of the first world war, many precognitive dreams were reported; none as specific as that of Monsignor Joseph de Lanyi, Bishop of Grosswardin, who dreamed that he saw his former pupil, the Archduke, in a chauffeur-driven car with his wife, facing a general in the opposite seat. They were driving through crowds, when two men stepped forward and fired on them. The vision appeared to arise out of a letter from the Archduke which de Lanyi read in his dream, saying that the assassination had taken place at Sarajevo. De Lanyi woke up trembling, noted the time – 4.30 A.M. – and wrote down his dream, telling his host and his mother about it later in the morning, before a telegram arrived giving the news.

Rudyard Kipling had one dream in which he was sure that he had 'passed beyond the bounds of ordinance', as he put it in *Something of Myself* (1937). He was standing in his best clothes, which he rarely wore, in a line of similarly-dressed men, facing another line across a vast hall, floored with rough-jointed stone slabs. On his left, some ceremony was taking place that he would have liked to see, but a fat man next to him blocked his view, and he could not step out of line until the ceremony ended, when the lines broke up and the space filled with people – at which point somebody came up to him, took his arm and said 'I want a word with you'; and he woke up.

Six weeks later Kipling, in his capacity as a member of the War Graves Commission, had to attend a ceremony at Westminster, where the Prince of Wales was to dedicate a plaque to the fallen. There, Kipling broke his dream: in front of him were the rough-jointed stone slabs; beside him, a fat man who blocked his view. 'But here is where I have been,' he told himself; and after the ceremony ended, and the two lines merged across the nave, a man came up to him, took his arm and said 'I want a word with you please' – on some trivial matter. For the sake of the 'weaker brethren', Kipling explained, he had not made use of the experience at the time; 'but how, and why,' he asked, 'had I been shown an unreleased roll of my life-film?'

Perhaps Kipling had been reading J. W. Dunne's *An Experiment with Time* (1927), in which the author related a succession of his own dreams of future events, and presented a theory to account for them by which life could be compared to a roll of film going through a projector; in dreams, he suggested, the mind can sometimes move forward to see what was on the roll of film before the projector – the present – is reached. The theory, however, was to make less impression than Dunne's account of the dreams themselves, in spite of the fact that he had not fulfilled one of Lambert's criteria; he had not related them to witnesses, to have them attested at the time.

Dunne was unknown, except as an aeronautical engineer and as the author of a book on fly-fishing. There was no reason to suppose that his account of some dreams he had had which had foretold future events in his life, rather inaccurately, would attract readers; but it did, it still does.

The dreams were for the most part fairly commonplace. In one, for example, he saw a horse plunging about in a field; suddenly he realized it was pursuing him, and he was trying frantically to reach a flight of wooden steps, to escape, when he woke up. The next day, on a fishing expedition with his brother, he found himself watching a horse in a field behaving in the same way as the one in his dream; he was just telling his brother about it when it got out of the field, and 'just as in the dream, it was thundering down the path towards the wooden steps'.

The reality was in a number of respects different from the dream. The field, the path and the steps were on the far side of the river; so there seemed no question of the horse pursuing them. As it happened, though, the horse swerved past the steps, and plunged into the river, coming towards them. They were sufficiently alarmed to pick up stones, ready for action: but 'the end was tame, for, on emerging from the water on our side, the animal merely looked at us, snorted and galloped off down a road'.

The same pattern emerged from most of Dunne's dreams; they contained what would turn out to be startlingly accurate images of what was going to happen, usually the following day, but coupled with distortions and inaccuracies. From this he constructed his theory that dreams are (or can be) erratic images of experience, past or future, displaced in time; and he went on to offer an elaborate theory of time to account for the displacement.

What impressed readers, however, was not Dunne's theorizing, but the fact that his dream experiences were so commonplace; it was easy for dreamers to identify with them. His belief too that anybody could have precognitive dreams and that in all probability everybody has them, but forgets them, was infectious. Put a pad and a pencil beside the bed, he suggested, and write down everything remembered from a dream immediately on waking. Hundreds, perhaps thousands, of people did and, like Dunne, experienced partly accurate, partly inaccurate, precognition. When, years later, J. B. Priestley invited TV viewers to contribute to a programme on Time, the flood of replies made him realize just how much influence Dunne had had: 'without his example, and his advice on the immediate recording of dreams,' he wrote, 'I suspect that at least a third of the best precognitive dreams I have been sent would never have come my way.'

Precognitive dreams continue to be reported to and filed by the SPR; but since the emphasis in research has switched from anecdote to experiment, they are rarely published. A recent exception has been the report in the *SPR Journal* of the experience of Mrs Lickiss, a social worker living in Hull. In a dream she saw a coffin in which lay a Mr G, whom she had not seen for about 16 years. After waking the next morning, she told her husband. That day, driving to her work along a main road, she braked to allow an estate car to come out of a side road, and was astonished to recognize the driver as 'Mr G'. Calling on friends who knew him, she told them about the way her dream had been broken, before going on to make her calls:

but when I reached home, I found a telephone message left urgently asking me to contact my friends. When I telephoned, it was to learn that after I had pulled up, to let the man in the estate car out of the side road, he had continued to the town. At the traffic lights, in the centre of the town, while stopping at red, he had suffered a heart attack and died there and then.

Mrs Lickiss's husband, and one of the friends who had heard her describe the breaking of her dream, confirmed to Brian Nisbet, the SPR member who checked the story, that it was correct. The friend, in particular, had good reason to remember it in detail, as she and 'Mr G' had at one time been very close friends, who might have married. Mrs Lickiss herself, though, had no reason to dream about 'Mr G'; she had seen him all those years before, but they had never actually met.

Less dramatic, but a good example of precognition because of the improbability of chance coincidence being responsible, is a case described in *Working with Dreams* (1979) by Montague Ullman and Nan Zimmerman. A woman woke herself and her husband up one morning by laughing out loud; in her dream, she explained, she had seen her sister put her hands in her coat pockets to show her that they were full of bottle caps. When her sister arrived for lunch that day she said, 'Look at what the boys put into my pockets!' Reaching into them, she pulled out two handfuls of bottle caps.

The precognitive category also houses presentiments and premonitions. The *Shorter Oxford English Dictionary* defines a presentiment as 'a vague expectation, seeming like a direct perception of something about to happen; an anticipation, foreboding (usually of something evil)'; a premonition, as 'a previous notification or warning of subsequent events; a forewarning'. As both tend to be used almost exclusively to describe feelings of nervousness, alarm, or dread, in colloquial usage they tend to be interchangeable. They are not necessarily precognitive: if a calamitous event follows, the foreboding may turn out to have been a subconscious realization of something done (or not done) which is going to have unfortunate results, such as forgetting an important appointment or leaving the gas on under an empty saucepan in the kitchen. And even when the event is of a kind which would suggest that the foreboding must have been psychic, unaccountable by any known way of transmitting alarm signals, it is rarely possible to relate it objectively to the event.

The first systematic attempt to find if precognition could be demonstrated in test conditions was made in France in the 1920s. Pascal Forthuny, a well-known French author, discovered that he had some psychic abilities, which he allowed researchers to test; and he proved to be particularly successful in what came to be described as 'chair tests'. His investigator, Eugene Osty, would take him to a lecture theatre and ask him to describe the person who, a few hours later, would be sitting in one of the chairs. Precautions were taken to ensure that when the audience arrived, there was no way in which the eventual occupant of the chair could have been tipped off where to sit, in advance; nevertheless Forthuny's descriptions were often accurate.

After the publication of J. W. Dunne's *An Experiment with Time* the Society for Psychical Research conducted an experiment to find whether volunteers, using Dunne's method of writing down their dreams each morning but also having the accounts witnessed, would produce positive results; the investigator reported they were inconclusive. At Duke University, however, J. B. Rhine was sufficiently impressed by Dunne's book, and by case histories of the kind which Dame Edith Lyttelton and H. F. Saltmarsh collected, to apply the card-guessing method to the investigation of precognition, by the simple procedure of asking subjects to guess not the card which had been turned up, but the next in the pack.

The results, though less impressive than for clairvoyance or telepathy, were positive; some subjects scored significantly above chance expectation, even when the cards were shuffled by a machine before each guess. But this posed a new question: as Gaither Pratt put it, 'if psychokinesis could influence the fall of dice in an experiment designed to test the PK hypothesis, what was to keep it from influencing the fall of the cards in the shuffling machine, and the fall of dice for the final cut of the pack?' A combination of psychokinesis and clairvoyance might then be held responsible for any excess of 'hits' over chance. So eventually the target pack was shuffled either before or immediately after the subject had made his calls; but the final order to be used was determined by a random cut made on the basis of a particular set of figures that would not be printed in the newspaper until the following day – market reports, say, or meteorological data of a kind which could not be known at the time of the task. Later even more sophisticated ways of eliminating other forms of ESP were introduced; but the trend was maintained 'towards a steady mounting of the evidence for precognition'.

When in the late 1930s Whately Carington, in the course of his experiments to see whether subjects could describe, or draw, the pictures he put up each evening, found that the number of 'hits' was above chance expectation not merely on the evening but also on the evening before, it occurred to him that precognition might be responsible; and also that some of the subjects S. G. Soal had tested for telepathy or clairvoyance with negative results might have been found to have scored positively, had precognition been taken into account. Soal allowed himself to be persuaded to go back over the records, which had been kept, to see if anybody whom he had tested had been scoring above chance on the next card to be turned up, and two subjects, he found, had had highly significant results if this time displacement were taken into consideration.

Resuming tests with one of them, Basil Shackleton, Soal found he could guess precognitively at a rate billions to one above chance – provided the agent looked at the cards: where precognitive clairvoyance, rather than telepathy, was being tested, the results were negative. When Shackleton was asked to make more rapid guesses, it was found that he was guessing *two* cards ahead. For some years, Soal's work was accepted by parapsychologists as the best proof of precognition which had been obtained. Unluckily for this assumption, it was eventually found that Soal appeared to have tampered with the figures for some experiments; and although it could not seriously be maintained that he had rigged all his results from the start, Soal's entire contribution was discredited.

In 1966 a huge coal tip in Wales, loosened by rain, obliterated part of the Welsh village of Aberfan, killing nearly 150 people, most of them schoolchildren. A psychiatrist, Dr J. C. Barker, was impressed by the number of people who reported having premonitions of the disaster. After collecting and checking them, he decided that, although there was no single clear-cut case where the premonitory vision had exactly corresponded with the reality, taken together they confirmed the existence of a precognitive element.

Could precognition be exploited in future, to give advance warning of such calamities? The London *Evening Standard* took up this idea, offering to provide a 'central clearing house' to which people who had alarming dreams could report. The following year a similar bureau was set up in New York. Both received some predictions which came close to the reality: in the spring of 1969 a New York resident sent in an account of the crash of a light aircraft with a number which he thought was N129N, or N429N, or N29N; the light plane in which Rocky Marciano was killed that summer was N3149X. There has not so far, however, been a case in which the report of a dream has led to action being taken that would fulfil the hope that such centres might save lives.

Other types of tests for precognition have been tried out since; one of them, by the physicist Dr Helmut Schmidt, exploited the discovery that although the rate of decay in radioactive strontium 90 is predictable – every twenty years, half of the atoms will have gone – the individual atoms disintegrate in a wholly random fashion. Schmidt set up a panel with coloured lights, each to be lit up in random order as individual atoms decayed, and invited students to guess which light would come on next. He found, as Rhine had done, a few stars; and with them he recorded over 60,000 guesses, their 'hits' exceeding chance expectation by odds of two billion to one. In some later trials the results were even better.

Another type of experiment which has produced positive findings is the work of the New York researcher Douglas Dean in the 1970s. Are certain businessmen successful, he wondered, because precognition enables them to foresee market trends? He invited some company managers to his laboratory, where they played with a one-armed bandit, trying to guess what symbol would turn up next. A comparison of their results with the companies' balance sheets for the previous year revealed that the companies of those who did best in the laboratory had in general also the highest profits.

In the 1950s chair tests of the kind that Forthuny had undertaken were resumed in Holland with the clairvoyant Gerard Croiset, who proved to be if anything even more proficient. In the experiments, conducted by Professor Tenhaeff, the chair number would be selected by a randomizing process, and Croiset would be told what the number was – but not where: it might be in a hall in some distant town. He would then describe the occupant-to-be: if it were a woman, her size, height, hair colour, what she would be wearing, and episodes from her past life. These predictions, sometimes made weeks before the meeting at which the test was to be made, would then be compared with the person who took the chair. Over two decades, Croiset proved to be a remarkably consistent forecaster in scores of trials, some of them conducted or monitored by sceptical investigators.

Predestination?

Of all the varieties of extra-sensory perception, precognition has been regarded as the most disturbing, because of the implication that coming events do not merely cast their shadows before; they are immutably fixed in advance. In his book on the occult sciences, Schopenhauer actually used a precognitive dream of his own to illustrate this contention.

Composing an important letter, he inadvertently picked up the ink-well instead of the sand-box; the ink ran all over the letter, and on to the floor. While the maid was trying to wash the ink off, she told him that she had dreamed what she was going to have to do, the night before; and when he suggested she must be making it up, she replied she had told his other servant, who slept in the same room, about the dream. To check, Schopenhauer called in the other servant and asked if she remembered what she had been told about the dream that morning. Yes, she replied. 'It had been about "washing an ink-spot off the floor here".'

Schopenhauer was impressed not only because for him it placed the reality of this type of dream 'beyond doubt', but also because it showed that his involuntary and unwelcome act was 'so necessary and so inevitably determined that its effect existed, several hours in advance, as a dream in the consciousness of another. Here appears in the clearest manner the truth of my proposition: everything that happens, happens of necessity.'

Schopenhauer had not paused to ask himself what might have happened if the servant had told him of the dream *before* he began to write the letter. The extent to which intervention is possible in such cases has been the subject of much speculation right down to the present day, as Louisa Rhine found. One of the accounts of a precognitive dream which was sent to her at Duke came from a young woman who in her dream had seen an aircraft crash at a place she knew, killing the pilot and setting a cottage on fire; the fire engine took the wrong road, and arrived too late to be of any use. That evening, hearing a plane overhead, she sensed it was the one which would crash, and begged her husband to warn the firemen which road they should take. He demurred; the plane crashed, killing the pilot and setting alight the cottage; and the fire engine duly took the wrong road.

Could she have prevented the crash, she asked? Or, failing that, at least have set the firemen right? But if she had intervened the dream would not have been of the future; in which case such dreams should not be used as evidence of predestination, but rather of the existence of at least a modicum of free will.

There have in fact been a great many accounts of dreams which, because they have given early warning of some danger, have enabled the dreamer to avert it. Foxe in his *Book of Martyrs* (1554) described how a member of a Protestant group in London in Queen Mary's reign dreamed twice in one night that a Queen's officer had arrested the deacon, and found a list of the three hundred members of the congregation. He warned the deacon; and although the deacon was inclined to scoff, he agreed to pass the list on. The following day a Queen's officer appeared and conducted a search; had the list been found, the entire congregation would have been at risk of the stake.

In his *Miscellanies* (1696), the diarist John Aubrey recounted the experience of a man he knew, Dr Hamey. Setting out on a visit to Italy, Hamey was stopped by the Governor at Dover, no reason being given. The ship, which sailed without him, was lost in a storm, and all the passengers drowned. On hearing the news the Governor explained that although he did not know Dr Hamey, he had had 'a perfect vision in a dream' of him, with a warning to stop him from sailing. Dr Hamey, Aubrey added, was a 'pious, good man', who would not have invented the tale.

When Tom Paine was leaving England for France at the time of the French Revolution to take the seat to which he had been elected in the Convention, he stayed *en route* with William Blake; and Blake, who believed that he was guided by spirits, was able to demonstrate, on this occasion, that he enjoyed psychic perceptions.

He told Paine he must leave at once, as he 'saw' that Pitt's agents were pursuing him with a warrant for his arrest; they arrived just after Paine's boat had sailed.

The *Journals* of the Societies for Psychical Research contain many examples of cases where use has been made of precognition, usually to avert some accident. On holiday in Scotland a Dr Robertson had sent his small daughter out for a walk when he 'distinctly heard a voice, as it were, within me, say, "Send for her back or something dreadful will happen to her." At the same moment I was seized with violent trembling, and a feeling of great terror took possession of me.' He despatched a servant after the girl, who brought her back unharmed. She had only been going to sit on stones on the beach, she told him, by the railway bridge, as she liked to listen to the noise the trains made as they passed over the arch. That afternoon Robertson heard that at the time she would have been on the beach, an engine and tender had come off the rails by the arch, falling on to the stones where his daughter would have been sitting.

In *Some Cases of Prediction* (1937) Dame Edith Lyttelton gave examples of precognitive dreams which had nudged the dreamer into taking action; as in the case of the woman manager of a chocolate packing department, with 30–40 girls to supervise, who dreamed about the chocolates 'all getting mixed up'. The following morning something moved her to go to one of the packers, who turned out to be putting cheap jellies in with the best gingers – an episode which the girl in question corroborated. 'I remember Miss Anderson telling me that she had a dream that the chocolates were being mixed wrongly.'

An engaging example of useful dream precognition in this collection came from Patty Alberigh-Mackay, who had taught at the Bloomsbury School of Art. One morning, before her class were to sit an exam, she 'saw', as if spread out on a wall, a geometry problem, which she realized she knew how to solve. She gave the problem, and its solution, to her students before the examination. The identical problem appeared in the geometry paper, with the result that all her students passed. The episode had taken place too long before for Patty to obtain corroboration from any member of her class; but her sister recalled her telling the story to the family at the time.

The most frequently reported category of precognitive dreams which prompt the dreamer to do something he would not otherwise have done, with gratifying results, are those which disclose in advance the winner of some sporting event, such as a horse race. Again, sceptics are inclined to argue that the only dreams of this kind which get publicity are those in which the dream winner actually wins; there may be hundreds which go unreported because the horse loses. But there are a few accounts for which precognition provides the most plausible explanation, such as the sequence John Godley, Lord Kilbracken, described in his *Tell Me the Next One* (1950).

While an undergraduate at Oxford after the war, Godley (he had not then succeeded to the title) dreamed that he saw the results of races in the next day's papers. As two of the winning horses were running the next day, he put some money on them and told friends to do the same; they won. A few days later, a similar dream brought him another winner; and another soon followed. When, a year later, he 'saw' the results of two races, he rang up the *Daily Mirror* to tell them about his 'double' – an action which was to change his life, as, when the horses won, it led to the offer of a job on the paper which he took, in spite of having just passed out top of more than a hundred candidates hoping to enter the Foreign Office.

Godley next dreamed a loser – but it would not have qualified as a precognitive dream, as he actually had money on the horse already. Once more, he dreamed a winner; and then, another 'double'. One of the horses won; the other led until the last fence, but stumbled there and came in third. Still, in the space of less than three years (excluding the loser he had backed) Godley had had eight wins out of nine. The names of the dream winners, admittedly, had not always been exactly the same as those of the actual horses, but they had been close – he had dreamed 'Tubermore', for example, when the horse's name was Tuberose. On the *Experiment with Time* model, too, such deviations could be expected. In other respects, Godley's dreams had fulfilled G.W. Lambert's criteria; in particular, he had begun to write down the names of the dream horses after waking and had them attested by friends before the races.

If precognition can be thought of as a potentially valuable source of information, either positively as in Godley's case, or negatively, in warning of danger, might not more use be made of it than is generally realized? In the 1950s an American researcher, William Cox, though of an ingenious way to test this hypothesis. Examining the records of railway accidents in which ten or more people had been injured, he found that in each of them, the number of passengers carried had been significantly fewer than the average which had been carried on the same train in the seven days before the accident. It was difficult to account for these findings, he suggested, except on the supposition that some of the potential passengers on the day of the accident had had a precognitive warning of some kind not to travel by that train.

In his *Foreknowledge* H. F. Saltmarsh offered three possibilities to account for precognition without having to accept a paranormal element. One is auto-suggestion: the feeling that something is going to happen, because of the dream, can lead the dreamer to take the very courses which will make it happen. The second is subliminal knowledge; as the subconscious has a range of knowledge 'wider and fuller than that of our normal consciousness', our normal consciousness can be deceived into thinking that information must be coming from a psychic source when in fact it lies hidden in our own minds. The third is hyperesthesia: hyperacuity of one or other of the senses. The first two of these could occur, Saltmarsh conceded, but at best they could account only for a very small proportion of the known cases of precognition; and hyperesthesia of the kind necessary to account for precognition is unlikely.

For those who feel compelled to accept the reality of extra-sensory perception but jib at precognition, simple telepathy has been advanced as an alternative: as when the writer of a letter thinks of the recipient, and the recipient, picking up his thought by anticipation, 'sees' the impending arrival of the letter. Some cases of precognition might well be accounted for in this way, Saltmarsh agreed, but not all; and he felt that the volume of evidence for precognition, 'so large and so impressive in regard to quality', had accumulated to the point where it had become unscientific to ignore it.

If the evidence for warnings given by precognition were accepted, he added, it also had to be accepted that the future was 'alterable' (he preferred to call it 'plastic') by 'free will action performed in the present'; he thus confirmed that people can be self-determining agents, morally responsible for their actions.

RETROCOGNITION

If, as now seems so well established, we can have precognitive glimpses of the future, it would seem logical for us occasionally to have retrocognitive glimpses of the past: scenes, that is, which we could not have known about, or inferred, in the ordinary way from books or other sources. But as the main function of those who can induce psychic experiences – shamans, seers, diviners – has been to give guidance about the future, the ability to peer back into the past has not been highly regarded.

Perhaps for this reason, although there have always been indications that information may flow through psychics about past events, it has seldom been considered significant, except in so far as it seems to provide evidence for survival, or for reincarnation. The spirits who 'control' or 'possess' mediums have often identified themselves as having previously lived on earth; but the tendency has been to regard the spirits as still living in the spirit, rather than to assume that the medium is shifting back in time in order to allow them to communicate.

Retrocognition could hardly be said to have become recognized in its own right until the publication in 1911 of *An Adventure* by two Oxford dons, Annie Moberly and Eleanor Jourdain (though they used pseudonyms: Miss Morison and Miss Lamont). It described how, on a visit to Versailles, they appeared to have been wafted back into the 18th century; what they saw were the grounds, buildings and people as they were in the days of Louis XVI and Marie Antoinette.

An Adventure excited considerable interest, and has continued to do so, with frequent new editions. It has also provoked criticism: on the one hand from Eleanor Sidgwick, wife of the founder of the Society for Psychical Research, who wrote a sniffy review ('it does not seem to us that, on the evidence before us, there is sufficient ground for supposing anything supernormal to have occurred at all'); on the other from sceptics, one of whom suggested that what the two ladies saw was a fancy dress party given by the Comte de Montesquiou, who was living nearby. Surveying the evidence in his *Hauntings and Apparitions* (1982) for the SPR's Centenary Series, however, Andrew MacKenzie has shown that Eleanor Sidgwick did not take into account some impressive confirmation for the reality of the ladies' hallucinatory experience; and also that the fancy dress party hypothesis, derived as it was from the discovery that such events had been held by the count, could not be sustained because the dates did not match – Montesquiou was living elsewhere at the time.

For anybody who is prepared to accept the possibility of the mind – two minds, in this case – moving backward in time, the evidence for the genuineness of *An Adventure* is considerably stronger than Moberly and Jourdain could make it, as details which they did not know about have since emerged to relate more closely what they saw (and heard – music) to what they would have seen had they taken the same walk in 1770.

Glimpses of the past of a similar kind have since been reported in the *SPR Journal*, some relating to specific events. In 1950 Miss F. E. Smith of Letham in Angus was driving home when her car skidded off the road; walking back for the rest of the way, in the rain, her dog began to growl and she saw men carrying torches, wearing clothes which were strange to her. They struck her as looking like men searching for their dead, after a battle, to bury them. There had indeed been a battle there, in A.D. 685, accounts of which fitted reasonably well with what Miss Smith had 'seen' which could not be attributed to anything that was actually happening at the time she was walking home.

The following year, two English women were on holiday near Dieppe when, early one morning, they both heard noises which 'sounded like a roar that ebbed and flowed, and we could distinctly hear the sounds of cries and shouts and gunfire'. After a time it stopped, but then started up again, the sounds becoming more distinctly that of dive bombers. The times of the two 'waves' of battle, it turned out, closely corresponded to those of the invasion of Dieppe in 1942; and as the two women found that nobody else had heard them, disturbingly loud though they had been, the case was presented by the Society's investigators as a possible dual auditory retrocognitive experience.

Objections were raised by sceptical SPR members in both cases: one because there was no independent confirmation, as nobody had been with Miss Smith at the time; the other because the two women might have taken the sounds of a dredger, working at the time, for the sounds of battle. And no case so far reported, in fact, has been free from such objections.

The great majority of reports of experiences attributable to retrocognition are in any case not recognizably linked to specific events. The most frequently reported experience is for the 'real world' to fade momentarily, and for a different one to be superimposed over it, as in a film flashback. A typical example was sent in to Celia Green and Charles McCreery, following their appeal for experiences of apparitions. A woman described how, on her way to work on a winter night as an office cleaner, the warehouse she was passing faded, giving way to a small old-fashioned house; the road turned to cobble-stones and she heard the clip-clop of horses' hooves. 'The feeling of elation and happiness was great for me'; she longed to see more, but suddenly the scene vanished and the warehouse reappeared: 'Oh, my disappointment at not being able to grasp it!' Nothing comparable, she added, had ever happened to her before or since.

Visions of this kind are quite commonly reported by children – to the alarm of their parents, who fear their child is 'seeing things'. Sir Kelvin Spencer, a former Chief Scientist to the Ministry of Fuel and Power, has recalled that as a child he used to 'see' people 'moving about around a long table at which others were seated, all of them clothed in a kind of dressing gown'. (He later identified them as monks in a refectory.) Although real to him, his nurse could not see them.

Occasionally, though it seems more rarely, adults have these passing visions of the past. Sir William Rees-Mogg, Chairman of the Arts Council and formerly editor of *The Times*, gives another example in his autobiographical *An Humbler Heaven* (1977). He was preparing to have a siesta one afternoon when 'momentarily I was walking on the left-hand side behind a coffin in Camley Church' (the church where his father was buried). 'The man in front of me was wearing a green greatcoat in a coarse heavy material I had never seen before; under my feet there was the crunch of straw or rushes, as though I had been walking in a barn.' Rees-Mogg did not know, at the time, that in the 18th century rushes were customarily spread on the floor of a church. The brief experience, Rees-Mogg admits, would not qualify as evidence for anybody except himself; but 'if for a half second – as I have reason to believe, but no one else does – I followed an 18th-century coffin, then I lived for that half second a century and a half before my own birth'.

For the most part, these experiences happen only once in a lifetime, but occasionally individuals appear who can induce them, usually while in a trance state. It was not uncommon for spiritualist mediums, under the influence of their 'controls', to appear to identify so closely with the 'communicator', the spirit of a dead person, that they seemed actually to become the dead person as he, or she, was in life; and occasionally a medium would become somebody in this way – transfiguration – whom she identified as herself in a past incarnation.

The Swiss psychologist Theodore Flournoy investigated a medium of this kind in the 1890s: 'Hélène Smith', who in her trances described her past lives on earth, as Marie Antoinette and as an Indian princess. Hélène, Flournoy was careful to emphasize, was in her everyday life not merely beautiful and intelligent, but also of 'irreproachable moral character'; he was sure that she would never consciously have deceived him. But in her trances, she was taken over by spirit 'guides' who, Flournoy found, were untrustworthy, dishing up information about past events which, when he checked it, was frequently false.

With Marie Antoinette, the discrepancies were easy to track down. With the Indian princess it was more difficult; but Flournoy eventually discovered an old book which confirmed that some, at least, of Hélène's visions were historically accurate. This disturbed the sceptical Flournoy. In his *From India to the Planet Mars* (1901) – Hélène thought she could visit Mars, in her trances: she brought back a ludicrous account of its inhabitants – he fell back on the hypothesis of 'cryptomnesia'. She might long before have read the old book, absorbed the contents, and then forgotten all about it. This was highly improbable, he had to admit; 'but though there is scarcely any choice, extravagance for extravagance, I still prefer the hypothesis which only involves natural possibilities to that which appeals to occult causes'. Soon after, what Flournoy witnessed on a visit to the physical medium Eusapia Palladino shook his scepticism about the occult; but he did not abandon his belief that cryptomnesia was responsible for much that was being attributed to retrocognition and reincarnation.

Cryptomnesia has presented psychical researchers with a problem ever since; but it cannot account for some cases of trance retrocognition, such as the story of 'Patience Worth', 'author' of some highly praised books which were published in the United States during the first world war. 'Patience' emerged during a ouija-board session in a town in the Middle West, becoming the spirit 'control' of Mrs Pearl Curran, who simply had to put her hand on the planchette for 'Patience' to throw off witty sayings, verses and eventually whole novels, all of a quality which Mrs Curran herself, who had had only a rudimentary education, could not match.

Another method which has been used to induce retrocognition is regression under hypnosis, first explored by Colonel Albert de Rochas around the turn of the century. Subjects could re-live what appeared to be episodes in their past lives, he found, though it was rarely possible to verify the episodes, or the lives, historically. Could the explanation be that these were not 'past lives' which were being re-lived, but instances of retrocognition, displaying the confusion familiar in dream precognition?

The bulk of the work done with hypnotically regressed subjects, however, has been done in connection with reincarnation, rather than retrocognition, which has largely been ignored by parapsychologists. It does not receive a section to itself in either Wolman's massive *Handbook of Parapsychology* (1977) or Grattan-Guinness's *Psychical Research* (1982), the survey prepared for the SPR's centenary, in both of which it is mentioned only in passing. One reason, Gertrude Schmeidler suggests in the *Handbook*, is that if subjects provide what appears to be information obtained psychically about past events, its accuracy can be checked only from the records; 'but with such records, clairvoyance is not precluded (even if the records are now buried and not yet known to us)'. Perhaps it is for this reason, she surmises, that no laboratory research on retrocognition has been published, such reports of it as there are coming from spontaneous cases.

Gertrude Schmeidler has, however, suggested a way in which retrocognition might be prised out from clairvoyance, for test purposes. Some records of ancient civilizations have resisted deciphering: if a subject succeeded in giving the key to the cypher by using retrocognitive faculty, this, she contends, would provide a strong argument for retrocognition, because the translation, if it proved accurate, 'would not have existed in the absence of his retrocognitive success'.

There is no clear-cut division between cases which are described as *déjà vu*, in which individuals feel 'I have been here before', and retrocognition; but the tendency is to apply *déjà vu* to cases where the feeling is reported with no explanation – as in John Buchan's *Memory Hold the Door* (1940), in which he recalled three such occasions.

It was not simply that he suddenly came across places which he felt he had been to before; there was also a hint of menace. On the first occasion in the South African bushveld, when he felt sure that something had come out at him from a thicket, he recognized: 'something had happened to me here; and was about to happen again'. It didn't happen, either then or on the two subsequent occasions.

In one, he was on his way out to a yacht in Scotland when he 'was switched back two centuries'. He was sure that something fateful had happened, and was about to happen again when he went on board (all that happened was a welcome with a glass of Scotch). In the other, while serving as Lord High Commissioner in Edinburgh, he was sitting in the garden of Holyrood House when he was suddenly transported to 'some Château of Touraine' in the Ronsard era, where he knew the stage had been set for some high drama in which he was to play a part; but before he could be summoned to play it, an ADC appeared to remind him that 'seventy provosts and bailies were invited to luncheon'.

Attempts have been made to account for *déjà vu* as 'identifying paramnesia'; the contention being that it represents a temporary displacement of brain function ('You know that feeling you sometimes feel of feeling you're feeling that something has happened which has happened before', as P. G. Wodehouse described it in *Young Men in Spats*; 'I believe doctors explain it by saying that the two halves of the brain aren't working strictly on the up-and-up'.) But the idea that one part of the brain is 'remembering' something, which the other part has registered a split second before, cannot account for those experiences where the experiencer not only sees the same scene, a winding road or the façade of a house, but can tell what is coming round the next corner, or inside the house.

In such cases it is, however, possible to attribute what has happened to precognition in a dream which has since been forgotten – though this is no consolation to sceptics. In his *On Time* (1982), Michael Shallis, describing *déjà vu* experiences, agrees that the effect could be the living-out of a precognitive dream; hence the element of knowing what is about to happen next and the total familiarity of the occasion. 'There seems to be a difference between these two temporal phenomena. In the cases I know, the recognition of the precognition is what is experienced. That is, the prior notification of the event is what is remembered, whereas in *déjà vu* the experience is one of actually having lived that moment before. *Déjà vu* seems more likely to be related to time slips, where the temporal displacement is into one's own life rather than into some other piece of the future.'

Reincarnation

The belief that a soul can inhabit a succession of different bodies, human or animal, is of very ancient lineage; and it is derived largely from experiences which suggest that simple precognition is insufficient to account for the memories of past lives, as in the remarkable series of case histories provided by the psychiatrist Arthur Guirdham. One of his patients, he found, had been troubled in her teens by extremely vivid dreams and visions of what seemed to be an earlier existence as a Cathar (Albigensian) in the Languedoc during the early 13th century. Visions of such intensity were then commonly regarded (as they sometimes still are) as delusions – the forerunners of insanity; so she wrote them down but kept them to herself. To check on her account, Guirdham passed it to M. Jean Duvernoy, the acknowledged French expert on the subject. Duvernoy replied expressing astonishment at Guirdham's detailed knowledge – though Guirdham had none: he had obtained it all from the notes which the girl had kept.

What impressed Guirdham still more was that Duvernoy, who initially pointed out a mistake – the girl had insisted that Cathar priests dressed in dark blue, whereas it was known they always wore black – wrote later to say that in editing a new book by an Inquisitor appointed to deal with the Cathars, he had discovered that the priests did sometimes wear dark blue. Earlier historians had been misled.

Guirdham subsequently found that he, too, had had a role in

his patient's Cathar life, as did a few other people with whom they came into contact, almost as if the reunion had been planned; and he related the story in *The Cathars and Reincarnation* (1970), showing how individuals living in the 20th century could 'see' and 'feel' themselves in their separate, earlier lives. But did this evidence necessarily demonstrate reincarnation? 'Is some other explanation, for instance that of thought-transference, applicable?' Guirdham asked. The answer must be 'no', he explained, because he had 'had nothing to transfer'; it was not until later on that he learned about the Cathars, and could compare his patient's account of his role in the 13th century, from her visions, with what he had been, and done, in his 13th-century incarnation.

This, however, does not settle the argument. If ESP is responsible for those experiences which appear to point to reincarnation, it is not necessarily through simple thought-reading. The alternative hypothesis is of retrocognition, operating with and through what Jung described as the collective unconscious. People with psychic powers, it is surmised, particularly when under hypnosis, can tune in to the past as if on some tape recording. In the process they can identify with one, or more, of the cast, and may be 'possessed' to the point of actual feelings, whether of love or of death.

More recently it has been discovered – or re-discovered – that when they are under hypnosis, it is relatively easy to direct subjects back to what seem to be past lives. There are now scores of case histories of the kind described in Jeffrey Iverson's *More Lives Than One?* (1976) based on tape recordings made by the psychiatrist Arnall Bloxham; and *Encounters with the Past* (1979), from the records of Joe Keeton. But they leave the issue as confused as ever.

On the one hand, considering the great number of past lives which have been identified – in the sense that the subject has given a name, a place and a date – there are very few cases in which the evidence for the existence of the individuals thus identified can be clearly established, let alone shown to have the characteristics established by the subject's behaviour at the time of the session under hypnosis; and where they can be established, the possibility of cryptomnesia lurks in the background. On the other hand, the subjects while under hypnosis often display characteristics which do relate to the period, even if not to any individual, and which cryptomnesia cannot account for.

In *The Search for Bridey Murphy* (1956) Morey Bernstein described how he had found a subject, Mrs Tighe, who, under hypnosis, could be regressed to a 'life' in the 19th century in which she spoke in a broad Irish brogue, and provided a mass of detail about her childhood. A best-seller, the book inevitably irritated sceptics, who were pleased to find, when certain leads which 'Bridey' gave were followed up, that there was no trace of any such person, whereas there *was* evidence that, as a child, Mrs Tighe might have picked up both the brogue and the details from a neighbour.

Parapsychologists had been suspicious of the case from the start because it had not been investigated through with standard monitoring; they could now settle for cryptomnesia. Sceptics preferred to think that Bernstein had been hoaxed (or perhaps was himself the hoaxer). Many of the details, however – the names of shops, for example, the descriptions of life at the time, and some of the slang expressions 'Bridey' used – could not be accounted for by what Mrs Tighe might have picked up as a child. After examining the evidence the philosopher Professor C. J. Ducasse of Brown University dismissed both cryptomnesia and the contentions of the sceptics as inadequate to explain away the wealth of detail which 'Bridey' had provided – though the details were insufficient, in his view, to prove that Mrs Tighe was a reincarnation of Bridey, 'nor do they establish a particularly strong case for it'.

A much stronger case for the reality of reincarnation has been built up by Ian Stevenson, Carlson Professor of Psychiatry at the University of Virginia Medical School. In his *Twenty Cases Suggestive of Reincarnation* (1966) he put forward a formidable dossier of evidence from studies he had made of the evidence, including first-hand investigations; and these have been supplemented since by additional examples. None of them is flawless: 'we cannot reasonably expect to find any single case that will provide conclusive proof of reincarnation', he admits, 'nor is such proof a likely result of all the cases considered together'. Nevertheless the cumulative effect is impressive. Before Stevenson's work began to appear, few parapsychologists would have been prepared to take reincarnation sufficiently seriously to study the evidence. Now, he believes, most parapsychologists realize that it is at least entitled to consideration as one of the possible explanations for some retrocognitive experiences, even if few of them would accept it as the most plausible.

3 PSYCHOKINESIS

Psychokinesis, commonly abbreviated to PK, is usually defined as denoting the action of mind upon matter without the agency of any known physical force. The term was introduced by Rhine, and caught on; but the older term 'telekinesis' (still occasionally encountered, and in use behind the Iron Curtain), indicating simply action at distance without the agency of any known physical force, is theoretically preferable, as the movements do not necessarily stem from any mental impulse.

Some commentators, such as Scott Rogo in his *Parapsychology* (1975), make the distinction between psychokinesis 'the direct action of mind over material objects', and telekinesis 'the spontaneous movement of objects without contact or observable force or energy'. Although this is open to the objection that in many cases there is no satisfactory way of making the distinction, it does at least intimate that there is one; nevertheless, since psychokinesis is beginning to become the colloquial usage, it is likely to hold on in both senses for the foreseeable future. It also embraces what a century ago came to be described as the physical phenomena of spiritualism.

Where did PK have its origins? In *The Soul of the White Ant* (1937), Marais drew attention to two mysteries which he could not account for in his capacity as a naturalist, and which suggest the possibility of psychokinetic forces at work. When flying termites emerged from their original colony to found new ones, he could pick them up by their wings and hold them, vigorously struggling to escape from his fingers. Yet the moment a female termite landed after her flight, which could range from a few feet to hundreds of yards, she discarded her wings 'by a lightning-like movement, so fast that we cannot follow it with the eye'; and when she was examined, there was no sign of any ruptured linkage to show how the wings had been attached to the body.

Marais also found stones weighing ten or twelve pounds, high up on termitaries, 'which could only have got there through elevation by the termites'. How, he wondered, could termites have lifted such weights?

In the twilight zone between tribal life and early civilizations there are some mysteries for which PK has been put forward as a possible explanation; notably for the way in which what are now regarded as monuments constructed by ancient proto-civilizations were erected, a subject which has aroused a great deal of speculation without any fully satisfactory hypothesis being advanced.

To judge from Homer, the reality of psychokinetic powers, whether wielded by the gods or by sorcerers, was taken for granted by the ancient Greeks; as it was in the Old Testament, where Moses turned rods into serpents, divided the Red Sea, and materialized manna in the wilderness. When one of the prophet Elisha's followers, cutting down wood near the River Jordan, accidentally let the borrowed axe-head fall into the river, Elisha caused it to float so that it could be picked out again. In the gospels, Jesus is credited with several psychokinetic feats, from his first miracle, the changing of water into wine for the wedding feast at Cana, to walking on the water. And when, later, the apostles were put in prison for preaching their new Christian faith, the doors were flung open to allow their escape; to the bewilderment of their jailers the next morning, as they found the doors still locked.

In the literature of Greece and Rome, PK effects of all kinds were taken to be the work of the gods, expressing their satisfaction or, more frequently, their wrath, often in the form of omens presaging the fate of rulers. And one type of omen has continued to be reported up to within living memory: accidents to royal or imperial insignia, particularly crowns.

When the father of King Edward IV was declaring himself Duke of York in the House of Lords, Aubrey recalled in his *Miscellanies,* a crown hanging in the chamber suddenly fell. At the same time, the crown which stood on top of Dover Castle fell, too – which was taken to be a prognostication that the British Crown would pass from one line to another. And when James II was entering Dublin in 1689, hoping to restore himself to the throne by rallying the Irish to his side, the mace-bearer in front of him stumbled; the cross upon the crown of the mace stuck fast between two stones in the street, which 'did much trouble King James himself'.

Aubrey would have relished a sequel; when the Royal Crown was being borne through London at King George V's funeral in 1936, the Maltese Cross which surmounts it fell off. 'Though not superstitious,' Edward VIII was to recall as Duke of Windsor after his abdication, 'I wondered whether it was a bad omen.' His reaction at the time – according to Lord Boothby, then a Conservative Party back-bencher, who was close by in the crowd – was to say, out loud, 'Christ! What's going to happen next?' 'That,' Walter Elliot – then Minister of Agriculture, who was with Boothby in the crowd – remarked, 'will be the motto of the new reign.' So it proved to be.

In early Christian communities, psychokinetic effects of all kinds were attributed to divine intervention by God, or his angels. Usually they were attributed to the fallen angels: Beelzebub and his demons. Phenomena such as levitations might be regarded as a sign of grace when they were witnessed by the admirers or colleagues of men or women with a reputation for holiness, or asceticism; but with few exceptions the levitators shunned publicity, for fear of falling victim either to the sin of pride or to the Inquisition, or both. Their feats were consequently rarely publicized until agitation began to have them beatified or canonized; and by then, the lapse of time and the desire to present an impressive dossier render many accounts of miracles suspect as hagiography.

During the Middle Ages, and thereafter until rationalist ideas took over, PK effects were usually attributed to the devil, acting either directly or through witches. Usually the phenomena were similar to those now familiar from accounts of poltergeist hauntings: as in the reports of a witchcraft trial held in Cork in 1661. The bewitched girl, witnesses claimed, had fits in which she was 'removed strangely, in the twinkling of an eye, out of her bed, sometimes into the bottom of a chest with linen, under all the linen, and the linen not at all disordered'. Sometimes she was transported up to the roof of the house, so that ladders had to be used to bring her down. Wherever she went, too, she was pursued by showers of stones; they could be seen hitting her, and then falling to the ground – where they vanished.

Occurrences of this kind, as Alfred Russel Wallace observed, can be found by the thousand in reports of witchcraft trials; and though many 'confessions' are suspect, obtained as they were under duress, some are impressive because of the number and status of the witnesses, who were not themselves threatened: 'When we find that phenomena of an exactly similar nature are witnessed in our own day by men of talent and education, whose prepossessions are all against them, this concurrence of ancient and modern testimony must be held to prove that some, at least, of the facts witnessed were realities.'

The Physical Phenomena of Spiritualism

Wallace was referring to 'the physical phenomena of spiritualism', as they had come to be called, and doubtless he had pre-eminently in mind the phenomena which Daniel Dunglas Home had demonstrated to him, and to the physicist William Crookes. Of the PK manifestations which Crookes recalled witnessing with the mediums he had investigated, almost all were produced by Home: movement of objects without physical contact (or without pressure); currents of air; changes of temperature; percussive sounds of various kinds; alteration in weights; levitations of furniture; levitations of people; musical instruments playing untouched by human hand; luminosities; materializations; 'direct writing'; phantom forms; and apports. And this list inadvertently omitted one of Home's specialities: immunity to fire.

What was witnessed at seances with Home, and with scores of other mediums, was significant not just in its own right, but because of the resemblances not only to the phenomena described at witchcraft trials, but also to the accounts of miracles and to the evidence which was being provided of the powers of tribal shamans. The physical phenomena of spiritualism would also have needed only minor modifications to be read as a description of a poltergeist at work. Psychokinesis, in other words, cannot easily be segregated from the physical phenomena associated with shamanism, miracles, witchcraft and hauntings – much though some parapsychologists would like it to be, if it enabled them to study it as an objective force, like magnetism.

Exteriorization

The commonest type of psychokinesis is sometimes described as 'exteriorization'. It is as if the people involved are the focus for PK energy of a kind which sporadically emerges to influence objects around them. Usually the individual is not aware of transmitting the energy, which may seem either pointless, or apparently directed by an intelligence other than that of the person who is the focus. A few people are capable of harnessing the energy, and directing it for specific purposes.

In perhaps its simplest form, the PK energy spreads out around the 'focus' in the way it did around Angélique Cottin, the 'electric girl' in the 1840s; when Angélique, a 14-year-old from a French village, went to sit down, furniture moved away from her, as if being pushed by invisible hands, and with such force that men could not hold it. A local landowner, hearing about the girl, decided to investigate and quickly realized that Angélique could not be physically responsible for the movements of objects around her, including a heavy bin which actually rose off the ground when she came near it. The explanation, he decided, must be that she had become charged with electricity.

Angélique was subjected to a series of tests locally, and then sent to Paris so that she could be investigated by members of the Academy of the Sciences. Dr Tanchou, who carried out the preliminary investigation, described how he had personally felt the forces playing around her; a chair had been wrenched from his hands, and 'a large and heavy sofa upon which I was seated was pushed with great force against the wall the moment the girl came to seat herself by me'. Satisfied that Angélique could not be using sleight-of-hand, Tanchou brought in some of his colleagues, including the leading French physicist of the time, François Arago, an outspoken rationalist. They watched furniture retreat from the advancing Angélique, chairs jerking out from under her if she tried to sit down, and a sofa backing away from her even when one of them was sitting on it.

It must be some electrical force, they decided, and prepared tests to try to find out how it operated. But as suddenly as they had come, the phenomena ceased. There was nothing the investigators could do except send Angélique home, and to pigeon-hole the reports which had been made up to that point. Later, the rumour spread that Angélique's tricks had been exposed; but as Guillaume Figuier showed in his *Histoire du Merveilleux* (1860), this was false. Figuier had been anxious to find a natural explanation for the phenomenon, but he could not stomach the allegation that Arago and the others had been either dishonest or utterly incompetent – which they would have had to have been, if the arguments of the 'preconceived disbelievers', as he described them, were taken seriously. In any case, he pointed out, similar effects had since been witnessed and reported in connection with another girl.

Similar effects have continued to be reported, from time to time. In 1928 Wilfred Batt, an 18-year-old English youth, began to create PK effects on the farm where he lived: iron bars bent; objects such as candlesticks and trays jumped up as he approached; the dining-room gong rang loudly when nobody was near it; and furniture 'danced' around the room in his presence. Batt was described as the 'electric boy' because although he could not understand what was happening to him, he felt as if electric shocks were going through him: 'I have the sensation that it is something inside me which causes the queer things to come about, in spite of myself.'

In 1983 Carol Compton, a Scots girl who had been a nanny in Italy, was brought up on charges of attempted murder and arson, following a series of fires which had broken out in homes in which she had been working. As she had not been detected in starting the fires, the evidence was circumstantial; the defence took the line that the crimes had not been proved, and although she was found guilty of arson, as she had already spent 17 months in prison, she was immediately released. The defence did not bring up the paranormal element in the case; but it emerged in the evidence of two witnesses. A fireman of long experience testified that he had never known a fire behave in the way that one of them did – leaving the table where it had started only slightly charred, while destroying furniture and cupboards around it. And a forensic scientist told the court that a mattress which had burned could not have been set alight in the manner the prosecution alleged; it had burned unnaturally downwards, rather than up.

Ironically, shortly before the trial of 'the witch', as some Italian papers had dubbed her, they were full of the case of another 'electric boy', who was having much the same experiences as Wilfred Batt. Professor Hans Bender, the leading authority on poltergeist phenomena, felt that Carol's case bore many of the hallmarks of PK exteriorization, and it would have been possible to make a good case for her acquittal on all charges on those grounds; but the defence understandably felt it was wiser to rely on obtaining an acquittal on the more serious charge, thereby virtually ensuring Carol's release even if she were convicted of arson.

Exteriorization can take many different forms. Often it has been associated with a death; sometimes with a reprieve. Arthur Koestler recalled how, at the age of 29, he found himself 'living on charity, a writer of rejected books and plays, a refugee and an outsider among my friends and comrades' – members of the Communist Party; and he decided to commit suicide. After he had turned on the gas tap and was settling down beside it, a book crashed down on his head from the wobbly shelf above, nearly breaking his nose: *The Second Brown Book*, with the story of the Reichstag trial. Either he had unconsciously kicked the shelf, he commented mischievously, 'or it was a case of the Dialectic producing a miracle'.

Examples of exteriorization providing useful information are unusual, but the American psychical researcher Hereward Carrington related one example. A friend of his, a 'very good and reliable' witness, wrote to him in 1918 to describe how he had arrived at the Vendome Hotel in Boston to pick up a very important letter, to find it had not arrived; and when it still had not arrived a fortnight later, he was just about to leave. He was sitting in his room reading when he saw what seemed to be the shadow of an arm and a hand make a sweeping motion just outside the ground glass door of his room; but when he looked out the corridor was empty. He went back to his book but then, a chest-of-drawers began 'to stir and creak as do articles in a ship when the waves are high'. Puzzled, he moved the chest-of-drawers to one side – and there was the letter: 'it had been pushed under the door by the bell-boy and pushed so hard that it had disappeared under the article of furniture'.

Exteriorization phenomena have often been associated with heightened tension. Koestler, again, cited a case in his autobiography: he was staying with his highly psychic (and emotionally disturbed) friend Maria; she warned him that something would occur to shake him. And at lunch a large picture hanging on the wall he was facing in the dining-room crashed on to the sideboard. When he went to look, the two picture hooks were still in the wall, solid and undamaged, and the picture wire was unbroken; he was able to hang the picture back in its former place, 'where it again came to rest as firmly and innocently as if it had always stayed there'.

Jung, too, provided a striking example of tension–exteriorization in his *Memories, Dreams, Reflections*, recalling an episode which preceded his break with Freud. Freud blew sometimes hot, sometimes cold, on accounts of psychic experiences; and on this occasion was deriding them. Jung, irritated, felt his diaphragm becoming a 'glowing vault', and suddenly so loud a report came from a bookcase in the room that both of them jumped to their feet. 'There!' Jung claimed, 'that is an example of a so-called catalytic exteriorization phenomenon.' When Freud dismissed this as bosh, 'You are mistaken, Herr Professor,' Jung told him. 'And to prove my point I now predict that there will be another loud report.' Sure enough, 'No sooner had I said the words than the same detonation went off in the bookcase.'

Out of about 10,000 cases of paranormal experiences in Louisa Rhine's collection, fewer than 200, she observed in *The Invisible Picture* (1981), had been classified as possibly psychokinetic. She felt, though, that this probably was not a fair representation of the frequency of their occurrence. Movements of objects, for example, are not always easy to attribute to PK with any confidence; in any case, there is much less of a disposition to accept the possibility of PK than of ESP.

Interestingly, however, when she analysed the PK cases they showed some marked resemblances. Nearly always, two people were involved: one who observed, or experienced, the effect; the other, at a distance, who was in a state of tension due to some crisis. Nearly always, too, the two people involved were relatives or friends 'so that the crisis of one would naturally produce an emotional response in the other'. And although the physical effects varied, they 'usually involved a household appliance, like a clock or picture'.

The same holds for anecdotal cases in history. One of the most frequently encountered varieties is enshrined in the old song 'The clock stopped, never to go again, when the old man died.'

Flammarion collected some examples, for *Death and its Mystery* (1922), including one which he claimed was well attested, though the family would not permit their names to be reported, in which a clock which had stopped when an old woman had died in 1913, and which could not be made to go again, suddenly started on the day her son died, without anybody having touched it. Another example, cited by Louisa Rhine, had been contributed by a citizen of Detroit, who dreamed one night that his grandmother was standing by his bed, calling him; when he woke up he found his dog, sleeping at the end of his bed, was in a disturbed state, so he turned on the light to find nothing the matter. It was four A.M., he noted. The next morning his grandmother was found dead in her bed, though there had been nothing to suggest she was unwell; and her clock had stopped at four.

Of mediums who have to some extent been able to produce PK effects voluntarily, only one has come within measurable distance of emulating Home's feats: the Brazilian, Carlos Mirabelli, who in the 1920s gave countless demonstrations of his ability in good light, and with numerous respectable witnesses, to produce apparitions of recently dead people which not merely looked and talked as they had done in their lives, but had pulses which could be felt to beat. Because South America was out of the main stream of psychical research, however, his accomplishments were not taken seriously in Britain or the United States; for nearly half a century psychokinesis, and in particular exteriorization of the kind associated with the physical phenomena of mediumship, became almost taboo – barring a few tests with dice throwing. Significantly, in Rosalind Heywood's balanced survey, *The Sixth Sense* (1959), psychokinesis was mentioned only in passing.

Ironically, the taboo was broken in the early 1970s in the way parapsychologists least welcomed: by the young Israeli Uri Geller. He had demonstrated an ability to bend forks and latchkeys by PK on television in the United States, but his real launching took place on a BBC programme, when he confounded the BBC's resident sceptic, Professor John Taylor, who confessed himself unable to detect any trickery. Even more striking was the flood of reports which arrived in the next few days from people all round the country who had found bent cutlery, or clocks – regarded as beyond repair – which had started up again in their homes: a display of mass exteriorization which was to be repeated whenever Geller was on television or radio.

Geller was pursued with venom by sceptics and conjurors, both claiming that he must be using sleight-of-hand; not even the fact that he was able successfully to pass certain tests was enough to impress them. What made it extremely unlikely that he was simply a prestidigitator, however, was the emergence of 'mini-Gellers' in countries all over the world, some of whom demonstrated metal-bending powers and a few of whom continue to do so. Although physicists remain divided, a number have been convinced by the evidence from experiments that they cannot any longer dismiss PK out of hand.

Experimental PK

The first attempt to devise and use equipment to test PK was made in the United States by Robert Hare, a former Professor of Chemistry, in the early 1850s. He experimented with a wooden board mounted on a fulcrum: one end fixed so that the volunteers who came to try to see if they had psychic powers could not physically shift it; the other end attached to a balance which would register any increase in the board's weight. The subjects could exert finger-tip pressure without influencing the pointer on the balance; if it moved, it could only be because they were exerting a psychic force. Some mediums, Hare found, were able to exert it without even touching the board; for one of them, the balance registered a change in the board's weight of eighteen pounds.

Hare became a convinced spiritualist, and as such, was greeted with derision by his former colleagues when he tried in 1854 to convince them that he had demonstrated the reality of the force. Johann Zöllner, Professor of Physics at Leipzig, fared no better with his test of the medium Henry Slade, though Slade's ability to move objects and furniture and make musical instruments play at a distance was testified to by some of the leading scientists in Germany – Zöllner himself, Gustav Fechner, Wilhelm Weber and Wilhelm Scheibner. The PK force showed a poltergeist-like propensity for mischief, unbuttoning Scheibner's jacket, and causing a table first to de-materialize and then to sail down from the ceiling, striking Zöllner on the head; but it nearly passed one test which has subsequently often been cited as the decisive way in which PK could be definitively proved. Slade was asked to see if he could interlink two wooden rings, each cut from a single piece of wood with no joins. The following morning the two rings were found, not linked, but wrapped around a table leg in a way they could not have been physically, except by taking the table to pieces.

All that Zöllner's *Transcendental Physics* (1879) did for him was to ruin his reputation and damage that of other witnesses – except that of Wilhelm Wundt, who claimed that he had not been fooled by Slade. Wundt's report at the time, however, indicated that, though he was unable to accept the implications of what he had witnessed – could it be that the laws of nature, he asked incredulously, were approaching the point 'where they shall be done away with?' – he had seen manifestations which he could not account for, such as the levitation of a table for which Slade could not have been physically responsible. If he were asked 'to express a conjecture as to how these experiments were performed', he had written, he would answer 'no'.

The next set of experiments to be reported were conducted by Alexander von Boutlerow, Professor of Chemistry (chemistry at the time had not split off from physics) at the University of St Petersburg. Using a dynamometer Boutlerow found that D. D. Home, who was on a visit to Russia, could increase the tension it recorded by up to 50 per cent.

A few months later William Crookes followed this up with a test using equipment similar to that with which Hare had experimented twenty years earlier. Home was required to see whether he could influence a spring balance attached to one end of a wooden board, Home's fingers being on the other end. Although the physical pressure of Home's fingers could not have been responsible, as soon as they were placed on the board the spring balance registered changes. Crookes and two colleagues – the lawyer Serjeant Cox and the astronomer William Huggins, who was later to be President of the Royal Society – reported that the tests appeared 'to establish the existence of a new force, in some unknown manner connected with the human organism'.

A succession of trials held with the Italian medium Eusapia Palladino by eminent scientists in Italy, Poland, Germany and France confirmed the existence of the new force. Again and again, from 1890 to 1910, she was able to show her investigators that she could move objects in distant parts of the room; chairs and tables came towards her, or away from her, as if attracted or repelled.

The most elaborate of the many investigations of Eusapia was conducted from 1904 to 1906 by Jules Courtier, Professor of Psychology at the Sorbonne, and witnessed by several eminent scientists, among them Richet, Bergson, Ballet, Perrin, d'Arsonval and the Curies. The reports recorded movements of objects at a distance from Eusapia and from the investigators controlling her, and musical instruments sounding. The investigators felt themselves being pinched; sometimes their hair was pulled, and the knots in their cravats untied. Pierre Curie described seeing and feeling a stool, which had been placed outside the circle of investigators, moving towards him and seemingly trying to climb upon him; and a small table which soared off the floor and into the circle made 'a pretty curve', as he put it, in its flight.

Later, three members of the SPR well-versed in conjuring tricks, and experienced at exposing spurious mediums, went to investigate Eusapia in Naples. To their chagrin, not merely was she able to produce PK phenomena while two of them were controlling her hands and feet and the third was observing: the raps, the sounding of musical instruments, the nudges and the movements of objects were most frequent in the sessions in which Eusapia's spirit 'control', being in good humour, allowed them to increase the amount of light, so that they could actually see that although she sometimes made convulsive movements, as if to push or pull objects at a distance, she was not physically pushing or pulling them when they moved.

The most elaborate tests ever undertaken of a medium were devised during the first world war by W. J. Crawford, a lecturer in engineering at Queen's University, Belfast. With the help of a weighing platform he found that the levitation of a table by the medium Kathleen Goligher appeared to be accomplished with the assistance of ectoplasmic 'rods', operating – sometimes visibly – on the cantilever principle, the 'rods' emanating from her, bouncing (as it were) off the floor to lift the table, and directing its movements while it floated. Her weight, he found, showed an increase during the levitations of roughly the amount which would have been expected if sufficient weights were being added to the scales to lift the table with a real, rather than a psychic, cantilever.

As with most mediums, Home being an exception, the forces emanating from the Goligher circle (Crawford thought the presence of the family circle increased Kathleen's generating powers) appeared to be directed by an independent and often mischievous intelligence. It was illustrated in the reports which Sir William Barrett, Whately Smith (who later changed his name to Carington) and others made following their investigations of the Goligher circle at Crawford's invitation. Both Barrett and a Belfast physician who accompanied him were encouraged to wrestle with a table which had been levitated within the circle; and in light good enough to see what they were doing, they were unable to force the table down to the floor. When Barrett sat on it, it swayed him about, eventually tipping him off. Smith had a similar experience some months later. He could just stop the floating table moving in any one direction, but it would then dart off in another; and he, too, could not push it down to the floor. When he saw a trumpet levitate and float towards him, separating into its two component parts, they resisted his efforts to twist them around.

After the first world war, several mediums demonstrated PK powers in laboratory conditions, the most successful being the Schneider brothers, who grew up in Braunau, the Austrian town where Hitler had been born a few years earlier. The evidence of Willy Schneider's ability to produce PK phenomena of various kinds – especially movements and levitations of objects at a distance from him and the assembled sitters, in light which, though subdued, was good enough for everybody present to observe what was happening – was provided not only by Baron Schrenck-Notzing and other psychical researchers, but by a procession of academics from a variety of disciplines (Schrenck's social position and wealth were a help here). Schrenck encouraged those who were sceptical, as many were, to suggest any additional precautions – apart from participating in the standard preliminary searches of the medium and the seance room. If they were interested, they could come again, with ideas for still more elaborate precautions. When Eric Dingwall arrived in 1922 to investigate Willy (and, by implication, Schrenck) on behalf of the SPR, he found three professors, two doctors and a general in the assembled company; and ascertained that in sixty earlier sittings, 27 professors, 18 doctors and 16 other savants, some of whom had attended several times, had testified to the genuineness of the phenomena – as Dingwall, hard though he was to convince, was himself to do. Not one of those who had attended, he added, had been able to suggest any way in which the phenomena could be accounted for naturally.

One of the most detailed and impressive accounts (or, rather, two accounts of the same occasion) of Willy Schneider's PK powers was written in 1922 by Thomas Mann – already an internationally-established author. Mann had arrived in a sceptical frame of mind; but in light good enough to reassure him that no known physical force could be responsible, a handkerchief which levitated off the floor began to change its shape while floating, as if it were being manipulated from the inside by a hand – the shape of knuckles could be observed, as protuberances. A bell, standing within Mann's vision on the floor, began to ring violently ('Any thought of a swindle in the sense of a conjuring trick is absurd,' he insisted. 'There was simply nobody there who could have rung the bell.')

Willy's younger brother, Rudi, had similar psychokinetic powers, which were to be tested in Paris in the early 1930s by Eugène Osty, Director of the *Institut Métaphysique*. Osty had been wary of physical mediums until convinced by phenomena produced by the Pole, Jean Guzik; but Guzik could produce them only in darkness. Such evidence, Osty realized, would never convince anybody who had not been present; and with the help of his son, a physicist, he worked out a foolproof way to detect psychokinesis and at the same time prevent fraud, even in total darkness. An infra-red projector sent invisible beams which would detect any movement in a target object, and in the process ring a bell and trigger off ultra-violet light in which a photograph would automatically be taken. This would reveal not only what, if anything, had happened to the object, but also whether the medium, or anyone else, had moved it with the help of physical force – say, a telescopic rod.

The method worked. Osty explained in his report that Rudi 'exteriorized' energy which was not visible, but which affected the infra-red rays, causing the bell to ring and the photographs to be taken, showing displacements of the targets and confirming that they were not caused by any physical intervention by Rudi. In any case, Osty found, the infra-red rays reacted differently when influenced by PK from the way they reacted to physical obstructions.

In further trials in London which followed, Harry Price, Lord Charles Hope, and others obtained confirmation of these results. So, later, did Hope and Lord Rayleigh. Price, however, furious over what he regarded as Hope's treachery in appropriating Rudi (and at Rudi's for allowing himself to be appropriated), produced evidence which, he claimed, showed that Rudi cheated. The evidence has recently been reviewed, and effectively demolished, by Anita Gregory in her *Anatomy of a Fraud* (1977), but at the time it looked damning; and as Price was still 'news' in Fleet Street terms, his 'exposure' received far wider publicity than the positive results of the Hope/Rayleigh series.

In the United States, the attention of psychical researchers in the 1920s was largely concentrated on 'Margery' – the medium Mina Crandon, who in seances in Boston produced most of the by this time familiar PK effects. As she produced them in near-darkness, however, she was unable to convince her many investigators that she and her husband were not supremely clever conjurors; and although she was not actually caught cheating (Houdini claimed to have caught her, but in fact 'Margery' – or her 'control', her deceased brother – caught *him* trying to 'plant' evidence which would have convicted her) the net result of her performances was a painful split in the ranks of psychical researchers between her supporters and her detractors.

Investigating Margery, the Rhines suspected her of cheating; and this helped to persuade them to switch to laboratory work of a kind they could better control. As Louisa Rhine was to recall in her *Mind Over Matter* (1970), the opportunity presented itself when a young man arrived at Duke claiming he could control the fall of dice by willpower – not all the time, he admitted, but on occasions when he was in a certain mental state, which he had learned to recognize. Rhine agreed to test him, and at the same time began tests with students along the same lines as those he had conducted with them for ESP, but using dice rather than cards. The number of times in which the dice fell as the students had 'willed' them to fall, he found, was significantly above chance expectation, the odds against chance being over a billion to one.

Similar experiments carried out in other centres in the United States and in Britain gave comparable results. The most remarkable trial was conducted by G. W. Fisk with his subject Dr Jessie Blunden, who lived in Devon. Dr Blunden threw the dice, 'willing' them to fall so that they would match the targets chosen by Fisk, who lived in Surrey. He did not tell her what those targets (selected by a randomizer) were until after her guesses had reached him. She had to guess telepathically, in other words, what the targets would be, and then 'will' the dice which she threw to match them. Over a period of six years, she 'willed' the dice sufficiently successfully for the odds against chance to stand at about 50,000 to one.

The introduction of electronic random event generators (REGs) improved the prospects for obtaining objective evidence for PK; and they were employed by the physicist Helmut Schmidt, using radioactive decay, 'nature's most elementary source of randomness'. Subjects were asked to try to 'will' his apparatus to take a particular direction – which could mean the decay had ceased to be random but was being influenced by the minds of the subjects. Again, the results attained by some of them were far better than chance.

In the Khrushchev era, when Western investigators were for a while allowed to meet Russian mediums, they were able to watch Nelya Kulagina – formerly a sergeant radio operator in a tank during the siege of Leningrad – and confirm that the reports of her PK abilities, which Soviet scientists had been making, were reliable. William A. McGarey, one of a team from the United States investigating psychic phenomena in Russia in 1970, described a session in which she obligingly caused several small objects to move across the tablecloth of a dining-room table. Small objects like a wedding ring, or the top of a condiment bottle, moved easily and rather quickly when she simply held her hands above them. Looking at the ring and moving her head slightly in a circular manner, she caused it to rotate on an invisible axis as it lay there on the cloth.

In one of the films taken of her, a ping-pong ball is shown levitating and hovering in the air for a few moments, before falling back on to the table. According to Gaither Pratt, another of the American investigators, the objects which Kulagina could move varied widely in material, shape and weight – a curiosity being that long objects, such as cigarettes, tended to move across the table while vertical, standing on end. Sometimes they progressed slowly and steadily, sometimes in fits and starts. Elaborate precautions were taken to ensure that she could not be using some device, such as a concealed magnet; as the investigators agreed, and the films taken confirmed, no known form of force could account for the movements.

In *The Geller Papers* (1976) edited by Charles Panati, several individuals and teams who had investigated Uri Geller's paranormal powers in the 1970s described their results, some briefly, some in detail. Geller's chief successes were with bending objects such as cutlery and keys with light stroking, sometimes without touching; but in addition he exerted an influence on electro-magnetic fields – causing compass needles to swing, for example. He also triggered poltergeist-type effects, including materializations and de-materializations. One of his achievements was to cause a permanent change in the shape of a piece of nitinol wire at the Naval Surface Weapons Centre in Maryland, a feat normally requiring re-shaping under tension at a temperature of about 900°F. The paper describing the experiment represented the first occasion the Defense Department released the results of parapsychological research for publication.

Sceptics, taking the line that scientists are notoriously gullible, demanded an investigation by conjurors. Arthur Zorka, a member of the Society of American Magicians, and a fellow-magician from Atlanta, Abb Dickson, undertook it. There was no way, Zorka reported, 'that any method of trickery could have been used to produce the effects under the conditions to which Geller was subjected', a verdict which Dickson endorsed. 'I was prepared to nail the guy,' Dickson wrote to Milbourne Christopher, the leading authority on prestidigitation in the United States, 'but the results were quite another story'; he had watched his key bend when Geller was merely touching, not holding, it – something, he knew, that no magician could duplicate except by substitution, which he was aware was impossible.

Not surprisingly, Geller lost interest in formal tests, as sceptics simply either ignored the results or offered increasingly implausible explanations of how he had tricked the investigators. Subsequently, however, 'mini-Gellers' in many parts of the world have produced distortions in metal under controlled conditions, as John Hasted, Professor of Experimental Physics at Birkbeck College, in the University of London, has described in *The Metal Benders* (1981). In the *SPR Journal* (October 1982) too, John L. Randall has described how he decided to try to replicate the 'nitinol' experiment which had been conducted with Geller with the help of one of the 'mini-Gellers', a schoolboy, Mark Briscoe. Nitinol was again used because of its 'memory'. Mark stroked it, gently: 'inexplicable deformations were observed, and the memory of the wire was permanently altered' – attempts to straighten it under heat proving as unsuccessful as they had with Geller, thereby confirming the verdict of the Naval Surface Weapons Centre. A do-it-yourself metal-bending kit which Julian Isaacs has invented has recently been enabling people who have some psychic powers to develop them, using bio-feedback, proving that crystals can be influenced in ways which cannot be attributed to any conjuring trick.

Adult metal-benders have also submitted to tests, with positive results: notably Jean-Pierre Girard in France, who managed to bend a steel bar enclosed in a glass tube. They have also obtained positive results in PK experiments of other kinds. In tests at the City University, London, conducted by Anita Gregory in 1978 on behalf of the SPR, Matthew Manning appeared to cause deflection of an infra-red ray similar to, even if less striking than, those which Rudi Schneider had obtained. In an experiment at the Stanford Research Institute, the New York artist and psychic Ingo Swann was challenged to see if he could influence the smooth flow of the recordings from a magnetometer which had been elaborately insulated. He promptly altered the 'ripple' on the chart to a 'wave'. This, the sceptical physicist in charge of the magnetometer claimed, must have been coincidence; to prove he was responsible for affecting the magnetometer, Swann must stop the ripple effect. Swann promptly did, for several seconds.

A promising line of PK experimentation, conducted since the early 1960s, has been described by John Thomas Richards in *SORRAT* (1982) – SORRAT being an acronym for the Society for Research on Rapport and Telekinesis – a body set up by John G. Neihardt, the 'Poet Laureate of the Plains States', in pursuance of his study of 'pragmatic mysticism'. As of old, the problem was to devise ways in which spontaneous PK events related to psychics could be monitored in a manner which would detect the use of physical force, conscious or unconscious. William Cox provided a solution: a sealed glass container, like a living-room aquarium turned upside-down, in which objects could be placed, with a cine-recorder attached which would be switched on automatically if any movement occurred in the tank in order to register what was happening.

The experiment proved only too successful. Among the movements recorded were 'direct writing' by a pen, a toy train moving back and forth, and leather rings first interlinking and then separating out again. There were also apports. As had so often happened in the past, some parapsychologists grew nervous, making no secret of their belief that it was all a hoax; and by 1983 believers and sceptics were divided in much the same way (though not so destructively) as they had been fifty years before over 'Margery'.

Even the sceptics, however, could not dispute that the methodology SORRAT had evolved is admirably suited to research into PK of a kind that anybody can do at home. The cine-record may not impress outsiders, because – as a demonstration at the SPR's centenary 1982 conference showed – faking is easy; but it will enable mediums or groups to experiment and check for themselves whether there is any PK activity, without having to sit around hour after hour waiting for it to occur.

Psi-blocking

All paranormal phenomena are naturally capricious, John L. Randall notes in his *Psychokinesis* (1982), particularly the psychokinetic type: 'in poltergeist cases, for example, objects usually move when the observer has turned his back for a moment, or when he is in the process of changing the film in his camera.'

It is not only in poltergeist cases that there has been 'psi-blocking' of investigation, of a kind which is apparently deliberate: and often it has been reported as taking the form of positive, rather than evasive, blocking. Randall cites cases where attempts to take a photograph or tape recording of a shaman have been frustrated by malfunctioning of the equipment, though it has worked smoothly before and after; and Laurens van der Post had much the same kind of story to tell about the time his team tried to film cave paintings in the Kalahari, which were protected, they were told, by the resident spirits.

The reports of investigations into physical mediumship or poltergeist activity frequently contain irritated comments about the fallibility of photographic equipment at crucial moments in tests, so that when, say, the investigators turn eagerly to a photograph which has been taken, to examine in detail some phenomenon they have all witnessed, it turns out to be blank. The two physicists who investigated the Rosenheim poltergeist in Germany in 1967–8 could count themselves fortunate to have caught some of its activities on videotape, in view of the fact that the movements not merely 'gave the impression of being under intelligent control' – as they put it – but also had 'a tendency to evade investigation'.

Perhaps the most detailed account of what began to look like systematic psi-blocking in a poltergeist case is in *This House is Haunted* (1980), by Guy Lyon Playfair. The house in question was in Enfield, in North London; and attempts to take recordings were frequently frustrated – the recorder would run at different speeds; a heavy microphone left its stand and fell to the floor; and when three cameras were set up in a bedroom to ensure total coverage, all three flashguns failed to fire – all three, it was found, had been drained of power simultaneously, though they had only just been charged.

When the product manager, the chief demonstrator and two employees of Pye Business Communications set up their own camera equipment, so that it would be possible to watch events in an upstairs bedroom from downstairs, the camera worked but the recorder – made by a different firm, but tested, and to all appearances working satisfactorily – suddenly went berserk: 'all the lights by the various buttons on the recorder came on together', which the demonstrator would have thought impossible; and the machine refused to wind the tape, jamming in a way he had never encountered before.

When Matthew Manning was making broadcasts, following the publication of his autobiographical account of the poltergeist experiences from his childhood, the failure of electrical and sound equipment and cameras was a constant accompaniment of his arrival in studios; as it also frequently was of Uri Geller's. Inevitably, sceptics have seized upon the failure of monitoring apparatus to perform its function on such occasions as justification for refusing to accept the evidence of eye-witnesses; but the failures have been reported so often, on so many diverse occasions, that psi-blocking has become a more plausible explanation than coincidence coupled with fraud.

PK Categories

Psychokinetic effects can be classified under four main heads. First, there are the physical effects: movement of objects at a distance, or without sufficient force being exercised to make them move; bending or breaking of objects; apports; 'direct writing'; and psychic photographs. Second, there are the physiological effects: ectoplasmic emanations and materializations; levitations; translocations; elongations; invulnerability; incombustibility; incorruptibility; and auras. Third, there are acoustic effects: raps and direct voices. And fourth, there are atmospheric effects: luminosities; changes of temperature and cold breezes; outbreaks of fire; liquefactions; and scents.

PHYSICAL EFFECTS

Movements of Objects

When, in the early 1850s, a drawing-room pastime became a fashionable craze, first in America and then throughout Europe, the procedure at sittings varied, but they were usually conducted by small groups: families (with their domestic servants, if they were considered suitable) and friends sitting round a card table – or a dining table, according to the number of sitters. The room would be in darkness, or near darkness; the group would put their finger tips lightly on the table and wait for something to happen.

The first indications were usually 'raps'; then the table would begin to shudder; 'a curious vibratory motion' as Wallace described it, 'almost like the shivering of a living animal. I could feel it up to my elbows.' Next, the table would begin to move: sometimes as if sliding along the floor, sometimes as if turning on one of its 'claws' (if it were that type). It might then rear up on two legs, or one; sometimes it would leave the floor altogether so that the 'sitters' found themselves compelled to stand to keep their fingers on top – which incidentally enabled them to make certain nobody was physically lifting the table from below.

It was not only the table which displayed PK on such occasions. Chairs would move up to, or away from, the sitters. Objects would fly around the room: musical instruments would sound as if being played by an invisible hand. But it was the movements of the tables that initially aroused fascinated interest, and then controversy.

Soon, it was obvious that tables really were behaving in this eccentric fashion. Too many men and women in society, in the professions and in the academic world, along with well-known writers who described their experiences, had attended sessions and come away convinced that trickery had been impossible. A 'natural' explanation was needed; and it was offered in a hypothesis which the physiologist W. B. Carpenter of London University had put forward to account for one of the features often noted in connection with the mesmeric trance state – relative weaklings were able to develop what for them, in their normal waking condition, would have seemed like superhuman strength: 'quasi-involuntary muscular action'. At that time, the existence of what would now be regarded as the subconscious was suspect as a hangover from the occultist belief in diabolic possession – as indeed was the trance state itself; but as Carpenter judged rightly, 'quasi-involuntary' would pass muster.

For Faraday – anxious, as he put it, to 'turn the tables on the table-turners', for their experiences, he feared, might promote a reaction against scientific rationalism – Carpenter's theory was just what he was looking for; and he set up an experiment which, he claimed in a letter to *The Times*, had demonstrated that quasi-involuntary muscular action was responsible for what the tables were doing. It is still sometimes cited as if it were a genuine rebuttal of the claims for table-turning. What it in fact did was show that a group of sitters might rotate a loose table-top without intending to. But the great majority of reports of sittings showed that what the tables did could not conceivably be accounted for on this basis; moving around the room, rearing up on two legs or one – let alone floating. And although the majority of the accounts of table-turning sessions lack independent confirmation, this cannot be claimed of the evidence for the similar effects at seances with Home or, later, Eusapia Palladino, both of which were attested by scores of witnesses of standing.

As a social pastime table-turning gradually went out of fashion, largely because it was time-consuming and often boring. Sometimes sitters waited in near darkness for a couple of hours before anything happened. Sometimes nothing did. The discovery that tables by their raps or their tilts could give what appeared to be replies from the spirits to questions tended to shift interest away from table-turning to table-rapping or table-tilting; and increasingly, reliance was placed on the presence at sittings of mediums who were able to get the spirits (and the tables) moving without protracted delays. Of these, the most celebrated was Home.

Born in Scotland, reared in the United States, Daniel Dunglas Home began to have psychic experiences as a youth, and was caught up in 'the psychic cloud', as Conan Doyle was to call it, which spread out from the Fox sisters' Hydesville experiences.

Returning to Britain for health reasons in his early twenties, Home found that his talents and his charm of manner procured him entry into society, and for the next twenty years he was to be the most celebrated medium in Europe.

His procedure varied little. He would go to the house where the seance was to be held, usually unaccompanied (except, occasionally, by his first wife during their happy but brief marriage). If any of the sitters wished to search him, Home complied before going to the seance room, which often he had not entered, or even seen, before. The sitters, usually around eight of them, would dispose themselves round a table, in the, by this time, familiar way, resting their finger tips on it. They would hear raps, and then feel the table begin to shudder, move around, rise up on two legs and leave the floor altogether.

Many other phenomena were reported. Home occasionally himself levitated, floating round the room. Disembodied hands could be seen and shaken; musical instruments played without a player; or Home would dabble in fire. Usually, though, it was a table which provided the focus for the gathering and whose movements convinced doubters that their scepticism had been misplaced – Thackeray, for one, and his friend Robert Bell, who in Thackeray's *Cornhill* magazine described a session with Home at which a small round table moved away from the sitters and appeared to be trying to climb up on a sofa: 'It slipped down at the first attempt, but again quietly resumed its task. It was exactly like a child trying to climb up a height.'

Movements of tables or other furniture were sometimes reported after seances had ended. The Scots writer Patrick Proctor Alexander, whose scepticism was banished by sessions which his friend Dr Doun had laid on for Home, went on to record what had happened after Home had left after a seance: one of the chairs in the room had travelled slowly across the carpet towards Doun. His wife, when she came in, thought he must have been dreaming; as if in rebuke, another chair approached them across the floor.

Among the scientists who participated in table-turning sessions was Wallace, who was initially incredulous, and then baffled. In his 'notes on personal evidence' in *The Scientific Aspect of the Supernatural* (1866) he cited, on one occasion, a small table on which the hands of four people, one of them himself, rose up vertically a foot from the floor, remaining suspended for about twenty seconds; enabling a friend of his, acting as an observer, to check that no force was being applied to the underside. On another, a chair in which somebody was sitting levitated with her in it; then moved away from her whenever she approached it; and finally appeared to become fixed to the floor, so that she could not move it – all this, in a room with two windows on a bright day. 'However strange and unreal these phenomena may seem to readers who have seen nothing of the kind,' Wallace remarked apologetically, 'I positively affirm that they are facts which really happened just as I have narrated them, and that there was not room for any possible trick or deception.'

Crookes participated in many table-turning sessions, usually with Home. In his summing-up of what he had witnessed, and experienced, he cited movements of furniture (his chair had been tugged around while he was sitting in it). He and the other sitters, too, had watched a small table move across a room, nobody being within touching distance of it. And he had seen levitations.

On one occasion I witnessed a chair, with a lady sitting on it, rise several inches from the ground. On another occasion, to avoid the suspicion of this being in some way performed by herself, the lady knelt on the chair in such a manner that its four feet were visible to us. It then rose about three inches, remained suspended for about ten seconds, and then slowly descended.

Why, sceptics had asked Crookes, was furniture usually involved in such manifestations? His business as a scientist, he used to reply, was to observe and record phenomena: his not to reason why – though he surmised that in rooms where seances were held, chairs and tables were always available for the forces to act upon, so it was not an unnatural choice.

Another table-turner was William James. He was mainly concerned with the messages spelled out by tilts; but on one occasion in 1908, following months of experiments, a table, after some of the usual tiltings with two or three legs off the ground, 'rose gently and with all four legs off the ground, to the height of six inches or more, to the great surprise of all of us and remained in the air two or three seconds, subsiding slowly to the ground'.

With materialism acquiring the status of a faith, however, table-turning became unfashionable; and the radio, and later television, made people increasingly reluctant to spend evenings waiting for manifestations which might not happen. As a pastime, it is still occasionally indulged in; but not often.

Towards the end of his career, Home agreed to formal tests. These were not, however, the earliest attempts to establish whether or not table-turning was a psychic phenomenon. In the mid-1850s Count Agenor de Gasparin did experiments which showed that a few individuals appeared to exercise an influence on tables, so that the tables moved and sometimes defied gravity without physical force being applied. De Gasparin, an internationally respected figure, sought to show in *Des Tables Tournantes* (1854) that table-turning ought to be, and could be, used for research in physics, indicating as it did the existence of forces which, he insisted, were not supernatural: they were simply unexplored and unexplained – an attitude shared by his friend Professor Marc Thury of Geneva, who carried out research along the same lines, coming to the conclusion that there is a force, which he described as 'ectenic', emanating from certain people, though not consciously directed by them. The concept of the subconscious mind as an independent element was yet to establish itself, but Thury came close to it with his hypothesis that the ectenic force was transmitted by the kind of dual personality which is illustrated in dreams, expressing, as they can do, an unconscious desire for what we do not consciously want.

By this time, however, researchers working along these lines were shifting away from research into table-turning as such to research with mediums to find what they could accomplish through the ectenic force, or telekinesis as it came to be called. Although table-turning continued to be demonstrated for psychical researchers, it was not until a century later that the pastime was made the subject of investigations using scientific equipment to record the movements of the table, to measure where possible the strength of the PK component, and also to preclude the possibility of physical pressure causing or supplementing the movements.

In the *Journal of the Society for Psychical Research* (September 1966) K. J. Batcheldor described how he had constructed an apparatus capable of providing an independent check on the movements of a table during experimental table-turning sessions, with lights, buzzers, luminous paint, weighing machines, cameras and other devices. Some 200 sittings were held, at seventy of which PK manifestations of various kinds were obtained. The tables, ranging in weight from two to forty pounds, behaved much as Victorian tables had done, promising activity by raps and tremors before beginning to slide, to tilt and sometimes to levitate. Although actual levitations occurred only in darkness, it was possible to watch the table's movements through the application of luminous paint; and the monitoring system would have revealed any physical pressure. 'There is no doubt whatever that in these levitations the table comes right off the floor,' Batcheldor commented. 'Unconscious muscular action is obviously ruled out, and hallucination is ruled out by the recorded buzzer.'

Batcheldor was well aware that his description, detailed though it was, would not convince a sceptic: 'I will be content,' he claimed, 'if I succeed in inducing some few of my readers to suspend disbelief for long enough to attempt sustained experimentation for themselves.' One researcher who was prepared to attempt it was Colin Brookes-Smith, who conducted table-turning sessions in the 1970s with even more sophisticated equipment, including the then latest scientific aid, data-tape recording, which made it possible to inter-relate the data obtained from the various monitoring instruments employed. Thus, when a sitter made a request, his voice and the table's reaction to it, whether through raps or movements, could be replayed; and if any sitter used physical force, he could be identified.

In his report to the SPR Brookes-Smith, like Batcheldor, emphasized that his work had been exploratory; the results could not be held to be definitive, but were sufficiently encouraging to suggest that this line of research was well worth pursuing. 'By adopting suitable procedures,' he felt, 'paranormal forces can be made available "by the pound", in repeatable experiments almost at any chosen time.' This was over-optimistic, partly because table-turning is still a time-consuming and often boring procedure – in many sessions in the 1980s, as in the 1850s, nothing happens; partly because it remains so hard to convince sceptics that tables can and do react to psychic forces. Nevertheless the evidence which Batcheldor and Brookes-Smith have provided, and which has continued to accumulate since, offers impressive confirmation of the findings of the Victorians.

An interesting feature of the sittings, which both investigators found and exploited, was the importance of a relaxed, even jolly atmosphere, with singing and jokes. It also helped, they realized, if one of the group cheated to start with, rapping or setting the table moving – much as it is easier to start a cold engine by running the car down-hill. The monitoring devices, revealing, as they subsequently do, who is cheating and what he is doing, also show that the movements continue when he stops; it is as if the table (or the combined ectenic force of the sitters) has warmed up.

Breaks and Bends

Reports of poltergeist hauntings occasionally contain accounts of objects mysteriously shattering, usually by falling on to a hard surface; metal being bent, or broken; or materials being damaged in a variety of ways. Manifestations of this kind have also occasionally occurred during seances, as if an overcharged atmosphere had built up. When Zöllner was investigating the medium Henry Slade in the 1870s, he was startled by a resounding explosion, and found that a wooden screen had split in two.

In his *Memories, Dreams, Reflections* Jung recalled an occasion when 'something happened which was to influence me profoundly': a report 'like a pistol shot', which turned out to have been caused by a table-top splitting in two. He was thunderstruck: 'a table of solid walnut that had dried out for seventy years – how could it split on a summer day in the relatively high degree of humidity characteristic of our climate?'

His mother thought it was an omen; and two weeks later, he found, after another 'deafening report', that a bread knife which had lain in a sideboard had broken. Its blade had snapped off in several pieces, in a way which an expert assured him could not have happened except by somebody deliberately breaking it into the pieces. Jung knew that this had not been the way it had happened; his realization that there might be some unexplained forces at work was to prompt him to investigate a young medium; and this led on to a lifetime's interest in the paranormal.

The investigators of the Rosenheim poltergeist in the late 1960s reported on a number of occasions finding electric light fixtures inexplicably twisted; and with the advent of Uri Geller, bends and fractures in household cutlery became a commonplace. Recently a new pastime has become popular in the United States: metal-bending parties, to which the guests bring forks and spoons, and seek to generate communal psychic energy of the kind traditionally associated with table-turning. The weird shapes, whorls and coils which result when the psychic component takes off (if it does) sometimes convince doubters that what they have taken to be conjuring tricks may be genuine, if their own spoons have undergone metamorphoses in their own hands.

Apports

In his *Encyclopedia* (1933) Nandor Fodor defined apports as 'arrival of various objects through an apparent penetration of matter' – one of the most baffling phenomena of spiritualism, he thought, the more so as the objects might be living: growing plants, animals, even people. He did not distinguish between apports which could be identified as having come from, say, another part of the house, and those which come from some unknown place, or perhaps simply out of thin air. But two parapsychologists, Erlunder Haraldsson and Karlis Osis, have recently made a distinction: 'in cases where paranormal creation of the object is assumed, the process is usually referred to as "materialization". When an existing object is "brought" by paranormal means from one place to another without visible means of travel, the phenomenon is called "teleportation", and the object is referred to as an "apport".' As it is often impossible, however, to say with certainty whether an object materializes or is teleported, the term apport has generally been used to describe the object whatever its source, teleportation being regarded as its mode of travel.

The historical evidence for apports comes mostly from accounts of spiritualist seances; but they featured earlier in reports of poltergeist hauntings, as they have continued to do. It seems likely, too, that the mesmerists encountered them in their research into the higher phenomena, but kept quiet about them for fear of exciting ridicule. Joseph Deleuze, one of the ablest and most conscientious of that early band of psychical researchers, cited apports among the mesmeric phenomena he had not dealt with in his published works because he considered 'it was not yet time to disclose them'.

In the table-turning era of the 1850s, however, and more particularly when professional mediums began to flourish, apports became a commonplace of seances. Wallace made a study of those which were produced by Miss Nichol, who, living as she did in the home of Wallace's sister, proved an ideal subject for investigation. Eventually, he found, she could produce them to order, fresh flowers being her speciality; as in a seance in 1867 when fifteen chrysanthemums suddenly appeared on the seance room table. Flowers were considered the ideal apport from the point of view of an investigator, as it was relatively easy to ensure that they had not been smuggled in; it was even better if they arrived dripping with water.

Apports were a frequent accompaniment of the seances held in the Speer household in London in the 1870s, with the spiritualist Stainton Moses as the medium. A former clergyman, forced by illness to leave his curacy, Moses had become a teacher at University College School; and while giving tuition to the children of Stanhope Speer, he began to have psychic experiences which he was eventually to bring under a measure of control in informal seances with the family. What he was unable to control, however, was the intrusion of apports. Objects would suddenly arrive on the table, though all doors and windows had been closed; sometimes hitting sitters as they passed, as if they had been thrown. Once, a heavy candlestick which ordinarily was on the mantelshelf of another room struck Moses 'a severe blow'.

People who knew Moses well, such as Myers, insisted that he was incapable of deception; and one of his pupils, Charlton Speer, was later to confirm that apports taken from other rooms had flowed in through closed and bolted doors – photographs, picture frames, books and other objects: 'how they came through the closed doors I cannot say, except by some process of de-materialization, but come they certainly did'.

Crookes had many experiences of apports, which he included in his list of the varieties of psychic phenomena in the category 'miscellaneous occurrences of a complex character'. On one occasion during a seance in the dark, he heard a hand-bell ringing as if somebody were circulating with it, until it fell beside him. When he picked it up he saw it *was* a bell, which he then found one of his sons had actually been playing with while the seance was in progress. There was no way in which the bell could have been transported by hand into the seance room, Crookes knew, as it was locked and he had the key.

In the course of a rigorously controlled investigation of Eusapia Palladino, Enrico Morselli and his colleagues found that objects –

nails, stones, flowers – frequently appeared in the course of tests. Ochorowicz had the same experience with Stanislawa Tomczyk, as did Schrenck-Notzing. On one occasion a branch of mimosa appeared, broken off from a plant which was in another part of Schrenck's house, to which Stanislawa had not had access; in any case, she had been searched, as she always was, before tests.

The most celebrated of human apports was Mrs Guppy, tele-ported in 1871 from her home in Highbury in North London into a seance in Lamb's Conduit Street. Although her re-materialization – still in her housegown – was vouched for by the respectable citizens at the seance, the story would have seemed too incredible to be taken seriously even if Mrs Guppy had not weighed twenty stone; as it was, it simply confirmed sceptics in their assumption that apports could all be accounted for in terms of illusion and trickery.

And not only sceptics. Even Home was disposed to take this view, on the surprising – coming from him – ground that matter surely could not go through matter. In *The Physical Phenomenon of Spiritualism* (1907) Hereward Carrington, too, thought that the historical evidence seemed 'to point to the conclusion that fraud and nothing but fraud has been operative throughout', though he felt bound to refer to the evidence to the contrary from Stainton Moses, 'that stumbling block to the rationalistic psychical researcher'. Richet conceded the strength of the evidence for matter to pass through matter, or to be created, but he too remained doubtful. Subsequently, apports were rarely considered in the works of scientifically-orientated psychical researchers, as distinct from spiritualists. In Stanley Krippner's *Advances in Parapsychological Research* (1977) they do not rate even a mention.

Recently, however, they have been forcing themselves on the notice of parapsychologists investigating metal-bending. Their recurrence has not been welcome: obviously, if objects can appear or disappear, materialize or de-materialize, the prospect of setting up fully controlled trials is hopelessly compromised, as the point of having laboratory-type investigations has been to eliminate such outside intervention. But Puthoff and Targ encountered apports while investigating Uri Geller at the Stanford Research Institute, capturing one of them – a wristwatch – on film; and John Hasted came across several in his investigation of 'mini-Gellers', most of them boys or girls who were claimed, or claimed themselves, to have psychokinetic powers.

Hasted accumulated a quantity of evidence about teleportation, which he has summarized in *The Metal-Benders* (1981). Objects can either appear or disappear – though obviously their appearance is more likely to be noticed. Appearance (reappearance, in the case of objects known to have been in another place) can take place on a surface, a floor or a table, or in mid-air – sometimes as if they are falling, or have been thrown. Occasionally a noise is heard, like a 'click' or 'ping', accompanying the teleportation. Occasionally too, the object when picked up is warm. 'It seems not to matter whether a solid wall lies in the path the object must take.' Hasted has found that 'sometimes the object passes from one room to another, even through closed doors, without being visible on the way. Sometimes the object does not reappear, but simply vanishes from within a closed capsule; sometimes an object reappears within a capsule.'

The only medium claiming to be able to produce apports at will who has been investigated recently is the guru Sai Baba. Haraldsson and Osis shared the prevailing view of teleportation and apports, that they were spurious, until they encountered him in Andhra Pradesh in the south of India while they were conducting research in the 1970s. Although Sai Baba declined to submit to formal tests – he claimed to use his paranormal powers only to help disciples in trouble, or to impress sceptics – he gave Haraldsson and Osis eleven interviews during which the phenomena occurred; objects appeared, ranging from 'holy ash' to a gold ring. Although the objects were usually unveiled in the way a conjuror who has 'palmed' a card displays it, there was nowhere for Sai Baba to have hidden them before producing them. He also caused a picture in a ring he had given to Osis to vanish, leaving the frame undamaged, though it was so constructed that the picture could not have simply fallen out.

On another occasion they watched Sai Baba materialize (or teleport) a bulky necklace, containing a variety of different stones, which could not have been 'palmed'. In all, they made twenty observations of what appeared to be paranormal phenomena while they were with him; and they were impressed by the fact that for forty years he had been producing apports in this way in all sorts of circumstances, indoors or outdoors, dressed in a way which made concealment of the objects impossible, without ever being detected in trickery. The 'holy ash', for example, which Sai Baba continually distributes on his walks, would immediately be detectable if he had to pull it out from any source in his clothing (they were careful also to satisfy themselves that there were no hidden pockets to provide such a source). Nor would he have been able to hide the oil or other liquid substances which he so often distributes.

'We realize that without adequate experimental conditions the evidence will never be conclusive,' Haraldsson and Osis admitted in their report in the *Journal of the American Society for Psychical Research* (January 1977); but they hoped that 'the variety and richness of the phenomena associated with Sai Baba may provide unique research opportunities for both Western and Indian scientists'. Their hope has yet to be fulfilled.

Direct Writing

There have been quite a number of reports of messages appearing, often on walls, sometimes on paper, which cannot have been written by a human hand. The description 'direct writing' is applied to them to distinguish them from the products of automatic writing.

The earliest example in history is the familiar biblical story of 'the writing on the wall'. While Belshazzar, King of the Chaldeans, was listening to the prophet Daniel denouncing him for 'lifting himself up against the Lord', he saw a human hand apparently detach itself and write, on the wall of the banqueting room, MENE MENE TEKEL UPHARSIN – the message intimating that Belshazzar had been weighed in the balances, and found wanting; he was killed the same night and his kingdom taken over by Darius.

Messages attributed to direct writing were to be encountered again in the Victorian era. Stainton Moses described how one day while he was receiving communications by automatic writing, loosely holding the pen which was producing the messages, 'in order to show me that the hand was a mere instrument not essential to the experiment, the pen was removed from the hand, and kept in position by the ray of light which was directed upon it', and the pen continued to write as before: 'I cried out in

143

astonishment, and was warned to keep still lest I should break the conditions.'

D. D. Home's disembodied hands were occasionally seen taking up a pen, and writing. On one occasion, at a seance for the Emperor Napoleon III, a hand which he had materialized used a pencil to write 'Napoleon' in – or so the Emperor asserted – the handwriting of his uncle Napoleon I.

A more commonly encountered form of direct writing in the Victorian period, however, was slate-writing, which enjoyed a vogue in the 1870s. The method which mediums generally used was to procure a slate of the kind children learned to draw on, put some chalk or pencil lead on it, and hold it up against the underside of a table (or with another slate on top of it), waiting until the scraping noises made by the writing ceased and then examining the spirit message.

'If we were to read carefully through the historical evidence for the phenomenon of slate-writing,' Carrington felt, 'we should find it to consist in one long and practically unbroken series of *exposés* of fraud and trickery, with no real evidence worth mentioning for the genuine manifestations of any supernormal power.' In this he was unfair, as some of the investigators of Slade, and of William Eglinton, conducted careful tests and reported that they could find no way in which they might be cheating. Some of the *exposés* to which Carrington referred, too, were not so much exposures of the mediums as demonstrations by conjurors of how easy it was to fake the messages. Nevertheless, slate-writing stood no chance of carrying conviction unless the lead, or chalk, could actually be seen to be writing; and this no medium of the period was able to demonstrate at will.

Direct writing has often been reported in connection with poltergeist hauntings, with messages appearing on the walls of locked, empty rooms. The most recent example has been described by Matthew Manning: a wall in a room in the Manning family's home became covered with signatures, apparently of men who had lived in the 17th and early 18th centuries. Some of them could be traced through parish registers; but whether or not the signatures were those of the men they purported to be has eluded discovery.

Psychic Photography

That psychic energy could influence photographic plates was originally surmised in the 1860s; some plates, when the negatives were developed, displayed indications that they were being tampered with in a variety of ways which the photographers either could not account for, or attributed to spirit influences. Sometimes it was as if unnoticed luminosities had been floating around the studio; sometimes there would be wraith-like forms; sometimes objects were visible which had not been in shot at the time the photograph was taken. There was no need actually to take a photograph, it was eventually discovered: pictures could be made to appear even while the plates remained in their wrappings. The presence of a medium, however, was usually needed; either one brought in or a photographer who himself had psychic powers.

Public interest in psychic photography was first aroused by the work of a Broadway photographer, William H. Mumler, whose speciality was spirit pictures. When in 1869 Mumler was brought up on a charge of false pretences, scores of respectable New York citizens offered to give evidence that the forms or faces which had appeared on the photographs he had taken were of deceased loved ones; one of the witnesses being Judge Edmonds, whose unblemished reputation had survived even the derisive publicity attendant upon his conversion to spiritualism.

That spirit forms should appear in photographs, Edmonds explained to the court, was not surprising. He had himself, in his judicial capacity, 'seen' a dead man whose property was the subject of the court case, and 'heard' him describe what had actually happened – a description subsequently verified. If a human mind could see spirits, there could be no reason why a camera should not pick them up, too. The jury, impressed, acquitted Mumler.

It proved to be all too easy to fake spirit pictures, however, and other court cases in which the photographer was found guilty soon brought the procedure into discredit. That all the numerous spirit photographers of the late Victorian era were rogues, though, was hard to believe, as Wallace pointed out: many were amateurs, not working for their income, but engaged in serious research. He cited three of them, working independently in different parts of the country, whose work had been tested with, he thought, 'absolutely conclusive' results.

Wallace also noted a couple of interesting features of spirit photography which had emerged from his study of their work. When the negatives were being developed, it was the spirit forms which invariably emerged first; 'the figures start out the moment the developing fluid touches them, while the figure of the sitter appears much later'. The other curiosity was that the spirit forms tended to be enveloped, apart from the face, in drapery. 'The conventional "white-sheeted ghost",' Wallace deduced. 'was not, then, all fancy, but had a foundation in fact.' Drapery, the supposition was, materialized more easily than the human form – a fact which, he felt, was significant, indicating the laws 'of a yet unknown chemistry'.

Impressive evidence for the genuineness of at least some spirit photographers also came from J. Traill Taylor, the leading photographer in Britain in the 1890s. Instead of accepting or rejecting them out of hand, Taylor decided to employ a simple but clever test: he would use two cameras, to make a stereoscopic picture, so that if a spirit form should appear (which he took to be unlikely) on both, it would be possible to check whether it was three-dimensional. To his astonishment, spirit forms did appear on both pictures, though he had not allowed the medium who was at the sitting to have access to the plates. But the forms were not in space, above the sitter's head, as they appeared on the positives. In both cases, they seemed to have been imprinted on the actual plate, like thumbprints. What, he wondered, could the explanation be? Were they crystallizations of thought? Had the light in the studio, and the lens, nothing to do with them? The whole subject had been 'mysterious enough on the hypothesis of an invisible spirit', he lamented – whether a thought projection, or an actual spirit, was 'really in the vicinity of the sitter': it was now 'a thousand times more so'.

As most prominent members of the SPR – the Sidgwicks and Podmore in particular – were convinced that spirit photography was a disreputable racket, few psychical researchers cared to risk their reputation even by testing spirit photographers, and they continued to have a dubious reputation. The setting-up in 1919 of a Society for the Study of Supernormal Pictures, with Conan Doyle as its most prominent member, promised a fresh approach to the subject; but members soon fell out over what could, and what could not, be admitted as evidence of the supernormal – and still more, over who was, and who was not, a genuine spirit photographer.

The most successful practitioner of the craft was William Hope, tested in 1916 by Crookes – who, as he wrote to remind Oliver

Lodge, had been a photographic expert in his youth. Hope, Crookes claimed, had had no opportunity to tamper with the plates, yet on one of them there was a clear likeness of Lady Crookes as she had looked ten years before. In the United States James Hyslop, too, was impressed by the evidence provided for the *Journal* of the American SPR, which he edited, by the Rev. Charles Cook, who had taken up psychic photography as a hobby, investigating the work of others. Some of the cases, notably those provided by the rich and religious Margaret du Pont Lee – whose Kodak kept on taking pictures of what appeared to be apports, in the sense that they were not there when the picture was taken – Cook found hard to explain except as paranormal, as he could think of no reason why Mrs Lee would wish to deceive him.

William Hope was 'exposed' as fraudulent by Harry Price in 1921; but the circumstances were dubious, and in view of Price's subsequent record his exposures could not be trusted. Their main aim was to obtain additional publicity for himself, and at the same time show himself off as a critical investigator. And, as Sudre emphasized, there were also tests of Hope's spirit photographs which gave positive results – at least to the point of producing recognizably human forms or faces. One was undertaken by a criminologist, and expert conjuror, Dr Lindsay Johnson, in 1921. Johnson brought all the equipment himself and – presumably aware of the earlier accusations against Hope – refused to allow him to come near it, except in a test where Hope was allowed to put his hands on a box which contained unexposed plates. Of eight photographs which Johnson took and developed, three had an 'extra' – as spirit forms had come to be called – two of them identifiably human. And on the unexposed plates in the box, two in the middle had 'extras' – 'one showed four heads of the same person, and the other a photograph which had appeared the day before' – evidence which sufficed to convince Johnson.

The most remarkable case of a spirit photograph in this period has been recalled by Air Marshal Sir Victor Goddard. A face appeared behind the men in the back row of a group photograph; and it was at once recognized as that of an airman who had accidentally killed himself by walking into an aircraft's whirling propeller a few days before. A copy of the photograph, taken immediately after the group had marched back from his funeral, was on Goddard's desk when he was writing his *Flight Towards Reality* in the early 1970s.

What little prospect the researchers had of getting psychic photography taken more seriously was dissipated in the course of a controversy in the early 1920s, aroused by the photographs taken by two children of fairies. In three of the pictures the fairies looked like paper cut-outs, and the fact that Conan Doyle, of all people, could have staked his reputation on such preposterous-looking pictures struck most of those who saw them as an indication that he must be growing senile; the 'Cottingley fairies' only succeeded in increasing the discredit into which psychic photography had slid.

As with so many other branches of psychical research, dispassionate investigation of paranormal aspects of photography was endlessly hampered by the divisions and rows between the spiritualists – who took for granted that spirits must be responsible for whatever appeared on negatives which could not be accounted for naturally – and a minority of interested investigators of the calibre of James Coates. In his *Photographing the Invisible* (1922) Coates argued that a distinction needed to be made between spirit photographs, which he mistrusted, and 'thoughtographs', obtained, as he put it, 'independently of the lens and of the camera', because he had satisfied himself they could be imposed on negatives which were still unexposed on the plate (or on the spool: by this time 'Box Brownies' had been introduced). Midway between Coates and the spiritualists, Stanley de Brath considered the possibility that the psychic imprint might be obtained by · thought-forms imposing themselves on the negatives; but he felt that this hypothesis was too far-fetched. If the existence of discarnate entities were conceded, he argued, the idea that they might be responsible, 'acting on some specially ideoplastic form of ectoplasm', was more plausible. Most members of the SPR, however, preferred to hold aloof from the controversy, as they still feared all kinds of paranormal photography were bogus. When the *SPR Journal* dealt with psychic photographers at all, it was to publish exposés: what could not easily be demolished was ignored, as in the case of T. Fukurai's remarkable *Clairvoyance and Thoughtography* (1931).

A Professor of Physics in a Japanese University, Fukurai had twenty years earlier tested a medium who, he found, could register thought impressions on unexposed photographic plates: but his attempts to convince colleagues that the medium's powers were genuine led only to his being forced out of his job. Coming to England in the 1920s, he conducted trials with William Hope; and on the strength of his years of research he came to the conclusion that they pointed to the existence of spiritual (but not necessarily spirit) powers, transcending what had been taken to be the physical laws of nature. A good medium, he had found, could produce pictures on photographic plates without the need of a camera, and he gave examples of this type of 'thoughtography' which were hard to dismiss, except on the assumption that Fukurai was a rogue – and that was rendered improbable by his past record, which had demonstrated his willingness to throw up a successful academic career in order to devote his life to research in this unpopular and unprofitable field.

Thoughtography was not seriously investigated again until the mid-1960s, when demonstrations which the young Ted Serios had begun to give in Chicago led to Jule Eisenbud, Clinical Professor of Psychology at the University of Colorado, being asked to lay on tests. From 1964–7, 'Ted worked with more than three dozen scientifically trained observers – physicians, physicists, physiologists, engineers and others – under a variety of conditions,' Eisenbud has recalled. 'During this period, over 400 normally inexplicable images on over 100 different themes were obtained, as well as hundreds of "blackies", prints from which light seemed inexplicably to have been totally or almost totally excluded, and "whities", prints rendered totally or almost totally white, as if markedly over-exposed in an equally inexplicable manner.'

There were problems. During the trials, Serios consumed 'several thousand quarts of hard liquor and beer, as heavy drinking turned out to be a regular part of the picture-taking ritual'; and this did not encourage belief in his trustworthiness. Serios also used what he called a 'gismo', an open cylinder which he could point at the camera, as if to concentrate his 'thought' on the negative; inevitably it led to the suspicion that trickery was involved. Eventually an article in a photographic magazine claimed that the writer had shown how the thoughtographs were being faked; and a number of well-known American conjurors gratefully displayed to audiences how Serios had been 'exposed'. Eisenbud thereupon issued an invitation to them to come to his laboratory and fake 'thoughtographs' successfully under the same controls as were still being applied with Serios. None of the conjurors cared to take up the gauntlet, even those who were sent personal invitations.

As Eisenbud has pointed out, the issue whether the 'gismo' could have been used to fake thoughtographs was in any case academic, as Serios had frequently shown that he could produce well-defined images on unexposed, well-wrapped film. It could not have been used for purposes of faking on the occasions when Serios had remained at a distance from the camera; and it could not have produced 'whities' by the hundred in conditions of total darkness. Serios was also able to produce images of randomly selected targets. If there was cheating, it would have to have been laid on with the collaboration of Eisenbud and numerous sceptical academic colleagues.

On several occasions in the 1970s, Uri Geller disconcerted photographers who had come to take pictures of him bending metal by offering to take a picture of himself sitting in front of a camera with the lens cap still on. The *News of the World*, irritated at a rival Sunday newspaper's feature on Geller, sent two photographers after Geller with instructions to try to 'see how he did what were taken to be his tricks' and if possible catch him in the act. Roy Stockdill, one of the most experienced of British press photographers, loaded his camera, left the cap both screwed and clipped on, and allowed Geller to 'photograph' himself, watching to ensure he did not try to remove the cap. The two photographers then packaged the undeveloped roll of film, put a seal on it, and sent it back to the *News of the World* office. Most of the negatives when developed were blanks; but among them were clear prints of Geller, good enough to be used in the paper the following Sunday.

PHYSIOLOGICAL EFFECTS

Ectoplasm

In the earliest accounts of ectoplasm, a term coined by Charles Richet, it usually made its initial appearance as a patch of mist, or a luminosity, which would gradually condense into a human hand, sometimes into features. A luminous cloud seemed to form, Crookes explained; 'then it becomes concentrated, takes on a shape and changes into a perfectly formed hand, of which the flesh seems as human as that of the people present'. At the wrist, though, or at the arm, it was as if the mist or luminous cloud remained as a base, until mediums appeared who could produce full-form materializations.

From some mediums, however, the ectoplasm appeared looking like muslin (as, in cases of fraud, it sometimes was found to be); emerging, as Gustave Geley put it following his research during and after the first world war with the medium 'Eva C', from her 'natural orifices' – usually her mouth, but sometimes her ears or her nipples (it could also come from her head, or her finger tips). When it emerged, 'there descends to her knees a cord of white substance of the thickness of two fingers. This ribbon takes under our eyes varying forms: that of a large perforated membrane with swellings and vacant spaces; it gathers itself together, retracts, swells and narrows again'. The colour varied, sometimes black, sometimes white, sometimes in between; and to the touch it was 'soft, and somewhat elastic' while it was spreading, later becoming 'hard, knotty and fibrous' so that it could be held in a human hand. Usually it emerged slowly from the medium; but it could appear, and disappear, in an instant.

The development of pseudopods – phantom ectoplasmic extensions, sprouting from the body of the medium – was one of the physical phenomena encountered by the researchers investigating Eusapia Palladino. 'How many legs and arms has she?' her first investigator, Ercole Chiaia, asked, challenging the criminologist

Cesare Lombroso to come and see for himself. 'We do not know. While her arms are held by incredulous spectators, we see other limbs coming into view.' Lombroso, himself incredulous, eventually consented to test Eusapia with three colleagues, admitting afterwards that he was 'quite ashamed and grieved' at having doubted Chiaia. He still doubted the spiritist interpretation of the facts, he insisted, 'but the facts exist, and I boast of being a slave to facts'.

In one of the tests Eusapia underwent at Cambridge in 1895 Mrs Frederic Myers was asked to hold the medium's feet; and while she was holding them, although the room was in near darkness, she could see the outline of Eusapia's back outlined against candlelight reflected from the ceiling. From the back, she wrote after the session, she saw two protuberances emerge 'like the neck of a swan', and also 'a kind of stump' coming from the hips. Actually to see pseudopods was unusual; but in most sessions with Eusapia the sitters felt them, in the form of nudges, pinches, and playful acts of a kind that gave the impression of being the work of an invisible arm and hand. 'We were hit on the back, and dug in the ribs, and this went on for several minutes,' J. J. Thomson – Professor of Experimental Physics at Cambridge, and soon to be the discoverer of the electron – reported. As he was controlling one of Eusapia's hands, with Lord Rayleigh controlling the other, he knew she could not have been using them. The conjuror John Maskelyne, who also attended one of the sessions at Cambridge, was to claim he had found out how she did her tricks, but from his account it is obvious that he had not; in spite of the fact that he and his son were controlling her hands, they had seen another hand which could not have been a dummy, and felt 'slaps and pokes'.

Early on in the investigations of Eusapia, a method had been found to explore what pseudopods consisted of, and what they were capable of doing, by putting a bowl of clay out of her reach in which she could make psychic imprints, as she frequently did, and as some later mediums were also to do. When Richet and Geley found that the Polish medium Franek Kluski could leave imprints, they devised a still more elaborate experiment: they asked him to see if he could materialize a hand in a bowl of paraffin wax, allow the wax to set around it, and then dematerialize the hand; which would – or should – leave a 'glove' mould in the wax which could be filled with plaster, and exhibited. Kluski needed darkness to produce his pseudopods, but his investigators were reassured, controlling his hands during tests, when they heard noises as if a hand was dabbling in the wax; and Kluski produced a variety of 'gloves' which, as they could check, could not have been made by his hands even if he had managed to elude their control. In any case, it would have been impossible for him to withdraw a hand after the wax had set. Houdini was to claim that he knew how the trick was done, by the substitution of a previously prepared bowl of wax. But as Geley pointed out, they had guarded against this by putting a soluble substance in the wax they bought, enabling them to check afterwards that no substitution had been made.

In Boston during the 1920s, 'Margery' – Mina Crandon – frequently was able to produce a thumbprint in a bowl of wax, which was identified as her deceased brother Walter's. Even Mrs Sidgwick was impressed, when the print was obtained at a seance in London. Unluckily for 'Margery', it was eventually found that thumbprints which had been appearing were not Walter's, but those of the Boston dentist who had originally demonstrated how the wax should be used to obtain good prints. This proved to be the final blow to the Crandons' reputation, as it was assumed they must have faked the prints all along. Mrs Sidgwick, however, pointed out that there was a sense in which the identity of the owner of the thumbprint was irrelevant; if 'Margery' succeeded in making a print in a wax bowl at a distance in any seance where she was strictly controlled, as she had been in London, it would suggest that a pseudopod must have been operating, no matter whose print it was.

Pseudopods might behave as if they were additional but invisible arms; or they might act as if they were agents tenuously linked to the body of the medium, and obeying the medium – or the medium's 'control'. Oliver Lodge, who had felt as well as seen Eusapia's 'ectoplasmic protuberances' in the tests he did with Richet and Ochorowicz, surmised that 'the filmy, visible thing' represented the 'connector or conveyor of the more active and important agency', its function being 'to maintain organic connection with the strong substantial mechanism which itself cannot be seen'; and he reminded colleagues who ridiculed the notion that an invisible conveyor could transmit the energy which caused tables to levitate, and perform other such feats, that magnetism and gravity had similar powers.

The nature of the relationship between materialized pseudopods and the physical anatomy of the medium has remained obscure. Mediums have often been reported as reacting to, say, physical pressure on a disembodied hand as they might be expected to react to the same pressure on their own hands. Although they could escape from a grasp by de-materializing the hand, a sudden snatch at a materialized pseudopod has often resulted in a gasp from the medium – which has naturally been taken to justify sceptics in their belief that the pseudopods are, literally, sleights-of-hand. But the American medium and psychical researcher, Dr F. H. Willis, who was later to become a distinguished Professor of Medicine in New York, recorded an experience which called for a different interpretation. While he was in a trance, a pseudopod hand emerged from him; and one of the sitters, thinking to teach him a lesson by stabbing at it with a knife, was gratified when Willis cried out in pain. But when he came out of his trance, and his hands were examined, they were not even scratched.

Materializations

Where objects materialize, they are usually put in the apport category, except where they are the adjuncts of materializing living forms – hands, faces, sometimes complete bodies – which emerge out of visible or invisible ectoplasm. The most striking versions are the 'full form' materializations, which resemble some apparitions in that they seem to correspond with living beings in every detail, including the clothes, which look and feel like real clothes.

Home once materialized a double of himself; but the first medium who under investigation began to produce a different person was Florence Cook, who in the early 1870s began to materialize the spirit form of her control, 'Katie King', in test conditions stringent enough to satisfy both the sceptical correspondent of the *Daily Telegraph* (when 'Katie' appeared while Florence was tied up with sealed knots, he reported, their seals were still unbroken after the seance) and the shrewd Russian investigator Alexandre Aksakov, whose *Animisme et Spiritisme* (1906) is one of the best sources of information about psychical research around the turn of the century.

Although Aksakov had satisfied himself that Florence was securely tied up in the 'cabinet' – a curtained recess in the corner of the seance room, in which she generated her psychic powers – he wanted to make absolutely sure that 'Katie' was a different being; so he asked her whether he might be permitted to see her and Florence at the same time. 'Katie', who was dressed in white, invited him to follow her into the 'cabinet', where, though 'Katie' had vanished, he saw Florence, dressed in black, in her chair. There was no way, he was satisfied, that any other person could have got into or out of the recess; and the bindings, knots and seals which tied her to the chair were intact.

What little chance there was of Florence's full-form materializations of 'Katie' converting sceptics was, however, soon lost. The medium Mrs Guppy was enraged that her mediumistic feats should have been put in the shade by her young rival: and William Volckman, who was soon to become Mrs Guppy's second husband, undertook to expose Florence by seizing 'Katie' when she appeared during a seance, which he did. According to the others who were present, 'Katie' de-materialized: they found Florence tied up in the 'cabinet', with her bonds, sealed with the Earl of Caithness's signet ring, still fixed. Volckman's version – that he had caught Florence, but owing to the intervention of her supporters had been unable to follow her and prove her fraud – was preferred by sceptics, and by the mediums who could not compete with her.

Both Volckman and the sceptics had tended to assume that if 'Katie' turned out to be solid, she must be 'Florence' in disguise. Crookes demonstrated to his own satisfaction that this was incorrect: that 'Katie', materialized, felt just the same to the touch as any other woman. To verify this, he – as he put it – 'asked her permission to clasp her in my arms', to which she consented. To Crookes this was the gesture of a gallant; but to sceptics, the notion of an eminent scientist testing the genuineness of materialization by an embrace was simply ludicrous. It also helped further to enrage rival mediums; and Crookes, finding himself the target of a campaign of calumny, abandoned research with mediums.

On some later occasions, a materialized spirit was grabbed and held, and found to be the medium. This happened to Mme d'Esperance, whose reputation was such that even Alfred Lehmann, a severe critic of spiritualism, suggested that as she was in a trance at the time she would not have been conscious of any deception. Aksakov, in desperation, offered another possibility: that a materialized form might in certain circumstances represent so much of the medium that the body would be absorbed into the materialization, rather than vice-versa.

A few years later a French girl, Marthe Béraud, was investigated at her home in Algeria by Charles Richet, and later in Paris by Mme Bisson and in Munich by Baron Schrenck-Notzing, both of whom produced massive books giving details of the seances, the precautions taken, the witnesses and the manifestations, with many photographs. The books, however, turned out to be counter-productive, partly because 'Eva C', as they called Marthe to preserve her anonymity, often produced two-dimensional materialized forms, which looked in the photographs like cardboard cut-outs; partly because the cut-outs resembled pictures which 'Eva' had seen in magazines. As Schrenck and Mme Bisson – and later Geley, who joined in the investigations – pointed out, the illustrations could not have been cut-outs, smuggled into the seance rooms, because they had watched the ectoplasm emerging to form itself into the two-dimensional shapes; and although the shapes resembled magazine pictures, they were not identical, but resembled inaccurate copies – which suggested to Geley that ectoplasm could be regarded as ideoplasm, as it could take its form from the unconscious mind of the medium.

'I have also,' Richet recalled in his *Thirty Years of Psychical Research* (1923), 'like Geley, Schrenck-Notzing and Mme Bisson, been able to see the first lineaments of materialization as they were formed. A kind of liquid, or pasty jelly, emerges from the mouth or the breast of Marthe which organizes itself by degrees, acquiring the shape of a face or a limb.'

Geley, who had given up a successful career as an orthodox scientist to devote himself to psychical research, began to investigate 'Eva' at a time when her powers were on the wane, and she produced no full-form materializations. But he often saw hands and well-formed human faces, which grew as he watched.

The materialized organs are not inert, but biologically alive. A well-materialized hand has the functional capacities of a normal hand. I have at different times been touched or grasped by its fingers. Well-constituted organs, with all the appearance of life, are often replaced by incomplete formations. Relief is often wanting, and the forms are flat. I have sometimes seen a hand or a face appear flat and then take to three dimensions, either completely or partly, as I looked.

When the forms were incomplete, Geley added, they were often smaller than natural size, which precluded substitution by the hands of the medium or of an accomplice. Scores of scientists and savants witnessed 'Eva's' materializations, and although she was frequently accused of cheating, she was never detected in deception during a seance. Richet, in particular – an eminent physiologist and in 1913 a Nobel Prize winner – was hardly likely to be deceived by real limbs masquerading as pseudopods; in any case, cameras were positioned to ensure that 'Eva' could not play tricks. It might seem to be the height of absurdity, Richet admitted, that living matter could form in this way 'which has the proper warmth, apparently a circulation of blood, and a physiological respiration', as well as a kind of psychic personality – 'in a word, a new human being! This is surely the climax of marvels! Nevertheless, it is a fact.'

Fact it might be to Richet and Geley, but as the materializations invariably de-materialized, it was hard to present witnesses with concrete proof; and on the few occasions when a residue appeared to be left, analysis proved unhelpful. Witnesses' testimonials consequently did little to impress the majority of scientists, who had either not been invited to 'Eva's' seances or had refused to accept invitations; and by the mid-1920s her powers were deserting her, marriage eventually withdrawing her from mediumship. By this time, however, a medium who could provide even more spectacular materializations was demonstrating them in South America: Carlos Mirabelli.

Mirabelli's full-form materializations were of deceased individuals known to the witnesses: something which had often been reported from spiritualist seances, but ordinarily in dark or very poorly lit rooms, whereas Mirabelli's appeared in full light, and in test conditions, before numerous investigators appointed to examine the claims. In the course of more than a hundred sessions, more than half of which were productive, Mirabelli performed in a locked and sealed room, tied up in a chair; and he materialized, among others, the child of one of the investigators, dressed in her burial clothes, and a bishop who had been drowned in a shipwreck.

They did not merely appear and fade away again; they were able to converse with the investigators, and to touch and be touched; a doctor present was able to feel the girl's pulse. These materializations were attested by scores of academics, prominent politicians, doctors and others, none of whom could offer any explanation other than that they were genuine; nor has any sceptic since been able to discover any evidence from the many witnesses still living to suggest that Mirabelli was involved in what would have been the most spectacular conjuring trick ever devised.

The question is often asked: why, if there were all these manifestations – ectoplasm, pseudopods, materializations – in Victorian times, and on until the 1930s, are they not still occurring today? There are many academic parapsychologists who believe that materializations of people were all spurious, and admit as much: others shrug their shoulders and confess they neither know nor care. So rarely have cases been heard of recently, let alone seriously investigated, that whereas in Fodor's *Encyclopedia* the entry under materialization was one of the longest, around ten thousand words, in Wolman's *Handbook of Parapsychology* (1977) it is not even mentioned, except as a historical curiosity, the writer of the section on the historical background to psychokinesis making no secret of his scepticism.

It is by no means certain, however, that materialization mediumship has gone into a decline. Reports of ectoplasm, pseudopods and occasional materializations are part of the stock-in-trade of Spiritualist journals the world over, even if they are no longer subjected to psychical research. The fact is that parapsychologists have tended to shy away from them, for fear of being contaminated by the fraud that is presumed to have been indelibly associated with them; and materializing mediums have themselves learned caution, because investigators have so often been interested only in exposures.

Levitations

Levitation occurs when objects, or people, rise into the air without physical force being applied, in defiance of gravitational pull. A magnet can levitate iron bars, but because it performs consistently, with a pulling power which can be measured objectively, magnetism is deemed outside the paranormal category. When objects rise and float without magnetic 'pull', they can be described as levitating; but the term is ordinarily taken to apply to the flights of humans.

In early Christian communities levitations were usually attributed to the devil. Demons, it was assumed, were lifting up the body of the person they had possessed. This applied even in the case of priests, monks and nuns. 'Much documentary evidence testifies to the bodily levitation of *demoniacs* (those allegedly possessed by demons or evil spirit entities),' Marc Cramer, a clinical psychologist who has made a study of the subject, has found; the earliest he has come across being an account in Thomas of Celano's *Lives of St Francis of Assisi*, describing a monk 'rigid all over, with his feet touching his head', who would be 'lifted up in the air to the height of a man's stature and then suddenly spring back to the earth'.

Numerous though such tales are, Cramer warns against too ready an acceptance of them because of the frequent outbreaks of mass hysteria, promoting delusions. But mass hysteria cannot account for the evidence in a few cases, notably that of Joseph of Copertino in the 17th century.

Few miracles in the history of the Catholic Church are as well attested as Joseph's levitations – 'flights' would be the more appropriate word. Of limited intelligence, perhaps even mentally retarded, he found it impossible to become a monk, eventually persuading the Franciscans to accept him as a lay Brother. He was assiduous in his duties and his devotions, scourging himself unmercifully; but he would have remained unknown had he not periodically taken off and floated around above the heads of his fellows. Mention of the name of the Blessed Virgin Mary was sometimes enough to raise him, so that he would be seen to fly by the entire congregation at mass. Once, he floated from the middle of the church to the high altar, covered with lighted candles; according to a member of the congregation, 'Brother Joseph flew and alighted among those candles, and threw down neither a candle nor a candlestick', remaining aloft for about fifteen minutes, 'kneeling and embracing the tabernacle'. On another occasion, walking in the monastery grounds, he soared up into the branches of an olive tree; unable to glide down, after his ecstasy had gone, he had to wait for a ladder to be brought out for him.

There was no question, in Joseph's case, of his feats being traded upon to impress the gullible public. His flights met with the disapproval of the authorities, who banned him from attending mass; he was investigated by the Inquisition; and strenuous efforts were made to prevent his becoming a cult figure. When it was suggested that he should be beatified, the Pope, Benedict XIV – who as Prospero Lambertini had written a balanced survey of the evidence for miracles, with shrewd advice on what should, and what should not, be regarded as miraculous – felt certain that the stories of Joseph's flights must be fantasies. When he came to study the case, however, he was compelled to admit the evidence was much too strong. Scores of eye-witnesses testified to seeing Joseph airborne, ranging from a previous Pope, Urban VIII, to the Lutheran Duke of Brunswick. The doctor who had attended Joseph on his death-bed, too, described how, when he arrived, the dying man was floating a few inches above the bed.

The contemporary accounts make it clear that Joseph did not deliberately induce his levitations. It was as if he became possessed, sometimes against his will (he had good reason to fear the wrath of the Inquisition if his flights should become embarrassing, as sometimes they did; on one occasion a slipper fell off his foot, while he was floating near the altar). Earlier, in the 16th century, Teresa of Avila, too, was worried when she found herself levitating; by her own account, she prayed to God to save her from further episodes. But when praying, she sometimes was observed to float for several minutes at a time. Often she was helpless to prevent herself from rising into the air. A bishop who was giving her communion observed that she had to clutch at a grille to hold herself down.

Levitations of the bewitched nuns were reported at the 'Devils of Loudun' trial: and, in considerable detail, in the evidence given about witchcraft at the Salem trials. Several Salem people reported having seen Margaret Rule, one of the supposed victims of the witches, lifted out of her bed 'wholly by an invisible force, a great way towards the top of the room where she lay': one witness had seen her thus floating 'when not only a strong person hath thrown his whole weight across her to pull her down, but several other persons have endeavoured with all their might to hinder her from being so raised up'.

D. D. Home levitated on several occasions. On one of them, Crookes 'saw him slowly rise up with a continuous gliding movement, and remain about six inches off the ground for several seconds, when he slowly descended'; on another, 'I was invited to come to him, when he rose eighteen inches off the ground, and I passed my hands under his feet, round him, and over his head when he was in the air.' Occasionally, the chair which Home was sitting in would levitate, his feet being off the floor. 'Less frequently the levitating power extended to those next to him. Once my wife was thus raised off the ground in her chair.'

The most famous of Home's levitations was when in the company of Lord Adare, the Master of Lindsay and a friend of theirs, he floated out of one window of a London house, and in at another. Sceptics then and since have devoted much time to showing how the flight could have been faked; but Home himself was in effect to dismiss it, and most of the other accounts of his levitations, as of no value for purposes of proof of the physical phenomena of his mediumship because they occurred in darkness. In his last book, *Lights and Shadows of Spiritualism*, he expressed regret that he had ever held seances in the dark – he rarely had – because of the discredit brought on spiritualism by mediums who had used darkness as a cover for sleight-of-hand.

Eusapia Palladino used occasionally to levitate during the investigations which European scientists made into her paranormal powers around the turn of the century; but although levitations of mediums have frequently been reported since in spiritualist journals, no medium has been able to produce them in conditions which would satisfy parapsychologists – let alone sceptics – as adequately controlled. Nevertheless, the historical evidence is extensive, and has occasionally been given unsolicited backing by sceptics.

The magician Harry Kellar, for example, whom Houdini admired, and who enjoyed showing audiences how mediums did their tricks, described how during a world tour in the 1870s he was watching a Zulu witch doctor go into a trance when suddenly 'to my intense amazement, the recumbent body slowly arose from the ground and floated upward in the air to the height of about three feet, where for a while it floated, moving up and down'. Doubtless to his even greater amazement, and chagrin, when in 1882 he challenged the medium Eglinton to perform some feat which no conjuror could repeat, Eglinton levitated, carrying

Kellar, holding his foot, into the air – an achievement which Kellar had to admit he could not account for.

Descriptions of what it feels like to levitate are hard to come by, but in the 16th century St Philip Neri was reported as saying that it was as if he had been caught hold of by somebody and 'wonderfully lifted'. Teresa of Avila's account is the more impressive in that it was written by her before her death and submitted to the Inquisition. It had been a 'very sore distress' to her, for fear it would occasion scandal, which was why she had forbidden nuns who saw her floating to speak of it: and it was also frightening; 'I confess that it threw me into great fear', so that she would find herself wrestling with the unseen power to try and keep her feet on the ground. But there could be 'great sweetness if unresisted', and she was sure that it was not a dream or an illusion: 'the senses are not lost; at least I was so much myself as to be able to see that I was being lifted up'.

Translocations

The tradition that individuals can be instantaneously translocated (or teleported), as if by magic, is of very long standing. Homer made frequent use of it in the *Odyssey*, where the gods were wont to intervene to rescue their favourites by pulling them out of danger. When Philip the Evangelist was told by an angel that he must interrupt his preaching mission to look for an Ethiopian in the desert, in order to baptize him, Philip was teleported back to Caesarea after he had fulfilled his task. And as late as the 17th century, the belief that people could be 'spirited away', usually by the fairies, remained widespread.

A 'learned friend' of Aubrey's described to him how a former Lord Duffus, walking in the fields near his home, 'was suddenly carried away, and found the next day in Paris, in the French king's cellar, with a silver cup in his hand'. Asked how he had come to be there, he could only say that he had heard a noise like a whirlwind and voices crying 'Horse and Hattock' – the fairy code for translocation; he had contributed his own 'Horse and Hattock', and found himself carried through the air to the cellar, where he had not hesitated to avail himself of the stock. Charitably, the French king not merely let him go but gave him the cup, which the family had kept, calling it 'the Fairy Cup'.

Even in this century, a number of cases of translocation have been reported, some with a surprising amount of attestation. In 1905 one of the children of the Pansini family in Italy began to have fits, in which he spoke languages he had not learned; apports began to manifest themselves in his presence, and his parents sent him to a seminary, where his psychic capabilities were confined to answering unspoken questions. When he came home at the age of ten, however, he and his younger brother began to have a succession of translocations which could not be accounted for: once, when he was in the Piazza in Kuvi at 1.35 P.M., he was found ten minutes later outside his uncle's house in Trani. According to Lapponi, who showed in his *Hypnotism and Spiritism* (1906) that he was far from credulous about such tales, the translocations, investigated for *Il Giornale d'Italia*, were attested by priests and doctors.

Carlos Mirabelli was reported by a number of citizens to have suddenly vanished from their presence, to find himself many miles distant; and in his autobiography Uri Geller has described how on November 9 1973, at around six P.M., he was on a New York street when suddenly he had the feeling that he was being sucked upward: a moment later, he was crashing through a porch screen at the home of his mentor Andrija Puharich in Ossining, 36 miles by road. As they telephoned the people he had just been with, there were witnesses to testify that he was in Ossining within minutes of their having seen him in New York.

Elongations

The human frame can ordinarily stretch an inch or two, simply by voluntary action (or enforced action, on the rack). But stretching to a markedly greater extent has frequently been reported of people in trance states.

Historically, elongations of this kind were attributed to possession by a god or a demon. In Virgil's description of Aeneas's visit to the Cumaean oracle, the sibyl's body is described as elongating when she went into her trance so that she could be possessed by Apollo; and the neo-Platonist theurgists in the third century A.D. reported similar experiences with mediums – 'sometimes their bodies seem to grow in height', Iamblichus observed. Elongations often feature in the data collected for canonization proceedings; and some of El Greco's paintings appear to illustrate the way saints were seen as 'stretched'.

Elongations were a common occurrence in Victorian spiritualist seances, the best attested being those of Home, who actually allowed sitters to take measurements. H. D. Jencken, a barrister, witnessed Home's elongations four times, measuring Home, who was ordinarily shorter than himself, by standing beside him. When Home was at full stretch (the extension apparently coming at his waist, as the clothes he was wearing separated out) Jencken hardly reached up to Home's shoulder.

At one of the test seances which Home undertook with Lord Adare and the Master of Lindsay, a journalist, H. T. Humphries, who was present, wrote that Home 'was seen by all of us to increase in height to the extent of some eight or ten inches'. The Master of Lindsay – a scientist soon to be elected to a Fellowship of the Royal Society – measured the elongated Home, standing up against a wall; 'not being satisfied with that, I put him in the middle of the room and placed a candle in front of him, so as to throw a shadow on the wall, which I also marked'. He then measured him when he came out of his trance, both against the wall and with the shadow; the difference was eleven inches. Adare emphasized that he had taken care to see that Home was not standing on tiptoe. The elongation, he and the others had satisfied themselves, came 'where the top of the hip bone and the short ribs separate'.

Elongations are still occasionally reported during seances; but no medium has been subjected to the kind of detailed test which Home permitted. Even Podmore, who could not accept the possibility of elongations, and felt compelled to offer some alternative explanation, could think of nothing more plausible than 'illusion, which Home may no doubt have eked out on occasion by such devices as slipping his feet half out of his boots and standing on tiptoe, or supporting himself on some convenient article of furniture' – a fair sample of the inanities to which Podmore, in his determination to reject all telekinetic phenomena, was reduced.

Invulnerability

The way in which the human body, in certain circumstances, can become resistant to violence is best documented in Carré de

Montgeron's account of the *convulsionnaires* of St Médard, in the outbreak of mass hysteria at the cemetery there in the 1830s. Watched by incredulous spectators, Sister Margaret allowed herself to be repeatedly struck by heavy blows, suffering no visible harm; and the twelve-year-old Gabrielle Moler could be beaten with mallets, and attacked with poles pointed at the end, without any sign of injury. Carré had taken the precaution of obtaining testimonies from witnesses, which showed that they were men of standing, some of them previously sceptical; and David Hume was to cite the evidence as the most convincing he had come across for miracles (though it did not convince him), observed as they had been 'upon the spot before judges of unquestioned integrity, attested by witnesses of credit and distinction in a learned age'.

George Gurdjieff used to demonstrate that he could confer invulnerability on his disciples. On one occasion which William Seabrook, among others, witnessed in New York in 1924, they were facing the audience on a stage when Gurdjieff ordered them to race forwards. The audience expected him to stop them when they reached the footlights, but he had turned his back. 'In the next split second an aerial human avalanche was flying through the air, across the orchestra, down among empty chairs, on the floor, bodies pell-mell, piled on top of each other, arms and legs sticking out in weird postures.' Yet when they finally sorted themselves out, on his order, 'it was evident that no arms, legs or necks had been broken – no one seemed to have suffered so much as a scratch or a bruise'.

Incombustibility

To Nandor Fodor, surveying the evidence for the paranormal in his *Encyclopedia*, the capacity of the human frame to render itself immune to fire – attaining immunity, that is, not just from the pain but from the actual symptoms of burning – was the most dramatic of all the phenomena. It also happens to be well-documented, from a variety of sources.

In many tribal communities it has long been taken for granted that the shaman can not only induce immunity to fire in himself, but can also confer it on members of the tribe. There are scores of accounts from explorers, missionaries and colonial officials of fire ceremonies: usually 'fire-walks' in which the tribal diviner leads his flock over white-hot stones, lava or ashes.

A tough-minded New Zealand magistrate, Colonel Gudgeon, described how in 1899 he and some friends went to watch a Maori fire-walk and were disconcerted to be invited to join – 'I hand my *mana*, my power, over to you.' It was like walking across an open oven, Gudgeon found; as his feet were tender, he feared that the skin would peel, 'yet all I really felt when the task was accomplished was a tingling sensation'. Only one of about two hundred people who did the walk was burned; 'he, it is said, was spoken to; but like Lot's wife, looked behind him – a thing against all rules'.

A more detailed investigation was carried out at this time by Dr T. N. Hocken, who brought with him a thermometer which could be suspended above the stones; it could register up to 400°F, but this, Hocken found, proved insufficient. He also examined the feet of the walkers, before and after – even, in some cases, applying his tongue, because sceptics had suggested that the immunity was secured by horny soles, perhaps treated with some chemical. Not so, Hocken found. The soles were flexible and had not been treated.

Historically, the earliest reference to incombustibility appears to be the story of Shadrach, Mesach and Abed-nego, cast, on King Nebuchadnezzar's orders, into the burning fiery furnace; it was so hot that it killed the jailers who put them in. Yet they were unharmed; Nebuchadnezzar and his court 'saw these men, upon whose bodies the fire had no power, nor was an hair of their heads singed, neither were their coats changed, nor had the smell of fire passed on them'.

Evidence of a different kind for incombustibility comes from the fact that in so many parts of the world, in so many eras, ordeal by heat has been used to decide whether accused persons are guilty or not guilty of crimes. It is hardly conceivable that the method should have been adopted – usually either plunging the hand in boiling water, or holding some red-hot piece of iron – or would have been maintained if it always pointed to guilt; still less that there should be so many accounts of people voluntarily offering to prove their innocence in this way, as the Thebans did in Sophocles' *Antigone*.

That faith could provide protection from fire became a Christian belief: a number of saints were reported to have illustrated this thesis. Catherine of Siena was rescued unharmed after falling, while in one of her trances, face down into burning coals; Bernadette was seen to put her hands into candle flames while in her ecstasies, and keep them there – on one occasion for as long as a quarter of an hour, according to Dr Dozous, who examined her afterwards and 'could not find the slightest trace of a burn anywhere'. Yet when he brought a lighted taper close to her, after she had come out of her trance, she reacted normally to it.

There do not appear to be any cases of people invoking such immunity when it would have been most welcome, while being burned at the stake; with the possible exception of the 17th-century Huguenot leader Claris, who according to his followers mounted a pyre and had it set alight, the flames reaching above his head while he continued to address them, before eventually descending without injury.

The first well-attested report of incombustibility features in Carré de Montgeron's account of the *convulsionnaires* of St Médard, at the tomb of the Jansenist François de Paris in the 1730s. A number of them displayed immunity to fire; one, Marie Souet, so successfully that she became known as *la salamandre*. Her performances, witnessed by ten respected citizens (two of them priests), included going so rigid in her trance state that she could be suspended head and heels over a violent fire, wrapped only in a sheet; she was roasted there for more than half an hour, the sheet showing no signs of burning, though it was actually in the flames. Gabrielle Moler was also flame-resistant. To prove there was no deception, she could either make her clothes incombustible, too, or allow her shoes to burn without any harm coming to her feet.

Even better attested are the fire-handling feats of Home. William Stainton Moses described how he had seen Home go into a trance; he 'ruffled his bushy hair until it stood out like a mop and then deliberately laid down and put his head in the bright wood fire'. Crookes, who was present on this and other occasions, satisfied himself that Home was not using a form of protection. After Home had carried around a glowing coal, Crookes examined his hand: 'I could detect no trace of injury to the skin, which was soft and delicate like a woman's. Neither were there signs of any preparations having been previously applied.'

Among others who confirmed Home's immunity to fire, Lord

Adare described watching him in a seance in 1868: 'after stirring the embers to a flame, kneeling down, he placed his face right among the burning coals, moving it about as though bathing it in water'. The novelist Mrs Samuel Carter Hall testified that she had seen Home place 'a huge lump of red-hot burning coal' on her husband's head:

I have often wondered since why I was not frightened; but I was not. I had perfect faith that he would not be injured. Someone said, 'Is it not hot?' Mr Hall answered 'Warm, but not hot.' Mr Home . . . then proceeded to draw up Mr Hall's white hair over the red coal; Mr Home drew the hair into a sort of pyramid, the coal, still red, showing beneath the hair.

Home then handed the coal to Mrs Hall, who also felt it was 'warm' – yet when she bent down to take a closer look at it, the heat coming from it was sufficiently intense to make her draw her face back.

The strength of the evidence for incombustibility in Home's case can be judged from the puerility of attempts to discredit it, as in Henry Evans's *The Spirit World Unmasked*. The coal, Evans claimed, must have been 'a piece of spongy platinum'; in a secret pocket of his coat, Home would have 'a small reservoir of hydrogen, with a tube coming down the sleeve'; at the appropriate moment Home would turn on the gas, and when the current of hydrogen impinged upon the piece of spongy platinum, the metal would become 'incandescent'. As Carrington pointed out in his *Physical Phenomena of Spiritualism* (1907), apart from the improbability of such a device fooling Crookes, the leading chemist/physicist of the era, the smell would immediately have given it away to everybody present. In any case, it could not account for the occasions when Home had handed the coal around (or, for that matter, when he had put it on Hall's head). Carrington might have added that on at least one occasion, when Home was handing round a coal, it burned the hand of one of the recipients, leaving the others unaffected. The hand, Lang – a friend of his – wrote years later, 'still bears the scar'.

In the 1880s, when the reality of the hypnotic trance state had at last been conceded, several experimenters reported that subjects put into a deep trance displayed heat resistance. If told that they were being touched with a pencil, when in fact they were being touched with red-hot metal, they would show no sign either of pain or, later, of the effects of a burn; conversely, if told they were being touched with red-hot metal when in fact they were being touched with a pencil, they would scream, and blisters would appear. Professional hypnotists still illustrate this with volunteer subjects, in performances in clubs; but no serious research has been undertaken recently into incombustibility using this technique.

Incorruptibility

The human body, it has long been believed, can in certain circumstances give off a smell indicating that it is provided with what might be described as paranormal protection. It may last after death, so that the body will not begin to decompose; and if exhumed, will be found as it was in life. In the *Iliad*, when Patroclus was killed his body was preserved from decay; and the same phenomenon has been recorded of many men and women in canonization procedures.

At some point, however, preservation of this kind became entangled with folklore about vampires, who were believed also to be spared physical putrefaction thanks to their nightly consumption of human blood; and bodily incorruptibility ceased to be regarded as necessarily an indicator of holiness. It was in any case difficult to prove that the preservation might not be the result of some atmospheric condition of the kind which can preserve the corpses in vaults, such as those of St Michan's in Dublin. Reports of the odour of sanctity and incorruptibility are now rarely encountered; but in view of the evidence for psychic incombustibility and invulnerability, perhaps they should be admitted in this paranormal category.

Auras

The belief that the human body emits radiations, of a kind which in certain circumstances can become visible, has been encountered in all civilizations. Under Christianity the general assumption was that the aura was linked with holiness – as in pictures of angels, saints and martyrs; but in the middle of the 19th century Baron Carl von Reichenbach, a chemist of distinction (he was the discoverer of creosote and of paraffin), decided after experiments with a sensitive that there was an electro-magnetic component, –

which he called od, or odyle, or the odic force – a variant of Mesmer's animal magnetism. A great deal of work was done by the Baron and others to try to establish the reality of the force, but as only sensitives could see the aura, and as they could not see it consistently under test conditions, he was never able to convince orthodox scientists of its existence.

Reichenbach's ideas have been incorporated in several theories since, notably in Wilhelm Reich's 'orgone'. The most recent research along the same lines has been into what has come to be known as 'the Kirlian effect', from its discoverers Semyon and Valentina Kirlian of Krasnodar in Russia. They were able to demonstrate the existence of auras around both organic and inorganic materials, constantly changing, in the case of anything living – whether a leaf or a finger tip.

These auras are not themselves in the paranormal category: as Professor Arthur Ellison has described them, they represent the process of 'obtaining lensless coloured pictures when an electric discharge is caused to take place between either a high voltage plate electrode and an earthed plate electrode, a colour film being placed between them together with an object on the emulsion side of the film; *or* between a high voltage plate electrode and a finger (or hand), a colour film being placed under the finger (or hand)'. When the process was being explored, however, the resulting films suggested the possibility that the auras are related to those which have so often been reported by psychics, or by ordinary men and women in the presence of somebody they regard with veneration.

Two specific claims have been made about the auras, and supported by photographs: that when a picture is taken of a leaf with a portion cut away, its missing piece may remain as an 'apparition', visible for a while – suggesting that a parallel process might be at work with humans after death; and that variations in the brightness and coloration of the auras can be used in the diagnosis of illness. Neither of these claims has been fully vindicated, as the 'ghost' has only been reported on rare occasions, and electrical engineers complain that the methods employed for diagnosis are insufficiently objective. Whether the Kirlian aura has any connection with the psychic auras of tradition remains to be established.

ACOUSTIC EFFECTS

An old folk-lore tradition links the moment of death with sounds; usually melancholy, such as in the howling of dogs or wolves (in countries where there are wolves to howl) or the screech of the banshee (in Ireland). Sometimes these hallucinatory noises turn out actually to be psychokinetically induced, as in the stories of the ringing, or tolling, of bells, when nobody is tugging at the bellpull.

Typical of such tales is one in Flammarion's collection. In 1622 Louis, brother and inseparable friend of St François de Sales, was at home with his family at the Château de Thuille when, around ten P.M., a bell which was in one of the turrets of the château began to ring. The rope which was used to sound the bell, they found, was not being pulled. After this had happened a number of times, Louis ordered that the rope should be taken off the bell; but still it rang, until the family in alarm began to pray. Later they heard that François, who was Bishop of Geneva and of Annecy, had died at eight o'clock that evening.

PK bell-ringing has also been reported on many occasions when there is no death to link it to; it is usually attributed to a poltergeist. Major Edward Moore, a Fellow of the Royal Society, described an outbreak of the kind in *Bealing's Bells* (1840) (an account which Wallace, a neighbour and friend of Moore's, felt sure could be trusted) telling how the household was plagued for months by bells being rung when no human hand was in a position to ring them.

Among the common physical phenomena of mediumship, too – as Wallace noted – were 'musical instruments, of various kinds, played without human agency, from a hand-bell to a closed piano'. He added that where conditions were favourable, 'original musical compositions of a very high character are produced. This occurred with Mr Home'. The psychokinetic playing of musical instruments was, in fact, one of Home's most impressive feats. There are many accounts by well-known men and women who attended his seances in light good enough to see the instrument, usually an accordion, being played as if by invisible hands, while Home was in his trance, sitting several feet away from it at the seance-room table.

With few exceptions, too, the sitters were impressed by the quality of the playing – though the compositions were not, as a rule, original; they were sentimental drawing-room songs, such as 'Home, Sweet Home' – an unfortunate choice as, though Home pronounced his name Scots-fashion, 'Hume', it gave his detractors a chance to mock him, as *Punch* did in 1860.

> Of itself his accordion to play will begin
> (If you won't look too hard at the works hid within . . .)
>
> Home, Home, great Home
> There's no case like Home.

When Crookes tested Home with the lawyer, Serjeant Cox, and the physicist, William Huggins, FRS, in attendance, one of the experiments was to find if an accordion (inspected to ensure that no works were hid within) would play in a cage, wired so that an electric current could be passed round it. Home held one end of the accordion, the end away from the keys; the three men saw the instrument begin to contract and expand, and to play notes, which it did when the current was switched on. It continued even when Home had withdrawn his hand; with nobody touching the keys, it played what Crookes described as 'a well-known sweet and plaintive melody', which 'it executed perfectly'.

Other instruments which have featured at seances (and still do) are musical boxes, which the spirits are challenged to start up and to stop; hand-bells, which they are challenged to ring; and the ubiquitous trumpets, endlessly reported as having floated around in the air over the heads of sitters at seances, sometimes producing 'direct voice' effects. But no medium since has come near to emulating Home's musical feats.

The commonest form the paranormal has taken is the production of noises which have usually been described as raps though, as Sudre noted, they display an infinite variety; 'there are noises of all kinds from the slightest cracking sound to a blow resembling that of a hammer on an anvil. They imitate, often on request, dance tunes being drummed by fingers, the steps of a man or the gallop of a horse, a ball bouncing, wood being sawed, a floor being polished, etc.'

From earliest times, these sounds have been taken to be a form of communication used by spirits – as they still are in tribal communities. Along with the movement of objects, they constitute the highest proportion of the phenomena reported in connection with poltergeists and an even higher proportion in other types of haunting.

They are also reported from most spiritualist seances. It was initially raps, in fact, which led to spiritism, the belief in the reality of spirits, developing into spiritualism, with its emphasis on communication with the spirits. In 1848 the young sisters Margaret and Kate Fox began to communicate with the spirit of a man who had been murdered in their home at Hydesville, New York – or so the raps claimed. At first a simple code was used, the spirits answering questions with one rap for yes, two for no, three for uncertain. But soon the questioners began to call down through the alphabet, enabling the spirit, by rapping at individual letters, to construct whole sentences.

Inevitably the sisters were accused of making the raps themselves by 'popping' their joints; but in a succession of trials they demonstrated that they could not be physically responsible for the sounds, which would be heard coming from different parts of the room. Soon, scores of mediums were conducting seances at which sitters could ask questions and, with the help of an alphabet, elicit replies from raps, usually coming from tables.

The celebrated mathematician Augustus de Morgan, first holder of the Chair of Mathematics at London University, described sessions he and his wife attended in the 1850s with Mrs W. R. Hayden. The 'raps', he was surprised to find, were 'clean, clear, faint sounds' of the kind knitting needles might make 'if dropped from a small distance on to a marble slab, and instantly checked by a damper of some kind'. He satisfied himself that Mrs Hayden could not herself be physically responsible either for the sounds, or for the rapped-out messages which correctly answered his unspoken questions. Although he remained reluctant to accept the spirit hypothesis, he expressed himself convinced that 'something or somebody was reading my thoughts'.

During the table-turning era, raps were often the first intimation that a spirit was ready to co-operate with the sitters, the sounds sometimes coming from the table itself, sometimes from different parts of the room. They were commonly heard at the seances given by D. D. Home. Investigating them, William Crookes felt that the popular term, raps, was misleading as the sounds ranged from light ticks through scratchings, and from twitterings to loud detonations.

Sometimes the raps pursued sitters back to their homes. Cromwell Varley, a Fellow of the Royal Society, had found it hard to believe the evidence of his own eyes when he attended a seance with Home; but he felt compelled to believe the evidence of his own ears when he continued to hear the raps in his drawing-room – and had a letter the next day from Home to say that the spirits had informed him they were going to perform there, for Varley's benefit.

In the early years of the 20th century, the French psychical researcher Joseph Maxwell (he had qualified both as a doctor and as a lawyer, becoming attorney general for the Bordeaux region: his descriptions of the phenomena are lucid, and his comments shrewd) made a careful study of raps, finding among other things that they were characteristic of the spirit who was claimed to be employing them. They sounded serious, with serious communicators; but 'light, precipitate raps, weak but abundant, represent certain personifications which we might call kill-joys, whose unwelcome intervention spoils the experience'.

With the introduction of the ouija board, communication with the spirits was speeded up to a point that messages sent through raps came to be regarded as unnecessarily laborious; but the spirits continued on occasion to use them to make, or underline, some point. When the Rev. Drayton Thomas was testing the most reliable of the British mediums in the years between the wars, Mrs Osborne Leonard, he suggested to Mrs Leonard's spirit 'control', 'Feda', that she should try to make her presence felt in his home, in the absence of Mrs Leonard, by raps; and one evening he heard a succession of thumps. When he next had a sitting with Mrs Leonard, 'Feda' claimed to have made the raps, and offered to prove it; she told him that when he returned home, he was to take out the fifth book from the left of the second shelf behind his study door, and look at the top of page 17. When Thomas got back to his study, which Mrs Leonard had never seen, he found that the book was a collection of Shakespeare's plays; and at the top of the page 'Feda' had nominated was the phrase 'I will not answer thee with words, but blows'.

The sound of blows, often powerful blows, has been reported not only from seances and hauntings, but also during investigations of physical mediums. When William Barrett went to investigate the Goligher circle in Belfast, taking with him a sceptical friend, a doctor, at the start of the seance they heard raps coming both from inside and from outside the circle. The raps answered their questions; and when the doctor asked if the raps might be made a little louder, the reply was 'a tremendous bang' which shook the room, followed by a noise like a bouncing ball, 'and of somebody sawing wood'.

Investigators in many parts of the world have heard raps. In his *Occult Science in India* (1875) Louis Jacolliot described how a celebrated fakir, Covindasamy, managed to make an 'immense bronze vase full of water', in Jacolliot's bungalow, rock to and fro without touching it, and also cause sounds to emanate from it, as if it were being struck with a steel rod. The sounds varied, at Jacolliot's request, to imitate a drum roll, or the stately ticking of a clock. What most served to convince Jacolliot that he could not have been deceived was that after Covindasamy promised him that the raps would return that night, they did, while he was in his room, coming from various directions – on the walls, ceiling, and out of a lampshade – while in the distance, he could see the fakir at prayer.

It proved if anything even harder, however, to convince sceptics that tables could make noises, let alone conduct intelligent conversations, than it was to convince them that tables might move without physical force being exerted upon them. Even Charles Kingsley, though he visualized reprimanding his four-year-old son, should he say that there were no such things as water babies, 'my dear little man, till you know a great deal more about Nature than Professor Owen and Professor Huxley put together, don't tell me about what cannot be', could go on to say that a deal table was, like man, 'fearfully and wonderfully made' – more fearfully and wonderfully made 'than if, as foxes say and geese believe, spirits could make it dance, or talk to you by rapping on it'.

Devout Christians, in fact, were at one with materialist agnostics. The materialists insisted that dead wood could not produce raps; the Christians, that God would not permit spirits to use so absurd a method of communication. Raps, too, happened to be relatively easy to produce fraudulently, as the physicist John Tyndall boasted; pretending that he was undertaking a serious investigation of spiritualism, he had made the raps himself in a seance in order to confuse the other sitters. And after forty years of giving seances Margaret Fox, by this time an alcoholic, confessing she had cheated, gave a public demonstration of the way she and her sister had 'popped' their joints in the past. But the sounds she was able to produce were unconvincing; the confession was easily accounted for by the fact that she was almost penniless: she had been tempted by an offer of $1500, a formidable sum in those days; and the confession was quickly retracted. In any case, the evidence for sounds coming out of tables, or walls or the open air, was by then too extensively documented to be jeopardized by any single hoax.

To the stock objection – if spirits can communicate with us, why do they use so primitive a method of communication? – spiritualists reply that before man invented the telephone and the radio, he had to make use of raps to communicate with other men at a distance: the telegraph. Whatever the explanation, 'the reality of these raps is of primary importance', Richet asserted. 'If it is established that mechanical vibrations can be produced in matter, at distance and without contact, and that these vibrations are intelligent, we have the truly far-reaching fact that there are in the universe human or non-human intelligences that can act directly on matter.' But since the shift away from the research with mediums, in the 1930s, parapsychologists have paid scant attention to them.

Missionaries seeking to make converts in tribal communities were sometimes disconcerted, listening to the tribal diviner, to hear what the tribe assumed were the voices of spirits coming not through the diviner's mouth, but apparently from some point in space – a phenomenon familiar to them from their Bibles, where the voice of the Lord himself could sometimes be heard. This was taken to be 'ventriloquism', which in its original sense meant that although the diviner was the medium through which the spirits communicated, they could talk or make other sounds independently of his vocal cords. With the spread of materialist physics, however, direct voice was deemed impossible. 'Ventriloquism', like 'magic' and 'conjuring', came to be identified with trickery; it was even seriously believed that a ventriloquist could 'throw' his voice so that it sounded as if it were coming from a distant point. Later, it came to be realized that the ventriloquist's skill consisted in distracting attention from his own lips, and deceiving audiences into thinking of the sounds as coming from his 'doll'.

In spiritualist seances, however, ventriloquism in its original sense was often reported. It was as if the spirit 'control' or a 'communicator', speaking through the medium in his trance, could speak not merely in its own voice, but from different parts of the room. Direct Voice communication became quite a frequent occurrence, in which some mediums specialized.

In the seances held by the Crandons in Boston in the 1920s, 'Margery' (Mina Crandon) had her deceased brother, Walter, as her 'control' and he often came up in direct voice, loud, strong and sometimes profane, as when he shouted unprintable abuse at Houdini for playing dirty tricks in the course of some tests Houdini was carrying out to find if 'Margery' was genuine – Houdini being convinced she was not.

Was it 'Walter' who spoke, or 'Margery' imitating him? A Boston resident, Dr Mark Richardson, suggested an experiment to settle the issue. He brought along a U–tube filled with water, with a mouthpiece into which 'Margery' was required to blow sufficiently hard to keep the water up to a certain level in the other part of the tube, thereby effectively preventing her from speaking. Yet 'Walter' came through as before.

'Margery', sceptics alleged, must have found a way to block off the tube, having raised the water level; so another device was introduced, a sound-proofed box containing a microphone, and placed in a different room. 'Walter' was invited to enter the box, and prove his independence of 'Mina's' vocal cords by relaying messages through the microphone, which he successfully did.

There have been other indications that sound (or hallucinations of sound) can come from a source other than a medium's own throat. Waldemar Bogoraz, a Russian investigator of shamanism in Siberia, employed a phonograph to check where disembodied voices were coming from; he was disconcerted to find that they sounded as if they came from a position directly in front of the receiver, though to him they had seemed to be coming from different parts of the hut. Later, W. J. Crawford made a report of a similar finding in his research with the Goligher circle.

In the late 1950s Friedrich Jurgensen found that extraneous matter was imposing itself, in a manner which he could not account for, on tape recordings; sometimes in the form of voices, though nobody was in the recording studio. Investigating the phenomenon, Konstantin Raudive, a Latvian refugee working as a psychologist in Germany, conducted experiments which, he claimed, demonstrated that these voices could emerge on tapes even when strict precautions had been taken to ensure that no extraneous sounds could be heard during the recording. They were not voices in the ordinary sense, so much as sounds which bore a certain resemblance to those made vocally, sometimes in cadences similar to those of speech, with the occasional recognizable word.

In 1971 a test was held in which engineers monitored recordings with their own tapes, in a way which would disclose if there was any sound in the supposedly sound-proofed studios while the Raudive tapes were being run. The monitoring instruments detected no sound; but the play-back revealed that the 'voices' had intervened on the Raudive tape.

Since then several experiments have recorded the 'voices'. Various suggestions have been put forward to account for them: that they represent PK effects emanating from human minds; that they are messages from beings in outer space; or that they represent the auditory equivalent of psychic photographs – spirit sounds invading tapes in the same way as spirit forms invade photographic negatives. Sufficient evidence has accumulated to make the sceptic's alternative proposition, that the intrusive sounds can be accounted for by radio transmissions behaving in anomalous ways, untenable; but the fact that the 'voices' rarely communicate information has meant that the initial interest shown in the work and theories of Jurgensen and Raudive has tended to wane.

Matthew Manning has reported a Raudive-type episode in his *In the Minds of Millions* (1977). On a blank tape, church bells came through when no church bells were audible to account for their reception. The next morning, the sound of the bells had disappeared from the tape.

ATMOSPHERIC EFFECTS

Perhaps the commonest side-effect reported at seances has been the experience of a chill in the air, or cold breezes. The temperature of the seance room, it has often been found, does not change: and sometimes the cold felt by some sitters is not felt by others, suggesting that the experience is often subjective; but on a few occasions, significant changes of temperature have been recorded; at one of Stainton Moses' seances with the Speer family, a thermometer showed a fall of 3°C, and after one of his tests of 'Stella C' Harry Price reported a fall of over 6°C. As Lodge observed, the fact that the temperature in such cases actually fell was significant, as although it is comparatively easy to make a room warmer by some form of trickery, it is much more difficult to make it cooler, provided the obvious precautions have been taken.

When Eusapia Palladino was producing her psychic phenomena, they were often accompanied by a cold breeze which, investigators found, appeared to emanate from her forehead. This was noticed both by Muensterberg and the conjuror Joseph Rinn in the course of the test before she was 'exposed'; and the explanations which they advanced – that she had a balloon under her armpit with a rubber tube drawn up through her hair, or that she put her hand to her mouth and blew – were manifestly implausible, as in either case the air would have been warmer.

Of the atmospheric effects associated with physical mediumship, one of the commonest are luminosities: 'sparks, stars, globes of light, luminous clouds etc.', as Wallace described them, which sometimes develop into forms but commonly float around.

'Under the strictest of test conditions I have seen a solid luminous body, the size and nearly the shape of a turkey's egg, float noiselessly about the room,' Crookes wrote in his *Researches into the Phenomena of Spiritualism* (1874). 'It was visible for more than ten minutes, and before it faded away it struck the table three times with a sound like that of a hard, solid body.' He added that

179

he had also communicated with a luminosity alphabetically 'by the flashing of a bright light a desired number of times'.

Dr Speer often observed lights floating around during seances with Stainton Moses, as did Geley in his investigation of the medium Franek Kluski. Apart from raps, in fact, luminosities probably constitute the commonest of seance-room phenomena.

Outbreaks of fire have quite often been reported during hauntings, but they are usually associated with poltergeist disturbances – as is liquefaction, in the form of showers of water, sometimes of excrement, in enclosed rooms. Liquefaction has also often been recorded in the form of tears, or blood, accumulating on, or dripping from, statues of Christian saints. The best known demonstration of the liquefying power of faith is the annual miracle, as it is taken to be by the Neapolitan faithful, when the clotted blood of St Januarius is seen to flow on his name-day. A celebrated naturalist, bold enough to put a finger into it and try the taste, pronounced it to be bat's urine. But there have been a few cases of weeping statues which have defied analysis of this or any other kind.

In 1670, 'not far from Cirencester, was an apparition', according to Aubrey. 'Being demanded, whether a good spirit or bad; returned no answer but disappeared with a curious perfume and most melodious twang.' Scents have very often been reported from haunted rooms – usually repulsive; but during seances, when they are also frequent, they are as a rule pleasant – 'like nothing of this earth's production', as Stainton Moses described them, 'ethereal, delicate and infinitely delightful'. Scents have also often been reported following a bereavement, as Rosamond Lehmann has described in *The Swan in the Evening* (1967).

4 GHOSTS

In his *Encyclopedia* (1933) Nandor Fodor defined a ghost as 'a deceased person or its image appearing to the living', adding that it was 'a popular term, which does not include apparitions of the living'. In colloquial usage, this is still broadly true; but psychical researchers have long since shunned the term, partly because it is too vague. Ghosts, phantoms, spectres – these and other terms bring up mind's-eye pictures derived from fairy tales, folklore and the kind of fears which the imagination of young children breeds. They are ill-defined, ranging from wispy transparent wraiths floating across a room, to conventionally-dressed and to all appearances real people whose unreality only becomes apparent when they vanish; from 'elementals', whose fearsome presence can be sensed but not seen, to a headless Anne Boleyn, walking the Bloody Tower with her head tucked underneath her arm.

The main reason for dissatisfaction with the term 'ghost', however, and its near synonyms, is that their colloquial use has helped to perpetuate the misunderstanding lamented by Professor H. H. Price, introducing G. N. M. Tyrrell's *Apparitions*, deriding 'the tea party question, "Do you believe in ghosts?"' This, in his view, was hopelessly ambiguous; 'but if we take it to mean, "Do you believe that people sometimes experience apparitions?" the answer is that they certainly do.'

The comparison can be traced back to classical times, when Cicero, Lucian and other sceptics were prepared to argue that ghost stories were the product of delusion or invention. Plutarch disagreed. Some people, he knew, thought that ghosts were the delusive visions of the credulous or the mentally unbalanced; but if men of strong and philosophic minds like Dion or Brutus could place so much faith in ghosts they had seen that they were prepared to describe them to friends, he saw no reason to doubt their reality.

Much the same division of opinion resurfaced in the 18th century; and by the end of it, 'believing in ghosts' had come to be widely regarded as a sign of immaturity. Ghost stories, Immanuel Kant observed, 'will always find *secret* believers, and will always be regarded *in public* with well-bred incredulity'. As a result, philosophy, though it dealt with all sorts of futile questions, was uneasy when dealing with ghosts, as the topic introduced 'certain facts that it cannot *doubt* without making itself ridiculous'. Kant was not prepared to go against the tide. Although in his correspondence he admitted a belief in immaterial beings, in public he adopted the role of the sceptic.

The reluctance of men such as Kant to face the facts squarely helped to establish the idea that there is a straight choice: either to believe in, or not to believe in, ghosts. Thus in 1814 the great chemist Chevreul (one of the few men who, eminent in their lifetimes, have lived to attend the commemoration of the centenary of their births), saw a phantom between two windows in his study. Frightened, he turned away: but when he looked back it was still there, as it was again, twice, when he summoned up the courage to look. Eventually he moved towards his bedroom, and it vanished. Soon afterwards he heard that at the time, a close friend who was to bequeath his library to Chevreul had died. 'If I had been superstitious,' Chevreul commented when he recounted the story, 'I might have thought the apparition real.'

But there is a sense in which an apparition of this kind may *be* real. It may have been an illusion – a trick of light and shadow – but it may also have been a hallucination, in which case it can be real to the person who is hallucinating – as Walter Scott realized. Resolutely determined though he was to put a natural interpretation on all the phenomena which he surveyed in his *Letters on Demonology and Witchcraft* (1830), he could not allow that the evidence for apparitions could be explained away in terms of illusion; he preferred to accept that the senses from various causes might become deranged 'and that, in such cases, men, in the literal sense, really *see* the empty and false forms, and hear the idle sounds which, in the more primitive state of society, are naturally enough referred to the action of demons or disembodied spirits'. Acceptance of apparitions on this basis had led 'one of the greatest poets of the present time' – Scott did not identify him – to reply to a lady who asked if he believed in ghosts, 'No, Madam: I have seen too many of them!'

Reassurance that an apparition could be literally seen and heard, however, was of no comfort if this were an indication of derangement of the senses; and during the 19th century the assumption was that hallucinations of any kind represented a warning of impending mental disturbance. Largely through the work of Edmund Gurney, collecting and checking upon the case histories which were published in his *Phantasms of the Living* (1886), and the later collection in the SPR's *Census of Hallucinations* (1894), it became apparent that the people who had hallucinatory experiences involving apparitions, far from displaying mental instability, were a fairly representative cross-section of the public. There were instances in which factors predisposing to seeing apparitions, grief, or anxiety, could be noted; but in most cases the hallucinations came, in Myers's words, 'at ordinary unexciting moments'; and even where they were linked to some disturbing event, such as the death of a close relative or friend, this usually could not have been responsible for the hallucination except psychically, as the apparition was so often the first intimation of the event.

The outcome of this work was that psychical researchers came to look upon ghosts as hallucinations. The distinction must be made, William James insisted in his *Principles of Psychology* (1890), between hallucinations and illusions (or delusions). 'Every hallucination is a perception, as good and true a sensation as if there were a real object there. The object happens *not* to be there: that is all.' This does not, of course, rule out the possibility that some sightings of ghosts have been due to delusions – or to something seen, or sensed, which is mistaken for a ghost. Nor does it rule out the possibility that hallucinations may have no psychic component. But where hallucinations are found to correspond to some event – the figure of a man being 'seen' or 'heard' by his wife, say, at the time he is dying, hundreds of miles away – Myers classified them as veridical: and although sceptics could claim that the hallucination of a person who at the moment was dying hundreds of miles away could be attributed to coincidence, in many cases a paranormal explanation – at least to anybody who accepted the possibility – was more plausible.

Myers suggested using the term 'phantasm' for such hallucinations, preferring it to 'phantom' or 'apparition' because they had acquired the connotation of visual experiences. The less well known term, Myers proposed, should be adopted to 'signify any hallucinatory impression, whatever sense – whether sight, hearing, touch, smell, taste or diffused sensibility – may happen to be affected'. 'Phantasm', however, did not catch on; and 'apparition', though colloquially it has continued to be used to signify something seen, has been adopted by parapsychologists to describe any hallucinatory impression of a person; and for simplicity, apparitions which are of recognizable men or women have commonly been put into three categories: apparitions of the living; apparitions of the dying; and apparitions of the dead.

The most accomplished medium in modern times: Daniel Dunglas Home (1833-1886)

The founders of
the Society for
Psychical
Research:

Sir William Barrett

Henry Sidgwick

Frederic Myers

Edmund Gurney

Four early Presidents of
the Society for Psychical
Research:

Andrew Lang

Sir William
Crookes

Lord Rayleigh

Sir Oliver Lodge

Four Presidents
of the Society for
Psychical
Research were
distinguished
European
scientists:

Camille
Flammarion

Charles Richet

Hans Driesch

Henri Bergson

The founders of modern parapsychology: *Above left:* William McDougall *Above right:* Joseph Banks Rhine *Below left:* Gardner Murphy *Below right:* Gaither Pratt

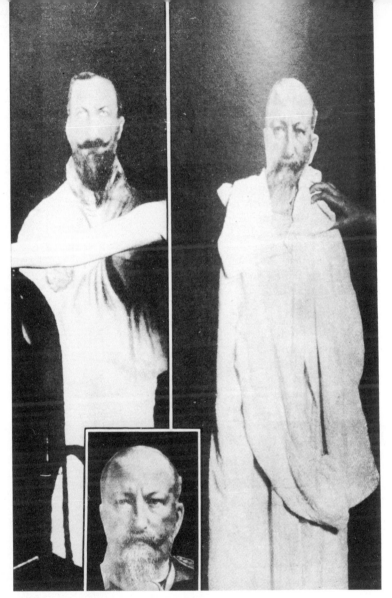

The fact that Marthe Béraud ('Eva C') produced materialisations which in photographs resembled cardboard cut-outs of well-known individuals inevitably aroused scepticism. But the life-size 'King of Bulgaria' (the real king is inset) could hardly have been swallowed and regurgitated, as sceptics alleged

Some of 'Eva C's' materialisations looked as if they were made out of chiffon, as her investigators discovered at the time

Franek Kluski, one of the Polish mediums investigated by Charles Richet and Gustav Geley, was able to materialise 'hands' in soluble wax, which could later be removed from the mould as 'gloves'. Houdini's claim that the trick was done by substitution was rebutted at the time

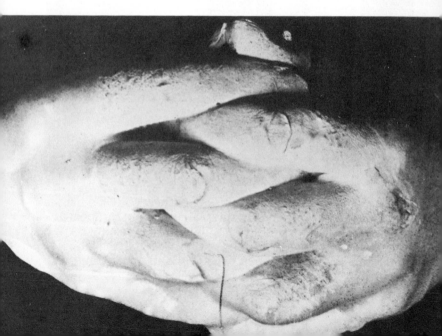

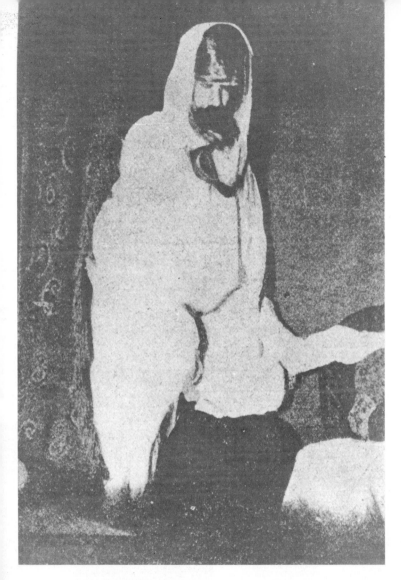

It is not surprising that Marthe Béraud's early 'full-form materialisations' were derided as fakes, when photographs revealed them looking like somebody at a fancy-dress party. But Charles Richet and the other sitters pointed out that Marthe (just visible at the right of the picture) could not have faked the phantom, as it had developed in their full view

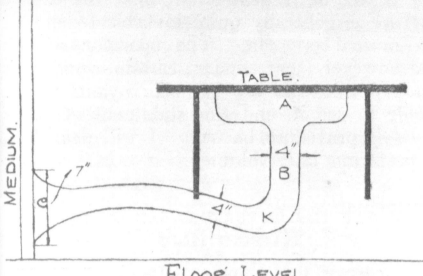

One of W J Crawford's illustrations of the way in which, in the course of careful experiments, he had observed that the medium Kathleen Goligher could levitate a table – initially using the floor as a cantilever. The flow of ectoplasm was sometimes visible, and could be photographed

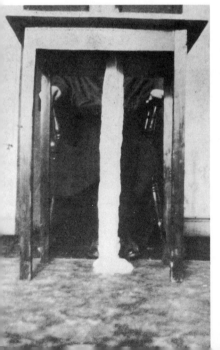

Stanislawa Tomczyk's speciality was levitating small objects between her hands, as if lifting them with an invisible thread. But her investigators were able to satisfy themselves that there was no thread

Houdini demonstrating his supposedly fraud-proof 'box'

Sometimes ectoplasm, flowing from 'Margery' gave her the appearance of somebody at the receiving end of a custard pie

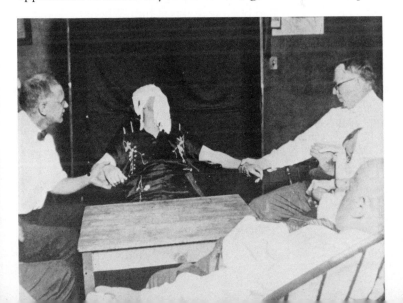

The group photograph described by Air Marshall Sir Victor Goddard in *Flight Towards Reality* and (inset) the face of the dead airman in close-up

When a medium informed Sir Oliver and Lady Lodge of a 'communication' from their son Raymond, who had been killed on the Western Front, he reported 'Raymond' as describing a group photograph taken before his death, in which somebody had been leaning on him. When the Lodges eventually saw the photograph, they were impressed: Raymond is seated on the ground, second from the right

W J Crawford and the medium he investigated, Kathleen Goligher

Eleanor Sidgwick and Mrs Osborne Leonard, the medium who was persuaded to give her exclusive services to the Society for Psychical Research

Examples of thought-transference: the Guthrie experiments in Liverpool. Original drawings are on the left in each case

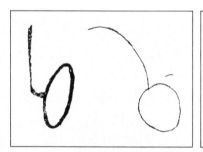

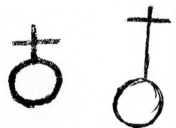

APPARITIONS

The evidence for the reality of veridical hallucinations of all three categories – living, dying, dead – is extensive and well-documented. Gurney, in particular, followed up the case histories he used in *Phantasms* with astonishing persistence: in *The Founders of Psychical Research* (1968) Alan Gauld estimated that he often wrote fifty or more letters a day to elucidate doubtful points or obtain additional attestation. Camille Flammarion's *The Unknown* (1900), and his later three-volume *Death and its Mystery* (1922), were less rigorously checked, and contained a few accounts later shown to be unreliable. Nevertheless a large proportion of the case histories he included came from people of substance – magistrates, men and women in the professions, in the civil service and in industry who were prepared to put their names to their accounts; and the overall impression from his collection, as from Eleanor Sidgwick's 1923 follow-up of the *Census*, is that the same kind of people were having much the same kind of encounters with apparitions as Gurney had found.

Since then, accounts of apparitions have been less frequently published, largely because the emphasis in parapsychology shifted to laboratory-style investigations; but findings presented in the *Journal of the American Society for Psychical Research* in 1962 suggest that if another Gurney were to surface in the US with the time, energy and means to conduct the same inquiry as he did a century ago, the same range of case histories would be collected there – as they have been, in Britain, by Celia Green and Charles McCreery, and presented in their *Apparitions* (1975).

Apparitions of the living are often called doppelgängers (the English equivalent, 'double-ganger', is now rarely seen). The term can apply to any apparition of a living person, but is most commonly applied in cases where an individual has what seems to be a persistent double, which is often encountered.

In a few cases, an individual has been seen in two places at once by several people. The best known account relates to Emélie

Sagée, a teacher at a school for young ladies in Livonia. During a period of over a year in the mid-1840s, she was frequently seen by her pupils inside their class room at the same time as they could 'see' her double outside in the school grounds. Sometimes while she was performing some action, such as writing with a chalk on a blackboard, her double would be seen to behave as if imitating her; but at other times the double acted independently – coming into a room, for example, and sitting down, while Emélie could be seen by the girls walking outside.

Emélie was highly regarded as a teacher, and although the stories of her 'bilocation' soon spread, and were accepted by the directors of the school, they were reluctant to get rid of her until parents, hearing about her, began to withdraw their daughters. She had often been sacked for the same reason from other schools, she lamented to the children; but there was nothing she could do about it. Investigating the tale, Robert Dale Owen claimed that in all his research into the subject he had not come across any example of the apparition of the living 'so remarkable and so incontrovertibly authentic as this'.

More often, the doppelgänger is encountered by people who have just left the person whose double it is; as happened often to Mrs Milman, wife of Archibald Milman, one of the senior secretaries in the Palace of Westminster in the 1890s. By her own account, she was afflicted – her own term for it – by a double. 'The other day a friend took leave of me in my work-room,' she told the London correspondent of *Le Temps*. 'Scarcely had he stepped out of the door, when he found me again on the landing of the stairway. Dumbfounded, he shrank aside to let me pass.' She had never seen her double, but she had heard it; and she had detected it opening doors.

Goethe once saw his own doppelgänger; and on another occasion, a friend's. Walking back with a companion to Weimar, Goethe suddenly stopped: 'If I weren't sure my friend Frederick is at this minute in Frankfurt,' he said, wonderingly, 'I'd swear it was he!' His companion, who saw nobody, became even more alarmed when Goethe said 'it *is* he!' and proceeded to address 'him', asking what 'he' was doing outside, wearing Goethe's own dressing-gown, nightcap and bedroom slippers, on the highway. When Goethe found his companion had seen nothing, he realized that it must have been a hallucination, and was worried in case it should portend that his friend was dead. But no: when Goethe got home he found Frederick sitting there. At first, he was alarmed, fearing it was another hallucination; he was relieved to hear Frederick explain that he had been soaked on the way to the house, and had to get out of his wet clothes.

There was an added twist to the story. Waiting for Goethe to arrive, Frederick had fallen asleep in an armchair and had dreamed that he had gone out to meet his friend, who had questioned him in much the same words that Goethe's companion had heard: 'You here, in Weimar? In my dressing-gown?'

Doppelgängers have not necessarily been respecters of scepticism. In *My Apprenticeship* (1926) the rationalist Beatrice Webb recalled how, when she was in her early twenties, 'for the first and last time', she had seen a ghost. Her sister had upbraided her for 'trying to be a blue-stocking when you are meant to be a pretty woman', and she had retaliated with abuse. Later that morning, when her sister came into her room, she had shouted at her to get out – only to remember, after the door was closed, that her sister had not been wearing her usual clothes. Her sister, she found, was not in the house; she had gone out earlier for a walk. Beatrice sat miserably, 'overcome with superstitious fear lest mishap had befallen her'; but her sister returned none the worse – and none the wiser, as Beatrice did not reveal to her why she had suddenly become penitent that day, until many years later.

Apparitions of the living are not always 'full form': there are accounts of hallucinations of faces. One was described by the naturalist and writer W. H. Hudson in *A Hind in Richmond Park* (1922). He was walking back to his London home when he saw a face he knew: 'so vividly seen that it could not have appeared a more real human face if the girl had actually come before me'. He was very fond of her, and wrote to her parents to inquire if all was well with her; they replied that there was nothing the matter. When he next met her mother, however, she told him that just before getting his letter, to their astonishment their daughter had broken out into a passionate revolt against their authority on a religious question; she had told them 'that she had prayed to Heaven to send me to her assistance – to protect and deliver her from them'.

A different type of doppelgänger which has often been reported is an invisible presence accompanying people, sometimes people who are under stress, and who feel vaguely comforted for having an invisible companion. In his autobiography (1919) the polar explorer Sir Ernest Shackleton recalled how during the 'long and racking ' 36-hour march he had to make with two companions over the glaciers of South Georgia, 'it seemed to me often that we were four, not three'. He said nothing at the time, but afterwards the other two men both confessed to having had the same impression. Shackleton admitted 'the dearth of human words, the roughness of mortal speech', in trying to describe what they had felt; 'but a record of our journeys would be incomplete without a reference to a subject very near to our hearts'.

The most engaging of all the accounts of an apparition of a living person seen by more than one person was provided for the SPR's *Census of Hallucinations* by S. R. Wilmot, a manufacturer from Bridgeport, Conn. *The City of Limerick,* on which he was returning across the Atlantic in 1863, ran into a fierce storm, and for eight days he could get little sleep. On the night when the gale abated, he slept, and dreamed that his wife came to the door in her nightdress; after hesitation, as if realizing he was not alone in the cabin, she 'stooped and kissed me, and after having caressed me a few moments she quietly withdrew'.

When Wilmot woke up, to his astonishment his cabin-mate, William J. Tait, 'a grave and religious man', was looking fixedly at him. 'You are a lucky fellow,' Tait said, 'to have a lady come to visit you like that!' Asked to explain himself, Tait described what he had seen, which corresponded with the dream.

Back in Bridgeport, no sooner was Wilmot alone with his wife than she asked, 'Did you receive my visit a week ago on Tuesday?' Hearing of the storm and of a wreck of another ship on the Atlantic crossing, she had lain awake out of worry; and at four in the morning of the day he had had his dream she had visualized herself crossing the stormy seas, finding the ship, and going to his stateroom. 'There was a man in the upper berth who looked straight at me, and for a moment I was afraid to come in, but at last I came up to you, bent over you, kissed you, pressed you in my arms; and then I went away.' The description she gave of the steamer and the stateroom, according to Wilmot, was 'correct in all its details'; and Wilmot's sister, who was also on *The City of Limerick,* confirmed that Tait had asked her whether it was she who had come down to see her brother.

Apparitions of the dying may not be the commonest type of veridical paranormal hallucination, but they tend to make the most impact. Usually they are either seen, or heard: but in some cases the percipient has both seen and heard the dying person.

In the booklet *The Return of Peter Grimm* which accompanied the production of the play of that name, David Belasco described how he had been moved to write it by his mother's coming to him at the time of her death. He was asleep in his New York home when he woke and 'saw' her, though he knew she was in San Francisco. She was standing by him, smiling, calling him by his boyhood name 'Davy, Davy, Davy', and telling him not to grieve, as all was well and she was happy; and then she vanished. Certain that this portended his mother was dead, he warned his family; and a few hours later a telegram arrived to say she had died 'at about the time I had seen her in my room. Later, I learned that just before she died she roused herself, smiled and three times murmured "Davy, Davy, Davy".' Thought-transference, he explained in the booklet, seemed to him a totally inadequate explanation, so 'after long brooding on the subject, I determined to write a play, in terms of what I conceived to be actuality, dealing with the return of the dead'.

The case most often cited of how 'real' an apparition of a dying person can be was described in 1918 in a letter from a young member of the Royal Flying Corps, James Larkin, to the father of a fellow officer, David McConnel. One afternoon Larkin was sitting in his room when the door opened 'with the usual noise and clatter which David always made. I heard his "Hello boy", and I turned round in my chair and saw him standing in the doorway, dressed in his flying clothes.' They exchanged a few words; 'I was looking at him the whole time he was speaking. He said, "Well, cheerio!", closed the door noisily and went out'. At, or very close to, the time 'David' was visiting his friend, Larkin heard later that day, he had lost control of the aircraft he was flying, crashed and been killed. Describing the episode for the benefit of the SPR, Larkin claimed that although he had heard of such happenings, he had never believed in them. He had always been sceptical; but could be sceptical no longer.

In the commonest type of apparition, however, the figure is seen, but does not communicate, except by its expression. While Ben Jonson was staying with his friend the Scots poet William

Drummond, the plague was raging in London. According to Drummond, who kept a record of their conversations, Jonson one day 'saw' his eldest son, then a child and in London, 'with the mark of a bloodie cross on his forehead, as if it had been cutted with a sword'; and soon afterwards came a letter to say the boy had died of the plague.

On the night of 22–23 July 1813, the Duchess of Abrantes, wife of Marshal Junot, who was in Geneva, awoke and 'saw distinctly, near my bed, Junot dressed in the same grey coat he wore the day of his departure', his face pale and profoundly sad, and 'what terrified me most was to see the apparition walking round my bed, and yet – heavens! – one of its legs was broken'. Junot, depressed by the defeat of his army in Spain (where he had received his title, following the capture of Abrantes) and at Napoleon's consequent coolness to him, had gone to stay at his father's house, and in his depression had thrown himself out of a window, breaking his leg. He died on 29 July.

Apparitions of the dying have quite often manifested themselves as if to fulfil a promise made during their lives. On 18 December 1799 Henry Brougham – later to be Lord Chancellor in the Whig Government which carried the Reform Act of 1832 – was enjoying a hot bath in a Scandinavian inn when, being about to get out of it, he turned to look at the chair on which he had put his clothes. Sitting on it was 'G', his most intimate friend at school and university. G and he had often discussed the possibility of survival in the spirit after death, 'and we actually committed the folly of drawing up an agreement, *written with our blood*, that whichever of us died the first should appear to the other, and thus resolve any doubts we had entertained of the "life after death".' After graduation G had gone to India; they had rarely corresponded; and Brougham had almost forgotten G until there 'he' was, on the chair. 'How I got out of the bath I know not, but on recovering my senses, I found myself sprawling on the floor' – the apparition having by this time disappeared.

That it was a dream, Brougham felt he could not doubt; yet the fact that he had had no communication with G for years, and that nothing had happened to bring him to mind, left him unable to get rid of the feeling that G must have died. When he was back in Edinburgh, a letter arrived from India 'announcing G's death, and stating that he had died on the 19th December'. Characteristically, Brougham described this as a 'singular coincidence'.

In a letter to Flammarion, the Princess de Montarcý recalled that her grandmother had always said that if they were not together when she was dying, 'I'll let you know I'm dead'. One evening at nine o'clock the princess's dog jumped up on her bed, 'howling as if he were being killed'; she looked up, and at the foot of her bed saw the apparition of her grandmother 'just as I had seen her last, but pale. She threw me a kiss, and disappeared.' The following morning, a telegram informed the princess that her grandmother had died between eight and nine the previous evening.

The argument for a paranormal element in such cases is obviously strengthened when there is some form of corroboration – such as, in the Junot instance, the broken leg. A similar type of case was narrated by Archdeacon Farler, who, one night in 1868, 'saw' a friend of his, a fellow-student, sitting at the foot of his bed, dripping water. Realizing it was a hallucination, Farler told the family with whom he was staying in Somerset what he had 'seen'; and a few days later they heard that his friend had been drowned while swimming off the Kent coast.

In 1863 Baroness de Boislève gave a dinner to, among others, General Fleury, Master of the Horse to the Emperor Napoleon III, and two judges. Her son Honoré was in the expeditionary force in Mexico, and she was relieved to hear from the General that there was nothing new from it to report. But at nine, when she went to the drawing-room to see if the coffee was ready, she gave a loud cry, and fainted. She had 'seen' her son, she explained when she recovered, in his uniform, but capless; his face 'a spectral pallor', and from his left eye, 'now a hideous hole, a trickle of blood flowed over his cheek'. A week later, the news came that Honoré had been killed by a Mexican bullet through his left eye: 'when the time difference was allowed for it was realized she had seen the apparition at the day and hour of his death'. And in this case, the story was unusually well-documented because the family doctor, a member of the Academy of the Sciences, sent in a report signed by all the distinguished guests who had been present.

An apparition described by the Canadian biologist and psychologist G. J. Romanes, a Fellow of the Royal Society, in a letter to Myers had no attestation, but it impressed Myers because

191

Romanes, though interested in what the psychical researchers were doing, was in the rationalist camp with Tyndall, Huxley and Darwin. It described how in 1878, at a time when Romanes believed himself to be awake, he saw the bedroom door open and a shrouded figure walk to the foot of his bed. 'Then with its two hands it suddenly parted the shroud over the face, revealing between its two hands the face of my sister.' When he exclaimed her name, she vanished. Although his sister was ill, Romanes had no idea that there was anything serious the matter with her; but when he called in Sir William Jenner, he was told she had only a few days to live, which proved correct. Myers commented that Romanes had more than once told him how deep an impression the incident had made on him; adding that there were other, unpublished circumstances which confirmed Romanes in the view that he had seen an apparition.

In a few cases, an apparition of somebody dying has been seen by more than one person. In 1785 two young officers, Sir John Sherbrook and George Wynyard (who was later to become a general), were sitting in Wynyard's room in barracks in Nova Scotia when a man whom Wynyard recognized as his brother John walked slowly through the room and into the bedroom. When they followed him, he was nowhere to be seen. Fearing the worst they made a note of the date, intending to keep the episode to themselves; but it quickly spread. When the next mail arrived from England, it disclosed that John Wynyard had died on the same day, and at the same time, as he had been 'seen' in the barrack room. Sherbrook had never seen John Wynyard in his lifetime; but in Piccadilly some time later he saw somebody so like the apparition that he could not resist the opportunity to introduce himself, and it turned out to be another Wynyard brother.

A case in Sir Ernest Bennett's collection was contributed by Miss Godley, daughter of Lord Kilbracken of Killegar in County Leitrim, Ireland. One afternoon she had been to visit Robert Bowes, an old farm labourer on the estate, who was ill. As she had broken her leg, she went in a donkey-trap, with a steward in front and her masseuse behind; and when she got to the cottage talked to Bowes through an open window. 'He sat up, and talked quite well, but said he would like to see the doctor.' On the way back the road ran beside a lake, and all three of them saw an old man with a white beard crossing to the other side, as if he were using a punt pole. Miss Godley could see no boat; when she asked the steward, he replied 'there is no boat'. Who, he asked, did she think it looked like? It looked to them all like Robert Bowes. When she got back she was about to write a note to the doctor when he arrived. He had just been to Bowes, he said; 'the old chap is dead'.

'Did Robert, as he left this world, cross to take a last look at his old haunts,' she mused, 'where he had worked all his life?' There was no boat on the lake, when they went to look; and he had been quite plainly seen by all three of them – as the steward and the masseuse ('I am not in the least given to seeing visions, but being of an extremely practical nature, I certainly saw the spectre') confirmed.

Apparitions of the dying have often been heard, rather than seen. There were so many accounts of auditory manifestations at the time of somebody's death sent to Flammarion that, he claimed, instead of devoting only a chapter to them he could easily have made a book out of them. Among his examples was one related by Carl Linné, better known as Linnaeus, generally regarded as the founder of modern botany. One night in 1766 he and his wife were awoken by the sound of someone walking up and down with heavy steps in his museum. He knew nobody could be there, as he had locked the doors and had the key with him. He recognized the sound of the footsteps: they were of his dearest friend Karl Clerk – 'it was his step, undoubtedly'. A few days later, he heard Clerk had died '*at precisely the same hour*'.

In his life of Sir Walter Scott, Lockhart included a letter describing 'a mysterious disturbance ' in his Selkirk house. Two nights earlier Scott and his wife had been woken up around two in the morning by a violent noise, 'like drawing heavy boards along the new part of the house'. He thought no more about it: but the next night, 'at the same witching hour, the very same noise occurred' – so alarming his wife that Scott got up, carrying a sword, to investigate; but nothing was out of order. Although Scott was baffled, he refused to admit the possibility of an apparition; 'if there was no entrance but the key-hole, I would warrant myself against the ghosts'. Scott did not then know it but, as Lockhart recalled, George Bullock, the designer and builder Scott had employed, had died 'at the very hour when Scott was roused by the "mysterious disturbance"'. According to Lockhart, this left a stronger impression on Scott than he was prepared to admit.

The likelihood that simple coincidence can account for cases of this kind is also reduced when what is 'heard' corresponds with what the dying person is subsequently found to have been saying. The editor of *Annales des Sciences Psychiques,* César de Vesme, described one such episode in 1907, when a Bordeaux woman was awakened three times by a voice calling her name, Jeanne, in anguish. Later, she was told that her former fiancé, who had been prevented from marrying her by his family, had died that night in Noyon, after several times crying out her name.

The commonest of all auditory hallucinations linked with somebody's death are raps or bangs. Alexandre Dumas the elder used to recall that although he was only three when his father died, they had adored each other; when it was realized that the father was dying, it had been deemed wise to have the child out of the way, and he had been sent to stay in another house. At midnight he and his young cousin were woken up '*by a loud blow struck on the door*' – an inner door, which nobody could have struck, as the outer doors were closed. Alexandre got up, saying he was going to open the door for his father, 'who's come to say good bye to us'; but his terrified cousin held him back. The next morning, he was told his father was dead; he had 'died at precisely the time at which this loud blow, of which I have spoken, had been struck upon the door!'

One of Flammarion's collection of auditory hallucinations is another instance of a promise to return on dying being fulfilled. A correspondent sent him an account of a girl, Clementine, who after a wretched life with a drunken father had decided to enter a convent. When her aunt, who had given Clementine refuge after she left her father, lamented that they would never meet again, the girl jestingly replied that as she knew she had not long to live, she would make her presence felt when she died: 'I know you are not afraid; I'll make an outrageous racket for you.' Some time afterwards her aunt, about to go to bed, heard a terrible uproar; the bricks of the house appeared to be knocking against one another, and the roof to have fallen in, but there was no sign of any damage. 'Clementine is dead', her aunt announced. The noise stopped; and the next day a telegram informed the household that Clementine had died at the hour they had heard the din.

194

Clairsentient hallucinations of the dying have only rarely been reported, but one case appeared in the *Annales des Sciences Psychiques* in 1919. In 1893 the commander of the training ship *Iphigènie*, sailing off Antibes, felt as if a child had got on to his bunk and kissed him; striking a light, he found nothing. When the *Iphigènie* reached Gibraltar, he heard that at the time of his hallucination his 2-year-old son had died of diphtheria; and when he met his family, they told him that his son had died kissing his father's photograph, saying 'Papa . . . boat . . . on the water'.

The oddest of all stories connected with apparitions of the dying was related in 1905 in an Italian journal devoted to psychical research, *Luce e Ombra*. In a light-hearted moment Count Charles Galateri, who believed in survival after death, and his friend M. Virgini, who did not, had agreed that whichever of them died first would tickle the other's feet. One night six years later Galateri's wife, in bed with him, complained that her foot was being tickled. When they pulled back the bedclothes, nothing could be found to account for the sensation; but when they had put out the candle the Countess exclaimed that she could see a young man with a colonial helmet on his head, looking at her husband and laughing. She was shocked to see that he had a terrible wound in his chest, and a broken knee; yet he waved at her husband – who could see nothing – 'with a satisfied air' before he vanished.

The next day the Countess told her friends about the experience; and a few days later the newspapers reported the death of Virgini in action against the Abyssinians, struck on the knee by a bullet, and then killed by another bullet in the chest. Repeating the story in *Annales des Sciences Psychiques* the following month, César de Vesme regretted that there had not been written attestation of the apparition before the news arrived of Virgini's death. But he knew personally the Galateri family, and some of the friends who had heard the Countess tell of her experience at the time; and he could vouch for their being trustworthy.

Another account of a pledge redeemed, in Flammarion's collection, concerned Beniamino Sirchia, a leading patriot in the Italian struggle for independence. He had jestingly told his friend and medical adviser Dr Vincenzo Caltagirone, a highly sceptical rationalist, that after his death he would try and return and break something in the doctor's room, preferably the hanging lamp above the table. A few months later the doctor and his sister, sitting in the room, heard taps on the lampshade, 'as if made by knuckles', a phenomenon repeated for four or five evenings, until eventually 'a loud sharp blow' broke the lamp's detachable china cap in two, though the pieces remained hanging. The next day, he heard a noise in the dining-room, as if the table had been struck with a stick. Half of the detachable cap was lying there, he found, *as if placed there by a human hand*'. The doctor had so far forgotten Sirchia's pledge that it did not occur to him to link it with what had been happening until a few days later, when he was told that Sirchia had died shortly before the tappings had first been heard. For all his rationalism, Caltagirone had to admit he was particularly impressed by the strange fact that when Sirchia's objective had been attained, 'as if to emphasize it, came the loud blow of announcement; and the deliberate placing of the half cap in a place where it could not have fallen naturally'.

Of other ways in which dying has been accompanied by what appear to be psychokinetic effects, among the commonest have been the stopping of clocks, and the falling of pictures of the dying person. In his *Minds and Motion* (1978) D. Scott Rogo recalls that when James Hyslop, who ran the American Society for Psychical Research, died in 1920, his daughter's watch stopped; and later when his old friend Dr Elwood Worcester, founder of the Emmanuel Movement, half facetiously challenged Hyslop to return after death, if he really was around in the spirit, one of the clocks in Worcester's home stopped and another began to chime incessantly for no reason, until Worcester was compelled to remove the chiming mechanism.

A 'truthful and sincere correspondent', Mlle Vera Kunzler of Naples, told Flammarion of the occasion when, at 10.30 A.M. on 12 February 1917, a portrait of her uncle, 'a large one which showed him in military uniform, detached itself from the wall, fell, and slid over the floor' coming to rest by her aunt's feet; when the nail and cord which had held up the picture were examined, there was nothing the matter with them. Convinced that something must have happened to her husband, who was at the Front, the aunt put a cross in red against the date. Three weeks later she was informed that he had been killed on the day, and at the time, of the picture's fall.

Most of the well-known and well-attested accounts of apparitions of the dead are associated with the places where they lived, and fall into the 'haunting' category; but there are some where the apparition of a dead person pays a visit elsewhere.

On the day the first world war ended Harold Owen, an officer on a Royal Navy cruiser, found it impossible to enter into the spirit of the festivities: 'something, I knew, was wrong. Monstrous depression clasped hold of me.' A few days later, when they sailed for the Cameroons, he went down to his cabin intending to write some letters and to his amazement he saw his poet brother, Wilfred Owen, sitting in his chair. 'He did not rise, I saw that he was involuntarily immobile; but his eyes, which had never left mine, were alive with the familiar look of trying to make me understand; when I spoke his whole face broke into the sweetest and most endearing dark smile.' Wilfred was in his army uniform: 'I remember thinking how out of place the khaki looked amongst the cabin furnishings. With this thought I must have turned my eyes away from him; when I looked again my chair was empty.' Soon, he was to hear that Wilfred had been killed in action on the Western Front, shortly before the armistice.

There have been many accounts of apparitions of the dead seeking to right some wrong. Aubrey described one, 'much talked of', which appeared to the sister of Dr Turbervile of Salisbury, telling her about the injustice done to the children of her marriage by the fact that their father, who after her death had married again, had broken the agreed settlement – and also telling her where it had been hidden; 'by which means right was done to the first wife's children' – an account which Turbervile affirmed was correct.

While Justinus Kerner was treating the 'Seeress of Prevorst' (and investigating her psychic powers), she complained to him that an apparition, a man with a squint, kept waking her up to tell her about some dubious financial transaction in his lifetime, for which another man had been unjustly blamed. The apparition told her where a document, clearing the name of the innocent man, would be found; and the description enabled Kerner to tell the local judge not merely where the document was, but what it would look like, even down to a 'small and long-standing bending of the corner of the paper'. The wronged man was no longer alive to enjoy his rehabilitation, but his widow could rejoice that his name had been cleared; and the spirit with the squint ceased to plague the Seeress with his importunities.

Another case of a similar nature was reported to, and checked by, Count Perovsky Petrovo-Solovovo, a keen but sceptical psychical researcher, and passed to Myers for his collection. Nicolai Pono-mareff and his son-in-law, Baron Basil von Driesen, had for some years been estranged. But after Ponomareff died, in the small hours of the morning before a liturgy was to be read for the repose of his soul, von Driesen was woken up by sounds outside his door; and when he struck a match, he 'saw' his father-in-law standing in front of the closed door in his dressing-gown. 'I have acted wrongly towards you,' the apparition said. 'Forgive me' – and he held out his hand – 'without this I do not feel at rest there.' The Baron seized the hand, 'which was long and cold', and shook it; the apparition moved away and disappeared.

The Baron, who was sceptical in such matters, initially attributed the apparition to his 'excited fancy'. But the service the next day was celebrated by the confessor to both men, whose name was also Basil; and following it, the priest took the Baron aside and told him, 'this night at three o'clock Nicolai Ponomareff appeared to me and begged me to reconcile him to you'. Perovsky contacted Fr Basil to find out whether the story was true; the priest assured him it was.

Another fairly commonly reported category of apparition is of people seen performing the same actions as they did when they were alive – as Robert Bowes was doing when Miss Godley saw him. Wilson Carlile, founder of the Church Army and Prebendary of St Paul's Cathedral, told Ernest Bennett of an occasion when, as a member of the congregation in a Woking parish church on a Sunday in 1932, he was about to offer his assistance during holy communion to the rector, as he was accustomed to do, when he saw that another clergyman, the Rev. Outram Marshal, an old friend, was assisting. But it transpired after the service that Marshal had *not* been assisting, he had died earlier that morning. The rector had been surprised when Carlile did not offer his services; and he assured Carlile that there had been no other clergyman. At first Carlile 'strongly asserted' that he had seen the surpliced man: only then did it dawn on him that 'it must have been Outram Marshal; God allowed him to help once again'.

Another dead person whose apparition continued to act as the living had done was the wife of Dr Eustace, Chairman of the Arundel Bench of Magistrates. A few weeks after his wife's death, he told Bennett, he had 'seen' her, standing on the lawn, looking at him with an expression which he interpreted as remonstrating with him for his doubts about survival after death. When he told his sister-in-law about the hallucination – as he regarded it; he shared the still far from uncommon fear that it might be the prelude to mental derangement – she replied that she had just met an old lady from the village who, at about the same time as Eustace had his hallucination, had been to a church service where his 'wife' had actually helped her – as she had often done before – to her seat, and later to the confessional. When the old lady was told this was impossible, as Mrs Eustace was dead, she refused to believe it.

Reports of animal apparitions are common: usually of pets who have died not long before they are 'seen' – or 'heard', as in the account in Celia Green and Charles McCreery's *Apparitions* (1975) by the owners of 'a very beloved old dog Snap', who, because of his age and stiffening joints, always went upstairs 'with the typical "ker-flop, ker-flop" noise they make when they put both front paws on one step and then take the hind feet up on to the same step'. The night after the dog had had to be put down, both his owner and her mother, in separate rooms, 'heard old Snap come "ker-flop, ker-flop" upstairs', at the same time.

'Snap' was never heard again; but some apparitions of pets have been reported as behaving as if they were haunting their old home. A large black cat used to be 'seen' quite frequently by a mother and her daughter, who decided not to tell anybody in case the house acquired the reputation of being haunted. Eventually, however, their 'daily' told them she thought she must be going daft as she kept thinking she saw a cat jump off a chair and run off. And when the mother, hearing of Celia Green's request for stories of apparitions, decided to write to tell her about the ghost cat, and mentioned it to her husband, he said 'Oh, *that* cat'. He had not said anything, he explained, in case it would make her nervous.

Folklore

A further category of apparitions are those which are familiar in folklore: fairies, gnomes, dryads, trolls, hobgoblins and many more. Whether they ought to be considered as paranormal phenomena, as distinct from fantasies, remains in contention:

many parapsychologists would dismiss them as a superstition. Others, however, accept that they may fall into the category of hallucinations, which certain people – those with psychic faculties – may be able to see, and even communicate with: sometimes even to photograph. Although the controversy about the photographs of the 'Cottingley fairies', which appeared with an article by Conan Doyle in the *Strand* magazine, has recently been terminated by the admission of the girls (now elderly ladies) who took them that they were faked, their explanation as to *why* they were faked remains that as children they did see the fairies, and used cut-outs only to 'prove' to their parents that the fairies were really there. As Doyle pointed out at the time, too, he had also been given a number of accounts by people of impeccable reputation of encounters they had had with fairies; and he offered, as an analogy, the notion that fairies might materialize and de-materialize on the same principle as an amphibian can move between land and water, disappearing from view when it sinks beneath the water's surface.

That 'seeing fairies' represents a hallucinatory experience is at least a plausible hypothesis; particularly as the type of fairy seen (or heard) tends to be related to expectations. Whether the varieties have any autonomous existence as discarnate entities or, as some students of the lore have surmised, should be regarded as nuclei, capable of taking different forms according to circumstances (and expectations) remains to be discovered.

It seems very likely that folklore tales, particularly 'fairy stories', condition people as young children to 'see' or 'hear' apparitions they would expect. The Irish 'see' leprechauns, and 'hear' banshees – species rarely, if ever, encountered in England. A commonly reported apparition in England is of a large black dog; in Ireland it is more commonly a wolfhound, sometimes seen, more often heard. But the temptation to explain apparitions away glibly as the product of childhood conditioning is sometimes upset by a case history. One of the contributors to the collection in Green and McCreery's *Apparitions* was an Englishwoman who, while staying in the West of Ireland, had taken her Cairn terrier for a walk when she suddenly 'heard the heavy panting breathing of an enormous dog' beside her. The terrier was terrified, its hair standing on end. This happened twice, in the same place; and the local vicar told her that she 'had undoubtedly heard and felt the presence of the Irish Wolf Hound, who was said to go for walks with people'.

HAUNTINGS

Hauntings are ordinarily so-called because they are experienced in a particular locality, often a dwelling. Haunted houses, Andrew Lang realized from his protracted study of the subject, 'have been familiar to man ever since he has owned a roof to cover his head'; they have been reported from tribesmen's huts and crofters' cottages, from monasteries and palaces; they featured in Egyptian papyri; St Augustine wrote about them as familiar occurrences; and Lang himself could provide many a carefully attested account from his own experience.

Surprisingly, in his experience visual apparitions featured only rarely. By far the most frequent manifestation of a haunting was a noise: 'the frou-frou or rustling sweep of a gown, footsteps, raps, thumps, groans, a sound as if all the heavy furniture was being knocked about, crashing of crockery and jingling of money'. Most of the noises could be relatively easily counterfeited, and some could be accounted for by natural causes, such as the creaking of old timber. But whereas it was easy to suggest that ghostly footsteps could be attributed to a joker, 'this explanation is rather more difficult when the steps pace a gallery, passing and repassing among curious inquirers'.

The 'creaking of old timber' explanation, Lang added, was also inadequate to explain how, in some accounts, some people could hear the sounds, while others could not; and he cited the experience of Admiral Lord St Vincent, who while staying with his sister did not hear the sounds which were terrifying her until she summoned up the courage to tell him; only then did he begin to hear them, too.

Agreeing with Lang that 'the essential characteristic of a true haunt is that it is related to a place', René Sudre in his *Treatise on Parapsychology* (1960) remarked that although the phenomena were often thought of as legendary, their frequency had not in fact decreased: 'even in modern scientific civilization haunted houses and places are reported in all countries'.

When the haunter is a phantom, ghost or spectre, Sudre asserted, it is not, contrary to tradition, 'dressed in a white shroud, but in the normal clothes it wore when alive'. Usually it is intangible, in that it cannot be grasped and can pass through walls or closed doors; usually, though not invariably, it ignores living people. In the majority of cases the haunting is connected with (or believed to be) a tragic event or a death. In his *Phenomena of Haunting* (1920) Ernesto Bozzano showed that of nearly four hundred cases he had studied, four out of five were of this kind (in 27 of them, walled-up corpses had been uncovered). Contrary to a common impression, however, Bozzano found that very few of the cases were related to the time, or the date, of the tragic event. Phantoms rarely kept anniversaries.

Accounts of hauntings appear in classical literature: Pliny the Younger tells the story of Athenodorus the philosopher who, hearing that a house was going cheaply in Athens because it was infested by a ghost wandering round in clanking chains, decided to take the risk and rent it. The ghost duly appeared; but Athenodorus had the good sense, when he saw that it was beckoning to him, to follow until it pointed to a place in the grounds. He informed the magistrates; they had the place dug up; a skeleton in chains was disinterred, taken away and given a proper burial; and Athenodorus could sleep undisturbed.

Ghost stories of this kind appear to have been commonplace in all eras; but by the 19th century it was becoming unfashionable to admit to believing them, even after personally experiencing the phenomena. In 'The Haunting of Lew House', for example, the Rev. Sabine Baring-Gould, author of the hymns 'Onward Christian Soldiers' and 'Now the Day is Over', described sights and sounds characteristic of hauntings, but felt compelled to explain them away. Members of his family had 'seen' the White Lady who haunted the avenue leading to his home, and the long gallery within; his mother had often heard her footsteps passing by the bedroom door, and had continued to hear them even when she had opened the bedroom door – thinking it was her husband – to look out, only to realize there was nobody there to make them. '*Rats* – that is my explanation', Baring-Gould insisted. When he and his wife both heard three heavy strokes 'as if made by a clenched fist' on the partition between their bedroom and his dressing room, the night before one of their children died, it was only 'the starting of the timber'. Even when Baring-Gould and his guests heard not just unaccountable footsteps, but steps 'with a dragging sound, as of a trailing silk or satin dress', he declined to take seriously the notion that the house really was haunted.

When the SPR was founded in 1882, one of its committees was established to investigate reports, 'resting on strong testimony', regarding disturbances in houses reputed to be haunted; and the committee was soon able to record that its search for such testimony had been 'fruitful beyond our expectations'. Of the numerous case histories proffered to the Society and carefully checked, the one reported as 'A Record of a Haunted House' in the Society's *Proceedings* in 1892 has generally been regarded as the most convincing because, as Andrew MacKenzie has observed in his *Hauntings and Apparitions* (1982), one of the Society's centenary series, the apparition of a tall woman in black was frequently seen by seventeen people, at different times – and heard by more than twenty.

The 'tall woman in black' moved around the Despard family's house in Cheltenham as if resident, and was sometimes mistaken for a guest by visitors who were unaware the house was haunted. What made the reports of such casual sightings in the house, or its grounds, impressive was their consistency; not just about the phantom's appearances, but also the fact that she held a handker-chief to the lower part of the face. Sometimes she would come into a room and stay for several minutes; when she walked out of it, she would sometimes be seen to do so independently by another of the family or a servant outside. Frequently, too, the family would hear sounds coming from parts of the house where nobody could be found. They consisted of walking up and down on the second-floor landing, of bumps against the doors of the bedrooms, and of the handles of the doors turning.

Sometimes the tall lady was seen at the same time by two or more people; at other times, one member of the family would see her, but not others. She was also seen by domestic servants – who were sometimes terrified, not surprisingly, as when they were engaged they were not warned that the house was haunted, or they would have been unlikely to come. Those who could be reassured soon became accustomed to the sounds, and occasionally to seeing the tall lady. Members of the family also came to take her almost for granted. One of them, Rosina Despard, tried her hand at some research, fastening fine string at varying heights across the stairs which the tall lady could be heard descending. They remained unbroken when the footsteps had reached the bottom, and twice Rosina actually saw the tall lady 'pass through the cords, leaving them intact'. Rosina also tried to feel the phantom: 'I have repeatedly followed it into a corner, when it disappeared; and have tried suddenly to pounce upon it, but have never succeeded in touching it.'

The accumulation of reports about the tall lady, over a period of seven years, made it difficult to dismiss the haunting as a delusion, or a hoax. Besides, as Andrew MacKenzie found, there is confirmation from other sources, including a letter written to the SPR in 1944 by a well-known solicitor, not a member of the Despard family, recalling how he, as a young boy, had seen the ghost on a number of occasions: 'a tall female figure dressed in black and with a handkerchief held to her face as if crying'. In his recollection – as in Rosina Despard's – '"she" was substantial' – not translucent. The solicitor, who identified himself but did not wish his name to be revealed, claimed that he clearly remembered two occasions: '(1) in the garden in bright sunlight walking about, and (2) in the drawing-room when we made a ring round her by joining hands, from which she appeared merely to walk out between two people and then disappeared'.

In spite of the wealth of evidence about haunting presented by Gurney, Myers and others towards the close of the 19th century, research into the subject remained suspect, and although the activities of the self-proclaimed ghost hunter, Harry Price, brought him a great deal of publicity in the years between the wars, it was of a kind which made most psychical researchers nervous, and discouraged people who might otherwise have contributed accounts of their experiences from doing so, for fear they would feature in the popular press.

A few well-known individuals, however, have had the courage to brave ridicule by affirming that they have had psychic experiences. One of them, L. A. G. Strong, who enjoyed a considerable reputation as a novelist in the years between the wars, described an occasion when he had seen a phantom who haunted the masters' residence at the Oxford preparatory school where Strong was teaching at the time. He saw a man with a brown moustache, carrying music under his arm, go into the room occupied by another master, Strong's friend W. S. Case. Assuming it was Case, who also had a moustache and could be expected to be carrying music, Strong went over to his room – and found nobody there. At this point, Case arrived. Realizing Strong looked odd, he asked what had happened; and when Strong told him, said 'Oh, that was Winford Allington. He was killed in 1917. He played the organ here before me. This was his room.'

Yet many people who had been convinced by personal experience of this kind of the reality of a haunting often declined to testify for the benefit of the Society for Psychical Research, as Bennett found when he was collecting material for his *Apparitions and Haunted Houses* (1939).

He managed to obtain a few good cases, including an unusual one, in that the apparition was seen by people who were unaware that it *was* an apparition, at the time. Fourteen people had come to tea one 1932 afternoon in a London suburb, with Mrs Blanche Hornsby; and four saw a man who looked to them as if he were something to do with the law. The first their hostess knew about it was when they asked afterwards who he was; and she had to tell them that no such man had been there. Curious, Mrs Hornsby rang up the others who had been present, and one, Dame Rachel Crowdy, principal commandant of the VADs in the first world war, gave her the same description as the others, telling her where the man had been sitting – 'she entirely declined to believe he was not there'. Dame Rachel corroborated Mrs Hornsby's account five years later. 'I noticed him rather specially because he was spending his time reading some papers, and I wondered how he could do it with all of us talking around him.' She still, she told Bennett, 'found it hard to believe that he was not one of the guests'.

Bennett regarded this as one of the best-attested cases he had come across. It was only rarely, however, that he was able to obtain attestation of this kind, much to his irritation, as he indicated when he related a narrative which he had been sent from the University of Leeds. It described how 'Mr H', cycling home one night along Wensleydale, saw a lady walking towards him wearing a crinoline-shaped ankle-length dress. This, he later heard from a friend, was 'the black lady', well-known to residents; and he was given the names of four of them, all men, who claimed to have seen her. Each confirmed that they had seen her, on the same lonely stretch of road. 'These men,' he told Bennett – he knew them all well – 'do not romance.' Nor, to judge by the sobriety of the account, did the author of it, who stressed that this was his only experience of the kind. But he could not induce any of the witnesses to give their accounts, even anonymously. Bennett ordinarily felt bound to exclude stories which were not formally attested by witnesses; but he included this one to show just how difficult it was to get such corroboration from people about experiences of hauntings, even when they were assured their identities would not be disclosed, for fear they might incur ridicule. '*Gegen Dummheit kämpfen die Götter vergebens!*' he sighed: against stupidity even the gods battle in vain.

Another reason for the decline of attested reports of hauntings, Bennett realized, was that there was no longer the same enthusiasm among members of the Society for Psychical Research for investigating cases. He cited the experience of the Bull family, who lived in Ramsbury, Wiltshire. In 1932, several months after his death, 'Grandpa' Bull began to appear to his family, in the clothes he had worn. All the family recognized him, as did visitors. Sometimes he appeared by day, sometimes by night; and he would stay around for as long as half an hour. The local vicar, called in, satisfied himself that the haunting was genuine, and eventually the case was brought to the SPR's attention, the vicar urging haste, as the cottage had been condemned as unsafe and the family were about to move; but the investigators – Lord Balfour and J. G. Piddington, both past Presidents of the Society – delayed too long. On the evidence available, Bennett felt, the case was unique: 'the figure which showed itself with such frequency seemed solid and life-like, and I do not know of any other narrative of this kind where the witnesses of a collective apparition were so numerous' – sometimes 'Grandpa Bull' had been seen by no fewer than nine people.

The evidence for the reality of haunting by apparitions, visible or invisible, is strengthened by the numerous accounts of the reactions of domestic animals when they have been involved: from Balaam's ass – which saw the Angel of the Lord barring the way and refused to proceed even when thrashed – down to the present day. The mastiff which belonged to the Wesley family used to 'bark and leap and snap' when the Epworth Rectory poltergeist was about to play its tricks, 'and that frequently before any person in the room heard any noise at all. But after two or three days he used to tremble, and creep away before the noise began. And by this time the family knew it was at hand; nor did the observation ever fail.' In the Cheltenham haunting, when the tall lady was around a retriever which spent its nights in the kitchen would sometimes be found in a terrified state in the morning. On two occasions a Skye terrier was seen to run to the foot of the stairs, wagging its tail; it 'jumped up, fawning as it would do if a person had been standing there, but suddenly slunk away with its tail between its legs and retreated, trembling, under a sofa'.

Describing his stay at 'the house on the lake' in *The Invisible Writing*, the second volume of his autobiography, Arthur Koestler recalled that when he went for a walk with his hostess, Maria Kloepfer, in 1935, her old mongrel dog Ricky suddenly stopped, 'and gave out a growl which then changed into a plaintive, long-drawn howl', its hair bristling. Maria hurried back to the house: it was the apparition of an uncle, she explained, who had sexually assaulted her, before dying, a schizophrenic, when she was three. He occasionally manifested himself, terrifyingly, advancing on her as if from three directions at once; but sometimes, as on this occasion, Ricky 'sensed the approach of the uncle before she saw him and warned her'.

Another author, Ann Bridge, has recalled in her *Moments of Knowing* (1970) how the horses which her family used to ride through Windsor Great Park would always shy violently when they came to a certain point on a roadside grass verge, 'to the point of leaving the grass for the road'. And while she was staying at Government House in the Isle of Man, on a visit she made there during the second world war, she noticed that every evening in the course of dinner the dogs would get up, growling, their hackles rising. 'It's only Lord So-and-so,' her host, Lord Granville, explained; 'he always comes in about this time.'

The dogs, however, welcomed another visitor, invisible to her or the Granvilles: 'They would suddenly jump up, race across towards the house and greet some invisible person with welcoming barks – and then follow him, walking up and down, up and down, on the flagged path which ran along under the house, sniffing at the level at which the hands of a tall man would hang, if he walked with them dangling at his side – it was most uncanny to watch them.'

POLTERGEISTS

The term 'poltergeist' – noisy and boisterous ghost – was picked up from the German in the 19th century and has stuck (in English; not in German, where *Spuk* has superseded it).

There is no clear-cut distinction between poltergeists and other types of ghosts, phantoms or elementals. But there are certain indicators, and as one of them is that the phenomena are so often associated with the presence of an individual 'focus', academic parapsychologists have been warming to the hypothesis that the forces involved are psychokinetic, exteriorized from the focus.

Some parapsychologists, in fact, prefer to use the term RSPK – recurrent spontaneous psychokinesis; and it is true that, just as there is no clear distinction at one end of the spectrum from spirit activities, at the other end there is no clear distinction from PK of the kind which, in currently its most familiar form, bends spoons or forks. But there is a middle ground in which simple PK, though it may be a factor, is inadequate to account for the manifestations. What appears to be a spirit entity behaves in certain characteristic ways, playing elaborate paranormal tricks as if with malice aforethought.

In a paper on 'Poltergeists, Old and New' (1910), Sir William Barrett listed the activities with which they have been associated in history. From his study of them he had found that the phenomena are sporadic, breaking out suddenly and disappearing after a few days or weeks. Poltergeists are rarely seen; but they appear to have some limited intelligence, as they answer questions with raps. They move objects – but abnormally; the objects 'slide about, rise in the air, move in eccentric paths, sometimes in a leisurely manner, often turn round in their career, and usually descend quietly without hurting the observers'. Sometimes, however, crockery is thrown about and broken. Tables, beds (and the people in them) are dragged around, or lifted into the air; stones are thrown; 'sometimes bells are continuously rung even if all the bell wires are removed. Noises of various kinds are heard, from footsteps to scratchings of walls, whispering or panting.' Often the disturbances were associated with the presence of children, and cease when the children are not in the house.

This list was incomplete, as Alan Gauld and Tony Cornell have shown in their *Poltergeists* (1979); there are also luminosities; incendiary effects (fires start up for no reason, usually, though not always, soon burning themselves out again); inundations of water, like rain, pouring down from the ceilings of rooms; tampering with electrical apparatus; ripping up of clothes; assaults – pinches and scratches; the opening of doors and windows; and the spreading of filth and excrement.

Writing in the 1911 edition of the *Encyclopedia Britannica* Andrew Lang conceded that the phenomena have often been faked; but 'to the student of human nature', he added, 'the most interesting point in the character of poltergeist phenomena is their appearance in the earliest stages of culture, their wide diffusion, and their astonishing uniformity'. The uniformity cannot be attributed to deliberate imitation on the part of hoaxers, because in so many cases the members of the households in which they have occurred, though they may have heard of poltergeists, have been unaware that the particular phenomena observed in their own case have been encountered before.

In most of the well-attested cases, too – of which there are scores – sleight-of-hand can be ruled out because the focus is commonly a child who could not conceivably have perfected the required skill as a conjuror. In any case, although the phenomena often do not occur in the absence of the child from the house, they are frequently reported as occurring in another room – or in the same room, but at a time when the child is under observation.

Poltergeist activity appears to have been observed in all communities, at all times. Anxious to show a Zanzibar tribe that Christians do not fear demons, Bishop Weston entered a hut reputed to be haunted, according to de Vesme's *Primitive Man* (1931); he was chastened to become the target of 'large pieces of earth violently plucked from the walls', which were thrown around, one of them striking him.

Medieval history is full of accounts of poltergeist-type activity, usually attributed to demons. They took a particular delight in harassing holy men and women in their monastery cells, plaguing them with loud noises, pinching and even scratching them, or covering them with showers of filth. There are also some reports of hauntings, foreshadowing those which are most commonly encountered today, where households were plagued by what Giraldus Cambrensis, encountering them while on a tour of Wales in the 12th century, described as 'foul spirits' which liked to mess clothes up in locked empty rooms, and to heap abuse on anybody who bandied words with them.

In his *Table Talk*, Martin Luther recalled how he had encountered a poltergeist when he was taken prisoner in 1521, and held in the castle of Wartburg, nobody being allowed to come near him except two youths who brought him his meals twice a day. One day they brought him a sack of nuts, which he put in a chest in his sitting-room; and that night, when he had gone to bed, 'it seemed to me all at once that the nuts had put themselves in motion; and, jumping about in the sack, and knocking violently against each other, came to the side of my bed to make noises at me'.

As they did no harm, Luther went to sleep, only to be woken up 'by a great noise on the stairs, which sounded as though somebody was tumbling a hundred barrels down them, one after another'. As the door at the bottom of the stairs was of iron, and fastened with chains, he realized it must be the devil: 'Well, be it so!' he said philosophically and, after prayer, returned to bed. He was moved to another part of the castle; but a woman who slept in the apartment he had vacated also heard such an uproar during the night 'that she thought there were a thousand devils in the place'.

The first attempt at a systematic investigation of a poltergeist haunting a private house was made by the Rev. Joseph Glanvill, one of Charles II's chaplains and a Fellow of the Royal Society, who in 1681 published an account of what has come to be known as 'the demon drummer of Tidworth'. The historian W. E. H. Lecky, the epitome of rationalism, conceded Glanvill's 'incomparable ability' and wrote of one of his works that it would be hard to find anything 'displaying less of credulity and superstition'; and Alan Gauld, after surveying both Glanvill's report and the rest of the source material, has concluded that although from a modern point of view Glanvill can be made to appear credulous, 'from a standpoint in his own time he can be seen to have made serious attempts at the critical sifting and assessment of his materials'.

The drummer – a beggar – had been extorting money with

the help of forged references; and a Tidworth magistrate, John Mompesson, had him committed to gaol, with forfeiture of the drum, which was taken to Mompesson's house. There, it began to play on its own, sometimes loud, sometimes so that the windows and beds shook, sometimes 'truly and sweetly'. Boards moved when nobody was touching them; 'in our presence and sight the chairs did walk about', Mompesson reported, 'the children's shoes were tossed over our heads'; and when the local clergyman came to join Mompesson in prayer, a staff was thrown at him and hit him, though 'a lock of wool could not fall more softly'. Sometimes the servants in their beds were lifted up to a great height, beds and all; then the beds would be laid down softly again.

When Glanvill went down to Tidworth to investigate, he was able to satisfy himself that some, at least, of the phenomena which had been reported were continuing, though the drumming had ceased. There were loud scratching noises which could not be accounted for by any trick; and the demon (as Glanvill assumed it must be) imitated noises he made, and then panted like a dog, so loudly that the room shook. A linen bag hanging in the room moved as if something living was inside it; Glanvill found it to be empty.

There could be no question of the drummer's being responsible, as he was again in gaol. Nor could anybody else have been playing his drum; early on in the haunting, Mompesson had burned it. Over the weeks while the manifestations continued many people had observed them; and although some had gone away disappointed, as nothing had happened while they were in the house, the testimony of those who were there when the 'drummer' was active makes it clear that neither Mompesson nor any of his household could have been responsible.

The Tidworth poltergeist is of interest for another reason. 'The present world treats all such stories with laughter and derision,' Glanvill lamented in his *Saducismus Triumphatus* (1681) – a survey of the evidence about witchcraft and apparitions – 'and is firmly convinced they should be scorned as a waste of time and old wives tales.' The world Glanvill was referring to was not rural England, where men and women were still being executed as witches, but the world of the members of the Royal Society, increasingly attracted to the notion that the discoveries of Newton, Boyle and others were establishing laws of nature of a kind which excluded the possibility of sounds coming from empty air, and objects moving with no physical force applied to them. But if what Mompesson described as happening could not happen, it followed that Mompesson, respected magistrate though he was. must be a trickster; and the Cambridge philosopher Henry More sent Glanvill a list of the allegations he had heard to that effect. Glanvill replied to them in detail in *A Whip for the Droll* (1668); Gauld gives the replies in full, but in brief – the allegations in italics – the replies ran:

Mompesson rented his house, and hoped to reduce its value. Mompesson owned the house.

It was a money-making device. Mompesson took no money, and had in fact been the loser because of the publicity.

The noise was made in the cellars. It was heard in all parts of the house.

An investigator who wanted to go down to the cellar was refused permission. He could have gone down, but preferred to send his servant.

The noise came from outside the house. It often came from the middle of rooms.

In addition, some of those visitors who went away without having witnessed any of the effects were apt to dismiss them. (This was like the Spaniard, Glanvill remarked, who having been six weeks in England without seeing the sun, reported that there was no sun in England.) And the rumour spread that when Mompesson was summoned to the Court to render account to Charles II, he had confessed it was all a hoax; an accusation which Mompesson was angrily to deny, pointing out that to have made such a confession would have convicted not only himself, but other respectable magistrates, and clergy, of perjury.

Gauld rightly stressed the importance of the correspondence between More and Glanvill, as it was an early example of the academic reaction against formerly acceptable ideas of spirits or demons as responsible for hauntings. Since manifestations of the Tidworth kind were no longer acceptable, sceptics had to find alternative explanations; and the more convincing the evidence that they were genuinely the product of some supernatural agency, the more necessary it became to impute dishonesty on the part of all concerned. This has since become a familiar pattern in connection not just with poltergeists, but with paranormal phenomena of all kinds; as has the subsequent spread of the rumour that the culprits, detected in cheating, have confessed.

Of the reports of poltergeists in the 18th century, two are still remembered. One, the haunting of Epworth Rectory, is celebrated mainly because it was the home of the Wesley family. The phenomena – noises and movements of objects – which John Wesley later described were not particularly striking, and he was writing years later; but they are consistent with other cases, and cannot be brushed aside as the product of a hoax. The other, the 'Cock Lane Ghost', attracted a great deal of attention at the time, and is remembered partly because it was investigated by, among others, Samuel Johnson and Oliver Goldsmith, but also because it has provided fuel for controversy over whether (as the investigators believed they had proved) it was a fraud.

In 1759 mysterious bangings and rappings began to disturb the residents of a house in Cock Lane, near Holborn; and a way was found to communicate with the ghost – taken to be the spirit of a woman who had lived in the house, but had died of smallpox – through a code. The ghost would reply to questions with a single rap for yes, two raps for no, and a scratching noise for no comment.

When investigated, however, the ghost proved both uncooperative, replying to some questions with falsehoods, and elusive, declining to perform when sceptics were around. ('As the ghost is a good deal offended by incredulity, the persons present are to conceal theirs,' Goldsmith remarked. 'Otherwise they must hear no ghost.') The unanimous verdict of the committee, expressed by Johnson, was that the daughter of the landlord, Richard Parsons, was the culprit; and his surmise that the child had 'some art of making or counterfeiting particular noises' was subsequently confirmed, when she was found trying to make them with a piece of wood. Parsons, who was assumed to be the guilty party, was sentenced to jail and the pillory.

The Cock Lane ghost then and later came to be cited as a classical example of a hoax which rebounded on its perpetrators – and also its investigators: Johnson, so far from coming out of the affair with credit for displaying robust common sense, was lampooned by his critics for having taken such obvious nonsense seriously. But the tale has features which suggest that at least in its early stages, poltergeist-type forces were operating. The case for the genuineness of some of the phenomena has since been put by Mrs de Morgan, wife of the eminent mathematician, in her *From Matter to Spirit* (1863), and by Andrew Lang in his *Cock Lane and Common Sense* (1894); and recently, more surprisingly, so sceptical a commentator as Trevor Hall has shown in *New Light on Old Ghosts* (1965) that he places more credence on the evidence for the reality of the paranormal element than he customarily does, surveying such episodes.

The majority of reports of poltergeists have shown them operating within a house; but there is one remarkable case where the house was the target of attack from a distance. In 1849 the official magazine of the French police described how, when demolition work was begun to open up a new street between the Sorbonne and the Pantheon, one inhabited house in the rue des Grés, near the excavations, had been assailed every evening, and throughout the night, 'by a hail of projectiles which, from their bulk, the violence with which they have been thrown, have done such destruction, that it has been laid open to the day, the woodwork of the doors and windows reduced to slivers, as if it had sustained a siege'. In vain had the police patrolled the whole area with guard dogs, and watched from rooftops; the projectiles could be seen coming over their heads, from considerable distances, but reaching the house with mathematical precision. Although the writer of the report expressed the hope that an explanation would be found, he recalled that on the occasions when there had been a rain of coins, evening after evening, in the rue de Montequiou, and 'when all the bells were rung in a house in the rue de Malte by an invisible hand', it had been found 'impossible to find a palpable cause'. No palpable cause was ever found for the assault on the rue des Grés.

The following year, a poltergeist which plagued the household of the Rev. Dr Eliakim Phelps in his rectory in Stamford, Connecticut, behaved in the more conventional pattern; to the consternation of visitors, who often witnessed the havoc. 'The contents of the pantry were emptied into the kitchen,' one of them reported; 'bags of salt, tin ware and heavier culinary articles were thrown in a promiscuous heap upon the floor.' Chairs moved around 'unimpelled by any visible agency', heavy marble-top tables reared up on two legs; and 'the large knocker of the outside door would thunder its fearful tones through the loud resounding hall, unmindful of the vain but rigid scrutiny to which it was subjected by incredulous and curious men'.

The rigid scrutiny did not protect Phelps and his family from slander. He had witnessed the effects 'hundreds and hundreds of times', he wrote to his friend Asa Mahan, the first President of Oberlin; so had 'scores of persons of the first standing in the community'; yet the newspapers were claiming that the mystery had been solved – it had all been a trick played by Phelps's children. On the contrary, 'with the most thorough investigation which I have been able to bestow on it, aided by gentlemen of the best talents, intelligence and sound judgement, in this and in many neighbouring towns, the cause of these strange phenomena remains undiscovered'.

William Barrett personally investigated some poltergeists in Ireland, in particular the 'Derrygonnelly ghost' which haunted a farmhouse near Enniskillen in Ulster. The manifestations seemed to centre on Maggie, the eldest daughter of the family, aged twenty; they included the usual rappings, scratchings, movements of objects, and stones falling inside closed rooms. The family, who were Protestants, one night hopefully put out an open Bible; by the morning, pages were torn out of it. A lamp blessed by the local Catholic priest fared no better: it disappeared.

When Barrett arrived in 1871 to investigate, he soon satisfied himself that no member of the household could be responsible for the noises he heard; and he witnessed 'a large pebble drop apparently from space in a room where the only culprit could have been myself, and certainly I did not throw it.' The ghost, Barrett was told, had answered questions put to it by rapping out replies. So

I mentally asked it, no word being spoken, to knock a certain number of times, and it did so. To avoid any error or delusion on my part, I put my hands in the side pockets of my overcoat and asked it to knock the number of fingers I had open. It correctly did so. Then, with a different number of fingers open each time, the experiment was repeated four times in succession, and four times I obtained absolutely the correct number of raps.

Chance coincidence, Barrett felt, was ruled out: 'the interesting fact remains that some telepathic rapport between the unseen agent and ourselves appears to exist, on this occasion at any rate.'

On this occasion, too, the unseen agent was abashed when the

Rev. Maxwell Close, who had accompanied Barrett, read aloud from the Scriptures. 'The noises were at first so great that we could hardly hear what was read; then as the solemn words of prayer were uttered, they subsided, and when the Lord's Prayer was joined in by all, a profound stillness fell on the whole cottage.' The poltergeist, silenced, troubled the family no more.

Experimental Evidence

Although the emphasis in parapsychology has been so heavily on laboratory-type experiments in the past half century, there has been one exception: the investigation of poltergeists. Although they cannot be moved to a lab., the fact that they so often hang around the same premises or the same person for weeks has encouraged some parapsychologists to bring the lab. to the poltergeist, when opportunity offers.

What they have found has been confirmation of the earlier anecdotal findings reported from Tidworth, or Epworth, or Cock Lane, or Derrygonnelly. It is as if poltergeists have a stock repertory, which can be varied according to the occasion, or the household, so that a particular haunting may be remembered for a particular type of malicious behaviour – as in what came to be described as 'the Bottle-Popping Mystery'.

In 1958 the Herrmanns in their Long Island home began to hear the noise of bottles popping, and would find when they went to investigate that bottles, in different rooms, had had their stoppers removed, the caps taken off or unscrewed, and the contents – shampoo, bleach, or wine – spilled. James Herrmann was a second world war veteran, and an airline executive; his wife was a former nurse; they were reluctant to accept that their house could be haunted, and their two children, a girl of thirteen and a boy of twelve, were suspected until it became obvious that they could not be responsible. After a week of the manifestations, Herrmann called in the police. The detectives sent to the house also thought at first that the children must be the culprits; but the children, they found, were often in a room when the bottles were being opened and emptied in other parts of the house.

Inevitably, the story of the bottle-popping ghost got into the papers; when J. B. Rhine heard about it, he asked Gaither Pratt, his most trusted assistant, to investigate; and Pratt invited the young W. G. Roll, later to become America's leading authority on poltergeists, to accompany him. Herrmann, who struck them as very balanced, told them how he had actually seen two bottles, which were on top of a table, moving – one of them falling into a sink, the other crashing to the floor. The moving, opening and spilling of bottles was not the poltergeist's only activity: a figurine was moved about, and eventually smashed; and periodically there were 'thumping' sounds. But as Roll was to describe it, 'the Herrmann poltergeist liked bottles'. The Herrmanns, being Catholics, hoped that filling bottles with holy water might prove to be a deterrent; but it was no help at all. 'In fact it probably made matters worse.'

While the investigators from Duke were in the house, bottles continued to pop, and fall, in rooms where they could satisfy themselves nobody was present. Analysis, too, showed that the bottles' contents had not been tampered with; and even if they had been, this would not have accounted for the fact that the bottle tops were so often found unscrewed. The son, James, could have been responsible for some of the incidents, and they only occurred when he was in or near the house; but in about a third of them neither he nor his sister was in a position to move the bottles, or the other objects affected.

After spending ten days with the family, Pratt and Roll ruled out any possibility that a family hoax was being perpetrated on the public. There was no conceivable reason to play it, and – as in Mompesson's case, at Tidworth – excellent reasons why they should fear the publicity, as well as the poltergeist. Fortunately for the Herrmanns, the presence of the visitors from Duke appeared to succeed where holy water and an exorcism ceremony had failed: the bottle-popping ceased. The Herrmanns for their part were relieved to feel that the whole episode could be looked upon as the first step towards a recategorization of poltergeist hauntings: 'at the end of our stay they had come to see the matter not as one for religion but for science'.

Roll felt that this 1958 Long Island case marked 'the dividing line between old and new poltergeists'. In this he was being unfair to earlier investigators – Mompesson, after all, had spread ashes over one of the rooms which the phantom haunted to see if it would leave any impressions: 'In the morning they found, in one place, the resemblance of a great Claw; in another of a lesser; some letters in another they could make nothing of, besides many Circles and Scratches in the Ashes.' Barrett, too, had conducted tests to find if the Derrygonnelly poltergeist could thought-read. And a controlled experiment had been conducted by Dr Xavier Dariex; he had delivered a paper on it to the first international psychological congress held in 1889, just before most academic psychologists turned their backs on psychical research, for fear it would damage their prospects of winning academic recognition for their faculty.

Investigating disturbances which took place every night in a room in a Paris house, Dariex invited colleagues to join him in locking and sealing up the room each night, and finding whether anything had happened in the room the following morning. On eight nights out of the ten set aside for the experiment, nothing happened; but on two of the nights, chairs were overturned. 'Without wishing to prejudge in any way the precise character of this force and draw positive conclusions,' Dariex and his colleagues concluded, 'we are inclined to think that the phenomena are of a psychic order.'

There have been several carefully monitored, well-attested and soberly documented investigations of poltergeists since, as Roll, Gauld and Cornell, and A. R. G. Owen in *Can We Explain the Poltergeist?* (1974) have shown. But one is outstanding: the case of the Rosenheim poltergeist, 'unique in that a series of spontaneous events, extending over a period of several months,' as Arthur Koestler described it in *The Challenge of Chance*, 'were actually observed and recorded by several teams of experts, under conditions resembling a planned laboratory experiment.'

The laboratory aspect was relatively easy to introduce because the poltergeist was infesting not a household, but a lawyer's office in the Bavarian town of Rosenheim. Initially it was the telephone system which went haywire, continuing to register quantities of calls which had clearly not been made, even after a complete overhaul. 'Telephones being what they are, the episode would hardly be worth recording', Koestler sardonically commented, had the lawyer not felt compelled to sue 'persons unknown' for fraud or embezzlement, which brought in the police. While they were investigating, neon tubes began to explode, and it was found that they were being twisted in their sockets. This in turn brought in the electricity company, which put the blame on surges in the current; but when the office supply was taken off the mains and put on to a generator, the surges continued, though nothing was the matter with the generator supply.

The observers were also treated to weird displays. Pictures would swing on their hooks, or turn face to the wall; one rotation of a picture was actually caught on a video tape which had been left running. Filing cabinet drawers came out, though unpulled, spilling their contents on the floor. A filing cabinet, weighing hundreds of pounds, moved out from the wall. And eventually, help was sought from two physicists, one from the Max Planck Institute.

Bender had no difficulty in finding the 'focus': one of the office secretaries. The poltergeist activity occurred only when she was in the office; and his inquiries revealed that something of the kind had happened to her before. She left; and the disturbances ceased.

The two physicists were left with a problem. The secretary, they had quickly realized, could not be directly physically responsible for the surges in the current, or for the registering of telephone calls which were not being dialled (the telephone company's monitoring had revealed not merely that the calls were an endless succession of requests for the time of day, but also that they were being dialled in a way which was not humanly possible). In their report, giving details of the elaborate gadgetry which had been used to ensure that neither the secretary nor anybody else could have been playing tricks, they were forced to admit that although investigated with all the known scientific means available, the events defied explanation in terms of conventional physics, and that they seemed to be carried out 'under intelligent control'.

The physicists' reports, and the programme on the subject put out on German television, led to a breakthrough in public opinion on the paranormal, reflected in opinion polls. The findings are so unpalatable to most scientists that they have as yet made little impression; but they constitute the most convincing proof yet obtained of the existence not simply of poltergeist phenomena, but of psychokinetic forces in general.

5 *DIVINATION*

Divination is the art, or craft, of obtaining information paranormally. It has been used in every community, in every era. Explorers and missionaries invariably found that the tribal shaman, medicine man or witch doctor was selected and groomed for his post because he had given indications that he had second sight; Bishop Callaway in his study of the Zulus insisted that the appropriate term for him was 'diviner', as the man's chief function was to relate and interpret the information which reached him by that means.

A diviner may 'see' into the past, or find out what is happening at a distance in the present, but the tendency has been to think of divination as foreseeing, and foretelling the future. In classical times, the chief function of the 'seer' was to find out what was going to happen, in order that due provision could be made for whatever was in store; but this led to some confusion, as the belief in seers rested on the assumption that the future was laid down – predestined. 'In order to account for divination, it is necessary to go back to the divinity, to destiny, to nature,' Quintus explained to his brother, in Cicero's treatise on the subject. Everything was governed by destiny; there was nothing in the future for which nature did not already contain the causes; 'let us add that since everything is ruled by destiny, if a mortal should exist capable of conceiving the connection between all causes he would never be mistaken' – a view echoed in the 19th century by the eminent mathematician Laplace.

This quite widely held view, however, contained the inherent contradiction that the future could not be so rigorously controlled by destiny, if destiny permitted those who could glimpse it – the seers, or ordinary men and women in dreams – to adopt some course of action which would alter it. And although the upholders of predestination have resorted to ingenious ruses to explain this away, divination has also commonly been regarded as indicating at least a limited measure of freedom of action – even though, as many a myth has intimated, the freedom may be illusory if destiny catches up later.

In *On Time*, Michael Shallis makes the point that divination is 'quite different from precognition. With the precognitive the future is seen, with divination an answer to a question is being sought.' Countless aids to the search have been adopted, and given what the coiners feel are the appropriate names. Some are colloquially familiar; others are now only rarely encountered – cheiromancy (palmistry); rhabdomancy (dowsing); oneiromancy (dream interpretation); and others, though they have been in common use – divination by tea-leaves in cups; by opening the Bible at random and looking at the passage upon which the forefinger falls; by consulting the entrails of sacrificial animals – either have no name, or none which has retained its place in the language.

Automatism

Divination is heavily reliant on automatism, which Myers defined as applying to activities made 'without the initiative, and generally without the concurrence, of conscious thought and will'; activities which he attributed to the action of 'submerged or subliminal elements in man's being'.

For convenience, he divided automatism into *sensory* and *motor*: 'on the one hand, the sights and sounds which we see and hear through some subliminal faculty rather than through the ordinary channels of sense; on the other hand, the motions which we perform, the words which we utter, moved in like manner by some unknown impulse from within'. But whatever the manner in which they manifested themselves, 'they will be seen to be *messages* from the subliminal to the supraliminal self: endeavours – conscious or unconscious – of submerged tracts of our personality to present to ordinary waking thought fragments of a knowledge which no ordinary waking thought could attain'.

Automatism, then, does not necessarily imply paranormal activity. It is often symptomatic of what are generally accepted to be psychological, or pathological, conditions – sleep-walking, for example – rather than psychic impulses. But because the symptoms so often appeared to be the work of a different personality, automatism used commonly to be attributed to gods or spirits possessing the individual for their own purposes: to talk through his mouth, dictate through his ear, or write with his hand.

Automatism still often presents itself as a form of possession. Spiritualists assume that the medium *is* possessed, by a spirit 'control'; and one of the last strongholds of belief in demons are the Christian churches, which employ exorcism to compel the demon or demons which have taken over to quit. But as Professor Ian Stevenson, Director of the Parapsychology Division at the University of Virginia, has pointed out, the information which automatism provides, whether through the senses or by movements, can be traced to three possible sources: '(a) material of normal provenance derived from what the subject has seen or heard (without necessarily being aware that this is the case); (b) information derived paranormally from living persons or from printed or other inanimate sources; and (c) communications from discarnate personalities.'

Material coming through from (a), Stevenson warns, is often mistaken for the productions of (b) or (c): 'we should remember that our minds are stored – one could say stuffed – with much more information than we ordinarily need or ever become consciously aware of'. The fact that the handwriting and the style – or the speed at which the material is transmitted – differ so much from the individual's norm has all too often encouraged the belief that the material is being fed in from an outside source; but experiments with altered states of consciousness have shown that the same features can easily be induced, suggesting that the subconscious (or perhaps a secondary personality embedded in it) is perfectly capable of, say, producing verses at speeds considerably exceeding the conscious mind's everyday ability to turn out prose.

But why should the subconscious be capable of turning out verse at all – let alone, as it has often done, turn out inspired poetry?

The instance which is most commonly cited is 'Kubla Khan', which came to Coleridge complete while he was in an opium-induced haze – though after he had been interrupted by a visitor, he found that the remaining lines had faded from his memory, never to be recalled. Later commentators have been able to show that the details in 'Kubla Khan', and in much of what Coleridge wrote, can be traced back to what he had read – sometimes to the point of plagiarism. But this would not account for the way in which they emerged in the poetic form they did, without his having to shape them. 'The authors of those great poems which

223

we admire do not attain to excellence through the rules of any art,' in Socrates' view; 'but they utter their beautiful melodies of verse in a state of inspiration and, as it were, possessed by a Spirit not their own.'

The verse, or the prose, or the musical compositions which composers have 'heard' in the mind's ear, cannot be differentiated from those which are transmitted through automatism – except by the mechanics of this process; the subconscious (or the forces operating through it) may choose different methods of gaining attention. Sometimes the words float into the mind 'as though from nowhere', as Siegfried Sassoon recalled about the writing of his most familiar poem. He jotted them down as if 'remembering rather than thinking. In this mindless, recollecting manner I wrote down my poem in a few minutes.' It was 'Everyone suddenly burst out singing', soon to become a stock anthology piece, almost as well known as Yeats's 'Innisfree'.

In cases of that kind it is easy to discount any paranormal component (though much more difficult to account for them satisfactorily on reductionist/behaviourist lines). The paranormal begins to sidle in, however, when the material arrives through the channels long associated with psychic phenomena: for example, through 'hearing voices'.

Many writers have admitted that their inspiration comes to them through voices in the inner ear, so that they can put down sentences as if from dictation; as Alfred de Musset did, and Blake, and Harriet Beecher Stowe – and Dickens (all that his characters said, according to G. H. Lewes, 'was distinctly *heard* by him', which initially disturbed him, but which he came to attribute to 'auditory hallucination'). The 18th-century musician Giuseppi Tartini, too, 'heard' a violin sonata he was trying to compose, in a dream, in the course of which he had sold his soul to the devil if the devil would finish it for him. (It is known as 'The Devil's Trill Sonata' to this day.)

Paranormal? The issue becomes even more complicated in cases where the material which emerges cannot easily be traced to any conceivable source of information. Dickens might get his dialogue through the inner ear, but it was the kind of dialogue he could have consciously written; not so the dialogue of 'Patience Worth's' characters, keeping as they did with such meticulous care to the words in use in the historical period they were supposedly living in – something which experts would have found it difficult to do.

There is a further complication, for anybody seeking to separate out the normal from the paranormal. Rosemary Brown has shown that she can produce pieces in the manner of Liszt and other composers, sufficiently impressively for some critics to accept that her belief – that the spirits of the composers are passing the pieces on to her – could be correct. But even if it is incorrect, the question still has to be answered: how does Mrs Brown, who has no appreciable musical talent, produce works which call for a skill considerably higher than that of simple imitation? Similarly, when Matthew Manning was extricating himself from the unwanted attentions of a poltergeist with the help of automatic writing, he began to produce drawings in the style of famous artists which not only were sufficiently well executed to compel some experts to admit that they looked more like originals than imitations, but were drawn in minutes, even in seconds.

In the present state of knowledge, these questions will have to remain unanswered; and with them, the extent to which the phenomenon of transcendence – the ability in certain states of mind to accomplish mental feats far beyond the normal capability – can be classified as paranormal. All that can reasonably be stated is that the mechanism by which transcendence operates is closely allied to that which is utilized by ESP and PK.

SENSORY AUTOMATISM

Mediumship

In all eras, in all communities, mediums have been employed as diviners, chiefly because of their assumed ability to communicate with the spirits or the gods. In theory they can be distinguished from 'sensitives', people who have the faculty of picking up psychic emanations – sensing, say, when a room is haunted; and from 'psychics', who have paranormal capabilities of various kinds, but who are not necessarily assumed to owe them to any spirit influence. In practice, however, the distinctions are blurred.

The earliest mediums were shamans, medicine men and witch doctors, chosen because they displayed indications that they could be intermediaries between the spirits and the tribe. The seers of classical antiquity were selected for the same reason, as were the sibyls who were available for consultations as oracles, and the Old Testament prophets. But the development of monotheism meant that independent mediumship of the kind practised by the witch of En-Dor, when she conjured up the spirit of Samuel for King Saul, came to be regarded as diabolic, equated with witchcraft, and punishable with death. And although the early Christians, St Paul in particular, regarded the ability to receive the communications of the Holy Spirit as the mark of divine grace, it was not long before the Church became frightened of mediumship, even when the mediums were devout Christians, for fear the devil would exploit their powers. It was not until the 18th century that it became safe to practise mediumship, as Swedenborg did.

So well known was Swedenborg's ability to help people with problems by taking the advice of the spirits that his most celebrated achievements were attested by numerous witnesses; such as the occasion when Mme Marteville, widow of the Dutch Ambassador to Sweden, was dunned for payment for a silver service which she was sure that her husband must have paid for in his lifetime, but for which she could not find the receipt. Three days after she had asked Swedenborg for his help, he informed her that he had been able to contact her dead husband, who had confirmed that he had paid the bill, and had said that the receipt would be found in a bureau in an upstairs room. Mme Marteville replied that she had cleared out the bureau and the receipt had not been in it; but her husband, according to Swedenborg, had told him there was a secret compartment, which she had not known about, containing private correspondence and the receipt. Accompanied by friends of hers who were present, they went to the upstairs room, opened the bureau, and found the secret compartment – and the receipt.

After the emergence of spiritualism as a cult, in the mid-19th century, the emphasis began to shift to mediumship of the type which is still widespread today, the chief function of the medium's spirit 'control' being to provide sitters with information about, or from, deceased friends or relations, either directly, or by bringing them on as 'communicators'. In such circumstances, most sitters were satisfied simply to establish communication, particularly if the 'control' or the 'communicator' could provide evidence of a convincing kind of survival after the death of the body, and the promise of meeting again in the after-life; and as spiritualism developed into a religion, psychical researchers began to concentrate more upon physical mediumship, and to explore PK in its various forms.

Periodically, however, feats of mental mediumship continued to be reported. In his *Animisme et Spiritisme* the tireless and resourceful Russian psychical researcher Alexandre Aksakov described how a deceased friend of Prince Wittgenstein's, General Baron de Korff, had suddenly and wholly unexpectedly communicated with him through a medium, asking him to tell the de Korff family where his will, hidden through malevolence, was to be found in a cupboard in the house where he had died. Wittgenstein had not even known that de Korff's heirs had been looking for the will, which was found in the cupboard indicated, and turned out to be of the greatest importance, not only for settling inheritance issues, but for the management of the family estate. 'Here is an occurrence,' Wittgenstein commented, 'that defies all scepticism.'

The divinatory power of some celebrated mental mediums have been extensively and rigorously vetted; in particular, Mrs Leonora Piper, a Boston housewife, who for about half a century gave seances in which she was able to give sitters intimate details about themselves and their past lives, of a kind which she could not have obtained without an elaborate network of agents – a network which the suspicious Richard Hodgson, investigating on behalf of the SPR, was compelled to admit did not exist. 'I agree with him absolutely,' William James wrote in 1898.

The medium has been under observation, much of the time under close observation, as to most of the conditions of her life, by a large number of persons, eager, many of them, to pounce upon any suspicious circumstance, for nearly fifteen years. During that time, not only has there not been one single suspicious circumstance remarked, but not one suggestion has ever been made from any quarter which might tend positively to explain how the medium, living the apparent life she leads, could possibly collect information about so many sitters by natural means.

In Britain, during and after the first world war, Mrs Osborne Leonard was put through many elaborate tests by members of the SPR, and she also was able to provide sitters with information of a kind that she could not conceivably have collected, except psychically. She, too, was never detected in any act which might have cast suspicion on her. Her 'control', Feda, who spoke in the voice of a young girl, appeared to relish being investigated, frequently volunteering her own proofs, often in the form of what came to be known as 'book tests'.

A typical example of her abilities in this connection was reported by Lord Glenconner. His son Edmund had been killed on the Somme; and at a seance that winter, 'Feda' passed a message from him to his father, telling him to look at page 37 of 'the ninth book on the third shelf counting from left to right in the bookcase on the right of the door in the drawing-room as you enter'. It had been a family joke that Glenconner, one of whose hobbies was forestry, was greatly disturbed by the depredations of beetles; he would go on and on about them during family walks. The book 'Feda' referred to turned out to be on trees; and the sentence at the bottom of p. 36, leading on into p. 37, was 'Sometimes you will see curious marks in the wood; these are caused by a tunnelling beetle, very injurious to the trees.'

If this had happened only once or twice, trickery would have been a plausible explanation; but 'Feda' did hundreds of such tests, and although she was often wrong, her success rate – in well over a third of cases, not counting partial 'hits' – was far above chance expectation, which could be measured by book tests taken in the same way, but with the selection made at random: the success rate in these control tests was around four per cent.

The introduction of the laboratory-orientated techniques of investigation in the 1930s shifted the emphasis of psychical research away from work with spiritualist mediums. Few of the student subjects who succeeded in the tests conducted at Duke University believed in spirit guidance, and the results which were achieved there did not suggest spirit intervention – if spirits had been at work, they would surely have intervened more dramatically, rather than simply pushing up correct guesses to a higher-than-chance level. Psychical research has since moved so far from investigation of a spirit component that Thalbourne in his *Glossary*, defining 'medium', describes it as a 'somewhat old-fashioned term'.

Spiritualist mediums are to be found in all Western countries; in some, as in Britain, there are many thousands of them. But it is now rare for individuals to be formally investigated; partly because most psychical researchers mistrust what they feel to be the mumbo-jumbo element in spiritualism; partly because the mediums themselves have come to believe that investigators are usually only interested in exposing them as fraudulent. The fact that Spiritualism is a religious faith, so that mediums often practise in churches, also militates against detached inquiry.

'Speaking in Tongues'

Automatism through the human voice is described colloquially as 'speaking in tongues', or 'the gift of tongues' – though less commonly now than it used to be, owing to the reduction in the number of people familiar with its source: 'they were all filled with the Holy Ghost, and began to speak with other tongues, as the Spirit gave them utterance'. In this case – Jesus's disciples meeting at Pentecost – the spectators were astonished because the disciples, though Galileans, spoke in languages they could not have been expected to know: 'how hear we every man in our own tongue, wherein we were born?' But automatism can also come through in an unknown language – sometimes in a language which appears to have been made up on the spot.

When the language is unknown, speaking in tongues is called

'glossolalia'. When the language is recognizable, Richet's term 'xenoglossy' is used. The paranormal enters into xenoglossy when the language is unknown to the speaker, or when the way in which it is spoken is far outside the speaker's normal capability. It is rarely easy to be certain that cryptomnesia can be ruled out: somebody who has heard a language spoken as a child, it can be argued, may have accumulated reserves of knowledge without realizing it. Still, this would rarely account for the fluency reported in many cases; and in others, there has been no opportunity for the child to pick up the language.

A typical case of spontaneous xenoglossy was described in 1857 by John Worth Edmonds, a New York judge whose daughter Laura was psychic. When a Greek visitor came to a party at their home, Laura's 'control' first gave him a description of a friend of his, unknown to the Edmonds, who had died some years before; and then began speaking to him in Greek, which Laura could not have picked up as a child. They carried on a conversation, partly in Greek, for an hour.

Laura's 'control' would also periodically speak through her in Spanish, and in American Indian; and mediums have frequently shown their ability to speak several different languages fluently, though not always accurately. In the 1920s the American medium George Valiantine carried on conversations in Russian, German, Spanish, and sufficiently idiomatic Welsh to impress a Welsh speaker who attended. The record of the Brazilian medium Carlos Mirabelli in this period was even more impressive; according to the committee of scientists who investigated him he spoke or wrote in nearly thirty languages, including Japanese and Syrian – and hieroglyphics.

In his *Polyglot Mediumship* (1932) Ernesto Bozzano gave thirty-five case histories of xenoglossy, some of which made the cryptomnesia explanation extremely implausible. In any case, he claimed, the voices occasionally transmitted information which could only have come through ESP. So far as he was concerned, the explanation must be either some form of omniscience which mediums could tap, or spirit possession – the spiritist hypothesis, in his view, being the more likely.

Psychometry

In *The Law of Psychic Phenomena*, published in Chicago in 1902, the psychical researcher Thomas Jay Hudson defined psychometry as 'the supposed power of the human mind to discern the history of inanimate objects by clairvoyance'. The term had been coined a few years earlier by a practising mesmerist, who had noted that touching or holding something appeared to encourage the emergence of the 'higher phenomena', so that the mesmerized subject could often reel off information about the owner, and past owners, of a watch, or a ring, or whatever it might be. Like so many other previously coined terms, it was later denounced as misleading; Richet called it 'hateful', and Sudre claimed that 'all modern researchers agree in finding the word ridiculous'; but, again like so many other terms, it has survived their objections (not surprisingly, as the best that Richet, so prolific an inventor in this area, could offer in its place was 'pragmatical cryptesthesia'). 'Psychoscopy' is today the only serious contender.

The two most celebrated exponents of the craft were contemporaries, though living on different sides of the Atlantic. When put into a hypnotic trance and given an object to hold, Madame Morel was often able to give the French investigator Eugène Osty a mass of detailed information in connection with it, which he used in his *Supernormal Faculties in Man* (1923), showing how it had helped to find missing people, or solve crimes. The information, he emphasized, had to be carefully sieved to get what was wanted. On one occasion, when he had brought some clothing with him belonging to a missing man, she first described somebody whom he began to recognize was himself, and then other people who were connected with the case, before giving a description of the missing man himself, and where he could be found. This could not have been through telepathic communication between him, as hypnotist, and Mme Morel, as subject, Osty pointed out, as he did not know the place which she described; but after a search, the man's body was found where she had said it would be found. And although she sometimes might pick up the wrong scent, as it were, from an object, Osty found that her characterization was always sound; that is, if she were describing Mlle A, who was connected with a case – but was not the person, Mlle B, whom he wanted her to describe – Mme Morel's description always fitted Mlle A, and was never confused with Mlle B.

The psychometric abilities of Mme Morel's contemporary 'Senora de Z' – Senora Maria Reyes de Zierold – were discovered by chance by Gustav Pagenstecher, a German doctor who had emigrated to Mexico. Treating her through hypnosis, he found that she displayed the 'higher phenomena', and her ability to 'see' clairvoyantly was enhanced if she were given an object to hold. Hearing about her, Walter Franklin Prince, who had just taken charge of the American Society for Psychical Research, decided to investigate, and found that she was even more startlingly clairvoyant than her reputation had suggested; her most striking feat being a description she gave of the associations of a letter he had brought with him. Without opening it she provided him with thirty-eight pieces of information relating not just to the contents, but to the writer, a clergyman; material which was not contained in the letter, and was unknown to Prince. On his return he checked on the information she had given and found that with the exception of three of her statements, which he was unable to verify, all of them had been accurate.

There have been many more recent cases where psychometrists have been called in to help solve mysteries. The most celebrated in recent times was the Dutch clairvoyant, Gerard Croiset, whose exploits have been chronicled in a biography by Jack Harrison Pollack (1964), his record being only marginally dented by some carping criticism by sceptics of some of the research undertaken by his mentor, Professor Tenhaeff. In addition to his work tracing missing people and helping the police, Croiset helped scholars seeking to identify archeological specimens by 'object reading' or psychoscopy. Picking up a tiny fragment of bone that had been found in a cave in Basutoland, Croiset in 1953 gave a 'reading' which astonished Dr Martin Valkhoff, Dean of the University of Witwatersrand, as it accurately described the cave, its inhabitants, its surroundings, and a religious ceremony connected with it, though no indication had been given to Croiset about its history.

Psychometry, as Professor Tenhaeff has pointed out, is simply a form of what he calls 'paragnosis' – the obtaining of knowledge through paranormal means – with the help of an object as an inductor; the psychic equivalent of a knot tied in a handkerchief to trigger recollection. 'Nor is it necessary for the psychoscopist to take the object in his hands. Many times the object is in another room, town, country or civilization. Distance and time are not factors.' The psychometrist may even find himself 'reading' an object he is about to be presented with.

Scrying

In Theodore Besterman's *Crystal-gazing* (1924) – an astonishingly erudite book, considering that Besterman, later to become Britain's leading bibliophile, was still in his teens when he wrote it – he defined scrying as 'a method of bringing into the consciousness of the scryer by means of a speculum, through one or more of the senses, the content of his subconscious; of rendering him more susceptible to the reception of telepathically-transmitted concepts; and of bringing into operation a latent and unknown faculty of perception'.

The 'speculum' could be any one of a great variety of aids to divination, as Andrew Lang found. He became interested in the subject when he encountered frequent references to the use of scrying by diviners in tribal communities, usually performed by children, who 'saw' pictures when they gazed into 'a crystal ball, a cup, a mirror, a blob of ink (in Egypt and India), a drop of blood (among the Maoris of New Zealand), a bowl of water (Red Indian), a pond (Roman and African), water in a glass bowl (in Fez), or almost any polished surface'.

In tribal communities, scrying with a bowl of water by the tribe's diviner has often been reported. In the Book of Genesis, Joseph used his silver cup for divination as well as for drinking. The practice was referred to by Chaucer, Spenser, Shakespeare and the Portuguese poet Camõens. And John Dee, astrologer and special agent to Queen Elizabeth I (whom she described as her 'ubiquitous eyes', and to whom she gave the same code name which, curiously, was given by Ian Fleming to James Bond – 007 – some four centuries later), used a crystal ball, among other things, to supplement his second sight.

The most celebrated example of divination by scrying in history is related in Saint-Simon's memoirs. In 1706 the Duc d'Orleans, about to set off for Italy, told Saint-Simon about an experiment he had conducted with the help of a young girl who lived at the home of his mistress, La Sery. A charlatan (Saint-Simon's term: he disapproved of Orleans' occult dabblings) had offered to answer any questions Orleans put to him provided that, as a go-between, he had a young and innocent child to gaze into a glass of water. He would tell her what to look for – as she proceeded to do. Suspicious, Orleans sent an attendant round to a neighbour, to find and report back what they were doing: when the child was asked to 'see' and describe what they were doing, her account tallied with the attendant's.

Rebuked by Saint-Simon, at this point in his tale, for wasting his time on such follies, Orleans replied that he was only beginning. The girl had been asked to describe the scene which would occur when Louis XIV died. Not merely had she accurately described the royal bedroom, though she had never even heard of Versailles; she had described the people round the bedside so well that Orleans was able to recognize all of them. There were, however, four members of the Court who should have been present but, according to the girl, were not. This had surprised Orleans, and it surprised Saint-Simon: 'we were at a loss to explain it'. But the event proved that the child had been right. At the time the seance took place, in 1706, 'these four members of the royal family were then full of health and strength: and they all died before the king' – eight years later.

In the 1890s Andrew Lang conducted tests of a Scots psychic of his acquaintance, 'Miss Angus', whom he asked to pick up what was in his mind, or in the minds of other people present, by scrying, which she frequently did. Sometimes straight telepathy might have accounted for what she saw; but often, Lang was convinced this could not have been the explanation.

In one instance Miss Angus described doings from three weeks to a fortnight old, of people in India, people whom she had never seen or heard of, but who were known to her 'sitter'. Her account, given on a Saturday, was corroborated by a letter from India which arrived next day, Sunday. In another case she described (about ten P.M.), what a lady, not known to her, but the daughter of a matron present (who was *not* the sitter) had been doing about 4 P.M. on the same day. Again, 'sitting' with one lady, Miss Angus described a singular set of scenes much in the mind, not of her 'sitter', but of a very unsympathetic stranger, who was reading a book at the other end of the room.

The French psychical researcher Joseph Maxwell recounted a number of interesting examples of the results of scrying in his *Metapsychical Phenomena* (1903). One psychic of his acquaintance, using a crystal ball, 'saw' a large steamer with a black, white and red flag, called (he thought) the *Leutschland*, surrounded by smoke and sinking, the passengers crowding to the upper deck. He told

Maxwell what he had seen; eight days later, Maxwell read that a boiler on the *Deutschland* had burst, with, it could be assumed, accompanying vapour and some panic among the passengers – though she had not in fact foundered.

The pictures 'seen' in a crystal ball, Lang surmised, are hallucinations of a kind similar to those some people experience in the state between sleeping and waking. Myers suggested that auto-hypnosis is responsible for them, and Barrett in his *Psychical Research* (1911) agreed; the gazer into a crystal ball is 'no doubt in a state of incipient hypnosis; detached from the surrounding impressions of the external world and awake to the impressions arising from his hidden or subliminal self. The crystal is a form of *autoscope*, not mechanical like the pendulum or dowsing-rod, but sensory.'

In a paper on 'Andrew Lang as psychical researcher', Alan Gauld admits that his experimental methods were casual, by modern investigative standards; but this, he feels, is not a reason for dismissing the results out of hand, and he suggests that the phenomenon 'is more than due for recognition'. Crystal-gazing, however, has acquired so sleazy a fair-ground image that few parapsychologists have been willing to take it seriously enough to investigate.

MOTOR AUTOMATISM

Automatic Writing

A medium, Alfred Russel Wallace explained, may write involuntarily

> . . . sometimes in a state of trance, and often on subjects which he is not thinking about, does not expect, and does not like. Occasionally definite and correct information is given of facts of which the medium has not, nor ever had, any knowledge. Sometimes future events are accurately predicted. The writing takes place either by the hand, or through a planchette. Often the handwriting changes. Sometimes it is written backwards; sometimes in languages which the medium does not understand.

Automatic writing is not in itself paranormal, so much as the outcome of a different level of consciousness. As Sudre commented, it is produced by hysterics and somnambulists as well as by people who are regarded as normal. A century ago, the researchers into hypnosis found it was possible to induce a condition in some subjects in which the answers they wrote automatically about what they were feeling, or hearing, were different from the answers they gave to the hypnotist's questions, which corresponded to whatever they had been *told* they were feeling by the hypnotist. This has been confirmed recently when hypnotized subjects who had been told they would not feel pain, although subjected to a painful experience, duly said they felt no pain, and showed no signs of feeling pain – while at the same time in automatic writing complaining that they were being hurt.

Whether there is a paranormal component or not is often difficult to determine, as in those cases where automatic writing provides information of a kind which is not in the writer's conscious knowledge, but where intuition or inspiration might be credited – as in the first recorded case of automatic writing: David's experience, when he was instructing Solomon how to build a Sanctuary. David provided 'the pattern of the porch, and of the houses thereof, and of the treasuries thereof, and of the upper chambers thereof, and of the inner parlours thereof, and of the place of the mercy seat' – the specifications all coming through the spirit: 'all this, said David, the Lord made me understand in writing, by his hand upon me'.

Automatic writing, however, did not become a standard technique of divination until spiritualists began to use it in the later 19th century. Most of the material which emerged was rhetorical and over-blown, but Stainton Moses' *Spirit Teachings* (1883), extracted from his notebooks, reveals considerable virtuosity in argument on the part of his spirit 'controls' and 'communicators'. (It was not his business, Moses observed, to define who these were: 'my interlocutors call themselves Spirits, perhaps because I so called them, and Spirits they are to me for my present purposes'.)

Quite often, however, the messages, though they could be attributed to the spirits, could also be accounted for by telepathy. When A. A. Liébeault, who with Professor Bernheim of Nancy was largely responsible for popularizing Braid's concept of hypnosis in France, was investigating examples of 'the higher phenomena' in the 1880s, one he recorded came from a patient, Mlle B, who had decided she would like to receive communications from the spirits, with the help of automatic writing. Within a couple of months she was able to write page after page of messages – 'all in well-chosen language, and with no erasures, while at the same time she maintained conversation with the people near her'. One morning in 1868 the urge came upon her to write, and the message contained the information that Marguerite was dead. Mlle B had a friend of that name, a colleague at the Coblenz School where they both taught. Inquiry revealed that Marguerite had died at about the time Mlle B was writing out the message.

Perhaps the most remarkable story in this context was related by David S. Bispham in *A Quaker Singer's Recollections*. Uncertain whether to commit himself to concerts, or try to secure an operatic role, he was pondering the problem while watching Baron Rudbeck, who had psychic powers, demonstrate planchette. It immediately spelled out 'Opera, by all means', though Bispham had not put the question, and was not himself touching the planchette.

In answer to his later spoken questions, he was told not only what operas to study, but which four parts he should concentrate upon: Amonasro, Wolfram, Kurwenal and Beckmesser; and study them he did. Two months later he had a message from the impresario Sir Augustus Harris, who had heard him sing in a concert; did he know the part of Beckmesser, and if he did, could he come at once to Covent Garden to rehearse it for a performance with, among others, Jean de Reszke and Madame Albani? The performance had to be postponed owing to the illness of de Reszke; but while his recovery was awaited, a message arrived from Hamburg to say that the baritone who was to take the part of Kurwenal the following evening was unable to come; did Bispham happen to know the part too?

'I may say without boasting,' Bispham claimed, 'for it is merely a matter of record, that for a number of years I had no rival in the part of Kurwenal, nor in the part of Beckmesser.' And not long after, he was asked to stand by to take the part of Amonasro, as Victor Maurel was indisposed – though as it happened, Maurel recovered sufficiently to be able to perform. 'When people say to me, "What but foolishness did anyone ever get out of planchette or any other so-called spiritistic advice?" I tell them the story.' Bispham concluded, 'My action in taking the advice I received – whence it came, I know not – resulted at the time in my being fully prepared for what I was asked to do.'

W. T. Stead claimed that he was able to exploit automatic writing for everyday purposes of communication, before the telephone became available for that purpose. Stead, editor of the *Pall Mall Gazette* and one of the foremost of campaigning journalists around the turn of the century, used to ask questions of people at a distance from whom he needed information, and allow them to 'use his hand' to reply. As an example of the method's utility, he cited an occasion when he had to meet one of his contributors from abroad at Redcar station. In his automatic writing, 'she' informed him she was in the train at Middlesbrough, and would be at Redcar at ten to three. When the train did not arrive, Stead tried again, receiving the message that it had been held up at Middlesbrough, but was now just about to reach Redcar. It duly arrived; and when he asked why the delay, she replied 'the train stopped so long at Middlesbrough, it seemed it would never start'.

Stead, however, had to admit that the messages' information

was not always so accurate, suffering sometimes from displacements. Once he received a report of a conversation which had taken place, details of which appeared to be wrong. It transpired later that they were in fact correct, but arose from a different conversation, which the woman who was 'using his hand' had had with somebody else.

Automatic writing was adopted by a few members of the SPR, around the turn of the century, as a convenient way of pursuing research in the home; and one of them, Mrs A. W. Verrall, a lecturer at Newnham College, Cambridge, had a curious instance of precognition. Twice within a week in December 1901 the name 'Marmontel' came up in her scripts, with meaningless – to her – comments attached: 'he was reading on a sofa or in bed – there was only a candle's light'; 'the book was lent, not his own'; 'Passy may help, *souvenirs de Passy*, or Fleury.' The following March she met a friend, who told her that he had borrowed Marmontel's *Memoirs* from the London Library in February, and had read it by candle-light in bed; in one episode in it, at Passy, Fleury had played a significant role. Mrs Verrall had never consciously heard of Marmontel at the time her automatic scripts appeared; and she had attestation that they had appeared before her meeting with her friend, because she had written to Eleanor Sidgwick to ask about Marmontel.

Automatic writing was used by the main contributors to the Society's 'cross-correspondences': Mrs Verrall; Mrs Piper, in Boston; and 'Mrs Holland' – the pseudonym used by Rudyard Kipling's sister Mrs Fleming – in India. Their scripts used to be sent into the SPR for filing; and the Secretary, Alice Johnson, eventually found that they contained material which suggested a common origin. It was as if 'Sidgwick', 'Myers' and 'Gurney' were collaborating in a scheme to show they had survived after death, by transmitting information of a kind which would not be appreciated by the mediums, such as classical allusions; allusions distributed among them, apparently meaningless in the individual scripts but acquiring consistency when the scripts were put together. Collaboration between the mediums, living as they did so far apart, could be ruled out.

What was to become the most celebrated of the cross-correspondences began with a message in automatic writing from Mrs Piper, purporting to come from 'Myers', telling Sir Oliver Lodge that he was to take the part of the poet, and 'Myers' would 'act as Faunus'. The message advised 'ask Verrall'; and Mrs Verrall, a classical scholar, explained that the reference was to a passage in Horace in which the poet thanked Faunus for protecting him from serious injury in an accident. A month later Lodge's son Raymond was killed in action on the Western Front. The following week Lady Lodge went with a French friend to a medium she had not met before, without disclosing her identity. In the course of the seance, which was directed towards her friend, the medium suddenly switched to her: a message was coming through from 'Raymond' who had met some friends of his father's. Could he name any of them: 'Yes: Myers.' Messages from 'Raymond' then began to come in from other mediums, some of a kind which were later shown to be veridical, as Lodge's *Raymond* (1916) described.

On an occasion when Sir Edward Marshall Hall, KC, who at the time of his death in 1927 was generally considered to be the ablest barrister of the day, was staying with his sister, her friend Miss K. Wingfield, another of the guests, agreed to demonstrate automatic writing. Asked by his sister to test her, Hall took out a letter he had received the previous day in his chambers in the Temple (and which he had not told his sister about), folded it up, put it in another envelope, and sealed it, before handing it to Miss Wingfield and asking where the letter came from. After a delay, a message came in automatic writing: 'The writer of that letter is dead'; and further questioning elicited the fact that he had died the previous day in South Africa.

The letter had come from Marshall Hall's brother in South Africa, posted three weeks before. Three weeks later, a letter arrived from South Africa to announce that his brother had been found dead on his bed, the day before the message came through automatic writing. 'If the phenomenon I have related can be explained by any natural process, I am ready to consider it,' Marshall Hall wrote in his introduction to a collection of Miss Wingfield's automatic writings, 'but until I am convinced otherwise, I shall continue to believe, and believe steadfastly, that the message of my brother's death was conveyed to me in mercy, by some influence outside this life.'

A recent example of divination by automatic writing has been given by Matthew Manning. When he was using it to release himself and his family from the attentions of his poltergeist, they light-heartedly decided to consult the spirit of his great-grandfather, Hayward Collins, who had been a racehorse owner, and ask whether he could tip the winners at a meeting the next day. They deliberately did not look to see what horses were running; nevertheless through Matthew's automatic writing 'great-grandfather' named six horses, which turned out to be runners: two came in first, one second, and two third, which would have netted a good each-way profit, had money been put on them. Later, 'great-grandfather' passed a further message about the Grand National:

Put your money on Red Rum which will come in first, and on Crisp which will come second. The third will be a tight spot so leave well alone.

Red Rum came first, Crisp second, and there was a photo-finish for third place.

Can automatism of this kind be a danger? Stevenson feels that the risks have been exaggerated. 'When automatic writing becomes compulsive writing, the person concerned should try to stop immediately,' he recommends; automatism can become a drug of addiction. But ill-effects are more likely to arise from vanity – the feeling of being admitted to a revelation, and the temptation to exploit it to found a cult:

I see no reason why interested persons should not try to develop themselves as automatic writers if they feel so inclined. I only remind them that they will be helped, not hindered, by informing themselves about the scientific investigations of automatic writing; we just need to stop adopting extreme positions about it, such as attributing all its products to psychopathology, or all of them to discarnate personalities. If we maintain the high critical standards of the best of our predecessors, we may yet obtain from automatic writing evidence of survival after death that improves on what they published.

Table-tilting

Collecting what he hoped would be damaging evidence against spiritism in the mid 1850s, the German theologian Franz Delitzsch uncovered the activities of a Jewish group in the early 17th century who had practised communication with the spirits by sitting round a table, and waiting for it to obey the spirits' promptings ('it springs up', an observer claimed, 'even when laden with many hundredweight'). Far from disturbing spiritists, this merely confirmed that what they were witnessing was not an illusion: tables really did obey the spirits, by tilting, or tipping, or rapping, to answer questions; with one tilt, or rap, say, for 'yes', two for 'no', and three for 'don't know'.

Used for divination, tables did not react as if they were simply automata, Lodge insisted. They appeared to develop personalities of their own. Hard though it was for anybody to believe who had not witnessed them performing, he had watched them 'convey touches of emotion and phases of intonation, so to speak, in a most successful manner'. Whereas any message transmitted by, say, a telegraph key was restricted, 'a light table, under these conditions, seems no longer inert, it behaves as if animated', he explained.

. . . somewhat perhaps as a violin or piano is animated by a skilled musician and schooled to his will – and the dramatic action thus attained is very remarkable. It can exhibit hesitations, it can display certainty; it can seek for information, it can convey it; it can apparently ponder before giving a reply; it can welcome a newcomer; it can indicate joy or sorrow, fun or gravity; it can keep time with a song as if joining in the chorus; and most notable of all, it can illustrate affection in an unmistakable manner.

The fact that tables acted in this way encouraged spiritualists in their belief that spirits must be responsible for the movements and the behaviour; but there was a catch. Questions might elicit correct answers from the spirit, often satisfying a sitter that information was being passed to him which could not be known to any of the others in the room. But when asked about their identity, the spirits tended to fall back on the names of deceased individuals who could not be traced; and they were suspiciously vague about conditions in the spirit world.

Occasionally, however, they provided useful information on a mundane level. In his autobiography *Sixty Years in the Wilderness* (1909) the journalist Sir Henry W. Lucy, best known for the long *Punch* series 'Toby, MP', recalled that when he and some friends decided to test the genuineness of the pastime, the spirit did nothing for the others, but introduced himself to Lucy as 'Charles

Dickens' (Dickens had died four years earlier), and told Lucy to call on his son Charles, editor of *Household Words*. Lucy thought it worth taking the advice; he went to see Charles, Jr, who commissioned him to write an article; and this launched him on what was to be his highly successful career. One other thing, too, intrigued him: Charles Dickens's writing, as spelled out by the tilts of the table, was 'playfully ungrammatical'. Only when Lucy read Forster's *Life* did he learn that in private correspondence, Dickens enjoyed being playfully ungrammatical.

Theodore Flournoy presented another example of useful information coming through table-tilting in his *Spiritism and Psychology* (1911). At a seance when Flournoy was present, a merchant, M. Ledoc, reacted to the occasion with 'a very rapid trembling'; soon, 'his whole body vibrated in unison with the table', which began to transmit messages. Initially they were incoherent, but eventually the table-tilting spelt out a sentence telling him he ought to go to his office: 'a telegram awaits you. It comes from Austria. It is very important.' Ledoc went to his office and found the telegram, which had arrived just before the seance began, and which indeed, 'proved to be very important – involving a transaction of about 60,000 francs'.

Flournoy declined to accept that this was a spirit communication. Ledoc, he pointed out, must have been expecting some such communication. What they had witnessed, Flournoy insisted, was no more than a product of 'cryptopsychism', the clothing of unconscious psychological processes in spiritualist garments. But he did not dispute the reality of the psychokinetic force moving the table; he attributed it to the psychic's PK.

The use of tables to pass messages began to die out when it was found that the ouija board provided a much faster means of communication. Although table-turning sessions have continued to be reported, from time to time, they have usually been held in order to witness the PK phenomena, rather than to make contact with the spirit world.

'Ouija'

Any flat, polished surface can be converted into a ouija board, the most practical being a round table small enough for sitters – usually no more than four or five – to reach to the other side.

Around the edge are placed the letters of the alphabet – not in order – and numbers from one to nine. Each of the sitters places a forefinger on a planchette, an upturned glass, or anything which will slide easily over the table-top; and after a time the 'traveller', as it has sometimes been described, will usually begin to move from letter to letter, spelling out words and sentences, often so quickly that it is not easy for a written record to be kept. The 'traveller' may answer questions, as if it is acting on behalf of a spirit (which it may identify); or it can simply take off on its own, as it were, providing information unasked. The material is often banal, but occasionally information will be provided which none of the sitters knows about, but which can subsequently be checked.

A version of the ouija board was in use as far back as the fourth century A.D.; on the same principle, but using a pendulum, held above the board, the movements of the pendulum 'bob' indicating the letters. Who was responsible for reviving it in Victorian times remains uncertain; but it has never since lost its fascination. In the late 1970s it topped the lists of the most popular Christmas buy in gift shops in the USA.

The most remarkable outcome of the use of a ouija board was the experience of Mrs Pearl Curran, a housewife in the American Middle West, during the first world war. Joining in sessions to please a friend, Mrs Curran was informed by a 'communicator' through the planchette that she now had a spirit 'control' – 'Patience Worth', a girl who had been killed by Red Indians in the 17th century. Mrs Curran was not a spiritualist, but she was intrigued by 'Patience's' personality, as were those who saw what Patience transmitted through the planchettes; poems and aphorisms, full of earthy humour. Eventually Patience produced *Telka*, the story of a girl who had lived in Britain in the Anglo-Saxon era, which not merely sold well as a book in its own right, but also baffled experts on the period because it was written almost entirely in words which, though up-dated, had been in use in the period. It would have been hard enough for the experts themselves to have been so consistent; and Mrs Curran was no expert, having had only a rudimentary education. Besides, the words poured out without the kind of pauses to think that an expert would have needed.

Later, 'Patience' was to write even more successful books: *The Sorry Tale*, around the life of Jesus; and *Hope Trueblood*, set in the

Victorian era. 'Either our concept of what we call the subconscious must be radically altered, so as to include potencies of which we hitherto had no knowledge,' Walter Franklin Prince commented after he had sifted all the evidence, 'or else some cause operating through, but not originating in, the subconsciousness of Mrs Curran must be acknowledged.'

In 1963 a New Yorker, Jane Roberts, experimenting with a ouija board, found that she was being plied with information by 'Seth', who was extremely knowledgeable in fields which she knew little or nothing about; and the books in which she described the experience made it hard to disagree with the verdict of Eugene Barnard of North Carolina State University, who investigated "Seth": 'I do not believe that Jane Roberts and "Seth" are the same person, or the same personality, or different facets of the same personality. Yet this only raises the question: is the Western scientific tradition which has held orthodox psychologists in thrall, capable of dealing with an issue of this kind?'

From the start of its use, controversy arose whether the movements of the 'traveller' should be put down to the unconscious muscular pressure, either exerted by one of the group (or all of the group, if they collectively were expecting the reply to a question), or to a spirit. Sceptics might maintain that the 'traveller' was moved by the *conscious* finger-tip pressure of some joker in the group, which could occasionally happen; but anybody who attended a number of sessions soon realized this explanation was inadequate.

In an attempt to settle the issue, Sir William Barrett set up a series of experiments in Dublin during the first world war: first, periodically shuffling the letters on the assumption that the individual (or group) unconscious mind, confused, would not be able to operate the 'traveller' with such facility; and then, when it was clear that shuffling made no appreciable difference, hiding the letters so that the subjects with their fingers on the 'traveller' could not see what it was spelling out. This, too, did not prevent the 'traveller' from forming coherent sentences, thereby demonstrating that if the group unconscious were responsible for the movements, it must have a paranormal dimension.

Dowsing

The mind's-eye picture of a dowser is of a man walking over fields holding in his hands the two ends of a forked hazel twig, its single end pointing out in front of him, waiting for it to dip or jerk when he passes over underground water. This method is still in common use, but many professional dowsers prefer a pendulum, or construct implements to their own specification – sometimes coat-hangers twisted to the desired shape, sometimes more sophisticated gadgets whose pointer, or pointers, can turn freely in sockets. The term divining 'rod' is still loosely used for any device employed in this form of divination; 'rhabdomancy' for the art.

The force that provides the dowser with his guidance acts differently for different people. Some individuals, when they are over an underground stream, feel the tip of the rod being pulled up: others feel it being pulled down. For others, it seems to jerk, or writhe. Where two L-shaped rods are used, one being held in each fist, they may swivel either outwards or inwards as indicators. Whatever method is used, an expert dowser reckons to be able to estimate not just where water is to be found, but its depth, its rate of flow, and whether or not it can be used for drinking, or for watering crops – or is unusable.

'Water divining' is often colloquially used as a synonym for dowsing, but dowsers can and often do search for metal, for archeological remains, for lost property, and for many other objects; and the dowsing faculty is quite common. The proportion of people who possess it is hard to estimate, as it does not necessarily display itself in tests; but if a dozen people are taken out to try their hand, one or two are likely to feel the twig's movements as they walk over an underground stream, while the rest will feel nothing. Most of them will feel something, though, if a practised dowser lays his hand on their wrists – sometimes even if he simply touches them – while they are experimenting.

Because divination with the aid of a forked hazel twig appears to be only a few centuries old, dowsing has sometimes been described as a recent development. In different forms, however, it has been found in many tribal communities, where sometimes a pendulum is used, sometimes a branch – Melanesian diviners held one out in front of them, giving witnesses the impression that it was pulling them along in the direction of the object or person they were seeking. Sometimes a cane, or a stick, fulfilled a similar function.

Divining 'rods' feature on several occasions in the Old Testament; they were regarded as acceptable if they were used in the service of the Lord, but denounced both by Moses and Hosea – it was 'whoredom', in Hosea's view – if they were employed by anybody who was not one of the Lord's prophets. This tradition lingered on into classical times; the priests at Hieropolis used to obtain information by putting an image of a god on their shoulders and waiting until it took charge and replied to their questions by movements – pulling them forwards for yes, backwards for no.

The Catholic Church banned any form of divination, discouraging priests as well as the laity from indulging in what was taken to be a diabolic practice; and Luther continued the tradition, including the use of a divining rod in his list of acts which broke the first commandment. It was not until the late 17th century that dowsers – the term came into circulation at the time to describe them – felt able to practise without fear of being arrested for witchcraft; and in 1692 the tracing of some criminals by a young dowser, Jacques Aymar, made him for a time almost a national hero in France, as his divining rod showed not only where the fugitives had stayed on their flight, but even the bottles out of which they had drunk, enabling their pursuers to track down and arrest one of them, who turned out to be the servant of the others.

During the 18th century, dowsing established itself in many countries, usually being practised by locals on about the social level of the local bonesetter. 'In Somersetshire, which is a county the most ill-watered in England,' de Quincey observed in the *Confessions of an English Opium-eater* (1822), 'upon building a house there arises uniformly a difficulty in selecting a proper spot for sinking a well. The remedy is to call in a set of local rhabdomantists.' They would traverse the site, holding a willow rod horizontally; wherever it dipped, water would be found. 'I have myself not only seen the process tried with success,' de Quincey asserted, 'but have witnessed the enormous trouble, delay and expense, accruing to those of the opposite faction who refused to benefit by this art.'

Useful though the local dowser often was to the aristocracy, gentry and newly-rich merchants, the rising tide of rationalism was bringing the dowser's art, like the bonesetter's, into disrepute with the opposite faction – scientists. But it retained a following, paradoxically, among priests, whose Church had for so long denounced it, and among soldiers, who might have been expected to scoff.

With belief in diabolic intervention fading, the Church's ban on divination ceased to be rigorously enforced, as Zschokke discovered when his interest in mining led him to investigate the methods then in use to discover seams of ore. 'In almost every canton in Switzerland,' he wrote, 'are found persons endowed with the mysterious natural gift of discovering by a peculiar sensation, the existence of subterranean waters, metals or fossils.' Sceptical, he tested some of them by taking them to places where he knew what lay underground, but they did not; and one who succeeded was 'a learned Abbot'. Another, a young woman, 'excelled all I have ever known'; in districts with which he was familiar she was never once wrong in her judgments. 'The results of the most careful observation,' he admitted, 'have compelled me at length to renounce the obstinate suspicion and incredulity I at first felt on this subject.'

Soldiers have often been forced to call upon the services of a dowser, for want of any hope of finding water; whether in camp on the North West Frontier or, in desperation, on Gallipoli, where Sapper Kelly immortalized himself with his achievements. In Germany after the second world war the water supply for a massive new military headquarters for the British army was located, against the recommendation of geologists, by an amateur dowser (he happened to be the army engineer in charge). 'Dowsers detect enemy's tunnels', a *New York Times* headline ran on 13 October 1967. The Marines in Vietnam, the correspondent explained, were using coat hangers bent into the shape of an L, one held in each fist: 'as the operator walks over the ground, they spread apart or point to hidden tunnels'. The method did not rate a mention in training or equipment manuals; but according to Marine officers, it had been used 'with marked success' by engineer units engaged in mine detection and tunnel destruction.

Major General James Scott Elliot, formerly GOC the 51st (Highland) Division, used to list his interests in *Who's Who* as the conventional 'polo, hunting, shooting, fishing, sailing'. After his retirement another hobby began to absorb him: dowsing – his particular interest being in the locating of archeological remains. His *Dowsing: One Man's Way* (1977) provided a lucid survey, primarily designed to help anybody who wanted to experiment with advice on what to expect and how to begin. And in particular, he emphasized how useful dowsing can be on a simple everyday level – for finding mislaid keys, for example.

Stories about dowsers succeeding where geological experts have failed are legion; some of them well-attested, as was a case featured in Christopher Bird's *The Divining Hand* (1979). The Misquamicut golf club in Rhode Island needed a steady supply of fresh water if it were to survive, and a hired professional driller failed to find it, though a pipe was sunk to the depth of 230 feet, much of it through rock, at considerable expense. A local dowser, called upon, obtained no reaction in the area which had been thought to be geologically the most promising, but the movements of his forked twig, he explained to the onlookers, pointed to a spot where, 23 feet down, there was a flow sufficient to provide the club with 34,000 gallons a day. He was a few feet out in his computation of the depth; and the flow turned out to be sufficient to fulfil only half of the club's needs. But as he had found another source, which was more than sufficient to cover them, this mattered little.

Insofar as dowsing is a form of divination, there is no reason in theory why it should not also be used for prediction; and, according to the British dowser Tom Graves, there has been at least one case which indicates that it can demonstrate precognition. Wanting to contact a friend who was moving round in London, a dowser first dowsed a street directory – which indicated a certain street – and then a directory of hotels in the street, before telephoning the hotel which triggered the dowsing reaction. His friend, he found, was not there; but he left a message for him. His friend duly rang him back; and they found that he had not decided to go to that hotel until *after* the dowser's pendulum had intimated where he could be contacted.

There are thousands of dowsers, most of them part-timers, semi-professionals, operating in countries all over the world. Along the northern shores of the Mediterranean the building boom has brought employment to them; many work on a 'no water, no payment' basis, which is more than contractors employing geological 'experts' are prepared to do. In the United States, companies dealing with water and pipe-laying employ dowsers as a matter of course. In Canada a dowser has been given an official appointment in the Ministry of Agriculture. And universities in the Soviet Union have spent a great deal of time and money seeking to find an explanation in terms of conventional bio-physics.

Why, then, is dowsing still unacceptable to most Western scientists?

There are two main reasons. Unless and until a force is discovered which can account for the phenomenon, it will remain suspect so long as scientists shy away from acceptance of anything which does not fit old materialist preconceptions. And in formal tests, dowsers who have an excellent track record in the field often fail. In books such as *Water Witching USA* (1959), by Evon Z. Vogt and Ray Hyman, the impression is given that all the evidence can be explained away either in natural terms – good dowsers intuitively and by practice know where to look – or in terms of deception and self-deception.

An explanation for the frequent failure of dowsers under test conditions is not hard to find; it is the same as for the failure of psychics in tests in other related fields – as in a case related by Ochorowicz. 'I do not feel quite master of myself in making this experiment,' a sensitive who had been asked to find and identify an object in a test explained to his investigator. The degree of success he could expect, he explained, depended upon whether he could get into a certain mental state; 'I then feel *isolated* from all around me. I hear nothing, I exist only in my fingers which, however, work without me. The more I reason, the less do I succeed.' Trials tend to distract dowsers: hence the failure rate.

Not all tests, however, have given negative results. Arthur Young in his *Autobiography* (1798) described how he had attended some which were held in Hyde Park of Captain Hoar's dowsing abilities by Sir Joseph Banks, the celebrated botanist. Banks thought Hoar had failed in one of them; 'but in the four trials I watched,' Young noted, 'and in which I knew he could not be acquainted with the direction of the pipes, he succeeded completely.'

Herbert Mayo, Professor of Physiology at King's College, London University, described some research into dowsing in his *Letters on the Truths Contained in the Popular Superstitions* (1851); the results had been so encouraging that he had formed the impression it could not be long before the divining rod 'will be a credit to the family of superstitions, for without any reduction, or slipping, or trimming, it may at once assume the rank of a new truth' –

provided that some explanation could be found for the force which moved the rod. But no explanation was found; and far from establishing itself, dowsing fell increasingly into disrepute.

Even relatively open-minded scientists, such as the anthropologist Edward Tylor, could not bring themselves to take seriously the proposition that the movements of the dowser's forked hazel twig were not deliberate, on the dowser's part; trying it for himself, Tylor 'noticed when I allowed my attention to stray, the rod would from time to time move in my hands in a way so lifelike that an uneducated person might well suppose the movement to be spontaneous'. And in the second volume of the *Proceedings* of the SPR in 1884, Edward R. Pease observed that both scientists and the public had long considered dowsing 'one of the black arts', even if a relatively harmless one in that it 'preys only upon men's pockets and does not imperil their liberty or their lives'.

From his own reading of the evidence, Pease thought there was a *prima facie* case for the investigation of dowsing; but that this was not the view of some of the leaders of the Society is clear from the dismissive references to it elsewhere in the records. William Barrett, however, felt it his duty to investigate – though as he was later to recall, he was not merely doubtful, but 'inclined to scoff at what seemed a mere relic of an ancient superstition'; he shared the view of most scientists that dowsers were 'merely clever charlatans, and the twisting of the rod a bit of stage play'. What he saw and read in the 1880s converted him: in particular a test staged by the Waterford Bacon factory. It had wasted a great deal of money having boreholes sunk on the advice of expert geologists; and it had sent for an English diviner, John Mullins, asking the Irish Geological Society to hold a watching brief. Its representative reported that after Mullins's rod had reacted so violently that it had snapped in his hands, a borehole had been sunk at the point he indicated, revealing a small fissure in the otherwise solid rock which had previously resisted progress. Through it, a source was tapped with a flow of up to 5,000 gallons an hour.

A more elaborate investigation was carried out in Paris shortly before the first world war by Armand Viré, a sceptical Professor of Geology, and reported to the Academy of the Sciences by the eminent physicist Jacques-Arsène d'Arsonval. Professionals and amateurs were invited to show what they could do, with varying degrees of success; but the results of one of the trials, Viré conceded, were impressive.

The dowsers were invited to see if they could trace the course which some tunnels took, around 100 metres below ground. Viré expected, and perhaps hoped, that the dowsers would trace the course on the surface which the tunnels took on the published map, as he knew the map to be inaccurate. But three of them (one was the Abbé Mermet, who was subsequently to develop radiesthesia – the use of the pendulum in medical diagnosis) followed the tunnel's bends, 'down to the smallest'; and their findings, when transferred to a correct map, exactly coincided.

The prejudice against acceptance of dowsing, however, was by this time too strong to be broken down by such evidence; and it remained, even though so distinguished a physicist as Sir J. J. Thomson, discoverer of the electron, pleaded for greater recognition. 'The divining rod is perhaps of all phenomena which may be thought to be psychical, the one most favourable for experiment,' he argued in his autobiography (1936). 'The motion of the rod is a mechanical effect, and gives the indication of the magnitude of the phenomenon. The conditions under which the effect occurs can be made definite and there is no lack of trustworthy people who possess the dowsing power; for these reasons I think such experiments are well worth making.' But the experiments which have been made since have never given consistent results; partly because of the old problem – that dowsers who have no difficulty in satisfying clients, week after week, cannot deliver the goods in tests; partly because neither orthodox researchers nor parapsychologists are any nearer to identifying the dowsing force.

Only in Russia where, thanks to the simple expedient of classifying dowsing as a branch of bio-physics, it has been possible to arrange for a programme to compare the results dowsers achieve with those of geologists using their own methods and equipment, has it been established that the dowsers obtain better results. According to an article in the *New Scientist* (8 February 1979) by David Patterson, a BBC producer who had the opportunity to visit the scene of one such trial, the proportion of dry wells sited by dowsing was half that of the geophysically-sited wells. Even in Russia, though, he noted that antipathy against dowsing remains strong in the scientific establishment 'for its lack of theoretical basis and alleged links with the occult'.

Perhaps the acid test will turn out to be financial, rather than scientific. Asked why Hoffman-LaRoche, the pharmaceutical company, employed a dowser whenever they were setting up new factories, their spokesman Dr Peter Treadwell replied, 'We use methods which are profitable, whether they are scientifically explainable or not. The dowsing method pays off.'

Granted that a dowsing sense exists, the question remains: what causes the movement of the divining rod? That some force acts on it can hardly be disputed, even by the most uncompromising of sceptics; a force which causes the rod to act as if it were performing independently of the dowser. In its commonest form, it feels as if an invisible hand were raising or depressing the tip of the rod, sometimes so powerfully that the dowser cannot resist it. Occasionally it looks as if the rod has taken on a life of its own, and is actually trying to escape from the dowser's grip.

This can leave a misleading impression, as some dowsers use their hands alone, the reaction to water being no more than a tremor (in some tribal communities, the diviner is described as a 'hand-trembler'): and most people experience no more than a twitch on the rod, or see a gentle twirl of the pendulum. But the more energetic displays have inevitably aroused interest, and provoked scepticism – as when Barrett initially assumed that the movements simply represented play-acting on the part of the dowser. The French chemist Chevreul, however, sceptical though he was of the pretensions of diviners, conceded in his book on the subject of divination and table-turning (1854) that rods and pendulums move as the result of a muscular action 'which is not the product of the will, but the result of a thought carried over to a phenomenon of the outside world' – the implication being that the 'thought' was not a conscious intention, but what would now be described as subconscious, a concept which had yet to establish itself in Chevreul's time.

For a while, spiritualists contended that the dowsing force must be the same force that moved tables. Wallace's surmise was that the rod was manipulated by discarnate intelligences – a view derided by Oliver Lodge: 'Does he suppose that a deceased person comes and bobs the stick?' In this, Lodge was being a little unfair, as the spiritualist theory was not quite so unsophisticated: the

Theosophist A. P. Sinnett preferred the idea that there might be 'some elemental agency at work', implying that dowsers could be mediums, rather than clairvoyants, and Barrett eventually was to concede the possibility that the movements of the rod were due to 'a force, or ectoplasm, emitted by the dowser' – though he did not himself accept that interpretation. The preferred view of most of the early psychic researchers, as expressed in the first contribution on the subject presented to the SPR after its foundation, was that as dowsers held the rods in a position of tension and unstable equilibrium, in order to pick up small movements, light muscular contractions could produce startling effects: 'the action of the rod may be caused by unconscious movements of the diviner's hands, due possibly to a sensation of chill on water-bearing spots or, possibly, merely to an unwritten practical science of the surface signs of hidden water'.

The main weakness in this hypothesis was that many dowsers did not (and do not) go out into the field until they had first done a preliminary dowse over a map of the area, from which the rod would pick up indications where to begin their search: and when Barrett began to investigate, he soon concluded that the information must be being picked up, as Richet had surmised, clairvoyantly.

Richet contended that clairvoyant information acted on muscles; not directly, but through the nervous system. Barrett agreed, arguing that all the rod's movements 'find their origin in the dowser's mind, that no physical theory can bear close consideration, and that the movements of the rod and of the dowser have no more direct relation to the discovery of, say, water than as giving physical and visible expression to a mental and abstract cognition'.

In writing this, however, Barrett was brushing aside evidence which did not fit. Two centuries earlier, a dowser had told Robert Boyle that when passing over a vein of ore, 'the motion of the hand did not at all contribute to the inclination of the rod, but that sometimes when he held it very fast it would bend so strongly as to break in his hand' – a phenomenon frequently reported since, along with accounts of dowsers who have felt the hazel twig rasping against the fulcrum of their fists, in its efforts to turn. Richet, too, had noted that in tests conducted in Toulouse, the handles of a divining rod had turned in the dowser's hands even when they were enclosed in sheaths; and also that in descriptions of the use of a technique by Chinese diviners, the handles of the T-shaped divining rods were not held, but lightly balanced on the diviner's open palms.

Evidence that muscular action could not account for the movements of a divining rod had been produced in London in the middle of the 19th century by John Obadiah Rutter, an engineer, who had rigged up a contraption which looked like a miniature fishing rod, with its base firmly held, and with a line from which a pendulum bob dangled, enclosed in a glass bowl. If psychics touched the base, Rutter was able to show, the 'bob' would move and answer questions. Unluckily for Rutter, his 'magnetoscope' either did not work for sceptics, or provided them with inaccurate answers, which enabled W. B. Carpenter magisterially to dismiss him.

It was not until the 1970s that a sophisticated experiment to test the force was mounted by Alvin B. Kaufman, an American electronics engineer, who decided that with modern instruments it should be possible at least to decide whether the force was muscular or external. Using what he described as a 'strain gauge bending beam', Kaufman found that the force was externally applied. The movements of the forked twig, he warned, still required explanation. 'We can say it is an effect of psychokinesis,' he noted – but what psychokinesis is remains unresolved. 'One thing is certain, however: the amount of psychokinetic (if such it is) energy is great, and dramatically evident. I have seen a forked twig, one arm held with pliers and the other resting on an open hand, actually tear off in the pliers.'

Whatever the nature of the force involved, dowsing clearly has some significant affinities with other types of automatism: in particular automatic writing. The dowser's rod, Barrett observed, serves the same purpose as the ouija board 'traveller'. Mrs Travers Smith, with whom Barrett carried out a number of experiments to try to find out more about the force moving the 'traveller' over a ouija board, found that, as in dowsing, if somebody felt no impulse coming through, it was sometimes enough if she laid her hand lightly on his: the planchette would begin to move.

Richet noted that some dowsers had tremors, or went into slight convulsions, as they walked over an underground stream – a symptom frequently observed with mediums entering their trances. And the link of mediumship with dowsing was to be illustrated in a curious case in the files of the SPR. In 1922 a spiritualist group in Flushing, in Holland, held a seance in which they used a dowsing device to pick out letters of the alphabet. Four of them knew no English, and the other two, very little; but the device spelled out (with hesitations and mis-spellings) a poem in English which, they found the next day, had been written out and mused upon by a boy in a nearby house at the time of the seance.

QUASI-MOTOR AUTOMATISM

Card-reading

There are certain types of divination which are not as a rule considered to be paranormal – not, certainly, by parapsychologists – but which have a paranormal element, at least in the way they are ordinarily practised. Basically they involve the interpretation of what appears to be a fortuitous distribution of the materials which the diviner is using. In their earliest known form, the tribal diviner cast small bones upon the ground, making his diagnosis from the pattern in which they fell and spread out in front of him. In early civilizations this was replaced by a variety of devices, the most familiar being consultation of the entrails of sacrificial animals. Playing-cards, or tea-leaves in the bottom of a cup, are still occasionally used; and recently divination with the more sophisticated Tarot cards and the I Ching have become fashionable.

There are two possible paranormal aspects of these techniques. In one, the diviner does not content himself with mechanical interpretation – does not, for example, say that because the bones or the tea-leaves take the form of a ship, the subject is going on a sea-voyage; or because two 'unlucky' cards are in conjunction, that there is going to be an accident. Instead, the diviner uses the pattern formed simply as a taking-off point for his imagination; liberating his mind, as it were, to admit ESP. In *The Sixth Sense* (1927) Joseph Sinel described a friend who read tea-leaves as invariably starting with 'the usual rigmarole about meeting a tall fair lady'; but his expression would then change as he began to exhibit clairvoyance, sometimes trivial, sometimes serious.

Divination of this kind is related to psychometry, the cards or tea-leaves being used to facilitate psychic rapport. But another possibility has recently been attracting more attention: that the act of shuffling the cards, or, in the case of I Ching, the act of throwing yarrow stalks or coins, is psychokinetically linked to the results obtained. The arrangement of the Tarot cards after they are dealt, or the passages in the I Ching indicated by the way in which the stalks or the coins have fallen, are believed in themselves to provide paranormal divination through synchronicity.

This represents an interesting throw-back to the idea that when 'the lot is cast into the lap', as Proverbs put it, 'the whole disposing thereof is of the Lord'. The idea that God might settle issues in this way surfaced from time to time, as Keith Thomas showed in his *Religion and the Decline of Magic* (1971); lots were to be cast only with great reverence, William Perkins wrote early in the 17th century, 'in that the disposition of them immediately cometh from the Lord, and their proper use is to decide great controversies' – among them, the decision whether or not to reprieve condemned persons who, if they drew the lucky ticket, sometimes found on it 'life given by God'.

Palmistry

Palmistry, too, can be held to fall in the same category as card divination; though with palms, there have been indications that the lines can be used, up to a point, for straightforward prediction. In 1964 an article in the *Lancet* claimed that the lines on the hand had 'great diagnostic value', a verdict echoed by the United States Department of Health a few months later: there was enough evidence, it announced, to justify serious research into the health indications provided by the human palm. Whether the simplistic indicators used by some professional palmists – the 'long life line means a long life' and such – have any validity has yet to be established; but in any case, most professional palmists combine straightforward analysis along traditional lines with clairvoyance, and it is not as a rule possible to distinguish between the two.

Countless stories are in circulation at any given time about individuals who have gone to a palmist as a joke, but have been given information about their lives, past, present and future, which has shaken their scepticism. Flammarion provided a typical example in *The Unknown* (1900). A group of volunteer soldiers during the siege of Paris, meeting a man who read palms, nervously asked him how they were going to fare. Three, he assured them, would come through unscathed. The fourth, however, would be hurt – but not by a weapon: he would suffer burns. A few months later, trying to move a barrel of petrol when it caught fire, he was severely burned down his side.

As a rule it is only when there is a twist of this kind to the prediction – the soldiers expecting, though fearing, to be wounded or even killed, and the only one to suffer being hurt in a domestic accident – that the predictions of a palmist are remembered; but Osbert Sitwell reported a macabre variant in *Great Morning* (1948). Some of his brother officers went to a celebrated palmist (whom Winston Churchill was reputed also to consult) in the hope of being told they would be happy in love and successful in their careers. One by one they saw her throw up her hands and admit she could not 'see' what would happen to them. 'To each individual to whom it was said, this seemed merely an excuse she had improvised for her failure; but when I was told by four or five persons of the same experience, I wondered what it could portend.' It was 1914. A few months later, he had a different cause for wonder: the officers had lost their lives on the Western Front.

Astrology

Until very recently, few psychical researchers would have considered astrology worthy of their attention. It did not rate a mention in Fodor's *Encyclopedia* (1933); and still does not qualify for an entry in Thalbourne's *Glossary* (1982). The assumption has been that 'the art of judging of the occult influences of the stars upon human affairs', as the *Shorter Oxford English Dictionary* defines it, has long since been discredited. Parapsychologists have tended, in this field at least, to side with 'the sceptics comprising the "educated public"' – as John Anthony West, writing in the *Encyclopedia of the Unexplained* (1974) described them – in believing astrology to be 'absolutely without foundation, a superstitious attempt by primitive man to read order into an essentially chaotic and meaningless universe, and to stave off the unknown through bogus divination'.

What has made astrology even more suspect is that, as West noted, 'a vast audience follows the daily horoscope in the newspapers and believes astrology to be a more or less valid system of fortune-telling' – something which astrologers, apart from those who write the predictions, are accustomed to deplore. But the daily horoscopes need not be laid at astrology's door. Most readers are ready to be told they should be careful with money, or patient with difficult relations, as homely advice worth paying attention to, without regarding it as an indication of Destiny ruling their lives from the planets.

West made the point that astrology once had a long and distinguished following, including Plato, Pythagoras, St Thomas Aquinas and Johann Kepler, who 'accepted astrology not as a means of foretelling the future but as a symbolic master plan of the structure and functioning of the universe'; adding that modern science has been discovering a great deal about the links between celestial and terrestrial events as experiments with living creatures reveal how they can be influenced by, say, the phases of the moon. But the decisive influence in restoring astrology to a measure of respectability has been the work of the French psychologist and statistician Michel Gauquelin and his wife Françoise.

Originally intending to demonstrate how unsatisfactory the evidence for astrology was, by subjecting the claims to careful statistical analysis, the Gauquelins found that in certain respects (though not in all) the traditional belief that personality can be influenced by the position of the planets at birth was borne out. 'Myths and astrological expectations of a rather vague sort would suggest a connection between the martial arts of competitive, assertive sport and Mars; the introverted saturnine personality of the scientist and Saturn; and the jovial, extroverted personality of the actor and Jupiter,' as Professor Hans Eysenck has put it. 'In essence, this is what the Gauquelins found, using thousands of sportsmen, actors and scientists in their determination to obtain objective, conclusive data.'

What the Gauquelins found was that people born 'under' a planet, in the sense of being born when it was at certain positions relative to them, were significantly more likely to become famous – athletes 'under' Mars, and so on. Eysenck, deeply sceptical, checked the Gauquelins' work by carrying out a similar study, with his wife's help, to find whether the same method would show a comparable difference between extroverts and introverts. His expectation was that there would be no correlation; but that if the Gauquelins were right, introverts would tend to be born under Saturn, extroverts under Mars or Jupiter – and so it turned out.

'To find some solid fact in the astrological field was surprising,' Eysenck has admitted, adding that it was 'not entirely welcome – we like to find our preconceptions confirmed'. Hoping for just this confirmation of sceptical preconceptions, Paul Kurtz, founder of the Committee for the Scientific Investigation of Claims for the Paranormal, embraced a research project in 1978 which, it was expected, would expose the Gauquelins' research results as false. To his chagrin, the test produced the same results as the Gauquelins. Alarmed that this would give a boost to serious psychical research, Kurtz and his committee opted for a cover-up, and it was not until five years later that the cover was blown by dissident members of the CSICOP, who felt that, whether or not the Gauquelins were correct, suppression of the confirmatory results was disgraceful. Kurtz was compelled to publish a humiliating climb-down in his journal, the *Skeptical Inquirer*.

Assuming that the Gauquelins' basic findings continue to be confirmed, the status of astrology will be radically altered. On the one hand, it will eventually have to be accepted that the casting of horoscopes can provide information about human beings of a kind which can be verified – not, indeed, as applicable to individuals, but as applicable to groups, on a predictable statistical level. To this extent it will become possible to claim that astrology, at least where it has been provided with confirmation along the lines the Gauquelins pioneered, should no longer stay in the paranormal category. A paranormal element remains, however, in that the demonstration of the relationship between birth and the position of the planets opens up again the debate on the extent and nature of cosmic influences, prompting a fresh look at earlier attempts to explain forces which have so far eluded explanation.

There also remains the possibility that astrology can be used to make predictions about individuals. The evidence for this is mainly anecdotal, but historically it is quite extensive, in tales such as the one recounted of Jean Stoeffler, who worked out from his horoscope that he was doomed to die on a certain day in 1530 from a blow on the head. Determined to take no risks, he decided to stay at home all day; but, reaching for a book on an upper shelf, he dislodged the shelf and its contents, which fell on his head and killed him.

In *On Time*, Michael Shallis has suggested that astrology may have more relevance for individuals than could be ascertained by analyses along the Gauquelins' lines. The map of the heavens produced for a horoscope, he believes, 'represents the quality of time that synchronistically is mirrored from the celestial pattern above to the terrestrial event below'. Astrology, in other words, is an a-causal system, which needs to be looked at in the light of the theories of synchronicity propounded by Kammerer, Jung and Pauli. The power of astrology lies in its a-causality, 'just as in Tarot the shuffling of the cards is the vital a-causal link', Shallis claims. 'The random moment of birth, even the random pattern of tea leaves in a cup, has qualities and an interconnectedness with the rest of nature, because nothing is really random in the sense of being meaningless.'

The Gauquelins' research, and the new interest being displayed by some parapsychologists in synchronicity, is reflected in *Psychical Research* (1982), the SPR's Centenary Symposium, which includes a section on astrology by Arthur T. Oram. 'The possibility of direct links between psychical research and astrology has not yet been investigated in depth,' he admits; but he believes that the chart of an individual can be a useful indication not only of personality factors but also of 'attitudes, relationships with people, approach to money, potential for development under these and many other headings, the timing and nature of major points of development or change, and so forth'. Astrology has been described as 'a kit of tools with which the individual approaches life'; it would make sense to start collecting data, he argues, 'so that the possibility of more specific relationships between psychical research and astrology can be investigated'.

6 *MAGIC*

The *Shorter Oxford English Dictionary* defines magic as 'the pretended art of influencing the course of events by compelling the agency of spiritual beings, or by bringing into operation some occult controlling principle of nature; sorcery, witchcraft'. With the spread of scepticism – of belief that the art, or craft, was a pretence – magic came to be regarded as legerdemain. 'Conjuring' went the same way. 'A conjurer,' Sir Edward Coke had laid down in 1644, 'is he that by the holy and powerful names of God invokes and conjures up the devil to consult with him, or do some act.' By the 19th century, a conjuror was a man who pulled rabbits out of a hat.

It may be too late to rescue magic, restoring it to its original sense; but there is no other obvious term except witchcraft, or sorcery, both of which have acquired some sinister connotations. Recently there has been a revival of interest in alchemy, largely due to the efforts of Jung; and a revival of witchcraft practised by small groups using what are believed to be traditional methods. But the only type of traditional magic which is at all widely practised is psychic healing.

Few recent claims to magical powers can be trusted; but according to William Seabrook, who was interested in the subject, Aleister Crowley actually demonstrated that he had them. After a lunch where Crowley had 'regaled himself with whitebait, steak tartare and creamcake, topped off with a Napoleon brandy', Crowley suggested they went for a stroll through New York – Seabrook to choose the route. As they were walking down Fifth Avenue, Crowley quietly synchronized his footsteps with a man walking ahead of them, before allowing his knees to buckle under him. As they did, the man ahead of them 'fell as if his legs had been shot out from under him'.

Describing the episode in his *Witchcraft* (1934), Seabrook said he had examined the possible natural explanations, finding none of them satisfactory. 'Behind the mumbo-jumbo', Seabrook felt,

Crowley had power: 'Whether it was the kind of power worth having, or of a kind that can ever in anybody's hands have any profound effect upon the world, or whether he always used it honestly, are questions outside any point I'm trying to make, and which I don't pretend to answer.'

Seabrook had some reservations about Crowley; none about George Gurdjieff, who certainly 'had power'. Seabrook met him in 1924, when he brought his disciples to the United States, to demonstrate how he could make them move or 'freeze' them by mental commands, 'like a group of perfectly trained zombies'.

This ability to induce freezing, sometimes described as 'glueing', ties in with a similar effect observed by the mesmerists and hypnotists. When the polar explorer William Scoresby turned his attention to mesmerism in the 1840s, he found with one subject that he could 'magnetize' the chair on which she was sitting, so that if he mentally informed her that she could not get out of it she would be unable to leave it until he released her, even after she had come out of her trance. Reading about Scoresby's experiments, the surgeon James Esdaile followed them up in India, finding that if he told a mesmerized subject to place his hands on the arms of his chair, and not to move them even when taken out of his trance, the subject would be astonished to find he could not release them. Freezing of this kind is now one of the standard gags of club hypnotists – a form of witchcraft.

Alchemy

'Was the alchemist a philosopher, deep in a mysterious study where he discovered the secrets of transmutation?' C. A. Burland asked in *The Arts of the Alchemist* (1967). 'Was he just a charlatan involved in a particularly fantastic kind of mumbo–jumbo? Was he simply a fore-runner of the scientists of today? Or had he an occult knowledge which we cannot hope to acquire in our materialist environment?'

The fact that such questions can be put by an authority on the subject is itself an indication of how little is known about alchemy. That the alchemist was not 'just a charlatan' is clear: nobody is likely to apply that description to Newton, or to Boyle, both of whom were fascinated by the subject. It seems probable that some alchemists found ways to tap paranormal sources in their researches in physics and chemistry – just as some physicists have been finding that a few psychics can tap paranormal forces to bend metal; but it has to be admitted that we do not have the evidence from which to provide a clear-cut picture of what alchemists could do.

Probably the only way in which alchemy can be profitably explored is the route Jung took, and described in *Memories, Dreams, Reflections*. Reading, with difficulty, the old texts, he thought some of them 'blatant nonsense'; but he was intrigued by others, and eventually began to realize their curious affinities with his analytical psychology: 'the experiences of the alchemists were, in a sense, my experiences, and their world was my world'.

When I pored over these old texts everything fell into place; the fantasy images, the empirical material I had gathered in my practice, and the conclusions I had drawn from it. I now began to understand what these psychic contents meant when seen in historical perspective. My understanding of their typical character, which had already begun with my investigation of myths, was deepened. The primordial images and the nature of the archetype took a central place in my researches, and it became clear to me that without history there can be no psychology, and certainly no psychology of the unconscious.

Alchemy, like the pursuit of Nirvana, cannot be studied dispassionately as an exact, or even as an inexact, science; it requires the subjective, even emotional, immersion of the student.

Witchcraft

In tribal communities, two categories of individual were assumed to have the ability to tap *mana*, the psychic force, so that they could 'see' what was happening or move objects at a distance: the witch doctor, who was expected to use his magical powers for the tribe's benefit, and the witch, or sorcerer, who was expected to use them for his own benefit. Witch doctor, in fact, meant witch diviner: the man employed to 'see' or 'smell out' witches.

Some anthropologists have made a distinction between sorcery, which they consider to be the use of certain techniques of magic, such as spells – which in theory at least, anybody could use; and witchcraft, where the magical powers resided in the witch – though he might use spells to strengthen them. But in both cases, the aim was to enlist paranormal forces for whatever purpose was in the mind of the witch, or sorcerer.

The assumption tended to be that anybody who employed magic in this way was being – or, at least, could be – anti-social; the Old Testament injunction 'thou shalt not suffer a witch to live' expressed an attitude which had long been held, and was to continue, enshrined in law, until the 18th century – in places, until even more recently. But in the Christian era witchcraft became confused with diabolism, so that in witch-hunts, the accusation was usually of liaisons with the devil.

With the gradual erosion of belief in spirits, demons included, witchcraft has ceased to be taken seriously; belief in it has survived chiefly in cult form, with people forming covens to observe certain rituals believed to be based upon a religion which long pre-dated Christianity. For a while, this belief obtained a measure of academic respectability through the publication of Margaret Murray's *The Witch Cult in Western Europe* (1921); but as a number of critics – notably Professor Norman Cohn in his *Europe's Inner Demons* (1975) – have shown, her thesis cannot be sustained in the light of historical research. The notion of witches practising in covens, and the rituals, turn out both to have been derived from forgeries put about by the Church to provide additional justification for its campaign against heresy in the Middle Ages.

The fact that somebody enjoys the ability to exploit paranormal forces no longer leads to his being regarded as a witch: he may simply be a medium, or a dowser, or a mini-Geller. Occasionally, however, a case history appears in which the phenomena described suggest that a few individuals can exercise the power to influence other people at a distance paranormally – which is what witches were traditionally expected to do.

In *Annales des Sciences Psychiques* Dr J. Gibotteau described how in 1899 he had observed this power in a patient of his, 'Bertha'. When he suddenly felt a spasm of uneasiness for no good reason, he would put it down to her playing a trick on him: she would admit as much on their next consultation. He also tested her by getting her to make pedestrians stumble, or hesitate and change direction, from his window.

Healing

Of all the forms of magic, healing has been the most important – at least until the development of scientific medicine began first to overshadow it, and then to cast doubt on its existence. It was always closely linked with divination – the use of paranormal faculties to ascertain the nature and cause of an illness, and to prescribe for it; but magic played a significant part in the procedure by which the illness was diagnosed and treated.

Healing, though, presents a problem; it is often impossible to separate out the psychological element, which is usually attributed to the effects of suggestion, from the paranormal. Only recently have tests been devised which enable investigators to begin to make the distinction; it can rarely be made with any confidence in connection with the historical evidence for paranormal healing, when the existence of a psychological therapeutic component always has to be allowed for. Paradoxically it may be significant even where magic is superficially dominant – for example, where ceremonial magical practices are being used, of a kind calculated to impress the gullible.

Dr Stanley Krippner of the Humanistic Psychology Institute in San Francisco, the leading American investigator in this field, divides folk healers (as he describes them) into five categories: shamans, spiritists, esoteric healers, sacramental healers, and intuitive healers. In practice, there is overlapping, but the classification has its uses.

One of the chief functions of the shaman, medicine man or witch doctor has always been to find by divination what is the matter with sick members of the tribe, what has caused their illnesses, and what should be done to cure them. Treatment has usually been undertaken in one of two ways: either by putting patients into a trance, with induced fits, dissociation and comas – as if to 'shake up' mind and body to get rid of the illness; or by prescribing herbal remedies. Even when the prescription is made not by the diviner, but by a tribal elder who is regarded as an expert herbalist, an element of magic has always been encountered in the form of a widespread belief, still lingering on in folklore, that the best way to find the appropriate herbal remedy is for the prescriber (or, sometimes, the patient) to go to find it – but not consciously to search for it; rather, to allow serendipity to guide the footsteps to the right place, where the herb will be found.

Both these traditional healing methods re-surfaced in early civilizations. Herbalism became linked to astrology – so that medicinal herbs had to be picked at certain phases of the moon;

trance healing took the form of 'stroking', in which magic passes were made over the bodies of the patients.

The most celebrated 'stroker' in history was the Irishman Valentine Greatrakes, who in the reign of King Charles II acquired an immense reputation, first in his own country and later in England, with scores of testimonials from men and women in society, impressing even those who came to scoff: 'I have seen deafness cured by his touch, grievous sores of many months date in a few days healed, obstructions and stoppings removed, and cancerous knots in the breast resolved,' the Rev. R. Dean wrote, after watching him over a period of three weeks, during which Greatrakes had treated about a thousand patients. 'Really there is something in it more than ordinary.' Nevertheless Dean did not believe the cures were miraculous; and it is still possible to argue that they were brought about by the power of suggestion.

At the time, there was much speculation over whether the effect was magnetic; and some strokers held magnets while they made their passes. As convulsions often followed, a few priests began to use magnets when exorcizing members of their flock who were presumed to be possessed by demons; and it was witnessing this procedure which put Mesmer on to his theory of animal magnetism as a curative current coming from the planets. In the way he used it, animal magnetism provoked shamanist-style dissociation and comas; and to this day there are still a few 'magnetizers' – as they sometimes describe themselves – using the same technique.

Mesmer's disciples, however, introduced a new development, which they described as autoscopy. One of their discoveries was that clairvoyant subjects could sometimes 'see' their own internal organs, and those of other people, making it possible to use their powers for clinical diagnosis. The commission set up by the French Academy of the Sciences in the late 1920s to investigate mesmerism found one such subject, 'Céline', who although ignorant of medical matters was able to provide diagnoses sufficiently accurate to impress her investigators; one, in particular, when she disputed the accepted medical findings about the nature of a patient's disorder, and at a subsequent post-mortem it was found that she had been right.

The commission's report, accepting that Céline and others could 'see' clairvoyantly what they could not see with their eyes, was rejected by the Academy; but examples of autoscopy have continued to be reported from time to time with subjects under hypnosis, or with mediums. The most striking practitioner of autoscopy in modern times has been George de la Warr, working near Oxford; the inventor of a 'camera' which, he claimed, could photograph internal organs of patients, disclosing what was the matter with them: a drop of the patient's blood placed on the 'camera' would suffice to produce results on film – an example of mechanized autoscopy.

De la Warr's hope was that the 'camera' would eventually provide evidence as objective as that of an X-ray photograph. In this he was to be disappointed; when the camera was independently tested by Brigadier R. Firebrace (formerly an interpreter at the wartime conferences between Churchill and Stalin), the tests indicated that the camera itself played no part in the process. The photographs, Firebrace agreed, sometimes provided pictures of what appeared to be internal organs of patients, and he was confident that they had not been obtained by fraud; but 'the available evidence tends to indicate that these photographic phenomena really constitute thought photography, or changes in the photographic emulsion brought about by the action of the human mind'.

Tribal diviners have ordinarily been spiritists, assuming that the information about cause and cure of illness comes from the spirit world; as also does the healing force, transmitted through patients while they are in their trances, or giving curative herbs their potency. This method received a temporary setback with the emergence of monotheism: in the Old Testament, the Israelites tended to assume that because illness was a mark of the Lord's displeasure, there was little point in the prophets trying to be healers. Jesus, however, revived the concept of healing through the spirit – the Holy Spirit – by explaining that it could be a reward for faith (healing was one of the gifts which St Paul attributed to the Holy Spirit's beneficence).

Ordinarily, healing of this kind was carried out through 'the laying on of hands', the assumption being that the hands of Jesus's disciples, and those to whom they passed on the healing gift, were channels through which the Holy Spirit exercised its therapeutic force. But the fears of the leaders of the Catholic Church in the Middle Ages that heresy might spread in the guise of spiritism led the Vatican to put a ban on healing by priests, with the exception of exorcism – the casting out of demons. Healing at shrines, attributable to the spirits of the dead saints and martyrs, was also allowed; but the laying on of hands, though it continued in ritual use, lost its healing significance.

Spiritist healing has continued to flourish in a few countries, notably in Brazil and in the Philippines. The most celebrated of Brazilian healers, 'Arigo', believed himself to be possessed by the spirit of a German, 'Dr Fritz', who told Arigo what was the matter with patients, and what to prescribe for them. 'Dr Fritz' also guided his hands when the prescription was surgery; using only an unsterilized kitchen knife, Arigo would remove tumours and then, halting the blood flow, seal the wound, leaving no scar. That these feats were genuine was attested by many respectable doctors who had come to investigate, assuming they would only see conjuring tricks. Among those who were impressed was Juscelino Kubitshek, President of Brazil, who had had a medical training at the Sorbonne.

In the Philippines, psychic surgery is usually conducted without a knife. The bodies of patients seemed to open up for Tony Agpaoa – the leading practitioner in recent years – and, as for 'Arigo', close again, leaving no trace of the wound. Agpaoa, too, was carefully investigated by, among others, Krippner. 'Psychic surgery', however, became for a few of the 'surgeons' a profitable racket, as an airline began regular flights for rich Americans suffering from diseases which orthodox medicine could not cure; and although some films taken of the operations have appeared to show that they are genuine, at least in the sense that the body is opened up and tumours removed, the fact that in some cases the 'tumours' turned out to have been 'palmed' by the healer, and then flourished for the benefit of the camera team, has led to psychic surgery's acquiring a seedy image – not wholly justified, Krippner and Alberto Villoldo insist in *The Realms of Psychic Healing* (1976).

There are a few psychic healers on the Philippine model in Europe, but easily the largest group in the spiritist category are the Spiritualists, who in recent years, particularly in Britain, have been adding healing to their repertoire. They believe their 'controls' are spirits, often of famous doctors in the past, who guide their hands to places on patients' bodies, the better to let the healing force come through to the affected organ. Or they form prayer groups, who give 'absent healing'. (Lady Chichester organized healing of this kind for her husband when he was diagnosed as a terminal lung cancer case: three years later he was to win the first solo trans-Atlantic yacht race.)

Esoteric healing developed from the use of magical devices by shamans and sorcerers; and gradually it came to be believed that the devices – spells, formulae, rituals – could be exploited in their own right without recourse to spirit intervention. Witches were generally consulted for cures, a tradition that still is occasionally to be found in rural areas where 'wise women' (as those who were not regarded as witches were called) are consulted about cures for disorders which resist orthodox medical treatment.

Although, in theory, belief in the healing powers of the Holy Spirit has remained in the creeds of the Christian Churches, it has been effectively supplanted by sacramental healing; the function of the priesthood being not to act as the healers, but to provide the setting in which God, through the Holy Spirit, could intervene, if suitably impressed by the faith of the sick or the prayers of their friends. Healing services, with formal prayers and ritual, became standard in the Catholic Church and in the Anglican communion, though they have never been extensively used by Protestants.

'The intuitive healer undergoes no special training or initiation,' Krippner explains, 'but responds to a call from God, or spontaneous begging to "lay on" hands or pray for the ill.' Often the discovery of healing powers is unrelated to any religious belief, though the greater majority of intuitive healers agree that there is some outside force which flows through them, and some take it to be divine. Others are content to regard it as unexplained.

In addition to Krippner's five categories of healing, there is radiesthesia: the use of certain techniques originally employed by tribal diviners to diagnose, prescribe for, and treat illness. In its most frequently encountered forms a pendulum is employed, in the same fashion as in dowsing. The most celebrated practitioner of the art, the Abbé Mermet, explained in his *Principles and Practice of Radiesthesia* (1935) that it was based on the assumption that all bodies, of all kinds, emit radiations: that the human body 'enters these fields of influence and becomes the seat of nervous reactions, of some kind of current, which flows through the hands'; and if a rod or pendulum is held in the hands 'the invisible flux is made manifest in the movements given to this object, which acts as a kind of indicator'. By holding the pendulum over the bodies of patients in hospitals, Mermet was able to diagnose what was the matter with them, and prescribe treatment, with an accuracy that confounded sceptical members of the medical profession.

Radionics came into existence largely as a result of the belief of some practitioners of radiesthesia that the technique could be made to provide more consistent and objective results if sophisticated equipment could be introduced to analyse the information conveyed by the 'current'. Gadgets of various kinds are employed to enable the practitioner to relate the movements of the pendulum (or some other divining aid) more specifically to disorders – even in the absence of the patients: it is enough if they send a drop of blood or a few hairs. Sometimes these 'black boxes', as they have come to be described in the press, are used simply to diagnose and prescribe; but practitioners have begun increasingly to use them for treatment, sending the 'current' back to the patient, on the analogy of absent healing.

Inevitably, the invention of the 'black boxes', initially in the United States, provoked the derision of the medical profession, and practitioners have been prosecuted and on occasion jailed. In Britain, however, a trial set up by the medical profession in 1924, and carried out by a committee of distinguished scientists led by Sir Thomas (later Lord) Horder, produced striking confirmation of the accuracy of the method as a diagnostic tool, compelling the committee to report that the claims for it had been established 'beyond any reasonable doubt'. The investigation, however, was not taken further.

The Paranormal in Medicine

Controversy has periodically arisen over the role, actual or potential, of the paranormal in conventional medicine: particularly in psychiatry. Several psycho-analysts have reported encountering ESP in their sessions with patients, including Freud. But he was ambivalent on the subject: he told Hereward Carrington that if he had his life to live again, he would devote it to psychic research; but he allowed himself to be persuaded by Ernest Jones not to publish his views on it for fear that it would make orthodoxy even more hostile.

Analysts, too, have been confronted with the same problem as psychical researchers: how to be sure that what appear to be extra-sensory exchanges with patients may not be accountable for by the transmission of sensory clues. Telepathy, as Jan Ehrenwald has noted, is 'not labelled with the criterion of uniqueness or specificity to pin-point its telepathic origin', and it is hard to distinguish from the effects of suggestion or unrecognized signals of the kind that facilitate thought-reading – coughs and sniffs and twitches. The evidence is consequently 'largely circumstantial and at best unproven'. Nevertheless it is extensive and it is beginning, he believes, 'to have a seminal influence upon the overall system of modern psychiatric thought'.

It can affect the course of psychiatric treatment in two ways, Dr James E. McHarg observes in 'Psychical Research and Psychiatry' in the SPR's Centenary volume (1982): in the form of apparently spontaneous episodes of ESP; or in actual connections between paranormal forces and illnesses.

Firstly, overtly paranormal phenomena, such as those of a poltergeist outbreak, may sometimes point very clearly to a disturbance in an individual or a group which is of sufficient intensity to be regarded as a psychiatric illness. Secondly, convincing explanations of a paranormal basis may sometimes be discovered for serious psychiatric illness which has hitherto been without plausible explanations and in which there have been no overt paranormal manifestations. Thirdly, distress and perplexity of such intensity as to require psychiatric referral is sometimes precipitated by an encounter with frankly paranormal phenomena, for example at a seance.

A better appreciation of the influence of paranormal forces, then, could provide a better understanding of some disorders, and of how to deal with them. When Matthew Manning was the focus of poltergeist phenomena as a boy, the psychic energy was eventually channelled into automatic writing and drawing, which provided him with a safety valve; and later into healing, using the laying on of hands, which he has made his career.

The lack of any established way of distinguishing between the psychological and the psychic element in healing has presented a problem for those who have hopes to undertake scientific research in this field. There was one type of trial, however, which it was realized might settle the issue whether or not a psychic force is involved: the inmates of a hospital ward were to be divided into two groups, one of which would be given absent healing, and the other left unprayed-for. If the absent healing group showed significant improvement compared to the unprayed-for, this would constitute *prima facie* evidence for the force's existence.

A trial along these lines was proposed in the 1940s by the psychologist Dr Robert Thouless, a member of the Council of the Society for Psychical Research. To exclude the possibility of psychological influences, he suggested that the names of the patients who were to be given absent healing would be given to the healer, but not to the patients nor to the hospital staff; and a healer volunteered to make the experiment. Hospitals, however, refused to co-operate 'because it would be contrary to medical principles to allow hospitalized patients to receive any kind of treatment without the patients' knowledge and consent'. Any doctor who had permitted such a trial even *with* the patients' knowledge and consent could in fact at that time have been struck off the Medical Register, as the General Medical Council had a ruling that patients must not be referred to anybody without medical or paramedical qualifications: and in his *Experimental Psychical Research* (1963) Thouless wrote that unless this problem could be solved, he did not see how there could be any experiments of a kind which would satisfy scientists.

In Canada, however, Dr Bernard Grad, a research biologist at McGill University, had by this time developed an ingenious alternative to research with humans: he was using laboratory mice. He anaesthetized them, made small 'nicks' in their skin, and divided them into two groups, one of which was 'treated' by a healer, Colonel Estebany, a former cavalry officer in the Hungarian army. (He simply held the box containing them in his hands.) The healing rate in the mice Estebany treated proved to be significantly faster than in the control group: as it was in a further trial, when individuals who did not have healing powers went through the same procedure, thereby providing control groups against which to measure the healer's success.

Estebany was also able to show that by laying his hands on a flask of enzymes, he could exert a marked influence on their activity. And later Matthew Manning, in a series of trials, influenced the growth rate of cancer cells *in vitro*. Ambrose and Olga Worrall, too, living in Baltimore, showed that they were able to speed up the rate of growth of rye grass in a laboratory 600 miles away by applying the techniques they ordinarily used for distant healing.

7 PSYCHIC STATES OF MIND

From earliest times, what are now regarded as paranormal phenomena have been associated with trance states – as they commonly were, and still are, in tribal communities. The term trance, however, has fallen into some disfavour, as it is both too positive in its implications – we tend to think of trances as implying total loss of awareness of surroundings – and too vague. The term 'altered states of consciousness' (ASCs) – a newcomer, coined by Professor Charles Tart of the University of California, Davis – is now preferred: also vague, but deliberately so, to cover the wide range of mental conditions which people can experience when they are not in what is taken to be normal consciousness: dissociation, trance, sleep, meditation and so on.

Parapsychologists commonly accept that ASCs are conducive to psychic phenomena: or, put the other way round, that the ordinary state of consciousness is *not* psi-conducive. The reason, Henri Bergson suggested in his *Matière et Mémoire* (1908), is that the function of the human brain is to sieve out information coming into it which is not of practical use before it reaches consciousness. Developing this hypothesis in his Presidential Address to the SPR in 1914, Bergson related it to ESP: extra-sensory promptings, he pointed out, might be urging a man in one direction at the time his conscious mind was telling him to go in another. In such circumstances, the sieving mechanism would be 'specially charged with the duty of throwing back into the unconscious the presentations so provoked, for they would be very embarrassing in everyday life'; nevertheless 'one or other of these presentations might yet at times pass through as contraband, especially if the inhibiting mechanism were functioning badly; and these again would be facts with which psychical research would be concerned'.

Sleep and Dreams

A commonly reported experience is to go to bed with a problem on the mind, 'sleep on it' and wake up the following morning with the solution. Whether the solution has been presented by a kind of reshuffling of data already in the mind, or is attributable to some psychic pick-up from the collective unconscious or a guardian spirit, cannot yet be determined, owing to the limitations of our present knowledge; and this also holds for those dreams which perform the same function. It is consequently often impossible to classify dreams as paranormal, even when the dreamers have been provided with information of a kind they are certain they did not know about: and this has tempted some sceptics to find 'natural' explanations to cover all eventualities.

In his commentary on witchcraft and magic, for example, Sir Walter Scott related the story, which he had found to be well-attested, of the dream of Mr Rutherford of Bowland, at a time when he was being prosecuted for arrears of tithe. He knew that his dead father had paid in a capital sum, in lieu of tithe; but could not find the documents to prove it. The night before he was due to go to Edinburgh to try and effect some compromise, his father appeared to him in a dream; told him the name of the attorney, since retired, who had dealt with the matter on his behalf; and said that as it was so long ago, the attorney might have forgotten, but would remember it 'by this token: that, when I came to pay his account, there was difficulty in getting change for a Portugal piece of gold, and we were forced to drink out the balance at a tavern'. The attorney, when Rutherford called on him, did not remember the transaction, 'but on mention of the Portugal piece of gold, the whole returned to his memory'; the papers were found; and Rutherford won his case. Nevertheless Scott felt that the dream represented nothing more than a belated jogging of Rutherford's memory of what his father had told him at the time.

Sceptics have sometimes been compelled to stretch 'natural' explanations to breaking-point. The French writer Alfred Maury reported that he had once had a protracted dream about the French Revolution, in which he was hauled before a revolutionary tribunal, and sentenced to the guillotine; at the point when the blade was about to fall, he was woken up by a blow on the neck from a falling rod which had been holding up a canopy over his bed. Rather than accept any precognitive element, he took this to illustrate the hypothesis that entire dreams last only seconds – just long enough, in this case, for instinct to warn the sleeper that the rod was falling. 'The error of theorists is that they wish to explain everything within the limits they themselves have set,' Flammarion complained; 'in all probability, in the light of our new psychic investigations, Alfred Maury here deceives himself.' That Maury had in fact deceived himself was to be recognized later when conventional investigators, exploring the rapid eye movements (REMs) associated with dreaming, finally demolished the 'over-in-an-instant' hypothesis.

There is a further problem in assessing the paranormal element, as Gurney, Myers and Podmore noted in *Phantasms* (1886):

Millions of people are dreaming every night; and in dreams, if anywhere, the range of possibilities seems infinite; can such positive conclusions be drawn from such a chaos of meaningless and fragmentary impressions? Must not we admit the force of the obvious *a priori* argument, that among the countless multitudes of dreams, one here and there is likely to correspond in time with an actual occurrence resembling the one dreamed of?

What cannot be disputed, however, is that dreams are the largest source of reports about the paranormal – in the sense that the people who have had the dreams have taken them to be telepathic, clairvoyant or precognitive. Surveying the range of evidence from reports of spontaneous cases in Wolman's *Handbook*, Robert L. Van de Castle admits that it is hard to make firm generalizations, but 'some recurrent threads of similarity can be traced through the fabric of the collated studies carried out during the past fifty years'; if all forms of ESP are included, a third or two-thirds of reports are about dreams, and they account for about a quarter of all reported telepathic experiences.

In the 1960s, an attempt was made to test for ESP in dreams at the Maimonides Medical Center in Brooklyn, New York, the results being reported in several articles and in *Dream Studies and Telepathy* by Montague Ullman and Stanley Krippner, with A. Vaughan (1970). The volunteer subjects had electrodes attached to their heads so that they could be monitored by an electro-encephalograph; whenever they were dreaming, their rapid eye movements (REMs) providing the indicator, an agent in another room would seek to transmit a target picture. After a few minutes, the subjects would be woken up and asked to relate what they could remember of their dreams, so that links, if any, with the target picture could be assessed, and in the morning they were shown several pictures, one of which had been the target, and asked which, if any, of them related to their dreams. The results, though not consistent, frequently indicated an ESP component in dreams significantly above chance expectation.

Another development which has attracted attention recently, and which may have psi implications, is the possibility that dreams may be put to use to solve problems. In a trial in the United States in 1974, 500 students were asked to find if they could solve a problem by sleeping on it: seven succeeded. In 1983 the *New Scientist* helped in a test devised by Morton Schatzman, publishing 'brain twisters' which readers were invited to try to solve in their sleep: several replied that they had been able to do so, their dreams having pointed to the answers.

Relaxation

In his *Mental Radio* (1930) Upton Sinclair described numerous tests he had conducted with his wife Mary, in which she was able to 'see' and draw pictures which were handed to her in opaque envelopes. Asked to describe how she did it, she admitted that this was difficult. To call it a state of simultaneous concentration and relaxation might sound contradictory; but when her mind was concentrated on the process, no effort was involved. It was 'a relaxation as restful, as seemingly "complete" as when I am in that state called normal sleep'. Perhaps, she surmised, we have more than one mind, one of which can be unconscious while the other takes over for a time.

Recently a method has been adopted by parapsychologists to promote relaxation: the Ganzfeld. It consists of devices designed to eliminate unwanted sensory stimulation: half ping-pong balls placed over the eyes, diffused lighting, and 'white noise' played through ear-pieces, the subjects being made as comfortable as possible during ESP tests. According to Carl Sargent – the first graduate to be awarded a Doctorate of Parapsychology at Cambridge University, who has conducted several experiments using the Ganzfeld – the method has a significantly higher success rate than tests conducted without it.

Dissociation

Although the term dissociation has been used in a narrower sense by some psychologists, in this context it is convenient to employ it loosely to describe those states where consciousness is not entirely lost, but where the mind wanders, as it were, as if partly split. This is quite a common experience in connection with automatic writing, where the writer may be able to keep up a conversation on one topic while the pen or planchette is churning out entirely unrelated material.

A limited measure of dissociation can be induced, or assisted, by what has sometimes been described as negative concentration: concentration, that is, upon eliminating distractions. 'When I am getting at the thing which I wish to discover, the only effort I make is a sort of effort of attention of a quite general kind,' Professor Gilbert Murray explained, describing how he picked up information in his telepathy game with his family. 'Any disturbance of our customary method, change of time and place, presence of strangers, controversy and especially noise, is apt to make things go wrong.'

Possession

Explorers who took the trouble to investigate tribal divination reported two main types. In one, the shaman went into a trance resembling sleep, coming out of it with the information he had obtained in it from the spirits; in the other, he appeared to be taken over by a different personality, which was assumed to be one of the spirits using him as a mouthpiece. The same assumption is made by most mediums, who, in their trances, lose their identity, and are taken over by a 'control'. In possession, 'there is a more or less complete substitution of personality', Myers explained, 'writing or speech being given by another spirit through the entranced organism'.

But does possession imply the taking over of the mind from outside? May it not reflect the existence of dual, or multiple, personality? The evidence for the interdependent existence of spirit 'controls' has repeatedly been challenged, often with success, as it was in the case of Mrs Piper's 'Dr Phinuit'. 'There seems no escape from the conclusion that the trance personalities of most mediums are secondary personalities of the mediums themselves,' Ian Stevenson has claimed in the *Journal* of the American SPR (1977). 'They thus resemble the secondary or multiple personalities manifesting in some mentally ill persons.'

In the Middle Ages, possession tended to be equated in the eyes of the Church with occupation by the devil, or his demons: the possessed risked being burned as witches, unless they could lay the blame on a sorcerer, as the nuns at Loudun did upon Urban Grandier. With the decline in belief in diabolism, possession came to be regarded as a form of insanity: its victims, though saved from torture and the stake, were often condemned to life-long incarceration in lunatic asylums. Induced possession, of the kind which began to flourish in the form of spiritualist mediumship, was taken to be spurious by conventional scientists, and was left to the psychical researchers to investigate; when the American psychologist Morton Prince was conducting his protracted and immensely thorough investigation of 'Sally Beauchamp' and her four different, independent, personalities, his findings initially appeared in the publications of the SPR.

Prince's *The Dissociation of a Personality* (1906) began the process by which multiple personality established itself as an accepted fact, rather than a superstition; and the first world war, with its numerous cases of 'hysterical fugue' – loss of memory, often coupled with the emergence of a different personality – among soldiers in the trenches, consolidated it. Subsequent case histories – the best known being 'Eve', described in a number of books and in a successful feature film – have been accepted by orthodox psychologists as if purged of any psychic taint. Nevertheless the links between multiple personality and mediumship are obvious. Ordinarily, mediums voluntarily induce what they still believe to be spirit possession, unlike 'Sally' and 'Eve', both of whom had alternative personalities who took over at whim. But many mediums find that their 'controls' occasionally, and sometimes frequently, come through with information when they are not asked for it. And whether the condition is regarded as being caused by the intrusion of split-off personalities or of spirits, a paranormal element may be encountered.

Hysteria

Hysteria has confusingly accumulated a number of different meanings, but in this context it can be regarded as the syndrome – a constellation of symptoms – commonly (though far from invariably) related to entry into a state of trance. Historically, the most frequently encountered symptoms have been convulsions, attributed to the entry of a spirit, god or demon, taking possession, and strange noises. As Iamblichus, the 3rd-century Greek philosopher, described it:

> Sometimes the body of the man is violently agitated, sometimes it is rigid and motionless. In some instances sweet music is heard, in others discordant and fearful sound. The body of the subject has been known to dilate and tower to a superhuman height, in other cases it has been lifted into the air. Frequently not merely the ordinary exercise of reason, but sensation and animal life would appear to have been suspended; and the subject has not felt the application of fire, has been pierced with spits, cut with knives, and not been sensible to pain.

Hysterical symptoms have since frequently been reported which to observers are paranormal – the invulnerability and incombustibility of the *convulsionnaires* of St Médard, for example. According to the French hypnotist Charles Lafontaine, an outbreak of mass hysteria in the Haute Savoie in the 1850s was sufficiently serious for the Government of the day to appoint a commission of inquiry; and it found that girls had been seen rising to the tops of trees with a facility that no climber could match, leaping, somersaulting and hanging head down; one of them, when on top of the highest tree, 'sprang from one to another just as a squirrel or a monkey might have done'. Reports of this kind, usually referring to 'superhuman' behaviour, have been quite common.

Outbreaks of mass hysteria at schools and other institutions, even when the symptoms are straightforward, sometimes seem to spread as if through some psychic contagion, the victims fainting and retching simultaneously. That this is not by simple imitation has been confirmed in reports of a recent outbreak in which babies in prams were among the victims – leading at the time to the assumption that some kind of a gas must have been responsible, which was found to be incorrect.

Induced Trances

Franz Mesmer's therapeutic technique was derived from the practice of shamans, who, treating patients, endeavoured to put them into a trance in order to shake off the spirits presumed to be plaguing them. Mesmer's assumption was that the procedure was justified even if the explanation was fallacious. Animal magnetism, he believed – a bio-magnetic force coming from space – could be channelled through patients with the magnetic 'passes', giving them the symptoms of hysteria, such as convulsions, and curing their disorders.

Mesmer's followers found that the convulsions were superfluous; the beneficial effects could be obtained by simple suggestion after the patient had been put into a mesmeric trance, and became the equivalent of a sleep-walker (such cases were described as 'somnambules'). In this condition, they found, some patients displayed the 'higher phenomena' – clairvoyance, 'travelling clairvoyance' and 'community of sensation', or 'exteriorization of sensibility', the ability to 'taste' and 'smell' what the mesmerist, in another room, was tasting and smelling.

It proved impossible, however, to convince scientists and the medical profession that the mesmeric trance existed, let alone that it could result in the appearance of the 'higher phenomena'. Even when surgeons demonstrated that they could amputate a limb without the patient's feeling pain – this, at a time when there were no anaesthetics – orthodox doctors claimed that the patients, well-paid by the mesmerist, were only pretending to feel no pain. When John Elliotson tried to secure recognition of the therapeutic value of hypnosis, he was sacked from University College Hospital, London, which he had helped to found. Induced trances did not begin to attract the attention of orthodox scientists until the 1840s, when the Scots practitioner James Braid provided an explanation which they could accept without feeling they were being lured into occultism.

Arguing that the mesmeric trance state was the product not of animal magnetism, but of a bio-physiological rapport between the mesmerist and the patient, James Braid, in his *Neurypnology* (1843), felt that this disposed of the 'higher phenomena', which, he thought, were contrary to the laws of nature and so could not be genuine. He was faced with a problem, however; some of his patients could 'see' objects held behind their backs. This, he was compelled to attribute to hyperacuity of the senses while in the state of hypnosis (as he named it); so that these few individuals, when hypnotized, could *feel* what was held behind them.

Noting the resemblance between the symptoms of possession, hysteria and those sometimes occurring when patients entered the trance state, Charcot, though accepting 'Braidism', came to the conclusion that hypnosis was an induced form of hystero-epilepsy; and it was in this guise that it was finally accepted by the French Academicians who for a hundred years had refused to accept that the mesmeric trance state existed. The research projects which proliferated in the 1880s not merely soon showed that the hystero-epilepsy theory was wrong – the trance could easily be induced in normal people without any symptoms of either hysteria or epilepsy; they also revealed that Braid had been wrong by producing numerous examples of 'community of sensation' which could not be accounted for by hyperacuity of the senses, as patients could 'see', 'hear', 'feel', 'taste' and 'smell' in circumstances which precluded the use of those senses as detectors. Then and later, a considerable quantity of evidence accumulated to show that hypnosis, like the mesmeric trance, could liberate the 'higher phenomena'. In his contribution to Wolman's *Handbook* on the subject of hypnosis, Charles Honorton, Director of Research, Division of Parapsychology and Psychophysics at the Maimonides Medical Center in Brooklyn, New York, groups them in four categories:

(a) transposition of the senses, including claims of eyeless vision and finger-reading.

(b) community of sensation, in which hypnotized subjects were reported to have responded to sensory stimuli presented by a distantly-located hypnotist.

(c) mental suggestion, in which the hypnotist is alleged to have exerted an influence on the subject's behaviour, while in a 'trance', post-hypnotically, or by hypnotic induction at a distance; and

(d) travelling clairvoyance, billet-reading, and claims of paranormal medical diagnosis.

Summarizing the results of recent ESP research using hypnosis, Honorton points out that, out of 42 series of trials, slightly over half have provided positive results, as against a chance expectation of five per cent. 'I believe the conclusion is now inescapable that hypnotic induction procedures enhance psi receptivity.'

The other common method of inducing trances is with the help of drugs.

When Columbus and his crew, and the explorers, missionaries and colonizers who came after them, were investigating the tribal customs of the American Indians, they were greatly struck by the way in which medicine men used a variety of drugs made from plants – cohoba, peyotl, jimsonweed, mushrooms, tobacco and morning glory among them – in order to induce the trance state for purposes of communication with the spirits. After watching the process, the chronicler Gonsalvo Fernando d'Oviedo Y Valdez described how the 'priest' (as he called the diviner) partook of the drug 'and then began his conjurations, calling aloud on the spirits; and then, highly agitated and furious, he was shaken by the most violent movements'. Later, when the diviner had calmed down, 'the chief, or some other, asked what they desired to know, and the spirit replied through the mouth of the inspired man in a manner perfectly exact'.

The Spaniards did not find it hard to believe that the information passed in this way could be 'perfectly exact', as they assumed that the devil was responsible for it, providing diviners with second sight to keep them, and the tribes, under his control. Wherever they colonized, they tried to stamp out divination, and the drug-taking associated with it. But it continued underground, to surface again when fear of the devil ceased to cause alarm; and in central and southern America diviners today use the same drugs (if they can obtain them), or newly discovered drugs, for the same purpose. As a Peruvian diviner recently told the anthropologist Douglas Sharon, a drug taken from a cactus initially causes slight dizziness, then a clearing of the faculties and a feeling of tranquillity: 'then comes a detachment, a type of visual force in the individual', inclusive of all the senses, 'including the sixth sense, the telepathic sense of transmitting oneself across time and matter'.

The Siberian shamans used the 'magic mushroom' – the fly agaric, which has been identified by some commentators with *soma*, the drink of the Vedic gods; and mushrooms with hallucinogenic properties have been exploited for divination in many other parts of the world. In Mexico recently, the American banker R. G. Wasson and his wife, pursuing their hobby of collecting hallucinogenic mushrooms, heard to their disappointment that the old gatherings where they were ceremonially eaten were no more; but they managed to find a woman who performed the rites under the mushroom's influence, and who had a reputation as a diviner, and they decided to test her by making inquiries about their son, who was in Boston. He was not in Boston, she told them: he was in New York, in a state of emotional crisis. He had joined the army, and would shortly be posted overseas, to Germany. When they returned to the United States they found their son had indeed been in New York for the week at the time of their seance with the diviner; that he had been in a state of emotional crisis, over a girl, and that he had joined the army. He was sent overseas – the diviner's only error – to Japan, rather than to Germany.

In the explosion of experimentation triggered off by the realization of the psychedelic properties of mescaline, especially after the publication of Aldous Huxley's *The Doors of Perception* (1954), there were countless reports of ESP while subjects were under the influence of drugs. In *The Varieties of Psychedelic Experience* (1966), for example, Robert Masters and Jean Houston gave several instances which they had encountered in the course of their work; and in tests LSD subjects either guessed correctly or gave close approximations of 'guides' (pictures in envelopes) at a level considerably higher than chance: 'out of 62 subjects tested, 48 approximated the guide's image two or more times out of ten. Five subjects approximated the guide's image seven and eight times out of ten.'

Investigating the experiences described by marijuana users in California, Charles Tart found in 1977 that almost one in three of them thought they had telepathic experiences. By examining the reports of over 1,000 experiments in the scientific journals, with more powerful psychedelic drugs, such as mescaline, he hoped to find additional evidence; but most of the experiments were methodologically flawed, he found, because in the investigators' desire to make their work scientifically rigorous they took no account of the subjects' individual differences – for example, differences of attitudes to drug-taking could obviously affect the results of experiments; but the experimenters often either had not attempted to discover them, or failed to take into account the possibility of strong subconscious feelings which subjects did not disclose. As a result, Tart felt compelled to admit that in spite of much apparently scientific research, this was in many ways 'a pre-scientific area'.

8 ANOMALOUS PHENOMENA

The term 'anomalous' has been coming into increasing use recently to describe phenomena which may not be paranormal in the usual sense, but which are unexplained – or which, although accepted as natural, have certain mystifying elements, as lightning has. It may seem illogical that incombustibility should be in one category, and spontaneous combustion in another; but psychical researchers who have accepted the paranormal reality of the former have tended to shy away from the latter – as they also used to do with UFOs, though recently these have been attracting more attention. So have spirits, after half-a-century during which most parapsychologists have averted their gaze from the subject, concentrating on types of research which would help to divorce psychical research from its original partner, spiritualism. As for synchronicity, it is anomalous in that it presents a proposition which does not fit conventional scientific thinking: some coincidences, it suggests, are brought about not by chance, but by paranormal, a-causal means.

Lightning

Lightning used to be regarded as one of the devices used by the gods to punish erring mortals, or simply to display their power. Benjamin Franklin's research, and later the investigations of Galvani, Faraday and the rest, established electricity as a force which obeyed the laws of nature. Nevertheless there is a great deal of evidence pointing to the existence of what might be described as behavioural quirks, as yet unaccountable in terms of conventional science.

Some of the caprices of lightning, in relation to people, were listed by Camille Flammarion in *The Unknown* (1900).

At one time a stroke of lightning sets fire to a man and blazes like a sheaf of straw; at another it reduces a man's hands to ashes, leaving the gloves intact; it fuses the links in an iron chain as the fire in a forge would do, and on the other hand it kills a huntsman without discharging what he holds in his hand; it melts an ear-ring without burning the skin; it consumes a person's clothing without doing him the slightest injury, or perhaps it only destroys his shoes or his hat; it photographs on the breast of a man an egg which he has taken from the top of a tree that it has struck; it gilds the pieces of silver in a pocket-book by gliding from one compartment to another, without the owner being aware of it.

The effects or non-effects of lightning, Flammarion argued, were much harder to explain than telepathy; why, then, should scientists reject telepathy out of hand?

Ball lightning presents similar incongruities. In *Lightning, Auroras, Nocturnal Lights and Related Luminous Phenomena* edited by William R. Corliss (1982), it is described as one of nature's most mysterious manifestations; the 'ball' may be the size of a pea, or of a house: it can change colour and shape; and it sometimes appears as a dynamic entity, in that 'it may glide silently past an observer, or it may inquisitively explore a room as if directed by intelligence'. No satisfactory explanation of the composition of ball lightning has been put forward, and it has sometimes been dismissed as a product of hallucination; but it has so often been described, and occasionally photographed, that its existence is today generally, if grudgingly, conceded; its eccentricities, like lightning's, being glossed over.

Spontaneous Combustion

Spontaneous combustion of human beings has yet to be accepted as a real, though inexplicable, phenomenon; but the evidence for its reality is considerably stronger than the evidence for ball lightning, as although both leave traces, those left by ball lightning are quite often accountable for in terms of, say, a practical joke – burns, and smoke – whereas those of spontaneous combustion generally show that it has occurred in ways which cannot be naturally explained.

Spontaneous human combustion, according to one of the leading American investigators of the phenomenon, Larry Arnold, is 'the process whereby a person suddenly ignites without contacting an external source of fire, and then may be reduced to ashes while nearby combustibles paradoxically escape largely unsinged'. It would often be hard to establish that even this incineration had taken place, were it not for the fact that 'the person who becomes a human fireball leaves behind an extremity or two – feet, ankles, maybe the lower legs, hands, perhaps a shrunken skull – and a mound of sweet-smelling powdery-ashed bone and tissue, burned more completely than a crematorium normally achieves'.

Even those who have studied the evidence in detail concede that one of the best descriptions of spontaneous combustion is fictional – Charles Dickens's, in *Bleak House*. Guppy and Weevle are talking together when Guppy, sitting on the window-sill, realizes his hands are defiled by a thick, yellow liquor, 'offensive to the touch and sight, and more offensive to the smell'. Puzzled, they go into the room where the old miser, Krook, lived; everything is as usual, with the miser's cap and coat on the back of a chair; but there is a suffocating vapour, and the walls and ceiling are coated with grease. The cat is snarling at something on the floor; they investigate, and find a small burnt patch.

Is it the cinder of a small charred and broken log of wood, sprinkled with white ashes, or is it coal? O Horror, he IS here! and this from which we run away, striking out the light and overturning one another into the street, is all that represents him.

The greasy walls, the absence of any damage to furniture, and the fragment of a limb – all these are the commonplaces of spontaneous combustion; and they demonstrate its reality, because a body cannot be incinerated in a room except at temperatures which would set alight the furniture, and even burn the whole house down. There are scores of well-attested cases, as Michael Harrison showed in *Fire From Heaven* (1976); and new ones are reported every few months.

In some of them the victim has actually survived. In 1974, Jack Angel, a prosperous travelling salesman, woke up in bed in an American hotel room to find himself badly burned – though the sheets were untouched. In hospital, he was diagnosed as having burned internally – rather than having been burned by some external source. So clear-cut was the evidence that his lawyers, understandably expecting to secure juicy damages for him if the hotel management or anybody else could be blamed, were compelled to give up the case in despair.

This is only one in a number of cases where an individual has realized that he is burning from inside, but has survived – a

Professor of Mathematics at Nashville University actually managed to put out the 'bright blue flame' which he saw emerging from his leg by patting it out with his hands. In the great majority of cases, however, the victim is reduced to a heap of ashes, but with part of a limb remaining, as if to prove this was spontaneous combustion, from the inside out.

Unidentified Flying Objects (UFOs)

'By UFO is understood a phenomenon which causes a percipient to report what seems to be a physical object, flying or capable of flight,' Hilary Evans, one of the leading British investigators of the subject, has offered as a tentative definition, 'but which neither he nor anybody else has yet been able satisfactorily to identify, as regards either its nature, origin or purpose, with any known object.'

There is also considerable confusion in the public mind, as Koestler noted in *Janus* (1978), 'between CETI (communication with extra-terrestrial intelligence), and UFOs (unidentified flying objects, vulgarly called flying saucers)' – a confusion which still haunts the issue. He might have added that there is also a confusion between the vulgarly called flying saucers, because that is what they look like, and UFOs, which come in many other shapes and sizes.

It has become difficult to dispute the existence of unidentified flying objects. Air Marshal Sir Victor Goddard, who coined the word 'ufology' in 1946 – he was then on the Allied Chiefs of Staff Advisory Committee in Washington – used to share the prevailing view that they were a publicity stunt (chiefly to sell a book); but he felt compelled to change his mind when he examined the evidence. As he wrote in *Flight Towards Reality* (1975):

Reports upon ten thousand thorough-going checks have furnished evidence which leads to two conclusions: the first is that only six per cent of so-called UFO sightings remain unsolved and unexplained; the second is that, of the unsolved residue – twelve thousand, unidentified by now – some surely were quite rightly held to be what they were claimed to be: objects of reality but unknown in origin and technicality, flying in the sky or nearby air, or landing on the ground.

Unluckily an investigation which the US Air Force sponsored in the 1960s, carried out by the University of Colorado, was found to have been blatantly rigged by the man in charge, as *Look* magazine revealed (May 1968). In a private memorandum, which was later leaked, he had explained that the committee would pretend, for the benefit of the public, to be conducting an objective study, 'but to the scientific community, would present the image of a group of non-believers trying their best to be objective'. It did; and no serious attempt at a reappraisal of the evidence has been made since.

If it is conceded that there are unidentified flying objects, the further question arises: are they in the paranormal category? If, as believers tend to assume, they are spaceships carrying 'ETs', it can be argued that they are not. But two alternative hypotheses have been put forward.

Diffidently, Jung thought the 'rumours of round objects that flash through the troposphere and stratosphere', and the possibility that they had a physical existence, were so significant that he felt compelled to repeat the warning note he had given before the outbreak of the first world war; 'as we know from ancient Egyptian history, they are manifestations of psychic changes'; changes in 'the constellation of psychic dominants, of the archetypes, or "gods" as they used to be called, which bring about, or accompany, long-lasting transformations of the collective psyche'. Jung admitted that to express such a view was unpopular, and put him in the company of those who liked to fantasize about 'signs and portents', but he had considered it his duty to express his worry.

The other hypothesis which has occasionally been put forward is that UFOs are, or can be, psychic in the same sense as apparitions, materializing and de-materializing. Ufologists insist that UFOs have often left traces – a burnt patch, say, where they have landed. 'Of course they are material – must be – and made of hardware – hard as nails,' as one of them put it. 'To that some might respond, "Why, certainly – but paraphysical in all their hardness,"' Victor Goddard commented, observing that the burnt up grass 'seems almost never to be there next day, when all that made them come to human consciousness of men like us has gone'. Nevertheless he was sufficiently impressed by the evidence to suggest that UFOs may be apports, common enough phenomena in the literature of the paranormal; in the astral world

. . . a world pervading ours, co-incident with ours – its denizens created by astral-mind imagining. That which they create can manifest materially as apports in a transient state of hardware here. If so, the hardware *will* leave marks where it has landed on the ground, before it flies away again, or is again etherealized.

Unidentified flying objects do not rate even a mention in Wolman's *Handbook of Parapsychology*; as Ivor Grattan-Guinness remarks in his brief commentary in the SPR's Centenary survey, 'ufology is anathema to many psychical researchers', and most even of those who accept their reality, at least on the psychic plane, would agree that they cannot yet be studied in the same way as other paranormal phenomena. They present the same problems to investigators, as, say, fairies, as a subject for research.

Spirits

The question which always shadows divination is whether the evidence points to the existence of discarnate entities of the type usually called spirits or whether it can be accounted for in terms of what has come to be described as 'super-ESP' – the proposition being that everything which has been done, said, seen and felt, at all times, is stored away in the equivalent of a cosmic computer, and can be tapped by mediums, psychics or sensitives, as well as, occasionally, by ordinary men and women without psychic prowess.

The arguments are complex; they have been soberly set out in Alan Gauld's *Mediumship and Survival* (1982). And on the evidence he feels that the super-ESP hypothesis 'will not suffice to explain the quantity of correct and appropriate information sometimes furnished'.

The basic case for the reality of spirits as the source of psychically-transmitted information has always been that the information is so often presented as if *by* an entity – whether in the form of a medium's 'control', and the 'communicators' introduced by the control, or in the behaviour of a poltergeist. On top of this, there have been the countless occasions when a medium has provided information which has appeared to come from deceased persons – as Swedenborg so often did.

In 1761 Queen Louisa Ulrica, sister of Frederick the Great, asked Swedenborg if he would try to contact her brother Augustus, who had been declared heir-apparent to Frederick but who had died. Swedenborg agreed to do so and he passed her a message from Augustus which, by her own account, nearly made her faint with shock: 'No one, except God,' she exclaimed, 'knows this secret.' The Queen prided herself on her contempt for superstitions; the whole tenor of her mind, one of the courtiers who recounted the story noted, was free from such weakness. But she had related to him what had happened with conviction, and when he appeared doubtful, reminded him she was not easily duped.

Even more difficult to explain in terms of ESP are certain features of mediumship, such as what have come to be known as 'drop-in communicators'. Quite often in seances, a 'communicator' will announce his presence, either through the 'control' or by taking over a planchette. Having introduced himself, he will provide information which can be checked, though none of the sitters has ever heard of him. And if the information is of a kind which can be verified only by consulting several different sources, it becomes a little difficult to explain it by telepathy on the part of the medium or the sitters.

Mediums and sitters usually have a common incentive to obtain information about some person or persons in whom they are interested; but as Professor Ian Stevenson has observed, in 'drop-in' cases 'the stronger motivation appears to lie with the communicators, and they sometimes state one. Thus with regard to both the selection of sources of correct information and the motive to communicate it, there seems to be an advantage in supposing that the communication does in fact come from a deceased person.'

Gauld has given a typical example. In seances held in the early 1950s a 'drop-in' communicator told sitters that he had been a 2nd Lieutenant in the Northumberland Fusiliers and the Tyneside Scottish; that he was tall, thin and dark, with large brown eyes; that he hung out in Leicester; and that he had died on 14 July 1916. All of this could be, and was, verified (he had even given the correct date upon which he was killed, which was incorrect in the War Office's list). It was unlikely, Gauld thought, that any surviving relative possessed all this information, so that it could be picked up from a single source by the medium through ESP.

Another significant feature of mediumship is that the medium sometimes appears to be taken over by the deceased 'communicator', to the point of beginning to resemble her, in various ways sometimes resembling transfiguration.

When Una Lady Troubridge and Radclyffe Hall (who was later to become notorious as the author of *The Well of Loneliness*) sat with Mrs Osborne Leonard, they noted the reproduction of the intonations, vocal mannerisms and other characteristics of the dead friend with whom 'Feda' had established communication; and sitters have often reported that the features of the medium have appeared to change, as if trying to reproduce the features of the 'communicators'. Impersonation of this kind, as Gauld points out, is a very different matter from knowing the mannerisms or features of a 'communicator' in ways which could reasonably be attributed to super-ESP. Even if mediums like Mrs Piper and Mrs Leonard had it all made available to them by ESP, 'there still remains an immense problem over how they translated the factual knowledge they were thus able to obtain into convincing impersonations of deceased people well-known to their sitters'.

But why, if the spirits have such powers, can they not put them to more effective and productive use? The stock argument has been that men and women are poor 'receivers': the medium distorts the message. And to the contention that belief in such beings represents a primitive stage in man's evolutionary mental development, Ernesto Bozzano in his books and articles between the wars advanced a counter-argument: that man began to be capable of sensing the spirit component only at a recent stage – just as he had only recently become capable of appreciating the beauty of works of art. Full appreciation might only be possible in the spirit – that is, after death; though perhaps at a later evolutionary stage man might move closer to it while on earth.

The case *for* the hypothesis of super-ESP (though the term had not then been introduced) was put by Alexandre Aksakov in his *Animisme et Spiritisme* (1906). He could not accept the sceptics' view that the evidence from mediumship could all be accounted for by delusion and fraud; but he was only too familiar with 'firstly, the obviously automatic character of so-called spiritualist manifestations and secondly, the frequent falsity – shameless and conspicuous – of their intellectual content'. Mediumistic phenomena, he decided, were produced not by spirits but by some force which 'can overstep the bounds of the body and can exert, either with or without the body, activities of a physical, nay even of a plastic, kind.'

Like Aksakov, the Swiss psychologist Theodore Flournoy

accepted that the material presented as if by 'controls' was not faked, nor was it necessarily bogus; but he attributed it to the way in which mediums, in the state of dissociation, entered 'a sort of infantile regression, a relapse into an inferior phase of psychic evolution, where his imagination naturally begins to imitate the discarnate, utilizing the resources of the subconscious'. And this idea, that 'controls' were products of dissociation, received striking confirmation when 'Dr Phinuit', Mrs Piper's control, who had claimed to have lived and worked as a physician in France, could not be traced in the records. Eventually, as if embarrassed at being detected in his deception, he faded out, to be replaced by other 'controls'.

'Once the idea is firmly grasped that part of our being is in possession of knowledge, of which another part is not conscious,' Dame Edith Lyttelton argued in *Our Superconscious Mind* (1931), 'and that occasionally fragments of that knowledge reach our consciousness in various and undependable ways, much of the confusion and some of the contradictory results of psychical happenings are accounted for'; among them, she suggested, 'dramatization' by a secondary personality. The mixture of truth and fiction that such personalities purveyed had commonly been attributed to the struggle between good and evil spirits, or to delusion, or to the fact that the communicating spirit's message was garbled in transit. Of these, she preferred the last interpretation; 'but if we concentrate on the idea that a part of our own mind is in the transmitter, and for some reason cannot be understood by the conscious mind in a normal way, but has to resort to all sorts of devices, some clumsy, some obscure, some clear enough, like dramatization, but all essentially unreliable, we begin to have an idea of the complexity of the process'. She was not, she insisted, rejecting the possibility that disembodied intelligences might also be at work; in fact the superconscious portion of the mind might be in touch with them, and transmit their communications. But the trivial nature of so many of the communications pointed 'not to messages from the discarnate, but to communications from a part of our own mind'.

Perhaps the most illuminating evidence in support of the super-ESP hypothesis has come from some experiments originally undertaken in the early 1970s by a group in Toronto. They decided to conjure up – literally, in the old sense of the term – a spirit; and to assist in the process they gave it a spurious historical identity. 'Philip', as he was called, responded to the challenge; table-tilting sessions eventually began to elicit replies in the form of messages by raps and tilts, 'Philip' taking on a personality of his own and inventing details about his life and times which none of the sitters had consciously thought of.

There are arguments, in short, on both sides. For the present, it seems best to remember Gauld's warning that in this and related areas, 'what we know stands in proportion to what we do not know as a bucketful does to the ocean. Certainty is not to be had, nor even a strong conviction that the area of one's uncertainty has been narrowed to a manageable compass.'

Synchronicity

Coincidences, Jung believed, could in certain circumstances have a relationship based neither on chance nor on simple cause and effect; and he offered as his hypothesis 'synchronicity', which he defined as 'a coincidence in time of two or more causally unrelated events which have the same or similar meaning'.

As an example, he cited an occasion when a patient was telling him of a dream she had had in which she had been given a golden scarab.

While she was telling me this dream I sat with my back to the closed window. Suddenly I heard a noise behind me, like a gentle tapping. I turned round and saw a flying insect knocking against the window pane from outside. I opened the window and caught the creature in the air as it flew in. It was the nearest analogy to a golden scarab that one finds in our latitudes, a scarabaeid beetle, which contrary to its usual habits had evidently felt an urge to get into a dark room at this particular moment.

The concept of synchronicity, Jung realized, necessitates acceptance of extra-sensory perception; an ordinary experience, causally explicable, is linked with a psychic experience, which cannot be explained in ordinary causal terms. It can be explained, he argued, if the existence of a collective unconscious is accepted, independent of space and time, and responsive to certain psychical conditions, such as heightened feelings, or certain 'numinous' occasions, such as dying.

Synchronicity, Jung claimed, is responsible for the results

obtained by people who consult the I Ching, or have their horoscopes cast; an idea upon which Michael Shallis has elaborated in *On Time*. Critics of astrology attack it because, they argue, there cannot be a causal link between somebody on earth and the position of the planets at the moment of birth. But there *is* no causal connection, Shallis argues: 'the power of astrology as a divinatory system lies in its a-causality, just as in Tarot the shuffling of the cards is the vital a-causal link'.

Leys

Shortly after the first world war Alfred Watkins argued in his *Early British Trackways* that pre-Roman roads in Britain were constructed in ways which suggested that they had the benefit of the same kind of occult inspiration as Stonehenge, or other megalithic monuments. These straight tracks, which he called leys, frequently bisected prehistoric sites and 'standing stones'; and this would make sense only if the structures were put up after the leys had been laid down.

As Tom Graves has pointed out in *Needles of Stone* (1978), the simple notion that these leys were tracks cannot easily be sustained, 'for they do strange things like dropping over precipices, taking the longest line over marshes, and recrossing the same river many times'. This suggests that the tracks which had given Watkins his idea must be afterthoughts; promoting the idea that leys represent lines of energy which were picked up by early man through some form of divination. Some confirmation has been lent to this theory by dowsers, who have found that they can trace leys. Ufologists, too, have claimed that sightings are related to leys; and there has been much speculation about the possibility that hauntings can be accounted for, to some extent, by the psychic energies released in leys. So far, however, the evidence is too fragmented for comfort.

BRIEF BIOGRAPHIES OF LEADING MEDIUMS, PSYCHICS AND PSYCHICAL RESEARCHERS

I have tried in this section to single out the men and women who have done most to establish psychic phenomena as worthy of study. Inevitably the choice has been to some extent subjective; but I have wanted to ensure that the leading mediums, psychics and psychical researchers are included, though space has not been available to include all the deserving. The living are not included: to have made a selection from them would have been invidious.

Aksakov, Alexandre (1832–1903)

Aksakov was the leading Russian investigator of the Victorian era. His descriptions of his investigations of mediums, such as Florence Cook and her full-form materializations, provide useful independent confirmation of the reports of Crookes and other psychical researchers. Attempting to account for what he witnessed, Aksakov evolved the theory that a materialized being is in a sense the medium's 'double', so that if a materialized form is caught and held, the fact that it turns out to be the body of the medium is not necessarily an indication of fraud: it may be fusion.

In a moving apologia for his life's work Aksakov admitted that he had relatively little to show for it in the way of proofs; 'but if it be, in the end, my lot to have laid one stone of the temple of the spirit, built up from century to century by men true of heart – this will be the highest, and the only, recompense which ever I strove to gain.'

Barrett, Sir William, FRS (1845–1926)

After working under Tyndall at the Royal Institution, Barrett was appointed Professor of Physics at the Royal College of Science in his home town of Dublin; and while there became interested in the 'higher phenomena' of mesmerism, demonstrated with children by a friend of his, who showed that while they were in their trances they reacted as the mesmerist did to sensations – feeling pain if he did, tasting what he tasted. A paper Barrett read on the subject infuriated some of the leading members of the British Association, who accused him of dragging spiritualism into its deliberations; but he continued his investigations of 'community of sensation', and also of a poltergeist haunting. Six years later, he was responsible for bringing a group of leading spiritualists together with Myers and Gurney, the meeting which led to the foundation of the Society for Psychical Research.

An indefatigable investigator, Barrett conducted the first full-scale investigation of dowsing on the Society's behalf, before becoming its President in 1904. Later, he carried out what remains the most sophisticated study of ouija board communications; and his report on his visit to Belfast to attend a seance with W. J. Crawford and the Goligher circle testified to the genuineness of the results which Crawford had been reporting. His books give a clear picture of the state of psychical research at the time; and his *Death-Bed Visions* (1926), published posthumously and attracting little attention at the time, has recently been shown to foreshadow the results of more systematic studies of the visions of people who have had near-death experiences.

Béraud, Marthe ('Eva C') (Dates unknown)
In 1905 Richet went to Algiers to investigate the physical mediumship of a young girl, Marthe Béraud, and returned to describe how he had watched ectoplasm emerging from her mouth, or sometimes independently of her, and forming into shapes, limbs, and sometimes a whole person. As usual, there were accusations of fraud, but they were from people who had not attended seances.

In the years leading up to the second world war 'Eva C', as she was called to preserve her anonymity, was investigated by Mme Bisson, in whose home she lived, and by Schrenck-Notzing, both of whom devoted large books to descriptions of the research; and during the war also by Geley. By that time her materializations had become, in her investigators' term, 'ideoplastic', resembling ideas or pictures which she had seen (sometimes they were two-dimensional), and in photographs they looked even more spurious than the three-dimensional ones had; but the descriptions by the investigators and by numerous witnesses they invited confirmed that in her hypnotically-induced trances 'Eva' produced the materializations gradually, so that they could be seen forming, developing, in a way that no fake ectoplasm could have formed and developed. Tested in London, she produced phenomena, but they were disappointing compared to the expectations; and in the mid-1920s, her powers having waned, she married and ceased to give seances. The later story that photographs were found showing that the phenomena were fraudulent has since been shown to be the result of a misunderstanding.

Bergson, Henri (1859–1941)
Although Bergson had little direct connection with psychical research, his hypothesis that the human brain's function is to act as a door-keeper, admitting to consciousness whatever is of most immediate usefulness, was greeted with relief by parapsychologists as helping to explain why extra-sensory communications only rarely break through.

In his Presidential Address to the SPR in 1913, Bergson explained that the five senses ordinarily have priority, dealing as they do with the here and now. But there might be a fringe of perceptions 'all ready to enter consciousness, and in fact entering it in certain exceptional cases, or in certain predisposed subjects'; and these messages may get through as 'contraband', especially when the inhibiting mechanism of the brain is functioning badly, as in trances. This proposition has won general acceptance among psychical researchers.

Bozzano, Ernesto (1862–1945)
One of the researchers who investigated Eusapia Palladino, Bozzano went on to become the leading parapsychologist in Italy in the Mussolini era, and to write some influential books. In particular, he was the most energetic campaigner for the spiritist interpretation of the phenomena of mediumship.

Brewster, Sir David (1781–1868)
The author of *Letters on Natural Magic* (1832), Brewster is still sometimes credited with having exposed Home, in the first set of tests Home did on his arrival in London in 1855. In fact a letter

which Brewster wrote immediately after the sittings showed how profoundly he had been impressed by phenomena; he 'could not conjecture how they could be produced by any kind of mechanism'. It was only later, when he realized his reputation as a purveyor of orthodox science would be at risk, that he pretended he had caught Home cheating. Twice in his lifetime Brewster was detected in false pretences: trying to claim the credit for inventions, w. 'n the help of anonymous articles which he had written to argue that he was the real inventor. But thanks to his services to the cause of orthodoxy he was not discredited; he ended up as Principal of Edinburgh University.

Carington, Whately (1884–1947)

While flying as a pilot in the Royal Flying Corps in the first world war, Whately Smith (as he was by birth) became interested in the mediumship of Mrs Leonard, and was also impressed by what he witnessed at a seance with W. J. Crawford and the Goligher circle – as he revealed in his *The Measurement of Emotion*, in which he suggested ways to use mathematics in this context, as well as in the *SPR Journal*. In 1924, while he was at the Air Ministry, he was one of the Horder team which investigated the Boyd 'emanometer' and eventually he threw up his job in the civil service to undertake fulltime psychical research on a tiny income.

Carington, as he had become, concentrated in the 1930s on finding ways to apply refined statistical methods, devising a project in which volunteers guessed pictures, rather than playing or Zener cards, and monitoring the results. The subjects scored 'hits', he found, significantly more often than chance expectation – not just on the day the picture was chosen, but also on the day before and the day after, as if precognition and retrocognition were involved, as he related in his *Telepathy* (1945).

Carrington, Hereward (1881–1958)

Although Carrington's initial interest lay chiefly in the study of the fraudulent methods which had been used by mediums, as his *Physical Phenomena of Spiritualism* (1907) showed, he encountered enough evidence for the genuineness of some of the phenomena to retain an open mind, and he was entirely convinced of the reality of Palladino's psychokinetic powers following his investigation of her with Feilding and Baggally in Naples. It was at his prompting that she went to the United States in 1910, there to be 'framed', in effect, by some of her investigators who were determined to expose her – as he showed in his account of her American seances.

Although at odds both with Hyslop and, later, Walter Prince, and therefore not identified with the American SPR, Carrington was the most energetic researcher in the United States in the years between the wars; eventually his type of work, mainly with individual mediums, was overshadowed by Rhine's. Carrington was one of the investigators selected by the *Scientific American* to vet contestants for their prize, offered in 1923, to anybody who could produce conclusive evidence of psychic phenomena, casting his vote in Palladino's favour, but failing to win over his colleagues on the committee. He was also a prolific writer of books on psychic phenomena in general. Some of them were light-weight, as in the case of his description of those which were associated with the first world war; but others were useful surveys. His attempts to set up research organizations designed to be more go-ahead than the American SPR were unsuccessful.

Cayce, Edgar (1877–1945)

Nobody has ever equalled Edgar Cayce as a psychic diagnostician. In his trances, he could discern what was the matter with people who came to him, even without actually seeing them, and prescribe for them; there are thousands of attested case histories relating to these 'readings' over the period of more than forty years in which he practised – taking no fees, for most of that period, to protect himself from prosecution. He was often investigated by sceptics, including Muensterberg, who backed out when he could find nothing to criticize; but unluckily Cayce was never asked by the American Society for Psychical Research, which between the wars was often in a state of turmoil, to co-operate in formal trials. One of the numerous books about him, by Doris Agee, deals specifically with the evidence for his paranormal powers.

Cook, Florence (1856–1904)

While teaching at a London school, the fifteen-year-old Florence Cook attracted poltergeist-type manifestations, to the dismay of her pupils' parents; the headmistress, highly though she rated Florence's services, had to dispense with them. Her services as a medium, however, were promptly in demand, as she turned out to be the best available for William Crookes, following D. D. Home's retirement in 1874. Her ability to produce full-form materializations of 'Katie King', her spirit 'control', was particularly impressive, as Aksakov testified; and an attempt by the lover of a rival medium to discredit her by demonstrating at a seance that 'Katie' was Florence in disguise, though it delighted sceptics, did not impress the other sitters. Crookes was to describe his research with her in sufficient detail to make it clear that she could not have been cheating except with his connivance – a hypothesis Trevor Hall in *The Spiritualists* (1962) gratefully accepted, implausibly arguing that they were lovers.

Florence Corner, as she became by marriage, continued to give seances and to produce materializations until the end of the century, when her powers waned.

Crandon, Mina (1888–1941)
Following a table-turning session in 1923 with friends and her husband, LeRoi Crandon, in their Boston home, Mina Crandon was found to have the psychic powers which were to make her the most famous, or notorious, physical medium in the United States. Investigated in the mid-1920s by William McDougall of Harvard, by the *Scientific American* committee, by E. J. Dingwall on behalf of the SPR, by a committee of Harvard graduates, and by members of the American SPR, 'Margery' (as she was widely known, from the pseudonym the *Scientific American* gave her) demonstrated a variety of psychokinetic phenomena which she believed were produced through the agency of her 'control', her deceased brother 'Walter', who spoke through her by 'direct voice' – and who roundly denounced Houdini for trying to cheat, in one session, to discredit her. Houdini later claimed to have exposed her; but this allegation was repudiated by his fellow investigators.

'Margery' was never detected in fraud, but frequently accused of it; and she was to be discredited when in 1934 thumbprints which 'Walter' claimed were his, and which were produced in wax in bowls outside her reach, were found to be that of a Boston dentist. As Eleanor Sidgwick pointed out, the essential point was not whose thumbprint appeared but whether or not 'Margery' was under effective control at the time – as on many occasions, including one in the SPR in London, she had appeared to be. Her reputation nevertheless received a blow from which it did not recover.

Crawford, William J. (1890–1920)

The most detailed and ingenious attempt to discover how psychic forces actually work was made by W. J. Crawford, a lecturer in engineering at Queen's College, Belfast, during the first world war. Finding that a Belfast family, the Golighers, were holding private seances during which table-turning and allied manifestations occurred, he managed to win their confidence, and to persuade them to allow him to undertake a variety of tests to find how the psychic forces, apparently emanating from, or through, one of the daughters of the family, Kate, operated so as to lift the table, or perform other actions. His three books remain the most impressive account of the mechanics of the physical phenomena of mediumship.

Although the bulk of Crawford's research was done with the family, some sittings were witnessed by observers; the accounts given by Sir William Barrett, Whately Smith (as Carington then was) and others effectively dispose of the inevitable accusations that Kathleen Goligher, or her family, were engaged in an elaborate fraud.

Crookes, Sir William, OM, FRS (1832–1919)

When in 1870 William Crookes, a young chemist and physicist who seven years earlier had been elected to the Royal Society following his discovery of the element thallium, announced that he was proposing to investigate spiritualist phenomena using scientific techniques and apparatus, his decision was hailed in the press as a breakthrough. When the following year, after investigating D. D. Home, he reported that Home really was able to move objects and play musical instruments without touching them, the enthusiasm promptly cooled, and sceptics condemned him as a dupe.

Crookes's researches with Home and other mediums represented the earliest systematic attempt to apply scientific methods in psychical research, and the results he obtained were striking. But internecine feuds among the mediums of the day led to the allegation, among other things, that he was a Don Juan, and in 1875 he decided to give up psychical research in favour of his investigations in more orthodox fields. Ironically, though, it was his work with mediums that led to his investigations with vacuum tubes, and his invention of the radiometer, which was to change the face of chemistry and physics and lead, in time, to the introduction of television. And although he abandoned psychical research, Crookes insisted in his Presidential Address to the British Association in 1898 that he had nothing to retract ('I adhere to my already published statements'), a position which he maintained to the end of his life.

Curran, Mrs Pearl ('Patience Worth') (1883–1937)

Of all the exponents of automatic writing Mrs Curran, from the American Middle West, is the most remarkable. During a ouija board session her hand on the planchette was taken over by 'Patience Worth' purporting to be the spirit of an English girl. 'Patience' wrote homespun prose, poetry and aphorisms, and in 1914 turned out a novel, *Telka*, about Anglo-Saxon England which created an academic sensation when it was found that 90 per cent of the vocabulary *was* Anglo-Saxon, a feat which would have taxed the capacity of an expert scholar – but the words had poured out through the planchette with great rapidity. And other novels which followed won commercial and critical success in their own right.

Although damned by Hyslop, Mrs Curran was investigated by Walter Prince in 1926, and he realized that the suggestions which had been put forward to account for her ability in conventional terms would not do: 'either our concept of what we call the subconscious must be radically altered, so as to include potencies of which we hitherto have had no knowledge, or else some cause operating through, but not originating in, the subconsciousness of Mrs Curran must be acknowledged'.

Doyle, Sir Arthur Conan (1858–1930)

In *The New Revelation* (1918) Conan Doyle described how he had originally been very sceptical about psychic phenomena, but had gradually been converted to acceptance of them; and during the first world war he had come to believe that they were 'something really tremendous, a breaking down of the walls between two worlds'. From then until his death he was deeply involved in spiritualism and in psychical research. Uncritical in his judgments, he was a constant source of worry to the SPR, whose leading members thought him too gullible. Shortly before his death he left the Society, complaining that it was dominated by sceptics. Oliver Lodge, no sceptic, lamented in an obituary that Doyle had become 'an almost undiscriminating enthusiast for what he believed to be spiritual truth'.

Driesch, Hans (1867–1941)

From his research as a biologist in the 1890s, Hans Driesch developed a Vitalist theory of 'entelechy', derived from Aristotle, based on the proposition that the materialists had been wrong; there were as yet undiscovered forces, one of them being 'a unifying non-material mind-like something' which provided processes with 'an ordering principle which does not add either energy or matter'. This brought him into contact with psychical researchers, and in 1926 he was elected President of the SPR. In his contribution to the 1925 symposium at Clark University he emphasized that entelechy did not create matter, but ordered pre-existing matter; and it was this ordering 'which we have to assume also in parapsychology', in connection with materialized forms.

Dunne, J. W. (1875–1949)

An Experiment with Time (1927) began with the assertion that it was 'not a book about occultism'. Dunne, with his background as an engineer, wanted to put across a theory he had evolved about Time, as a consequence of a succession of dreams which had given him glimpses of the future, and he was anxious that it should be regarded as a theoretical scientific contribution rather than as an addition to psychic lore. In this he was to be disappointed; his theory found few takers. But his dreams – and, more particularly, his recommendation that anybody who cared to keep pad and pencil beside his bed, in order to jot down everything remembered of dreams on wakening, could expect to get similar results – were to provide evidence for precognition which to this day has made more impression on the public than anything which parapsychologists have been able to produce. The book has remained in print, with only an occasional gap, ever since.

Edmonds, John Worth (1816–1874)

In 1851 Edmonds, a New York judge, attended a table-turning seance, and was startled to observe the table's antics. Deciding to investigate, in the expectation of finding some trickery ('no cavil was too captious for me to resort to; no scrutiny too rigid or impertinent for me to institute; no inquiry too intrusive for me to make'), he eventually satisfied himself that the phenomena were genuine, and courageously jeopardized his reputation by admitting as much in print. Although this provoked ridicule, such was his reputation for integrity and fairness on the Bench that his right to continue on it was not seriously challenged.

Elliotson, John (1785–1865)

One of the founders of University College Hospital, John Elliotson had won a big reputation when, in the late 1830s, he was introduced to mesmerism, and began both to practise it and to give demonstrations of its effects. Ordered to stop them by the hospital authorities, he preferred to resign; and his work was discredited by a test in which the editor of the *Lancet*, Thomas Wakley, appeared to show that he had been a dupe. In fact the results of the test were misleading; in retrospect Elliotson's researches into the 'higher phenomena' of mesmerism produced significant results. The *Zoist*, too, which he founded in 1843, is one of the most interesting psychic periodicals of any era. And his setback did not damage his reputation. He was the model for Thackeray's 'Dr Goodenough' – *Pendennis* was dedicated to him; Dickens said that if his life were in danger, it would be to Elliotson that he would entrust it.

'Eva C' – see Béraud, Marthe

Feilding, the Hon. Everard (1867–1936)

Of all the investigators in the SPR in the early part of the century, Feilding emerges in retrospect as one of the sanest and most reliable in his judgments. Sceptical, particularly about the physical phenomena, he had exposed some spurious mediums before he went to Naples with Carrington and Baggally, there to find that his suspicions of Eusapia Palladino had been unfounded, and to present one of the most convincing accounts ever written of a series of trials, published in the *SPR Journal* in 1909. Subsequently he investigated Stanislawa Tomczyk on the Society's behalf. Although the phenomena were not striking, he was impressed by Stanislawa, whom he later married.

'One of the keenest and most acute critics that this country has ever produced, he possessed a unique charm, and his sense of humour invariably saved him from the excess into which others fell when they had become convinced,' Dingwall, who knew him well, was to recall. 'His scepticism was extreme, although it was modified by an attitude of open-mindedness and an unwillingness to accept critical comments when they were unaccompanied by properly-adduced evidence.' That he never became President of the Society is one of the indications of its domination by less flexible minds.

Flammarion, Camille (1842–1925)

When Flammarion founded the Société Astronomique in Paris in 1887, astronomy had the public image of a remote discipline, of no interest except to its professional practitioners; by the time he died, largely due to his own writings, it had been transformed, with hundreds of amateurs making observations from their own homes. But throughout his career, he was also involved in psychical research – it was he who, in *Des Forces Naturelles Inconnues* (1866), popularized the term 'psychic', which he had coined.

Flammarion's collections of anecdotes about the paranormal, published in *The Unknown* (1900) and in the three-volume *Death and its Mystery* (1922), carried on the procedure adopted by Gurney in *Phantasms*; and although Flammarion did not check the case histories with the care Gurney had given them, they nevertheless contain a fascinating range of evidence, many of the accounts sent in by well-known men and women of the period. Flammarion was elected President of the SPR in 1923.

Flournoy, Theodore (1854–1921)

One of the most able and perceptive psychologists of his era, as his correspondence with William James reveals, Flournoy's scepticism about mediums was modified by his experiences when investigating 'Hélène Smith' in his home town, Geneva. Describing them in *From India to the Planet Mars* (1901), he showed how most of the information she gave him in her trances from what she took to be her past incarnations was rubbish; but some of it was hard to explain away even by cryptomnesia, and he was sure that she was honest. Later, when he joined in tests of Eusapia Palladino, he became convinced her phenomena were genuine.

His *Spiritism and Psychology* (1911) provided a useful survey of the evidence from the point of view of an investigator who had become convinced of the reality of paranormal phenomena, but continued to reject the spiritist interpretation.

Fox, Margaret (1838–1893) and Kate (1841–1892)

The birth, or re-birth, of Spiritualism is commonly dated from the time in 1848 when Margaret and Kate, daughters of a farmer in Hydesville, New York, began to answer the rappings of what was taken to be a ghost, and obtained replies. Soon, they were producing raps on their own; and later, more striking physical manifestations, in particular movements and levitations of seance-room tables, which were to trigger off the table-turning craze in the United States and Europe.

Margaret later became Mrs Kane, and rarely gave seances; Kate became Mrs Jencken, and worked for a while in London with Crookes, to his satisfaction (she also impressed Home, which was unusual, as he had little time for most of his fellow-mediums). But in the 1880s, both of their husbands having died, Margaret became an alcoholic, and in a well-publicized meeting in New York confessed to having been a cheat throughout her career – which Kate did not contest. Margaret's attempt to show how she had cheated, however, consisted of nothing more than some feeble raps; and she was soon to retract her confession, explaining that the sum of $1500 dollars (about $15,000 in today's money) offered for it had been too much for a penniless woman to resist; and she resumed her mediumship.

Fodor, Nandor (1895–1964)

A Hungarian journalist, Fodor became interested in psychic phenomena through reading Carrington's *Physical Phenomena of Spiritualism*, and worked for a while with Carrington in the United States before returning to Europe to become Lord Rothermere's aide, in the 1930s. In that capacity he compiled his monumental *Encyclopedia of Psychic Science*, the first attempt at such a work, setting a high standard, though it appeared too soon to recognize the revolution taking place as a result of Rhine's research projects at Duke. After some frustrating experiences as a psychical researcher in Britain, Fodor returned to the United States to take up another of his interests, psycho-analysis, of which he became a leading practitioner; but he retained his keen interest in psychical research until his death.

Freud, Sigmund (1856–1939)

Visiting Freud in 1909, Jung asked him what he thought about psychic phenomena; 'because of his materialistic prejudice, he rejected this entire complex of questions as nonsensical'. But Freud on this subject was ambivalent; from time to time he had intimations of telepathy with patients, and did not lose hope of finding some materialist explanation.

Asked by Hereward Carrington in 1921 to become co-editor of a journal devoted to psychic phenomena, Freud declined, but with the comment, 'If I had my life to live over again I should devote myself to psychical research rather than psycho-analysis'; and that same year he wrote a paper on the subject, speculating about the possible evolutionary background of telepathy. His future biographer Ernest Jones persuaded him not to publish it, for fear it would give further ammunition to the critics of psycho-analysis; and in 1929 Freud actually denied that he had made the statement Carrington attributed to him: 'I said nothing to justify his assertion.' But as Carrington had kept the letter, he was able to show that Freud's recollection was at fault.

Like Jung, Freud was a corresponding member of the SPR; and his paper on telepathy, published posthumously, appears in his collected works.

Garrett, Eileen (1893–1970)

The most accomplished and best-known of mediums in recent times, Eileen Garrett trained as a medium in the London College of Psychic Science under Hewat McKenzie, creating surprise among the College's clients, used to a very different type of medium, when found she was 'very modern, Eton-cropped and humorous', as one of them described her. She willingly allowed herself to be tested by Rhine at Duke, where she produced positive scores, and by Soal in London, where they were negative; but her most striking performance in the 1930s was at the seances when communication was established with the captain of the ill-fated airship R 101, after it had crashed in France, described in detail in John G. Fuller's *The Airmen Who Would Not Die* (1979).

Later, after the second world war, she was to set up the Parapsychological Foundation in New York, and to be a generous patron of psychical researchers.

de Gasparin, Count Agenor (1810–1871)

As a scholar, politician (he was a member of the National Assembly) and liberal, de Gasparin had established an enviable reputation during the reign of Louis Philippe; but he left France in sympathy with Louis after the 1848 rising and settled in Switzerland, where he was to conduct the first scientific trials of table-turning, linking up the table to a weighing machine so that the pressures involved could be measured. His *Des Tables Tournantes* (1854) presented a lucid, careful description of the results, which he had arranged to be monitored by independent witnesses.

Geley, Gustave (1868–1924)

Following a successful career as a medical student, Geley for a time practised medicine; but his Vitalist opinions roused an interest in psychical research, as they did with Bergson, Driesch and McDougall. During the first world war he investigated the medium 'Eva C', and after it became the Director of the *Institut Métapsychique* in Paris, displaying unbounded energy in setting up controlled trials of both mental and physical mediums, and persuading scientists and savants to attend in order to see for themselves that the results were not obtained by trickery. His books, along with those of Schrenck-Notzing and Mme Bisson, constitute the most detailed evidence there is for the reality of ectoplasmic materialized forms.

'The heroic stage of metapsychics would seem to be nearing its end,' he felt able to boast in 1923. If anybody had been capable of convincing conventional scientists that the materializations were genuine, it would have been Geley; but he was killed soon after in a flying accident. 'A philosophic thinker of no small magnitude,' Oliver Lodge thought, praising his conscientiousness and 'his exemplary simplicity, his rare faculty of reconciling the enthusiasm of the investigator with the reflective wisdom of the savant'.

Glanvill, Joseph, FRS (1636–1680)

It seems reasonable to credit Glanvill with being the first person to try to investigate the paranormal scientifically, or at least shrewdly, as his *Saducismus Triumphatus* (1681) shows. One of Charles II's chaplains, he believed that supernatural manifestations were meaningful and should be investigated to relate them to religious beliefs. His report of his investigation of the 'Demon Drummer of Tidworth' is written with a detachment unusual in that period.

Gurney, Edmund (1847–1888)

Four years Frederic Myers's junior, in 1872 Edmund Gurney was made a Fellow of Trinity College, Cambridge, where he impressed Henry Sidgwick (and George Eliot, who thought his mind 'as beautiful as his face', and appears to have made him the model for Daniel Deronda). When the SPR was founded, he became joint-Hon. Secretary with Myers, and embarked upon the Society's first major investigation, into the evidence for apparitions. His energy was prodigious; Alan Gauld, examining the records for his book on the Society's founders, discovered that Gurney would write as many as fifty letters a day in his own hand to check on details in the case histories sent in, and also where necessary visit the correspondents. *Phantasms of the Living* (1886), in which Myers and Podmore were his co-authors, was mainly his work, and remains his monument, though he also contributed valuable articles on hypnosis and other subjects in the SPR's *Proceedings*. His death two years later at the age of only forty was a severe blow to the Society.

Heywood, Rosalind (1895–1980)

From childhood Rosalind was psychic, her experiences tending to take the form of what she described as 'orders', virtually compelling her to take some action, often against her inclination. With her husband she established communication by telepathy which at times proved almost as useful as would normally be established by telephone, as she described in *The Infinite Hive* (1964). Her earlier survey of psychical research, *The Sixth Sense* (1959), represented a breakthrough in that it excited the admiration of a wide range of readers, from Arnold Toynbee and Sir Julian Huxley to the *New Scientist*'s critic – the measure of her ability to present the evidence dispassionately but sympathetically, and a reflection of her own engaging personality.

Hodgson, Richard (1855–1905)

After Gurney's death Richard Hodgson, an Australian, became with Podmore the most energetic of the younger members of the SPR. For a time he was best known for his scepticism, which manifested itself in an exposure of Mme Blavatsky; followed, in 1895, by what appeared to be an exposure of Eusapia Palladino, but which simply exposed his own inability to accept the possibility of psychokinesis. He met his match in Mrs Piper, when he went to Boston to try to revive the dormant American SPR; although he put detectives on her to catch her out, he was eventually convinced that she was genuine.

'As a *man*, Hodgson was splendid, a real man,' William James wrote to Flournoy; but he had become obsessed with Mrs Piper, 'cared too little for other clues, and continued working with her when all the sides of her mediumship were amply exhibited'. As a result, Hodgson had never written the books he had planned, and he had been so much of a one-man-band, James thought, that his death would probably mean the winding-up of the American SPR – as it would have done, had Hyslop not come to the rescue.

Home, Daniel Dunglas (1833–1886)

If a contest were held to select the most influential medium of modern times, the winner would surely be Daniel Home. Mirabelli produced some even more spectacular manifestations, and Palladino succeeded in test conditions of a kind which Home did not have to face; but his record over twenty years in seances with many of the best known men and women of the era remains unsurpassed.

As a boy, in the United States, he began to have psychic experiences, and in the early 1850s became known for his ability to move objects at a distance, and produce materializations – usually a disembodied hand which could be shaken by the sitters. Soon, he was levitating tables, and occasionally himself; and another of his specialities was the playing at a distance of musical instruments (most witnesses agreed that the music was soulful). In Europe, to which he returned (he had been born in Scotland) in 1855 for his health, he gave seances for the Emperor Napoleon III and the Tsar, as well as for scores of men and women in society, in the professions and in the academic world; their most significant feature being that they were ordinarily held in light good enough for sitters to satisfy themselves that neither he nor anybody else was producing the effects physically, as a mass of testimony by eye-witnesses confirmed. In the early 1870s he was tested by scientists, von Boutlerow in Moscow and Crookes in London, providing convincing evidence of his psychokinetic ability; but in 1873 ill-health forced him to retire to the Continent, and to give up seances.

In a letter to Home, Crookes lamented that he had sacrificed much for the cause of spiritualism, only to be met 'with little but calumny, slander, backbiting and abuse from Spiritualists'; but 'I look upon you as one of the real friends I have, and I would not spare any trouble to retain your friendship and good opinion'. Throughout his life, Home inspired such confidence in most of his friends; and he was never detected in any deception.

Houdini, Harry (1874–1926)

Born Erich Weiss (the stage name was a token of admiration for the great French conjuror Robert-Houdin), Houdini passionately loved his mother, and longed to communicate with her after her death; but the failure of mediums, including Lady Doyle, to convince him that the communications they provided were genuine led to a reaction. In the last few years of his life much of his time was devoted to exposures of Spiritualist mediums, whom he took to be cheats, by abandoning his normal routine of escaping from bonds or containers and showing how they might do their tricks. Salutary though the demonstrations could be, Houdini eventually became so paranoid on the subject that he too began to fake exposures, as he did with 'Margery' (his pamphlet showing how he claimed to have caught her out was repudiated by the other investigators who had been present at the time on behalf of the *Scientific American*); and his reputation as a reliable debunker of the paranormal is undeserved.

Huggins, Sir William, OM, FRS (1824–1910)

When Crookes elected to test Home, he had with him as witnesses a lawyer, Serjeant Cox, and an astronomer, William Huggins, both of whom confirmed that the report Crookes made of the trial was correct. W. B. Carpenter, seeking to demolish the report, wrote (anonymously) in the *Quarterly Review* that Huggins was not a scientist, but a brewer, and only an amateur astronomer.

The Fellows of the Royal Society clearly disagreed: he had already been elected to a Fellowship, and was later to be President. But in a memoir his wife was to explain that she had insisted he should abandon psychical research when she married him, as she felt it was bad for his reputation.

Hume, David (1711–1776)

In an essay written in 1750, Hume advanced the argument that miracles, which he defined as violations of the laws of nature, could not occur. 'As a firm and unalterable experience has established these laws, the proof against a miracle, from the very nature of the fact, is as entire as any argument from experience can possibly be imagined.' So long as it was held that miracles are violations of the laws of nature, Hume's dictum had some force; but it cannot be applied to phenomena categorized as paranormal – i.e. natural, though unexplained. In any case, physicists have been compelled to abandon the concept of 'laws', replacing them with the more flexible concept of 'models'. As for Hume's backup contention that 'the uniform experience of mankind' amounts to a proof that miracles do not happen, it is irrelevant, as paranormal experiences are continually being reported.

Hyslop, James Hervey (1854–1920)

Hyslop was Professor of Logic at Columbia University when his interest in psychic phenomena prompted him to throw up his job and take on the running of the American SPR, following Hodgson's death. Like Hodgson, he rejected physical mediumship, though he claimed that this was not so much because he was unable to accept the reality of the phenomena, as because he thought them the product of hysteria – of diseased minds; so he declined to have anything to do with Eusapia Palladino when Carrington brought her to the United States. He also denounced 'Patience Worth's' productions in intemperate language. Nevertheless he revitalized the American Society, and ran it almost single-handed for fifteen years.

James, William (1842–1910)

Originally trained in medicine, William James was appointed a lecturer in anatomy at Harvard in 1872; but ten years later switched to philosophy, becoming a professor in 1885. By that time his early materialism had been banished, largely through friendship with Myers; and in 1887 he began to investigate Mrs Piper, initially assuming that she must gain her information 'by ordinary means, such as confederates', but eventually realizing that her mediumship was genuine, though leaving open the issue whence her information reached her.

Conventional science, he told the members of the SPR in his 1896 Presidential Address, had come to be identified with narrow mechanism: psychical research had 'restored continuity to history'. In his Giffard Lectures, later published as *The Varieties of Religious Experience*, he developed this theme, recalling that 'the whole array of Christian saints and heresiarchs, including the greatest, the Bernards, the Loyolas, the Luthers, the Foxes, the Wesleys, had their visions, voices, rapt conditions, guiding impressions and "openings", because they enjoyed exalted sensibility, and to such things persons of exalted sensibility are liable'.

In his last report on psychical research, published in the *American Magazine* in October 1909, James felt bound to admit that for all the hours which he had spent investigating psychical phenomena, he felt he was no 'further' than he had been at the beginning; 'and I confess that at times I have been tempted to believe that the Creator has eternally intended this department of nature to remain *baffling*, to prompt our curiosities and hopes and suspicions all in equal measure'. However, he could not believe that the phenomena had all been put in simply as a form of divine mockery: 'my deeper belief is that we psychical researchers have been too precipitate with our hopes, and that we must expect to mark progress not by quarter centuries but by half centuries or whole centuries'. Time has proved him right.

Joan of Arc (1411–1431)

Joan, several commentators have argued, must have suffered from schizophrenia. It is the measure of the distortions which conventional psychiatric procedures have imposed that such a diagnosis can be put forward, let alone taken seriously. She was a medium, and by all contemporary accounts, whether written by her friends or her foes, an exceptionally gifted one, as her 'voices' provided her with information which would today be categorized as telepathic, clairvoyant and precognitive.

Joseph of Copertino (1603–1663)

Of all the accounts of levitation by men or women, in the Vatican records, none are so well-attested as those of the 'flying monk' – the friar Joseph of Copertino. Making every allowance for exaggeration, Eric Dingwall had to admit, after an initially sceptical study of the records, that the weight and the range of testimony, from peasants to Pope Urban VIII, from curious spectators to heretics (the Lutheran Duke of Brunswick became a convert to Catholicism after he had seen Joseph floating in the air) is too great to be dismissed as hagiography.

What makes the case for Joseph's levitations stronger is that initially they brought him no credit in his Franciscan order. Doubtless his superiors would have been more impressed if he had been a man of greater intelligence: Joseph was a simpleton. Besides, his exploits were an embarrassment: flying, as he sometimes did, over the heads of the congregation at Mass. He was disciplined – though it could hardly have been more rigorous than the scourgings he gave himself; he was investigated by the Inquisition; and for a time he was banned from attending Mass on occasions when the public were present. But the levitations continued to be witnessed, even at the time when he was dying; the doctor reported that, 'rapt in ecstasy', he had remained 'actually suspended in mid-air' for a quarter of an hour. The numerous testimonies to his levitations, many of them written in his lifetime, did not suffice at first to convince the Vatican that he deserved canonization; but this was secured for him half-a-century later.

Jung, Carl (1875–1961)

Jung's interest in psychic phenomena manifested itself in various ways throughout his life, as he made clear in his *Memories, Dreams, Reflections*. While he was a student, 'something happened which was destined to influence me profoundly': a report 'like a pistol shot' when a dining table at his home split apart, for no discernible reason. Later, following another deafening report, a breadknife was found to have snapped into small pieces. 'Exteriorization' continued to intrigue him, after the occasion when similar reports occurred while he was in a tense situation with Freud; poltergeists, he came to believe, were 'exteriorized effects of unconscious complexes' – as he told the SPR, of which he was a corresponding member, in a paper he wrote in 1920: he saw 'no proof whatever of the existence of real spirits'.

Thirty years later, however, in a revised version he was more cautious; the advances of the nuclear physicists had opened up the possibility of a 'transpsychic reality immediately underlying the psyche'. They had also led him to speculate on the subject of synchronicity, which was to restore interest in the possibility of p. 'nnormal (in the sense of a-causal) coincidences. A review of his ideas in relation to the paranormal was provided by Aniela Jaffé in *Science and ESP* edited by J. R. Smythies (1967).

Kardec, Allan (1803–1869)
Born Hyppolite Rivail, Kardec was a French doctor who in the mid-19th century embraced Spiritualism and converted Flammarion, among others, to acceptance of the reality of psychic phenomena. His influence in Europe was soon to wane, but it remains powerful in Brazil, where *Kardecismo* is one of the officially recognized varieties of spiritism.

Koestler, Arthur (1905–1983)
Throughout his life, Arthur Koestler had psychic experiences, though he maintained that he was not himself psychic. As a boy he was in demand for table-turning sessions in Budapest, and experienced what he described as the 'oceanic sense', a mystical liberation from mundane cares which was to return while he was under sentence of death in a Seville jail, after he had been captured by the advancing Franco forces. The experience determined him to devote his writing to an attempt to assimilate it with conventional science – as he sought to do in *Darkness at Noon* (1940).

Its resounding success had the effect of precipitating him into the political arena, where he remained, so far as the public were concerned, until in the 1950s he reverted to the quest to assimilate mystical experiences with science. At first he concentrated on demolishing materialist foundations, in assaults on behaviourism, neo-Darwinism and other products of mechanistic theory; but in his *Roots of Coincidence* (1972) he set out the case for acceptance of the reality of paranormal phenomena; and in *The Challenge of Chance* (1973) he effectively introduced a new element into psychical research with his study of coincidences, relating them to the 'synchronicity' hypotheses of Kammerer and Jung.

Shortly before his death, Koestler supervised a series of sophisticated experiments in 'mood induced changes of weight', in the hope of elucidating some of the mysteries of levitation. In his will, he left his entire property to found a Chair of Parapsychology, the first in Britain, which Edinburgh University has accepted. The Koestler Foundation, of which he was one of the founders, exists to promote research in parapsychology and other fields which have been starved of resources because of orthodox scientists' unwillingness to take them seriously.

Lambertini, Prospero (1675–1758)

As Archbishop of Bologna, Lambertini wrote *De Canonisatione*, a study of miracles derived from his experience in the job of *Promotor Fidei*, or Devil's Advocate. It marked a watershed in the Catholic Church's attitude to the miraculous, accepting that the divine will could manifest itself through supernatural agencies, but warning that there were natural manifestations which could be mistakenly identified as supernatural, and also that there were phenomena which had traditionally been placed in the supernatural category, but which with the advance of science might be transferred – people might have 'knowledge of things to come, things past, present events distant in space' without God or the devil being directly involved.

Holding such views, Lambertini opposed the beatification of Joseph of Copertino. Later, as Pope Benedict XIV, he realized the strength of the testimony; so numerous and respectable were the witnesses to 'the famous upliftings' that he gave way. As his biographer, Renée Haynes, has shown in *Philosopher King* (1970), the guidelines which he laid down for the assessment of what could, and what could not, be regarded as miraculous are still broadly followed by the Vatican.

Lang, Andrew (1843–1912)

Novelist, historian, anthropologist, expert on folklore and folk custom, Lang was never in the mainstream of psychical research, but his books were more widely read than any of the mainstreamers, and they contained a mass of testimony about various types of paranormal phenomena. In particular, he emphasized the similarity between those which had been reported from tribal communities and those which were being reported from Spiritualist seances – mediumship, levitations, raps, poltergeists, and so on.

Lang was the first to see through the pretensions of *The Golden Bough*, mocking Fraser's fanciful hypotheses; unluckily it was Fraser whom the public listened to, in spite of Lang's demolition. Probably this was largely because Lang, though always readable, was too prolific, never settling down to write a comprehensive treatise on any of the themes he was dealing with. His accounts of his experiments with a friend who was a scryer, using a crystal ball, are a good example of his critical but sympathetic approach, as are his descriptions of research into fire-walks.

He became President of the SPR in 1911, the year before his death – predicted, he himself noted, by what he described as a 'hereditary hallucination' – he saw a phantom cat which traditionally appeared to members of his family who were about to die. In his case, however, death was postponed for another few months.

Leonard, Gladys Osborne (1882–1968)

Of all the mediums who have submitted to investigation by psychical researchers, Mrs Leonard has the most impressive record. Initially becoming known to the SPR through information she passed to Sir Oliver and Lady Lodge from their son, following Raymond's death in action on the Western Front, she accepted a retainer from the Society to work exclusively for its members, and to undertake a variety of tests, as she was to do for the next forty years.

Her investigators as a result 'were able to study mediumship in the least unattractive conditions', as Rosalind Heywood recalled in *The Sixth Sense*, 'for her helpfulness made friends of the most hostile critics, and no detective ever caught her swerving one inch from the path of honesty.' Her most striking results were obtained in 'proxy' sessions, where the sitters did not know anything more than the name of the individuals they were proxies for: nevertheless Mrs Leonard was frequently able to provide evidence purporting to come from deceased friends or relatives of the people concerned, which the SPR could check.

Lodge, Sir Oliver, FRS (1851–1940)

Appointed Professor of Physics at Liverpool University in 1881, Lodge 'found a series of facts that were unpalatable and mainly neglected by scientific men', as he was to recall in his *Past Years* (1931); and for all their unpalatability, he 'felt them worthy of attention'. He participated in what are still recognized as carefully monitored tests for 'community of sensation' in Liverpool; checked on Mrs Piper when she visited Britain; and with Richet and Ochorowicz conducted an investigation of Eusapia Palladino with results which convinced them that her PK powers were genuine.

Appointed Principal of the new University of Birmingham in 1900, he became President of the SPR the following year, and received his knighthood for his services to physics (which had won him an international reputation) and to higher education, while still in that office. Originally sceptical of the spiritualist interpretation of the phenomena, his *Survival of Man* (1909) showed that he accepted the spiritualist case (though not its religious implications); and his *Raymond* (1916) provided evidence for survival of a more detailed type than had been obtained from mediums before.

On his retirement from his university post, Lodge continued to devote much of his time to the SPR (of which he was to become joint President, with Mrs Sidgwick, in its jubilee year of 1932) and to spiritualism, on which he was an accomplished lecturer. At the same time, he remained in close touch with scientific developments, becoming one of the best known voices on the new medium, the wireless, describing them.

Lombroso, Cesare (1836–1909)
Professor of Psychiatry at the University of Turin, Lombroso had already established an international reputation as the founder of the new branch of science, Criminology, when he wrote jestingly in 1888 that with so much flux in the domain of psychology, he and his friends might even be proved wrong in their contempt for spiritualism. Challenged to come to Naples to test Eusapia Palladino, he for a while backed out; but three years later, when he accepted the challenge, he was compelled to accept that he had been wrong. He was ashamed, he wrote, to have 'opposed with so much tenacity the possibility of so-called spiritist facts. I say the facts, because I am still opposed to the theory. But the facts exist, and I boast of being a slave to facts.' He was later to cease to be opposed to the spiritist theory, expounding his case in *After Death, What?*, published in the year of his death.

McDougall, William, FRS (1871–1938)

While Wilde Reader in Mental Psychology at Oxford University, William McDougall wrote *Body and Mind* (1911), including a section in which he presented a dualist theory and boldly endorsed the existence of telepathy; and after the war he became President of the SPR. His term of office, however, was brief, as he was offered the Chair of Psychology at Harvard, using his years there to promote psychical research, and himself investigating 'Margery' – though with reluctance, as he could not bring himself to accept the physical phenomena of mediumship. Moving to Duke University in 1927, he was responsible for employing J. B. Rhine and supporting him in his new-style research, as well as starting up the *Journal of Parapsychology*.

In his contribution to the Clark University symposium on psychical research in 1925, McDougall produced a spirited defence of the subject as an academic discipline, far surpassing all others 'in respect of the character discipline which it affords' – requiring, as it did, 'a perfectly controlled temper, and a large and understanding tolerance of human weaknesses'. But he recognized from his long experience that 'both the scientific world and the general public will react with strong emotional bias to any conclusion'.

'Margery' – see Crandon, Mina

Mirabelli, Carlos (1899–1951)

In some respects, Mirabelli was the most remarkable physical medium in recent history, outshining even Home in his ability to produce phenomena – in particular full-form materializations of people who had died not long before – in test conditions. Unluckily he was never fully investigated by Western parapsychologists, whose tendency then (and to a considerable extent since) was to brush aside the evidence, well-attested though it was, on the ground that psychical researchers in Brazil lacked the experience and the scientific know-how to provide reliable findings.

Morselli, Enrico (1852–1929)

A deeply sceptical Professor of Neurology, Morselli decided to investigate Eusapia Palladino in 1901 with a view to exposing her. He had been a leading campaigner against spiritualism, and as 'one of the foremost leaders of Italian science' – Flournoy's description

– his professional and personal attitudes did not dispose him 'to tolerate any infringements of known biological laws'. But having managed to attend a seance without disclosing his identity, he was so impressed by what he witnessed that he conducted a series of trials with positive results, followed up by a second, five years later, and described in detail in *Psicologia e Spiritismo* (1908). The results were vouched for by other leading Italian scientists, and by the most eminent of Italian journalists of the day, Luigi Barzini.

Moses, Stainton (1839–1892)

Holding a curacy in an Anglican parish, Moses was compelled by ill-health to resign, and to take up work as the tutor of the children of a London doctor, Stanhope Speer. In the course of it he began to have psychic experiences – rappings, table-tiltings, luminosities, apports, psychic odours and so on. The products of his automatic writing, and his spiritualist views, were presented in a number of books and articles by 'B. A. Oxon.' but he made no attempt to seek publicity for his powers. Nor did he submit himself for formal testing. Nevertheless his friends felt that the scrupulous care with which he refrained from publicizing his gift, and his almost saintly reputation – Myers claimed he had never heard anybody 'with even the slightest acquaintance with Mr Moses impugn his sincerity' – compensated for his unwillingness to subject it to laboratory-type scrutiny. Furthermore, Myers added, it was clear from the Speer family's attestation that Moses could not have cheated without their collusion – and what would have been the point of having bogus seances, week after week, if the results were only to be circulated privately?

Murphy, Gardner (1890–1975)

Murphy's grandfather happened to be Mrs Piper's lawyer in Boston, so that he grew up knowing her reputation; and reading Barrett's *Psychical Research* confirmed him in the belief that there must be something worth exploring in this field. At Harvard under McDougall, he investigated 'Margery'; and conducted trans-ocean telepathy trials with Warcollier; and although a severe illness interrupted his research, he made an important contribution to the Clark University Symposium – emphasizing the problems which

325

had been and would continue to be encountered in laboratory-type investigations – before he decided to concentrate for a while on more conventional research.

The temporary withdrawal proved advantageous: Murphy acquired the reputation which led to his appointment as Director of Research at the Menninger Foundation, visiting professorships, and in 1943 the Presidency of the American Psychological Association, reflecting his emergence as one of the leading academic psychologists in the United States. In 1948 he felt able to confront the American Association for the Advancement of Science with a paper on the place of parapsychology among the sciences; and the following year he became President of the SPR, emphasizing in his Address the need to regard psi as inherent in relationships between people – not just in individuals. The esteem and affection in which he was held can be judged from the *Journal* of the American Society for Psychical Research's January 1980 issue, entirely devoted to tributes honouring his memory.

Murray, Gilbert, OM (1866–1957)
Regius Professor of Greek at Oxford University, Murray became President of the SPR in 1915, and in his Presidential Address described how his interest had been stimulated by a version of a Victorian parlour game which was played in his home with family and friends. He would be sent out of the room, while they thought of a phrase, or episode, or quotation; when he was summoned back, he showed he could guess it correctly (or part correctly) two times out of three, as the records the family kept confirmed.

The family continued to play the game from time to time throughout his life, with similar results; and although for a time he thought that hyperacuity of hearing might be the explanation, he confirmed in his second Presidential Address in 1952 that this did not fit the evidence. He must have telepathic powers, he believed, which could be tapped, for these occasions. Like Moses, he declined to have formal tests, feeling that the atmosphere would be inhibiting; but his reputation, both public – he founded the League of Nations Union – and among his friends, rendered suspicions implausible. He would hardly have risked the ignominy, year after year, of being caught cheating by members of his family.

Myers, Frederic (1843–1901)

Around the year 1873 'at the crest, one may say, of perhaps the highest wave of materialism which has ever swept over these shores', a small group of friends at Cambridge decided that the issues involved 'must be fought out in a way more thorough than the champions either of religion or of materialism had yet suggested'. Thus Myers – one of the group – recalled how, with Sidgwick and Gurney, he had begun to investigate mediums. He and Gurney were to become joint Hon. Secretaries of the SPR when it was formed nine years later; and until his death he was one of the most energetic investigators, and the most articulate expounder of the need for a middle course between orthodox materialism and orthodox religion.

Myers's *Human Personality and its Survival of Bodily Death*, edited and published posthumously in 1903, remains the most important single work in the parapsychology canon. Indeed it may yet be recognized as one of the seminal works in psychology, ranging as it does far beyond the confines of conventional psychological thinking, with many insights into borderland phenomena, dreams, multiple personality, hypnosis, hallucination, as well as telepathy; and valuable speculation about the manner in which psychic communications reach consciousness – arriving, he surmised, through an unspecialized and as yet unidentified channel, but working up through one of the senses, through the hands in dowsing, or the eyes in scrying.

These 'motor-automatisms', as he described them, would eventually be seen to have a common link in spite of their variety of forms: 'they will be seen to be messages from the subliminal self: endeavours, conscious or unconscious, of submerged traits of our personality to present, to our waking thought, fragments of knowledge which no ordinary waking thought could attain' – a view parapsychologists now most commonly accept. Gradually, too, conventional psychologists are coming to realize that his concept of the subliminal mind, as he thought of it, 'a gold mine as well as a rubbish heap', is more illuminating than Freud's narrower concept of the unconscious.

Nostradamus (1503–1566)

Michel de Nostradame trained as a physician; but when a plague killed his wife and children he became disillusioned with conventional medicine, and took to travel. In the course of it he found he was clairvoyant; and in his trance states he produced convoluted cabalistic quatrains which sometimes predicted future events with uncanny accuracy, as James Laver showed in his biography (1942). Some of the more abstruse speculative interpretations of Nostradamus's obscurities have since been effectively demolished, but there remains a residue of precognitive material which is hard to dismiss.

Ochorowicz, Julian (1850–1918)

As a young man Ochorowicz, Assistant Professor of Philosophy and Psychology at Lemberg in Poland, decided that he would subject telepathy to rigorous controlled trials with a view to demonstrating that it did not exist. In his *Mental Suggestion*, originally published in French in 1887, he described with painful honesty the gradual process by which his research eventually convinced him that telepathy does exist. He collaborated with Richet in the investigation of 'Mme B' at Le Havre; undertook a carefully mounted investigation of Eusapia Palladino in Poland (as well as witnessing her demonstrations in Italy and France); and was the chief investigator of Stanislawa Tomczyk in the years leading up to the first world war. His reports leave no doubt of his determination to apply the energy which he had originally devoted to discrediting psychical research to exploring paranormal phenomena, with a view to achieving a better understanding of them.

Osty, Eugene (1874–1938)

One of the most detailed accounts of experiments with mediums to try to find whence their information is obtained was Osty's *Supernormal Faculties in Man*, the French version of which was published in 1923. Succeeding Geley as Director of the *Institut Métapsychique*, for a time he concentrated on research into the mental phenomena; but in 1930 he invited Rudi Schneider to undertake trials at the *Institut*, monitoring his psychokinetic abilities in darkness with the help of an infra-red beam, designed to reveal any attempt to move objects physically, and ultra-violet light for photography. If an object moved, the plan was, the movement would trigger off a picture. In these conditions objects moved while Rudi could be seen to be in his place, out of reach; and the results are considered by parapsychologists to be among the most convincing achieved in controlled tests of PK.

Palladino, Eusapia (1854–1918)

In 1888 Ercole Chiaia, a former cavalry officer under Garibaldi, issued a challenge to Cesare Lombroso to investigate a peasant woman, Eusapia Palladino, who had made a big reputation as a physical medium in Naples. This was to be the start of a series of trials all over Europe, witnessed by many of the most eminent scientists of the day. In the great majority of them she produced phenomena – levitations of tables, movements of objects, the nudging or pinching of sitters, and so on – often in light good enough to convince her investigators that the force involved must be psychic, or at any rate could not be accounted for in any conventional scientific terms.

If allowed to evade the control over her hands or her feet, Eusapia in her seances would take advantage of the opportunity. As she explained, when in her trances she had no control over her actions. Unluckily for her reputation then and since, on occasion researchers allowed her such liberty and used it to accuse her of fraud, as Hodgson did in Cambridge in 1895, and Muensterberg in Boston in 1910. Read in conjunction with the other reports, however, these 'exposures' are unsatisfactory. In particular Morselli's trials in Italy, and the systematic tests carried out by Richet, Lodge and Ochorowicz in France in 1894, are hard to explain away; as are the reports of Jules Courtier of trials in Paris in 1905–8 (when the witnesses included such eminent scientists as d'Arsonval, Bergson, the Curies, Perrin and Richet) and the immensely thorough investigation in Naples which followed, by three men with experience of unmasking bogus mediums, Feilding, Carrington and Baggally, on behalf of the SPR.

'Tables, we knew, or thought we knew, do not go into the air by themselves,' Feilding wrote in his report, and for a time, 'although we saw them do so, we still refused to believe that they did'. But in the end, they were compelled to believe – particularly as it was in the sittings 'when our precautions were most complete and the light strongest, that the phenomena were the most numerous'.

Piper, Mrs Leonora (1857–1950)

William James's mother-in-law, knowing of his interest in psychical research, told him in 1885 about a medium she had visited in

Boston, who had given her details about the family circle, purporting to come through her spirit control, 'Dr Phinuit'. Suspicious, James went to investigate, and eventually realized that his initial assumption, that Mrs Piper had taken the trouble to find out the details with the help of a network of agents, had been wrong; he reported to the SPR that he had been compelled 'to believe that she has supernormal powers' by the wealth of evidence she (or 'Dr Phinuit') provided which no agency could have collected for her.

'Dr Phinuit' turned out to be something of a fraud: his description of his earthly life in France turned out to be false. But other 'controls' replaced him, and the information they provided remained tellingly accurate, as Richard Hodgson found when he came out to Boston to investigate. His scepticism, deeper than James's, led him to put detectives on Mrs Piper; but he, too, eventually had to admit that she could not be obtaining the information, which came through in her trances, by natural means.

Mrs Piper was one of the contributors to the SPR 'cross-correspondences'; it was she who produced the warning to Lodge that he was soon to suffer a blow, shortly before the death of his son Raymond. Her record remained unblemished by any episode where she could have been accused of deception; and like Mrs Leonard's, her long career, and the many sitters who testified to the accuracy of the information provided, makes it hard to avoid the conclusion that it came through psychic channels, though whether the spirits or 'super-ESP' were involved remains in contention.

Podmore, Frank (1856–1910)

With Hodgson, Podmore was one of the most energetic and capable of the younger generation of psychical researchers attracted to the SPR when it was founded, and he did valuable work helping Myers and Gurney in its early stages. He also conducted research into the history of psychic phenomena, the first person to do so, becoming the chief chronicler on the Society's behalf. His writings, though, were marred by his prejudices. He could accept telepathy, and was convinced by Hodgson's reports from Boston that Mrs Piper's mediumship was genuine, but he could not accept telekinesis, which led him not merely to reject the evidence for poltergeists, and about Eusapia Palladino, but also to condemn all the historical evidence for physical mediumship which had been collected – though he could not find any serious flaw in the accounts of Home's seances. His books, therefore, though they contained much useful information, became flawed by his growing and almost rancorous determination to demolish the case for PK, which prompted him to include and sometimes to accept unreliable sources of information, where they suited him.

Pratt, J. Gaither (1910–1979)

One of Rhine's students, Pratt became his assistant, carrying out some of the most useful of the trials of ESP at Duke in the 1930s. His books and articles throughout his career reflected his shrewdness – and much else. His career was remarkable in three respects, Professor Ian Stevenson noted in an obituary. First, the number of years – almost fifty – he had devoted to psychical research. 'Second, no one has surpassed him in the diversity of the aspects of parapsychology that he studied. And, third, he brought to everything he did a high standard that has rarely been equalled in our field.'

Price, Harry (1881–1948)

Easily the most celebrated psychical researcher in Britain in the years between the wars, Price's reputation has since slumped, because of evidence of the way in which he allowed his passion for publicity to prompt him to fraud. Ironically, although suspicion rests on his conduct of the once celebrated investigation of the Borley Rectory phenomena, the only cases in which it now seems clear that he cheated were both 'exposures' of mediums, designed to reassure the public and fellow researchers that he was not to be regarded as gullible. It is almost certain that he framed the spirit photographer William Hope in 1921; and detective work by Anita Gregory of the SPR half a century after Price claimed to have exposed Rudi Schneider has demonstrated beyond doubt that it was Price who cheated. As a result the mass of evidence which he collected from his work with mediums, some of it well documented, has lost its value.

Prince, Walter Franklin (1863–1934)

The investigator of one of the most celebrated of multiple personality cases, 'Doris Fischer', Prince, an Episcopalian clergyman, sent his evidence to Hyslop, who printed it in the *Journal* of the

American SPR; and on Hyslop's death, Prince succeeded him in charge of that Society. Like McDougall, he accepted mental, but not physical, mediumship; and although he did some useful research, notably with Dr Pagenstecher and 'Mme de Z.' in Mexico, his prejudice made him an unfortunate choice as one of the *Scientific American's* team investigating 'Margery'. According to another of the investigators, James Malcolm Bird, Prince was 'one of those people in whom rugged intellectual honesty sticks out all over, like spines on a cactus'; his judgments were sound, except where his prejudices rendered him incapable of detachment. His books remain very readable, in particular *Noted Witnesses for Psychic Occurrences* (1928) and *The Enchanted Boundary* (1930).

Rayleigh, Lord, OM, FRS (1842–1919)
John William Strutt, third Baron Rayleigh, was one of the Trinity, Cambridge, group who from the start dominated the SPR. Cavendish Professor of Physics, he was elected President of the British Association in 1884, and twenty years later won a Nobel Prize. Marriage with Evelyn Balfour, sister of Eleanor Sidgwick, brought him into contact with psychical research; he investigated Mrs Jencken (the former Kate Fox) and, on her visit to Cambridge, Eusapia Palladino.

In his Presidential Address to the SPR in 1919 Rayleigh recalled that he had witnessed an exhibition of hypnotism as a young man, when hypnosis was still being dismissed out of hand by orthodox scientists; and this had convinced him that 'what was, or at any rate had recently been, orthodox opinion might be quite wrong'. Scientists, he urged, should concern themselves with phenomena which lay just outside convention's boundaries.

Rayleigh, Lord, FRS (1875–1947)
Robert John, the fourth baron, son of the above, followed his father into physics, becoming Professor at Imperial College, London. He was involved in the London investigation of Rudi Schneider, and in his Presidential Address to the Society in 1937 he reminded his fellow scientists that difficult though it might be for them to accept the evidence from psychical research, 'physical science has had to make adjustments of that kind often enough in the last few decades, and it would be rash to conclude that we have reached finality'.

Rhine, Joseph Banks (1895–1980)

By temperament sceptical, and by training a botanist, Rhine realized the limitations of the scientific materialism prevailing in the 1920s through reading Bergson, and was drawn to psychical research through reading Myers. After some false starts, he found a base at Duke University, where with the help of packs of 25 cards, with five different patterns, designed by his colleague Dr K.F. Zener, he began to test students to find whether any of them could guess correctly at a rate significantly better than chance expectation (five correct guesses). Some could guess six, or more, consistently enough over long runs to demonstrate that the odds against chance were thousands, even millions, to one; and with the publication of the results in the monograph *Extra-Sensory Perception* in 1934 Rhine and his research quickly established at first a national, and then an international, reputation.

For the next 45 years Rhine was to remain, in the eyes of the public, the leading parapsychologist. The concept of a parapsychologist, in fact, as distinct from a psychical researcher – the one seeking to demonstrate the phenomena in controlled conditions, the other being more concerned to investigate spontaneous cases – stems from his work. His chief contribution was to enable parapsychology to establish itself, albeit slowly, as an academic discipline, accepted in universities. Personally and professionally, Brian Mackenzie has recalled in his survey of Rhine's place in the history of the subject – contributed to the memorial volume *J. B. Rhine: on the Frontiers of Science* (1982) – that Rhine's attributes 'included experimental skills, a commitment to the importance and legitimacy of the field, confidence in the applicability of scientific methods to its problems, a favourable institutional setting, and a forceful personality that inspired enthusiasm and commitment'.

Rhine, Louisa (1892–1983)

Louisa Rhine collaborated with her husband J. B. Rhine throughout his career, first at Duke and then, on his retirement, at the Foundation for Research on the Nature of Man, which was set up nearby in Durham, NC, and complemented his research by collecting and analysing the cases of spontaneous psi, contributed from sources in the US and all over the world. Her surveys, *Hidden Channels of the Mind* (1961) and *The Invisible Picture* (1981),

333

are of particular value because they redress the balance which Rhine's work tipped in favour of experimental studies.

Richet, Charles (1850–1935)
For over half a century, from the awakening of interest in psychical research in France in the 1870s to the Rhine era, Richet was the dominant force in the field in Europe, first as an investigator and later as its elder statesman. Psychologist (with Pierre Janet and others, he helped to establish psychology as an academic discipline) and physiologist (in 1912 he won a Nobel Prize for his discoveries in connection with what has since come to be recognized as allergy) Richet refused to allow his conventional reputation to inhibit the expression of his opinions about paranormal phenomena, set out at length in 1922 in the book which was published in English the following year as *Thirty Years of Psychical Research*.

His interest initially aroused by encountering the 'higher phenomena' while he was investigating hypnosis in Paris, Richet was the first to experiment, nearly half a century before Rhine, with card-guessing games to test for telepathy. For some years sceptical about the physical phenomena of mediumship, he was converted to acceptance following careful and protracted trials of Eusapia Palladino; in 1899 he apologized to Crookes, in a paper read to the SPR, for his earlier attitude to Crookes's reports about Home and others, which he had laughed at 'as heartily as almost everyone else was doing'. It was his visit to Algiers and his articles in the *Revue Métapsychique*, which he had founded, that first established 'Eva C's' mediumship; and his eminence in orthodox science enabled him in 1922 to confront the Academy of the Sciences with the evidence for psychic phenomena.

Almost to the last, Richet remained doggedly a materialist, assuming that ectoplasm (a term he coined) was a natural, though unexplained, substance formed much as mist is formed from droplets of water by a fall of temperature. But in a letter to Lodge in 1932 he indicated that he was wavering; although not a spiritualist in the Conan Doyle mould, he wrote, 'I am insensibly approaching your ideas'. And according to Bozzano, he finally became convinced by the evidence for Survival.

Schrenck-Notzing, Baron Albert von (1862–1929)
Like Richet, Schrenck was initially attracted to the study of psychical phenomena through investigation of the 'higher phenomena' of hypnotism; and thanks to his and his wife's private means

he was able to concentrate on investigating them. His chief interest was in the physical phenomena, first with Eusapia Palladino; then with 'Eva C'; and, in the 1920s, with the Scheider brothers. His *Phenomena of Materialization*, published in Munich in 1913, translated and put out in an expanded version in English in 1920, remains the most detailed account of the experiments of the time; and the care which he took to make them as carefully controlled as possible was attested by even so critical an observer as Eric Dingwall.

Sidgwick, Eleanor (1845–1936)

Eleanor Sidgwick shared many of her husband's qualities. Granddaughter of Lord Salisbury, sister of Arthur and Gerald Balfour, she became a don at (and later Principal of) Newnham College, Cambridge. For a time she stayed in the background of the SPR, though editing its *Journal* in the 1890s, and joining its Council in 1901. Shortly before her retirement as Principal of Newnham she became Hon. Secretary, and then President, as if indicating that the time for such discretion was past; and, effectively, she ran the Society from her husband's death in 1900 to her own – though in the 1930s her influence lay mainly in the fact that Council members were in general of her persuasion.

Like her husband, she was hostile to physical mediumship, and as a result kept the Society at arm's length from the investigations of Crawford, Schrenck, Geley and others. Her surveys of the evidence on telepathy, apparitions and the 'cross-correspondences' were reasonably detached, exemplifying, in Renée Haynes's words, 'her clarity of thought, her energy and her enormous industry'; but her prejudices led to disagreements and divisions within the Society which severely weakened it in the years between the wars.

Sidgwick, Henry (1838–1900)

Made a Fellow of Trinity College, Cambridge, in 1859, Sidgwick resigned ten years later because his conscience was troubled by the need to subscribe to the Anglican Church to hold the post; and throughout his life he was highly regarded for his integrity, as well as for his academic distinction as a philosopher. With Myers, Gurney, Lord Rayleigh and the Balfours he began to investigate mediums in the 1870s, and was the natural choice as President of the newly-formed Society for Psychical Research in 1882.

In that capacity he investigated mediums, though usually with relatively disappointing results; 'I heard him say, the year before his death,' William James was to recall, 'that if anyone had told him at the outset that after twenty years he would be in the same identical state of doubt and balance that he started with, he would have deemed the prophecy incredible.'

Partly this seems to have stemmed from an unconquerable aversion to the physical phenomena; in spite of witnessing some of them during an investigation of Eusapia Palladino, he reacted with obvious relief to Hodgson's 'exposure', laying down not merely that all the evidence in her favour could be dismissed, but also that she should not again be tested on the Society's behalf. But it was also as if he was unconsciously what came later to be called a 'psi-inhibitor'; 'the liberal heart which he possessed,' James noted, 'had to work with an intellect which acted destructively on almost every particular object of belief that was offered to its acceptance.' His importance lay less in his contribution as a researcher than, as Professor C. D. Broad put it, for 'the weight which his known intelligence and integrity gave to the serious study of the subject'.

Soal, S. G. (1890–1975)
A lecturer in mathematics in Queen Mary College, London, Soal combined acceptance of the genuineness of individual mediums with scepticism about the results obtained at Duke in the early 1930s; and when trials for ESP he carried out in London gave negative results, he acquired the reputation of a sceptic. Persuaded by Carington to go through the results again, however, to see if any of them provided evidence for precognition, he found that they did. Two subjects, Basil Shackleton and Mrs Stewart, had a level of precognitive 'hits' far higher than chance expectation.

Further work with them after the war appeared to confirm the earlier findings, and for a while Soal's tests were regarded as the most conclusive evidence for precognition which had been presented; but doubts surfaced about his procedure, and the advent of the computer age enabled checks to be made which showed that he had not used the tables of random numbers in quite the way he had claimed. Whether he consciously fudged them, to improve the results, or had some other motive – he was by all accounts a very odd character – remains uncertain; but the discovery has led to all his results being rejected, though the early work with Carington was clearly genuine.

Swedenborg, Emanuel (1688–1722)

When Swedenborg was almost fifty years old, after a career of astonishing diversity, he had a vision of the Lord, in which the Lord informed him that he was to be the chosen expounder of the Bible for the benefit of the human race. There followed an outpouring of works in automatic writing – or at least taken down, as Swedenborg claimed, from spirit dictation ('I am but the secretary'). Periodically, too, he had visions, some providing him with second sight, as in the episode which so fascinated Kant, when Swedenborg 'saw' the fire raging through Stockholm while he was at Gothenburg, 300 miles away, describing it in accurate detail.

As Dingwall pointed out in his essay on Swedenborg in *Very Peculiar People* (1950), this and other stories of Swedenborg's mediumship lack contemporary attestation in the form of reports made at or immediately after the event; but Kant did at least obtain independent confirmation from a friend whom he asked to check the story a few months later.

Thomson, Sir John Joseph, OM, FRS (1856–1940)

Another product of Trinity, Cambridge, Thomson succeeded Lord Rayleigh as Cavendish Professor of Experimental Physics in 1884 and, thirteen years later, in what *Chambers's Biographical Dictionary* describes as 'the greatest revolution in physics since Newton', demonstrated that there were electrons two thousand times smaller in mass than what had till then been taken to be the smallest atomic particles. A member of the SPR, Thomson was one of the investigators of Eusapia Palladino when she was in Cambridge, and was impressed by what he witnessed. He remained one of the Society's Vice-Presidents until his death, urging in his *Recollections and Reflections* (1936) that scientists should investigate dowsing ('the divining rod is perhaps of all phenomena which may be thought to be psychical, the one most favourable for experiment'), describing the issue of the possible existence of communication with the dead as 'of transcendental importance', and echoing Eleanor Sidgwick by pointing out that if telepathy existed among the living it helped to bridge this divide; 'if the apparatus of the senses is not used in one case, why should it be needed in another?'

Tyrrell, G. N. M. (1879–1952)

An electrical engineer, Tyrrell worked with Marconi. After the first world war, he found that his adopted daughter Gertrude had psychic abilities, and together they embarked on a series of tests in which Tyrrell experimented with different methods to see if they could find protocols which would satisfy the demands of sceptics; with a measure of success, but only to find that there were elements, such as the state of mind of the psychic, which had to be allowed for, and which sceptics declined to accept. His *Science and Psychical Phenomena* (1938), *Apparitions* (1943) and *The Personality of Man* (1946) remain as testimonies to his ability.

Noting that, like Carington, he had thrown up a promising career to devote himself to psychical research, Rosalind Heywood recalled that 'he had that rare combination of qualities needed to evoke and to interpret psi: scientific training, the power to generalize from a number of apparently unrelated particulars, and an encouraging personality which never inhibited a timid percipient's ESP'.

Varley, Cromwell (1828–1883)

Although, as an engineer who was involved in the laying of the first trans-Atlantic cable, Varley was made a Fellow of the Royal Society in 1871, he was 'a man for whose contribution to cable telegraphy', according to Lodge, 'Lord Kelvin in later life frequently said he had not received a due meed of recognition and approbation'. Nor has he received it for being the first scientist to conduct research with Home. Some years before Crookes, Varley attended a Home session, recalling afterwards that although he had been too staggered by what he witnessed to feel satisfied that it had been genuine, he was later convinced, the same day, by the fact that when he returned to his home he heard similar raps to those he had heard earlier, though he was alone; and the next morning had a letter from Home to say that the spirits had reported making them.

Vasiliev, L. L. (1891–1966)

It seems likely that, in time, Vasiliev will be recognized as one of the most important figures in the history of parapsychology. In his *Experiments in Distant Influence*, published in Russia in 1962 and in its English translation the following year, Vasiliev – Professor of Physiology at the University of Leningrad – described trials he had made with subjects to find, among other things, if they could be put into a hypnotic trance at a distance by telepathy; and he found that this was possible.

For the present, descriptions of psychical research emanating from Russia need to be taken with reserve; but Professor Eysenck has expressed cautious satisfaction with the protocol of the experiments, and Vasiliev's translator, Anita Gregory, regarded them as 'among the few classical investigations of telepathy', open to some criticism, but representing pioneering work 'of the utmost importance'.

Wallace, Alfred Russel, OM (1823–1913)

Most people today remember Wallace, if at all, as the man who nearly beat Darwin to the draw over the theory of the origin of the species, but who magnanimously withdrew his claim when he realized that Darwin had been working on it for years. Wallace, however, was also one of the earliest investigators of mediums. Earlier, as a young schoolmaster, he had found that some of his pupils could demonstrate community of sensation; and in the 1860s, impressed by what he had witnessed of physical mediumship, he did his best to persuade sceptical colleagues and friends to take it seriously, setting out his views in a paper on the scientific aspects of the supernatural.

Wallace joined with Crookes in 1870 to investigate Home and other mediums; but though he became a member of the SPR, he was soon disenchanted, complaining that its leaders were too sceptical. Not that he wished to convert the public through his own writings; 'neither I nor any other well-instructed Spiritualist expects anything of the kind', he wrote. 'We ask our readers not for belief, but for doubt of their own infallibility on this question; we ask for enquiry and patient experiment before hastily concluding that we are, all of us, mere dupes and idiots, as regards a subject to which we have devoted our best mental faculties and powers of observation for many years.'

Zöllner, Johann (1834–1882)

Of all the eminent men whose reputation has been undone by his decision to take psychical research seriously, Zöllner is perhaps the most unfortunate. A Professor of Physics and Astronomy, he was widely regarded as one of the leading scientists of his time; and his theory of the fourth dimension had aroused international interest. Believing that physical mediumship could provide evidence which would support the theory, he undertook to investigate the medium Henry Slade in a series of trials in 1877–8, attended by distinguished contemporaries – Wilhelm Weber, Wilhelm Scheibner and Gustav Fechner. The phenomena, described in Zöllner's *Transcendental Physics*, published in German in 1879, were striking, providing the evidence he had hoped for. But Weber, though at the time he admitted they could not be accounted for naturally, later retracted; and Zöllner's death enabled sceptics to claim not merely that he had been duped, but that he had gone off his head – falsely, as those who knew him insisted.

BIBLIOGRAPHY

The works listed here are those which are referred to in the text, (except for a few which contain only an isolated episode relating to the paranormal) along with some which will be of use to anybody following up a particular theme. Where a book has been translated, the English title is given. The place and date of publication are ordinarily of the first edition, except for one or two older works, whose initial publication date is given in brackets.

Adare, Lord, *Experiences with D. D. Home*, London, 1869.

Aksakov, Alexandre, *Animisme et Spiritisme*, Paris, 1906.

Alexander, P. P., *Spiritualism*, Edinburgh, 1971.

Angoff, Allan, and Barth, Diana, *Parapsychology and Anthropology*, New York, 1974.

Ashby, Robert, *Guidebook for the Study of Psychical Research*, London, 1972.

Aubrey, John, *Miscellanies*, London, 1696.

Barrett, Sir William, *On the Threshold of a New World of Thought*, London, 1908; revised as *On the Threshold of the Unseen*, London, 1920.

Barrett, Sir William, *Psychical Research*, London, 1911.

Barrett, Sir William, *Death-Bed Visions*, London, 1926.

Barrett, Sir William and Besterman, Theodore, *The Divining Rod*, London, 1926.

Beloff, John (ed.), *New Directions in Parapsychology*, London, 1974.

Bennett, Sir Ernest, *Apparitions and Haunted Houses*, London, 1939.

Bergson, Henri, *Creative Evolution*, London, 1911.

Bergson, Henri, *Matter and Memory*, London, 1911.

Bernstein, Morey, *The Search for Bridey Murphy*, New York, 1956.

Besterman, Theodore, *Crystal-gazing*, London, 1924.

Bird, Christopher, *The Divining Hand*, New York, 1979.

Blackmore, Susan J., *Beyond the Body*, London, 1982.

Boirac, Emil, *The Psychology of the Future*, London, 1919.

Bouché-Leclerc, *Divination dans l'Antiquité*, Paris, 1879.

Bowles, Norma, and Hynds, Fran, *Psi Search*, New York, 1978.

Bozzano, Ernesto, *Phenomena of Haunting*, London, 1920.

Bozzano, Ernesto, *Discarnate Influences on Human Life*, London, 1938.

Bozzano, Ernesto, *Polyglot Mediumship (Xenoglossy)*, London, 1932.

Braid, James, *Neurypnology*, London, 1843.

Braid, James, *Magic, Witchcraft, Animal Magnetism*, London, 1852.

Brath, Stanley de, *Psychical Research, Science and Religion*, London, 1925.

Braude, Stephen, *ESP and Psychokinesis*, Philadelphia, 1979.

Brewster, Sir David, *Letters on Natural Magic*, London, 1832.

Bridge, Ann, *Moments of Knowing*, London, 1970.

Britten, Emma H., *Nineteenth Century Miracles*, New York, 1884.

Broad, Charlie D., *Religion, Philosophy and Psychical Research*, London, 1953.

Broad, Charlie D., *Lectures on Psychical Research*, London, 1962.

Brougham, Lord, *Life and Times*, London, 1971.

Brown, Slater, *The Heyday of Spiritualism*, New York, 1970.

Buchan, John, *Memory Hold the Door*, London, 1940.

Buchanan, Joseph R., *Manual of Psychometry*, Boston, 1893.

Burland, C. A., *The Arts of the Alchemist*, London, 1967.

Burt, Cyril, *Psychology and Psychical Research*, London, 1968.

Callaway, Henry, *The Religious System of the Amazulu*, Cape Town, 1868.

Capron, E. W., *Modern Spiritualism*, Boston, 1855.

Carington, Whately, *Telepathy*, London, 1945.

Carré de Montgeron, *La Verité des Miracles . . . par l'Intercession de M. de Paris*, Utrecht, 1737.

Carrington, Hereward, *The Physical Phenomena of Spiritualism*, New York, 1907.

Carrington, Hereward, *The American Seances with Eusapia Palladino*, New York, 1954.

Cavendish, R. (ed.), *Encyclopedia of the Unexplained*, New York, 1974.

Cayce, Edgar, *On ESP* (ed. Doris Agee), New York, 1969.

Chastenet de Puységur, A., *Mémoir du Magnétisme Animal*, Lyon, 1786.

Chevreul, Michel-Eugène, *De la Baguette Divinatoire et des Tables Tournantes*, Paris, 1854.

Christie-Murray, David, *Reincarnation*, London, 1981.

CIBA, *ESP: a CIBA Foundation Symposium*, New York, 1966.

Cicero, *On Divination*, London, 1876.

Coates, James, *Photographing the Invisible*, London, 1922.

Cohn, Norman, *Europe's Inner Demons*, London, 1975.

Collins, H. M., and Pinch, T. J., *The Social Construction of Extraordinary Science*, London, 1982.

Collyer, Robert H., *Automatic Writing*, London, 1876.

Coover, J. E., *Experiments in Psychical Research*, Stanford, 1917.

Corliss, William R., *Lightning, Auroras, Nocturnal Lights and Related Luminous Phenomena*, London, 1982.

Coxhead, Nona, *Mindpower*, London, 1976.

Crawford, William J., *The Reality of Psychic Phenomena*, London, 1916.

Crawford, William J., *Experiments in Psychic Science*, London, 1919.

Crawford, William J., *Psychic Structures of the Goligher Circle*, London, 1921.

Crookes, William, *Researches in the Phenomena of Spiritualism*, London, 1874.

Crowe, Catherine, *The Night Side of Nature*, London, 1848.

Cumberland, Stuart, *A Thought-reader's Thoughts*, London, 1888.

David-Neel, Alexandra, *Magic and Mystery in Tibet*, London, 1936.

Dean, Douglas, *et al.*, *Executive ESP*, New York, 1974.

Deleuze, J. P. F., *Histoire Critique du Magnétisme Animal*, Paris, 1819.

De Morgan, Mrs, *From Matter to Spirit*, London, 1863.

Dingwall, Eric J., *Some Human Oddities*, London, 1947.

Dingwall, Eric J., *Very Peculiar People*, London, 1950.

Dingwall, Eric J. (ed.), *Abnormal Hypnotic Phenomena*, London, 1967.

Dodds, E. R., *Supernormal Phenomena in Classical Antiquity*, London, 1971.

Doyle, Conan, *The New Revelation*, London, 1918.

Doyle, Conan, *The History of Spiritualism*, London, 1926.

Doyle, Conan, *The Edge of the Unknown*, London, 1930.

Driesch, Hans, *Psychical Research*, London, 1933.

Duchatel, E., and Warcollier, René, *Les Miracles de la Volonté*, Paris, 1914.

Dunne, J. W., *An Experiment with Time*, London, 1927.

Dupotet de Sennevoy, J. D., *An Introduction to the Study of Animal Magnetism*, London, 1838.

Du Prel, Carl, *The Philosophy of Mysticism*, London, 1889.

Easlea, Brian, *Witch-hunting, Magic and the New Philosophy*, Brighton, 1980.

Edmonds, John Worth, *Spiritual Tracts*, New York, 1858.

Ehrenwald, Jan, *Telepathy and Medical Psychology*, New York, 1948.

Eisenbud, Jule, *The World of Ted Serios*, New York, 1967.

Eisenbud, Jule, *Paranormal Foreknowledge*, New York, 1982.

Eliade, Mircea, *Shamanism*, New York, 1964.

Eliade, Mircea, *From Primitive to Zen*, London, 1967.

Elliott, G. Maurice, *The Bible in Psychic History*, London, 1959.

Elliot, James Scott, *Dowsing: One Man's Way*, Jersey, Ch. I., 1977.

Ennemoser, Joseph, *The History of Magic*, London, 1893 (1843).

Esdaile, James, *Natural and Mesmeric Clairvoyance*, London, 1852.

Eysenck, Hans, *Sense and Nonsense in Psychology*, London, 1957.

Eysenck, Hans, and Sargent, Carl, *Explaining the Unexplained*, London, 1982.

Eysenck, Hans, and Nias, D. K. B., *Astrology: Science or Superstition?*, London, 1982.

Ferguson, Marilyn, *The Aquarian Conspiracy*, New York, 1980.

Figuier, Guillaume, *Histoire du Merveilleux*, Paris, 1860.

Flammarion, Camille, *Des Forces Naturelles Inconnues*, Paris, 1866.

Flammarion, Camille, *The Unknown*, New York, 1900.

Flammarion, Camille, *Death and its Mystery*, London, 1922.

Flournoy, Theodore, *From India to the Planet Mars*, New York, 1901.

Flournoy, Theodore, *Spiritism and Psychology*, New York, 1911.

Fodor, Nandor, *Encyclopedia of Psychic Science*, London, 1934.

Fort, Charles, *The Book of the Damned*, New York, 1919.

France, Vicomte Henri de, *The Modern Dowser*, London, 1930.

Fukurai, T., *Clairvoyance and Thoughtography*, London, 1931.

Fuller, John G., *The Airmen Who Would Not Die*, New York, 1979.

Garrett, Eileen, *Telepathy*, New York, 1941.
Garrett, Eileen, *Adventures in the Supernormal*, New York, 1949.
Gasparin, A. de, *A Treatise on Turning Tables*, London, 1857.
Gauquelin, Michel, *The Truth about Astrology*, Oxford, 1983.
Gauld, Alan, *The Founders of Psychical Research*, London, 1968.
Gauld, Alan, *Mediumship and Survival*, London, 1982.
Gauld, Alan, and Cornell, A. D., *Poltergeists*, London, 1979.
Geley, Gustave, *From the Unconscious to the Conscious*, London, 1920.
Geley, Gustave, *Clairvoyance and Materialisation*, London, 1927.
Geller, Uri, *My Story*, New York, 1975.
Glanvill, Joseph, *A Whip for the Droll*, London, 1668.
Glanvill, Joseph, *Saducismus Triumphatus*, London, 1681.
Goddard, Sir Victor, *Flight Towards Reality*, London, 1975.
Godley, John, *Tell Me the Next One*, London, 1950.
Godley, John, *Living Like a Lord*, London, 1955.
Gooch, Stan, *Creatures from Inner Space*, London, 1984.
Grasset, Joseph, *The Marvels Beyond Science*, New York, 1910.
Grattan-Guinness, Ivor (ed.), *Psychical Research*, London, 1982.
Graves, Tom, *Needles of Stone*, London, 1978.
Green, Celia, *Out of the Body Experiences*, Oxford, 1968.
Green, Celia, and McCreery, Charles, *Apparitions*, London, 1975.
Gregory, Anita, *Anatomy of a Fraud*, London, 1977.
Gregory, William, *Letters on Animal Magnetism*, London, 1851.
Gris, Henry, and Dick, William, *The New Soviet Psychic Discoveries*, New York, 1978.
Guirdham, Arthur, *Cosmic Factors in Disease*, London, 1963.
Guirdham, Arthur, *The Cathars and Reincarnation*, London, 1970.
Gurney, Edmund, Myers, Frederic, and Podmore, Frank, *Phantasms of the Living*, London, 1886.

Halifax, Lord, *Ghost Book*, London, 1936 (vol. 2, 1937).
Hall, Trevor, *The Spiritualist*, London, 1962.
Hall, Trevor, *New Light on Old Ghosts*, London, 1965.
Halliday, W. R., *Greek Divination*, London, 1913.
Hansel, C.E.M., *ESP*, New York, 1966.
Hansel, C.E.M., *ESP and Parapsychology*, New York, 1980.

Hardy, Sir Alister, *The Living Stream*, London, 1965.

Hardy, Sir Alister, Harvie, Robert, and Koestler, Arthur, *The Challenge of Chance*, London, 1973.

Hare, Robert, *Experimental Investigation*, New York, 1858.

Harrison, Michael, *Fire from Heaven*, London, 1976.

Hasted, John, *The Metal Benders*, London, 1981.

Haynes, Renée, *The Hidden Springs*, London, 1961.

Haynes, Renée, *The Seeing Eye, the Seeing I*, London, 1976.

Haynes, Renée, *Philosopher King*, London, 1970.

Haynes, Renée, *The Society for Psychical Research*, London, 1982.

Heine, H. G., *The Vital Sense*, London, 1960.

Heywood, Rosalind, *The Sixth Sense*, London, 1959.

Heywood, Rosalind, *The Infinite Hive*, London, 1964.

Hitching, Francis, *Pendulum: the Psi Connection*, London, 1977.

Holms, Campbell, *The Facts of Psychic Science*, London, 1925.

Holroyd, Stuart, *Psi and the Consciousness Explosion*, London, 1977.

Home, D. D., *Lights and Shadows of Spiritualism*, London, 1877.

Houdini, Harry, *A Magician among the Spirits*, New York, 1924.

Howitt, William, *The History of the Supernatural*, London, 1863.

Hudson, Thomas Jay, *The Law of Psychic Phenomena*, Chicago, 1902.

Hume, David, *Essays*, London, 1875 (1750).

Huxley, Aldous, *The Devils of Loudun*, London, 1952.

Huxley, Aldous, *The Doors of Perception*, London, 1954.

Hyslop, James, *Enigmas of Psychical Research*, London, 1906.

Hyslop, James, *Contact with the Other World*, New York, 1919.

Iamblichus, *The Mysteries*, London, 1895.

Iamblichus, *Theurgia*, New York, 1911.

Inglis, Brian, *Natural and Supernatural*, London, 1977.

Inglis, Brian, *Science and Parascience*, London, 1984.

Inglis, Brian, and West, Ruth, *The Alternative Health Guide*, London, 1983.

Iverson, Jeffrey, *More Lives Than One?*, London, 1976.

Jacolliot, Louis, *Occult Science in India*, London, 1884 (1875).

James, William, *The Varieties of Religious Experience*, New York, 1890.

James, William, *Collected Essays*, London, 1920.

James, William, *On Psychical Research* (ed. G. Murphy and R. Ballou), New York, 1960.

Johnson, Raynor C., *The Imprisoned Splendour*, London, 1953.

Joire, Paul, *Psychical and Supernormal Phenomena*, London, 1916.

Jung, Carl, *Memories, Dreams, Reflections*, London, 1963.

Kant, Immanuel, *Dreams of a Spirit Seer*, London, 1900 (1766).

Kardec, Allan, *Le Livre des Esprits*, Paris, 1862.

Keeton, Joe (and Moss, Peter), *Encounters with the Past*, London, 1979.

Kerner, Justinus, *The Secrets of Prevorst*, London, 1845 (1829).

Kipling, Rudyard, *Something of Myself*, London, 1937.

Koestler, Arthur, *The Roots of Coincidence*, London, 1972.

Koestler, Arthur, *The Challenge of Chance*, London, 1973.

Koestler, Arthur, *Janus*, London, 1978.

Krippner, Stanley, *Advances in Parapsychological Research*, New York, 1977.

Krippner, Stanley (ed.), *Psychoenergetic Systems*, New York, 1979.

Krippner, Stanley, and Villoldo, Alberto, *The Realms of Psychic Healing*, New York, 1976.

Lafontaine, C., *Mémoires d'un Magnétiseur*, Paris, 1866.

Lang, Andrew, *Cock Lane and Common Sense*, London, 1894.

Lang, Andrew, *The Book of Dreams and Ghosts*, London, 1897.

Lang, Andrew, *Magic and Religion*, London, 1901.

Lapponi, Joseph, *Hypnotism and Spiritism*, London, 1906.

Lavater, Lewes, *Of Ghosts*, 1929 (1572).

Laver, James, *Nostradamus*, London, 1952.

Leeds, Morton, and Murphy, Gardner, *The Paranormal and the Normal*, Metuchen, NJ, 1980.

Leonard, Gladys Osborne, *My Life in Two Worlds*, London, 1931.

Leroy, Olivier, *La Raison Primitive*, Paris, 1927.

Leroy, Olivier, *Levitation*, London, 1928.

Leroy, Olivier, *Les Hommes Salamandres*, Paris, 1931.

LeShan, L., *The Medium, the Mystic and the Physicist*, New York, 1974.

Levi, Eliphas, *The History of Magic*, London, 1913.

Lewis, C. S., *Miracles*, London, 1947.

Litvag, I., *Singer in the Shadows: the Strange Case of Patience Worth*, New York, 1972.

Lodge, Oliver, *Survival of Man*, London, 1909.

Lodge, Oliver, *Raymond*, London, 1916.

Lodge, Oliver, *Past Years*, London, 1931.

Lodge, Oliver, *My Philosophy*, London, 1933.

Lombroso, Cesare, *After Death, What?*, London, 1909.

Long, Max Freedom, *The Secret Science behind Miracles*, Vista, Calif., 1948.

Lowell, Perceval, *Occult Japan*, Boston, 1895.

Lucy, Sir Henry W., *Sixty Years in the Wilderness*, London, 1909.

Ludwig, Jan (ed.), *Philosophy and Parapsychology*, Buffalo N. Y., 1978.

Lyttelton, Edith, *Our Superconscious Minds*, London, 1931.

Lyttelton, Edith, *Some Cases of Prediction*, London, 1937.

McConnell, R. A., *ESP Curriculum Guide*, New York, 1971.

McConnell, R. A., *An Introduction to Parapsychology in the Context of Science*, Pittsburgh, 1983.

McCreery, Charles, *Science, Philosophy and ESP*, London, 1967.

McCreery, Charles, *Psychical Phenomena and the Physical World*, London, 1973.

McDougall, William, *Body and Mind*, London, 1911.

McDougall, William, *The Riddle of Life*, London, 1938.

MacKenzie, Andrew, *Hauntings and Apparitions*, London, 1982.

McRae, Ronald M., *Mind Wars*, New York, 1984.

Maeterlinck, Maurice, *The Unknown Guest*, London, 1914.

Mann, Thomas, *Three Essays*, London, 1932.

Manning, Matthew, *The Link*, London, 1975.

Manning, Matthew, *In the Minds of Millions*, London, 1977.

Marais, Eugène, *The Soul of the White Ant*, London, 1937.

Marks, David, and Kamman, Richard, *The Psychology of the Psychic*, Buffalo N. Y., 1981.

Masters, Robert, and Houston, Jean, *The Varieties of Psychedelic Experience*, 1966.

Mathieu, P-F, *Histoire des Miraculés et des Convulsionnaires de St Médard*, Paris, 1864.

Mauskopf, Seymour H., and McVaugh, Michael R., *The Elusive Science*, Baltimore, 1980.

Maxwell, Joseph, *Metapsychical Phenomena*, London, 1903.

Mayo, Herbert, *Letters on the Truths Contained in the Popular Superstitions*, London, 1851.

Medhurst, R. G., *Crookes and the Spirit World*, London, 1972.

Mercer, J. E., *Alchemy*, London, 1921.

Mermet, Abbé, *Principles and Practice of Radiesthesia*, London, 1935.

Mesmer, Franz, *Mémoires sur la Découverte du Magnétisme Animal*, Paris, 1779.

Middleton, John (ed.), *Magic, Witchcraft and Curing*, New York, 1967.

Mitchell, Edgar D., *Psychic Exploration*, New York, 1974.

Moberly, C. A., and Jourdain, E. F., *An Adventure*, London, 1911.

Monroe, Robert, *Journeys Out of the Body*, New York, 1971.

Moor, Edward, *Bealing's Bells*, Woodbridge, 1841.

Moore, R. L., *In Search of White Crows*, London, 1977.

Moses, Stainton, *Higher Aspects of Spiritualism*, London, 1880.

Moses, Stainton, *Spirit Teaching*, London, 1883.

Moss, Thelma, *The Probability of the Impossible*, London, 1976.

Muldoon, Sylvan, and Carrington, Hereward, *The Projection of the Astral Body*, London, 1929.

Murchison, Carl (ed.), *The Case For and Against Psychical Belief*, Clark University, 1927.

Murray, Margaret, *The Witch Cult in Western Europe*, Oxford, 1921.

Murphy, Gardner, *The Challenge of Psychical Research*, New York, 1961.

Myers, Frederic, *Human Personality and its Survival of Bodily Death*, London, 1903.

Nelson, Geoffrey K., *Spiritualism and Society*, London, 1969.

Nichols, Beverley, *Powers That Be*, London, 1966.

Ochorowicz, Julian, *Mental Suggestion*, New York, 1891.

Oesterreich, T. K., *Occultism and Modern Science*, London, 1923.

Ostrander, Sheila, and Schroeder, Lynn, *Psi: Psychic Discoveries behind the Iron Curtain*, New York, 1970.

Ostrander, Sheila, and Schroeder, Lynn, *The ESP Papers*, New York, 1976.

Osty, Eugène, *Supernormal Faculties in Man*, London, 1923.

Owen, A. R. G., *Can We Explain the Poltergeist?*, New York, 1974.

Owen, A. R. G., *Psychic Mysteries of Canada*, New York, 1975.

Owen, Robert Dale, *Footfalls on the Boundary of Another World*, London, 1861.

Owen, Robert Dale, *The Debatable Land*, New York, 1874.

Palmer, E. Clephan, *The Riddle of Spiritualism*, London, 1927.

Palmstierna, Erik, *Horizons of Immortality*, London, 1937.

Panati, Charles, *Supersenses*, New York, 1974.

Panati, Charles (ed.), *The Geller Papers*, Boston, 1976.

Pauwels, Louis, and Bergier, Jacques, *The Morning of the Magicians*, New York, 1968 (1960).

Pedler, Kit, *Mind Over Matter*, London, 1981.

Piper, Alta, *The Life and Work of Mrs Piper*, London, 1929.

Playfair, Guy Lyon, *The Flying Cow*, London, 1975.

Playfair, Guy Lyon, *This House is Haunted*, London, 1980.

Podmore, Frank, *Apparitions and Thought Transference*, London, 1894.

Podmore, Frank, *Studies in Psychical Research*, London, 1897.

Podmore, Frank, *The Naturalisation of the Supernatural*, London, 1908.

Pollack, Jack H., *Croiset the Clairvoyant*, New York, 1964.

Pratt, J. Gaither, *Parapsychology*, New York, 1964.

Pratt, J. Gaither, *ESP Research Today*, Metuchen, NJ, 1973.

Price, Harry, *Fifty Years of Psychical Research*, London, 1939.

Priestley, J. B., *Man and Time*, London, 1964.

Prince, Morton, *The Dissociation of a Personality*, New York, 1906.

Prince, W. F., *The Case of Patience Worth*, Boston, 1926.

Prince, W. F., *Noted Witnesses for Psychic Occurrences*, Boston, 1928.

Prince, W. F., *The Enchanted Boundary*, Boston, 1930.

Puthoff, Harold, and Targ, Russell, *Mind-Reach*, New York, 1977.

Randall, John, *Parapsychology and the Nature of Life*, London, 1975.

Randall, John, *Psychokinesis*, London, 1982.

Randles, Jenny, *UFO Reality*, London, 1983.

Rao, K. R. (ed.), *J. B. Rhine: On the Frontiers of Science*, Jefferson, North Carolina, 1982.

Rees–Mogg, William, *An Humbler Heaven*, London, 1977.

Reichenbach, Carl von, *The Odic Force* (ed. F. D. O'Byrne), London, 1976.

Rhine, J. B., *Extra-Sensory Perception*, Boston, 1934.

Rhine, J. B., *New Frontiers of the Mind*, New York, 1937.

Rhine, J. B., *The Reach of the Mind*, New York, 1947.

Rhine, Louisa, *Hidden Channels of the Mind*, New York, 1961.

Rhine, Louisa, *Mind Over Matter*, New York, 1970.

Rhine, Louisa, *The Invisible Picture*, Metuchen, NJ, 1981.

Richards, John T., *SORRAT*, Metuchen, NJ, 1982.

Richet, Charles, *Thirty Years of Psychical Research*, London, 1923.

Richet, Charles, *Our Sixth Sense*, London, 1930.

Richet, Charles, *L'Avenir et la Prémonition*, Paris, 1931.

Rochas, Albert de, *L'Extériorisation de la Sensibilité*, Paris, 1895.

Rogo, D. Scott, *Parapsychology: a Century of Inquiry*, New York, 1975.

Rogo, D. Scott, *Mind Beyond the Body*, New York, 1978.

Roll, W. G., *The Poltergeist*, New York, 1972.

Romains, Jules, *Eyeless Sight*, London, 1924.

Rose, Ronald, *Living Magic*, London, 1957.

Rose, Ronald, *South Seas Magic*, London, 1959.

Saintyves, Pierre, *La Force Magique*, Paris, 1914.

Salter, W. H., *Ghosts and Apparitions*, London, 1938.

Saltmarsh, H. F., *Evidence of Personal Survival from Cross-Correspondences*, London, 1938.

Saltmarsh, H. F., *Foreknowledge*, London, 1938.

Sargent, Epes, *The Scientific Basis of Spiritualism*, Boston, 1881.

Schatzman, Morton, *The Story of Ruth*, London 1980.

Schmeidler, Gertrude, *Extrasensory Perception*, New York, 1969.

Schmeidler, Gertrude (ed.), *Parapsychology*, Metuchen, NJ, 1976.

Schrenck-Notzing, Baron von, *Phenomena of Materialisation*, London, 1920.

Scott, Walter, *Letters on Demonology and Witchcraft*, London, 1830.

Scott Elliot, J., *Dowsing: One Man's Way*, Jersey, 1977.

Seabrook, William, *Witchcraft*, New York, 1934.

Shallis, Michael, *On Time*, London, 1982.

Sinclair, Upton, *Mental Radio*, New York, 1930.

Sinel, Joseph, *The Sixth Sense*, London, 1927.

Smith, Susie, *The Mediumship of Mrs Leonard*, New York, 1964.

Smythies, J. R. (ed.), *Science and ESP*, London, 1967.

Soal, S. G., and Bateman, F., *Modern Experiments in Telepathy*, London, 1954.

Society for Psychical Research, *Census of Hallucinations*, London, 1894.

Stevenson, Ian, *Twenty Cases Suggestive of Reincarnation*, Virginia University, 1966.

Sudre, René, *Treatise on Parapsychology*, London, 1960.

Targ, Russell, and Harary, Keith, *The Mind Race*, New York, 1984.

Tart, Charles, *Altered States of Consciousness*, New York, 1969.

Tenhaeff, W. H. C., *Telepathy and Clairvoyance*, Springfield, Ill., 1972.

Teresa of Avila, St, *Life*, London, 1870.

Thakur, S. (ed.), *Philosophy and Psychical Research*, London, 1976.

Thalbourne, Michael A., *A Glossary of Terms Used in Parapsychology*, London, 1983.

Thomas, C. Drayton, *Life Beyond Death*, London, 1928.

Thomas, Keith, *Religion and the Decline of Magic*, London, 1971.

Thomson, William A. R., *Faiths that Heal*, London, 1980.

Thouless, Robert H., *Experimental Psychical Research*, London, 1963.

Thouless, Robert H., *From Anecdote to Experiment in Psychical Research*, London, 1972.

Thurston, Herbert, *Modern Spiritualism*, London, 1928.

Thurston, Herbert, *The Physical Phenomena of Mysticism*, London, 1952.

Tietze, Thomas R., *Margery*, New York, 1973.

Tischner, Rudolf, *Telepathy and Clairvoyance*, London, 1925.

Tyrrell, G. N. M., *Science and Psychical Phenomena*, London, 1938.

Tyrrell, G. N. M., *Apparitions*, London, 1943.

Tyrrell, G. N. M., *The Personality of Man*, London, 1946.

Ullman, Montague, and Krippner, Stanley, *Dream Studies and Telepathy*, New York, 1970.

Ullman, Montague, and Zimmerman, Nan, *Working with Dreams*, New York, 1979.

Van der Post, Laurens, *Heart of the Hunter*, London, 1961.

Van der Post, Laurens, *The Lost World of the Kalahari*, London, 1958.

Van Over, Raymond (ed.), *Psychology and Extrasensory Perception*, New York, 1972.

Vasiliev, L. L., *Experiments in Distant Influence*, London, 1963.

Vesme, César de, *Primitive Man*, London, 1931.

Vesme, César de, *Experimental Spiritualism*, London, 1931.

Vogt, Evon Z., and Hyman, Ray, *Water Witching USA*, Chicago, 1959.

Wallace, Alfred Russel, *The Scientific Aspect of the Supernatural*, London, 1866.

Wallace, Alfred Russel, *On Miracles and Modern Spiritualism*, London, 1875.

Warcollier, René, *Experiments in Telepathy* (ed. G. Murphy), London, 1939.

Watkins, Alfred, *Early British Trackways*, London, 1922.

Watson, Lyall, *Supernature*, London, 1973.

Watson, Lyall, *Lifetide*, London, 1979.

West, D. J., *Psychical Research Today*, London, 1954.

White, Rhea, *Surveys in Parapsychology*, Metuchen, NJ, 1976.

White, Rhea, and Dale, Laura, *Parapsychology: Sources of Information*, Metuchen, NJ, 1973.

Wiesinger, Alois, *Occult Phenomena in the Light of Theology*, London, 1957.

Wilson, Colin, *The Occult*, London, 1973.

Wolman, Benjamin B. (ed.), *Handbook of Parapsychology*, New York, 1977.

Worrall, Ambrose A., and Worrall, Olga, *Explore Your Psychic World*, New York, 1970.

Yost, Caspar S., *Patience Worth*, New York, 1917.

Zohar, Danah, *Through the Time Barrier*, London, 1983.

Zöllner, Johann, *Transcendental Physics*, London, 1882 (1879).

Zorab, G., *Bibliography of Parapsychology*, New York, 1957.

INDEX

Aberfan: premonitions of disaster 93

Abrantes, Duchess of: sees apparition of dying Marshal Junot 190

Acoustic effects 171–8; bell-ringing 171, 178; disembodied voices 176–8; music 171–2; raps 172–6

Adare, Lord 161, 164; on Home's incombustibility 167–8

Agpaoa, Tony: conducts psychic surgery 270

Aksakov, Alexandre 23, 73, 156, 300; *Animisme et Spiritisme* 154, 227, 296; concept of super-ESP 296; investigates Florence Cook's 'materialization' 154–5

Albani, Madame 238

Alberigh-Mackay, Patty: precognition of examination question 97

Albert, Prince Consort 18

Alchemy 264–5

Alexander, Patrick Proctor 134

Altered States of Consciousness (ASCs) 277

American Association for the Advancement of Science 27

American Society for Psychical Research 232

Animal magnetism 16–18, 283–4; inquiry into 17–18

Annales des Sciences Psychiques 266; records precognitive experience 79

Anomalous phenomena 289–99

Apollonius of Tyana: 'sees' assassination of Domitian 48

Apparitions 181–99 *passim*; appearances: of animals 199; of dead brother to George Wynyard 192; of dead farm labourer to Miss Godley 192–3; of dead friend to Archdeacon Farler 191; of dead friend to James Larkin 189; of dead friend to Wilson Carlile 198; of dead grandmother to Princess de Montarcy 191; of dead seeking to right wrong 197–8; of dead son to

Baroness de Boislève 191; of dead son to Ben Jonson 189–90; of dying sister to G. J. Romanes 191–2; of wife to Dr Eustace 198–9; of wife to S. R. Wilmot 188; in folklore 199–200; pledge-redeeming 194–6

Apports 139–43; accompaniment of seances 139, 140–41; defined 139

Arago, François 115

Arigo: as spiritist healer 270

Aristotle 24

Arnold, Larry: on spontaneous combustion 290–91

Astrology 259–62; scepticism about 259

Atmospheric effects 179–80; cold breezes 179; liquefaction 180; luminosities 179–80; outbreaks of fire 180; scents 180

Aubrey, John: *Miscellanies* 96, 112; on apparition seeking to right wrong 197; on scent from apparition 180; on translocation 162; reports PK incident 112

Auras 169–70

Automatism 222–5; motor 206, 236–56; possession in 223; quasi-motor 257–62; sensory 206, 226–35

Bacon, Sir Francis: on testing for ESP 35

Balfour, Lord 206

Ballet, Dr 121

Banks, Sir Joseph 250

Baring-Gould, Rev. Sabine: sceptical about ghosts 202–3

Barker, Dr J.C. 93

Barnard, Eugene 245

Barrett, Sir William 42, 122–3, 175, 300–1; investigates dowsing 251, 253–4, 255; investigates ouija board 245; investigates poltergeists 215–16, 218; investigates telepathy 68–9; *Psychical Research* 235

355